D0079406

Theories of Organizational Stress

Theories of Organizational Stress

Cary L. Cooper

Manchester School of Management
The University of Manchester Institute of Science and
    Technology (UMIST)
Manchester
UK

OXFORD UNIVERSITY PRESS
1998

Oxford University Press, Great Clarendon Street, Oxford OX2 6DP

Oxford New York

Athens Auckland Bangkok Bogotá Buenos Aires Calcutta
Cape Town Chennai Dar es Salaam Delhi Florence Hong Kong Istanbul
Karachi Kuala Lumpur Madrid Melbourne Mexico City Mumbai
Nairobi Paris São Paulo Singapore Taipei Tokyo Toronto Warsaw

and associated companies in
Berlin Ibadan

Published in the United States
by Oxford University Press Inc., New York

First published 1998

British Library Cataloguing in Publication Data
Data available

Library of Congress Cataloging in Publication Data
Cooper, Cary L.
Theories of organizational stress / Cary L. Cooper.
p. cm.
Includes bibliographical references (p.   ).
1. Job stress. 2. Industrial hygiene. 3. Stress management.
I. Title.
HF5548.85.C658 1998 158.7—dc21 98–35996
ISBN 0–19–852279–7

1 3 5 7 9 10 8 6 4 2

Typeset by Hope Services (Abingdon) Ltd.
Printed in Great Britain
on acid-free paper by
Biddles Ltd.,
Guildford and King's Lynn

Preface: Stress in Organizations—Theoretical and Empirical Approaches

Lennart Levi

This volume is about stress in organizations and of theories and practice in that field, intended to facilitate the analysis of its causes and characteristics, and its effects in a number of areas, but also ways to cope with it, therapeutically, and/or preventively.

History of the Stress Concept

Originally, the concept of stress derives from everyday clinical practice. Some 70 years ago, a young student sat in the lecture theatre at the Medical Department of the German University of Prague attending a lecture on the symptoms typical of various diseases.

The lecturer demonstrated patients with early stages of various infectious diseases, among other disorders. He described the symptoms common to many of these diseases—pain in the joints, enlargement to the spleen, disturbances of gastrointestinal function, proteinuria, skin rash—and the problems they therefore caused in diagnostic work. This similarity in the clinical picture, he pointed out, makes it particularly important to discover the *specific* characteristics of each pathological entity, i.e. the *typical* features of each individual disease.

The young student, *Hans Selye* (1907–82), subsequently originator of the biological concept of stress, remembered thinking (Selye, 1964): 'Every disorder certainly has its *typical* features which must naturally be considered. But how come that so different diseases also have so many features *in common?*' For want of a better name, he referred to the latter as 'The Syndrome of Just Being Sick'.

Some ten years passed. Selye had moved from Prague to Montreal, Canada, where—at the McGill University—he conducted a study involving injection of ovarian and placental extracts into rats, in search of a new hormone. He found that his intervention, indeed, induced a triad of organic changes: adrenal cortical hypertrophy, bleeding ulcers in the gatrointestinal tract, and involution of the thymolymphatic system. To control for confounding influences, he later injected control animals with extracts of kidney, skin, spleen, and other tissues. To his great surprise, he found that these injections also produced essentially the same triad of organic changes. Could this similarity in reaction to so different extracts be due to a common 'tissue hormone'?

To test this hypothesis, he now injected, not any extract, but simply formalin—and was even more surprised to find the same triad, once again. True, the rats reacted in a specific manner to each injection, but there were also features that were common to all interventions. Selye turned to his tutor to discuss the nature of this peculiar *stereotypy*, this *generality*, this lowest common denominator in the organism's way of reacting to so different stimuli. In response, the senior scientist advised him to abandon this line of inquiry. He simply interpreted Selye's findings as a result of—*impurities* in the extracts.

Knowing that this could not be the case, Selye continued exposing his rats to a wide variety of stimuli, and in July 1936 he published his first brief article in *Nature*, on 'A syndrome produced by diverse nocuous agents' (Selye, 1936). The article is about 35 column-centimetres long and does not mention the word 'stress'. But it describes for the first time this generality, this stereotypy in the organism's propensity to react to widely different chemical, physical, and biological stimuli. It was later found that this holds true also for cold, heat, X-rays, noise, pain, bleeding, and muscular work (Selye, 1964).

Selye now sought a suitable term for the newly discovered phenomenon and intended to choose an analogy from engineering. In a common dictionary, *stress* is defined as 'a force which deforms bodies'. What *happens* in 'the bodies' in question, for example the tension in the girders of a bridge when a train, a column of lorries or a number of cars cross the bridge, is called 'strain'. Although this tension varies from case to case, the term 'strain' is used to describe it in all these instances. It was precisely this type of stereotypy that Selye wanted to describe. Seeking an analogy from engineering he believed 'the tension in the girder of the bridge' was called 'stress'. This is not so. It is called 'strain'. But Selye, who was born in the Austro-Hungarian double monarchy, educated in Prague and emigrated to Montreal, misinterpreted the English terminology and named the phenomenon stress, thereby spoiling the analogy with everyday and technological language and—much to his own regret—causing a great deal of subsequent confusion.

Numerous attempts have been made to abandon the use of the term stress on the grounds that it is an abstraction which does not correspond to clinical reality, that there is a confusion between the stimulus ('stressor', according to Selye), the response, the non-specific component of that response ('stress', according to Selye), and the stimulus-response interaction. Selye countered that stress is admittedly an abstraction and not easy to define, but these are faults it shares with many other terms that are none the less indispensable in biology—for example, life, death, health, and disease.

What, then, is stress? According to Selye, it is the *lowest common denominator* in the organism's reactions to every conceivable kind of stressor exposure, challenge and demand or, in other words, the stereotypy, the general features in the organism's reaction to all kinds of stressors. Stress *is* thus an abstraction. It is very difficult to *observe* stress, since Selye does not base the definition on the entire reaction but only on its *non-specific* features, those that are common to all types of loads and demands.

Another way to define and describe the phenomenon 'stress' is by referring to what Selye used to call 'the rate of wear and tear in the organism'.

As stated above, many attempts have been made since 1936 to abandon the concept of stress. Yet it is alive and flourishing all over the world, as shown by an important report commissioned by the American National Academy of Sciences, *Stress and Human Health* (Elliott and Eisdorfer, 1982), a summary of the results of teamwork by about a hundred scientists, and, most recently, by the numerous papers presented at the 'Stress of Life' Congress held in Budapest in July 1997 to commemorate the 90th anniversary of Hans Selye's birth (Csermely, 1997).

However, it has also been shown that differing *perceptions* of stressors result in different patterns of neuroendocrine activation (cf. Henry, 1993). An easily and successfully handled challenge elicits noradrenaline and testosterone rises. With increasing anxiety, active coping shifts to a more passive mode, with concomitant adrenaline, prolactin, renin, and free fatty acids increase. As the distress grows, cortisol augments.

Occupational Stress in Europe

What do we know about occupational stressors, stress, and health in the fifteen European Union member states?

The most recent data come from the Second European Survey of Working Conditions, conducted by the European Foundation in early 1996.

Its report (Paoli, 1997) calls attention to the pronounced transformation of European working life from the industrial to the service sector, with a consequent change in job profile: introduction of new technology (one third of the workforce uses computers) and more client-oriented jobs (49 percent of the workers indicate permanent and direct contact with clients or patients). Work organization has also changed, with new management models, teamwork, just-in-time, and TQM.

Interacting with these and other situational factors, there is also a change in the European workforce profile. European workers are getting older; they are more often working on fixed term or temporary contracts; there is a rapid growth in the proportion of female workers; the traditional employee–employer relationship is slowly disappearing; and the unemployment rate remains very high.

According to this survey (Paoli, 1997) 45 percent of the 147 million workers in the EU Member States report having monotonous tasks; 44 percent no task rotation; 50 percent short, repetitive tasks; 35 percent no influence on task order; and 28 percent no influence on work rhythm; while 54 percent work at a very high speed, and 56 percent to tight deadlines.

Thirty percent complain of backache, 28 percent of stress, 20 percent of fatigue, 17 percent of muscular pains and 13 percent of headaches.

Under the European Union Framework Directive (89/391/EEC), employers have a

duty to ensure the safety and health of workers in every aspect related to the work, on basis of the following general principles of prevention:

- avoiding risks;
- evaluating the risks which cannot be avoided;
- combating the risks at source;
- adapting the work to the individual, especially as regards the design of workplaces, the choices of work equipment and the choice of working and production methods, with a view, in particular, to alleviating monotonous work and work at a predetermined work rate and to reducing their effects on health;
- developing a coherent overall prevention policy which covers technology, organization of work, working conditions, social relationships and the influence of factors related to the working environment.

The awareness that occupational stressors and stress-related ill-health do constitute serious problems for all parties on the labour market was expressed in an authoritative way in its ninth session by the joint ILO/WHO Committee on Occupational Health already in 1984. Its report entitled *Psychosocial Factors at Work: Recognition and Control* was subsequently endorsed by the Governing Body of ILO and the Executive Board of WHO and thereby became the first policy document for activities in this field worldwide (ILO, 1986). In 1992, based on a series of WHO and/or ILO-sponsored consultations (cf. Kalimo *et al.*, 1987), ILO published its major report on 'Preventing Stress at Work' (ILO, 1992).

Against this background, the European Commission issued an Orientation Document for its Ad Hoc Group (AHG) on 'Work-Related Stress', providing the following reasons for its endeavours:

- stress at work may lead to mental or physical ill-health;
- also stress that is not work-related can manifest itself in the workplace;
- the human and economic costs of such stress are very high to all concerned;
- such costs should therefore be reduced by preventing work-related stress.

Based on this mandate, the AHG issued its Draft Opinion (Doc. 5501/2/96). The latter was discussed at the Plenary meeting of the EU Advisory Committee for Safety, Hygiene and Health Protection at Work and accepted unanimously, in late November, 1996.

Its recommendations (European Commission, 1997) include support for

- Research on work, stress and health.
- A Guidance Note for National Guidelines.
- Exchange of information on Work-Related Stress.
- Education, and training.

The key paragraph of the current (Fourth) EU Framework Programme (for research) indicates that 'the Union is giving priority to projects which are likely to have a direct impact in terms of *competitiveness* and *quality of life* (my italics) and will therefore respond to the concerns of European enterprises and citizens'. A related approach also seems to be well founded in the area of prevention of work-related stress in European and other enterprises.

In a globalized market, new forms of work organizations and workplace partnerships are developing rapidly. In order to monitor and analyze the rapid change and their implications for the European occupational environment and workers' health and well-being, the European Foundation has commissioned a series of studies, including an EPOC-survey (Employee Direct Participation in Organizational Change, EPOC, 1997). These studies aim at the development of a 'European Social Model', based on what Peters (1987) referred to as 'committed, flexible, multi-skilled, constantly re-trained people, joined together in self-managed teams'. Such a European model is regarded as the 'only realistic alternative to the model of a highly deregulated labour market combined with a low-wage employment growth' associated with the USA (EPOC, 1997). The report categorizes and describes the nature and extent of direct worker participation, the motives for it, its links with organizational strategies, and its effects both on key business performance indicators and on employee health and well-being. It further describes the regulation of direct participation, qualification, and training for such participation, and remuneration systems utilized.

Some concern is expressed but no data provided on a possible down-side of such participation in the form of work intensification, stress, and self-exploitation.

A Model of Occupational Stress

Common occupational stressors arise from social arrangements at work, are mediated through perception, appraisal, and experience (higher nervous processes) and include: structures and processes in the total work environment (e.g. over- or underload, low decision latitude) that can elicit pathogenic effects. Individual determinants of the propensity of human beings to appraise and react to such stimuli include personality, customs, and attitudes. Stressor-induced physiological, psychological and behavioral mechanisms (e.g. functional disturbance in hormone production; anxiety; risk-taking behavior) are activated, leading to work-stress-related mental and physical disease; and decrease in well-being, satisfaction, and quality of life. These interactions can be visualized in an ecological model (see Figure 1); (Kagan and Levi, 1975; European Commission, 1997).

The occupational situation with all its social structures and processes as appraised by the individual worker, gives rise to stimuli (box 1), that interact with the psychobiological program (box 2). The process is modified by interacting variables, e.g. social support; coping repertoire (box 6). The resulting responses are in some cases provoked by a wide variety of situations, and/or in almost any individual, and/or are related to morbidity in general—the non-specific stress response as described above. Other responses are more specific. Some do not relate to various aspects of health, whereas others do. The latter have diverse expression as pathogenic mechanisms (box 3)—such as feelings of anxiety, depression, and distress, abuse of alcohol and drugs, or disturbances in lipid metabolism. These mechanisms are known or suspected to cause either precursors of disease (box 4), or disease itself (box 5). Predisposing interacting variables may promote this sequence of events, while

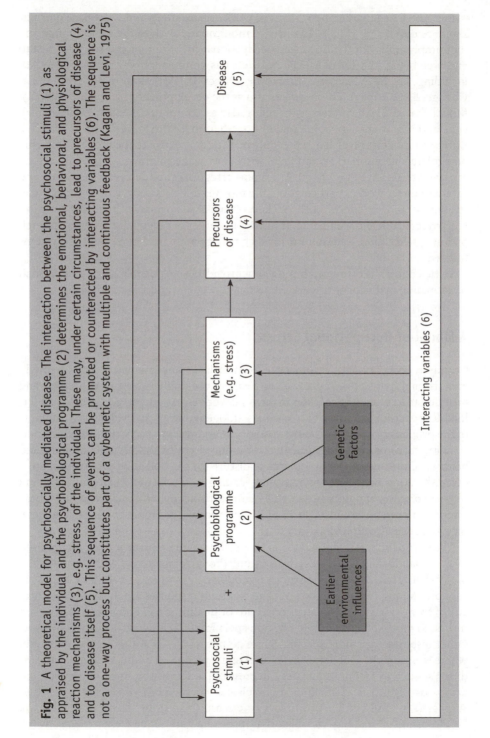

Fig. 1 A theoretical model for psychosocially mediated disease. The interaction between the psychosocial stimuli (1) as appraised by the individual and the psychobiological programme (2) determines the emotional, behavioral, and physiological reaction mechanisms (3), e.g. stress, of the individual. These may, under certain circumstances, lead to precursors of disease (4) and to disease itself (5). This sequence of events can be promoted or counteracted by interacting variables (6). The sequence is not a one-way process but constitutes part of a cybernetic system with multiple and continuous feedback (Kagan and Levi, 1975)

protective interacting factors—adequate coping and/or social support—may counteract it (box 6).

All of these processes take place in a man-environment ecosystem (see Figure 1). The process just described is not a one-way flow but constitutes a cybernetic system with continuous feedback. Accordingly, if disease (or social disintegration) has occurred in an individual (or a group), this has repercussions on occupational structures and processes and on the resulting psychosocial stimuli (box 1), individual and group characteristics (box 2), and on interacting variables (box 6).

What we need to know is the *content* of each of these 'boxes', their *interrelationships*, and the *dynamics* of the entire system. This knowledge could be implemented when considering occupational stress management, other preventive approaches but also for monitoring and research purposes.

A complementary model often referred to as the 'demand–control–support' model is described in great detail by Karasek and Theorell (1990). A third one is Siegrist's (1996) 'effort-reward-imbalance' model. In my opinion, these three models supplement one another. Although they originally focused on the relation between working life on one hand and workers' health and well-being on the other, they can also be adapted to the organizational system components referred to by the EPOC group (see above).

As pointed out recently by Greene (1997), the scientific enterprise is full of experts on specialist areas but woefully short of people with a more unified world-view. I believe that this volume gives examples of the eminent scientists that exist in our field of work that are both able and willing to cope with the unavoidable difficulties created by applying such a comprehensive and integrative approach.

References

Csermely, P. (ed.) (1997) *Stress of Life—Stress and Adaptation from Molecules to Man*. Book of Abtracts from the International Congress of Stress, Budapest, 1–5 July, 1997.

Elliott, G. R. and Eisdorfer, C. (eds.) (1982) *Stress and Human Health—Analysis and Implications of Research*. A study by the Institute of Medicine/National Academy of Sciences. New York: Springer.

EPOC (1997) *New Forms of Work Organisation. Can Europe Realise its Potential?* Results of a survey of direct employee participation in Europe. Dublin: European Foundation.

European Commission (1997) *Report on Work-Related Stress*. The Advisory Committee for Safety, Hygiene and Health Protection at Work. Luxembourg.

Greene, M. T. (1997) 'What cannot be said in science', *Nature*, 388: 619–20.

Henry, J. P. (1993) 'Biological Basis of the Stress Response', NIPS, 8: 69–73.

International Labour Office (ILO) (1986) *Psychosocial Factors at Work: Recognition and Control*. Report of the Joint ILO/WHO Committee on Occupational Health. Ninth Session. Geneva: ILO.

International Labour Office (ILO) (1992) 'Preventing stress at work', *Conditions of Work Digest* 1992, 11.

Kagan, A. R. and Levi, L. (1975) Health and environment—psychosocial stimuli: a review. In: L. Levi (ed.) *Society, Stress and Disease—Childhood and Adolescence* (pp. 241–260). Oxford: Oxford University Press.

Kalimo, R., El-Batawi, M. A. and Cooper, C. L. (eds.) (1987) *Psychosocial Factors at Work and their Relation to Health*. Geneva: World Health Organization.

Karasek, R. and Theorell, T. (1990) *Healthy Work—Stress: Productivity and the Reconstruction of Working Life*. New York: Basic Books.

Paoli, P. (1997) *Working conditions in Europe. The Second European Survey on Working Conditions*. Dublin: European Foundation.

Peters, T. (1987) *Thriving on Chaos: Handbook for a Management Revolution*. London: Macmillan.

Selye, H. (1936) 'A syndrome produced by diverse nocuous agents', *Nature*, 138, 32.

Selye, H. (1964) *From Dream to Discovery*. New York: McGraw Hill.

Siegrist, J. (1996) 'Adverse health effects of high effort/low reward conditions', *Journal of Occupational Health and Psychology*, 1, 27–41.

Contents

Figures

Tables

Contributors

Terry Beehr
Psychology Department
Central Michigan University
Sloan Hall
Mount Pleasant MI 48859
USA

Robert D. Caplan
Department of Psychology
George Washington University
USA

Cary L. Cooper
Manchester School of Management
UMIST
PO Box 88
Manchester M60 1QD
UK

Tom Cummings
Department of Management and Organization
University of Southern California
Los Angeles CA 90089–1421
USA

Jeff Edwards
Kenan-Flagler Business School
University of North Carolina
Chapel Hill NC 27599–3490
USA

Doris Fay
Fakulteit der Psychologie
Arbeids-en Organisatiepsychologie
Roetersstraat 15
1018 WB Amsterdam
The Netherlands

Michael Frese
Faculteit der Psychologie
Universiteit van Amsterdam
Roetersstraat 15
1018 WB Amsterdam
The Netherlands

Lennart Levi
Professor Emeritus of Psychosocial Medicine
PO Box 220
S–171 77 Stockholm
Sweden

Christina Maslach
Department of Psychology
University of California
3210 Tolman Hall
Berkeley
CA 94720
USA

Joe McGrath
Department of Psychology
University of Illinois
Champaign IL 61820
USA

Debra L. Nelson
Oklahoma State University
Department of Management
College of Business Administration
Stillwater OK 74078
USA

Jonathan D. Quick
World Health Organization
CH–1211 Geneva 27
Switzerland

James Campbell Quick
The University of Texas at Arlington
Box 19467
Arlington TX 76019–0467
USA

Marc Schabracq
Faculteit der Psychologie
Universiteit van Amsterdam
Roetersstraat 15
1018 WB Amsterdam
The Netherlands

Ellen I. Shupe
Grand Valley State University
1 Campus Drive
Allendale
MI 49401–9403
USA

Contributors

Johannes Siegrist
Medinizinische Einrichtungen
Institut für Medizinische Soziologie
Heinrich Heine Universität Düsseldorf
Postfach 10 10 07
D–40225 Düsseldorf
Germany

Sabine Sonnentag
Faculteit der Psychologie
Universiteit van Amsterdam
Roetersstraat 15
1018 WB Amsterdam
The Netherlands

Paul Spector
Department of Psychology
University of South Florida
Tampa FL 33620
USA

Töres Torell
National Institute for Psychosocial Factors and
Health
Box 230
S–171 77 Stockholm
Sweden

R. Van Harrison
Institute for Social Research
University of Michigan
G–1105 Towsley Center
Ann Arbor MI 48109–0201
USA

Introduction

Cary L. Cooper

Studs Terkel (1972), in his acclaimed book *Working*, suggested nearly thirty years ago that

work, is, by its very nature, about violence—to the spirit as well as to the body. It is about ulcers as well as accidents, about shouting matches as well as fistfights, about nervous breakdowns as well as kicking the dog around. It is, above all (or beneath all), about daily humiliations. To survive the day is triumph enough for the walking wounded among the great many of us.

To this day, the costs of occupational stress are still present and growing, as the very nature of work is dramatically changing. It has been estimated that the cost of stress to American organizations, assessed by absenteeism, reduced productivity, compensation claims, health insurance and direct medical expenses is in the region of $150 billion per year (Karasek and Theorell, 1990). In the UK, the Confederation of British Industry recently calculated that the costs of sickness absence to the UK economy was over £12 billion, of which around 50 percent has been estimated to be stress related, while the British Heart Foundation found that over 21 percent of all male absence and 45 percent of all premature deaths at work are due to heart and circulatory disease, in which stress plays a significant role. A report by the Nordic Council of Ministers (Lunde-Jensen, 1994) calculated the economic costs of work related sickness and accidents in the Nordic countries, estimating the costs in Denmark to be 2.5 percent of GNP per annum and in Norway to be 10 percent of GNP. In the European Union, the costs of stress to organizations and countries is estimated to be between 5–10 percent of GNP per annum (Cooper *et al.*, 1996).

Not only is workplace stress costly, but it is a growing problem as organizations throughout the Western world and beyond dramatically downsize, outsource, and develop less secure employment contracts. Many organizations are now smaller, with fewer people doing more and feeling much less secure. New technology has added the burden of information overload as well as accelerating the pace of work with demands for a greater immediacy of response (e.g. WWW, faxes, emails, etc.). This 'second wave' industrial revolution of contingent working, short-term contracts, portfolio careers and ultimately virtual organizations, has spawned a mountain of research in the cognate area of occupational stress, together with numerous books and stress-specific journals (e.g. *Stress Medicine, Work and Stress, International Journal of Stress Management*) in the field.

Much of the recent research (e.g. Cooper and Payne, 1988; Sauter and Murphy, 1995; Cooper, 1996) in occupational stress has concentrated on identifying occupational or organizational sources of stress as they relate to adverse strain indicators (e.g. job dissatisfaction, mental ill health, sickness absence, etc.) and in highlighting the potential individual difference variables or moderators in the stress–strain process. Empirical research in the field, however, has massively outstripped our ability to understand the implications of that research, to put it into some kind of conceptual framework for the purposes of trying to develop appropriate theories which could help us to understand the mechanisms of stress and to frame our interventions.

The purpose of this volume, therefore, is to provide under one umbrella a range of theories of organizational stress from some of the leading international researchers in the field. It is hoped that this will help to build the necessary theoretical frameworks for future research and encourage more systematic approaches to organizational stress interventions. Each chapter is divided into several parts: an exposition of the theory, research linked to it, and how this theory could be applied to occupational/organizational stress prevention or interventions. Future research on the theory is also considered in some of the chapters.

In the spirit of allowing maximum autonomy/decision latitude to these distinguished authors, each chapter is meant to be a discrete theoretical contribution, with implications of the stand-alone theory for future research and stress prevention/management. The intention of this volume is not to synthesize these conceptual models into one grand theory, but to allow researchers and practitioners in the field of organizational stress the opportunity of exploring a range of conceptual models to frame their future activities. These theories extend from complex and multidimensional paradigms to those exploring the relationship between a limited number of constructs.

We start the book with a comprehensive meta-model theory of occupational stress by Terry Beehr, in which he highlights many of the factors that impinge on the stress–strain process. He argues that organizations which are characterized by environmental uncertainty will make it difficult for people to achieve their objectives, as well as maintaining any sense of personal well-being. This depends to some extent on temporal concerns, like the chronic nature of the stressors, and on the coping mechanisms of the people involved. From this multi-faceted meta-model, we turn to one of the earliest espoused conceptual models in the field, the person–environment fit theory. In this chapter, Jeff Edwards, Roberts Caplan, and Van Harrison explore the significance of the misfit between the person and the environment. This theory identifies two types of fit: the fit between the demands of the environment and the abilities of the person and the fit between the needs of the person and the supplies in the environment that relate to the person's needs. As the authors emphasize, stress arises when environmental supplies do not meet the person's needs or when environmental demands exceed the person's abilities. This theory has been extended and developed much further since its early origins, and the chapter highlights the comprehensive research output to support its underlying premises. It also explores the coping responses directed at the individual and the environment when there is a mismatch. Given the significance of this theory in the literature, directions for future research in P–E fit theory are explored.

Another theory that has received widespread attention is burnout. Christina Maslach has played a major role in developing this multidimensional theory over the years, particularly for people-orientated professions (e.g. education, health care). Burnout is defined by the three dimensions of exhaustion, cynicism, and inefficacy. In this chapter Maslach describes several new theoretical developments, explores key patterns in the empirical research, and discusses the implications of the theory for stress prevention and intervention.

Ellen Shupe and Joe McGrath develop a dynamic, adaptive process theory at two levels: at the level of a single 'potential stress event or condition' and at the level of overall stress on the system at any given time. As the authors suggest, four linking processes are involved: the appraisal, choice, performance, and outcome process. They then apply this theory to sojourners, 'individuals who are spending a considerable period of time in a culture foreign to them'. This is a dynamic model, reflecting stress resistance as well as stress residues, which lead on neatly to a cybernetic of system control theory of stress by Tom Cummings and Cary Cooper. Although this theory provides a person–environment framework, its perspective emphasizes time, information, and feedback as essential constructs underlying the stress cycle from the detection of strain, through the choice of adjustment processes to cope with the threat situation, and on to the subsequent feedback about coping effects. It recognizes that coping behavior is purposeful, directed by the knowledge of its previous effects. Jeff Edwards follows this with an extension of the cybernetic model, viewing stress, coping and well-being as critical elements of a negative feedback loop. In this theory, stress is about discrepancies between perceptions and desires, which damages well-being and stimulates coping. The author 'organizes multiple feedback loops into a hierarchy in which loops at higher levels activate loops at lower levels, and efforts to resolve these at different levels have different consequences'. This theory is graphically illustrated by uniquely applying it to the work and family domain.

From cybernetics to a control theory, we explore in Paul Spector's chapter how perceived control 'moderates relations between the objective environment and the individual perception'. The author suggests that 'people who perceive control will be less likely to interpret an environmental condition or event as a job stressor'. On the other hand, perceived control is also affected by locus of control and self-strains, and emotions are said to mediate other job strains. This really does help us to put control into both a person and environment perspective. Leading on from control, we explore the complex interplay of workplace stresses and two performance concepts of innovation and personal initiative in a theory by Doris Faye, Sabine Sonnentag, and Michael Frese. This theory uses an action theory framework and explores the negative effects of stressors on innovation and personal initiative. The interrelationships between workplace stressors and these two performance characteristics are explored in a feedback loop type of paradigm.

Again focusing on a two factor conceptual framework, Johannes Siegrist describes an effort–reward model of stress. The imbalance between effort (both intrinsic and extrinsic) and reward is the critical relationship in terms of adverse health effects. At one extreme we have high reward and low effort, at the other low reward and high effort; it is the imbalance in these dimensions which creates disequilibrium according to the theory. Evidence is provided that supports the author's conceptual framework. This chapter is followed by a complementary theory in the demands/control/support model of Karasek. In this chapter, Töres Theorell tries to bring together the effort–reward and demand–control approaches within an organizational context, together with their impact on psychophysiological and cardiovascular outcome measures, and how these might be linked to individual differences factors. Theorell not only discusses the interface of the two theories but also their application in terms of organizational stress management.

The final two chapters explore more holistic approaches. Marc Schabracq's ethological theory of stress is about integrity, the semi-permanent system of relevant assumptions, meaning, images, goals, rules, etc. Integrity is meant to enable a person to control his or her functioning and environment. The author suggests that underdevelopment of and infringements on integrity cause stress. As these stressors are all characterized by a kind of loss, attention is paid to 'wisdom' as a conglomerate of abilities to cope with such potential losses. And finally, Jim Quick, Jonathan Quick, and Deborah Nelson conclude the book with a theory of preventative stress management in organizations, which essentially tries to overlay the constructs of public health and preventative stress management model. The chapter also presents ideographic research from two major organizations and concludes by discussing Sisyphus, dynamic self-reliance, and the relationship of theory, beliefs, and observations.

This book is a compendium of theory rich in diversity and range, exploring many of the issues central to organizational stress. As we enter the next millennium, with all the complexities and changes taking place in the work environment, and in society generally, it is important to begin to understand the linkages in the stress–strain process and what role individual differences plays in the dynamic. Research in occupational stress in the future depends on us better understanding the processes that make people ill at work, if we are to adequately intervene and enhance well-being. In all of this, if we are to distance ourselves from Studs Terkel's definition of 'work' at the beginning of this introduction, we must keep the words of Kornhauser in his book *The Mental Health of the Industrial Worker* firmly in our minds:

Mental health is not so much a freedom from specific frustrations as it is an overall balanced relationship to the world, which permits a person to maintain a realistic, positive belief in himself and his purposeful activities. Insofar as his entire job and life situation facilitate and support such feelings of adequacy, inner security, and meaningfulness of his existence, it can be presumed that his mental health will tend to be good. What is important in a negative way is not any single characteristic of his situation but everything that deprives the person of purpose and zest, that leaves him with negative feelings about himself, with anxieties, tensions, a sense of lostness, emptiness, and futility (Kornhauser, 1965).

References

Cooper, C. L. (1996) *Handbook of Stress, Medicine and Health*. Boca Raton, Florida: CRC Press.

Cooper, C. L. and Payne, R. (1988) *Causes, Coping and Consequences of Stress at Work*. Chichester: John Wiley & Sons.

Cooper, C. L., Liukkonen, P. and Cartwright, S. (1996) *Stress Prevention in the Workplace: Assessing the Costs and Benefits to Organizations*. Dublin: European Foundation for the Improvement of Living and Working Conditions.

Karasek, R. and Theorell, T. (1990) *Healthy Work: Stress, Productivity and the Reconstruction of Working Life*. New York: John Wiley & Sons.

Kornhauser, A. (1965) *The Mental Health of the Industrial Worker*. New York: John Wiley & Sons.

Lunde-Jensen, P. (1994) 'The Costs of Occupational Accidents and Work-related Sickness in the Nordic Countries', *Janus*, 18 (4), 25–26.

Sauter, S. and Murphy, L. (1995) *Organizational Risk Factors for Job Stress*. Washington DC: APA.

Terkel, S. (1972) *Working*. New York: Avon Books.

1

··

An Organizational Psychology Meta-Model of Occupational Stress

Terry Beehr

Facet Models of Occupational Stress

There are many approaches to occupational stress. They involve somewhat different types of causal and affected variables, and they also use different labels for them. The language used in describing stress-related variables can be confusing because of both inconsistent usage by professionals working in the area and the use of stress terms by the public at large (Jex *et al.*, 1992). Therefore, to make clear and consistent the way key terms are used in this chapter, the following definitions are offered: *stressors* are stress-producing events or conditions (also called SPEC's; Beehr and McGrath, 1992; 1996; McGrath and Beehr, 1990) in the work environment; *strains* are the individuals' responses to such stressor stimuli that are deemed harmful to themselves (i.e. poor mental or physical health or well-being); and *stress* is a more general term describing situations in which stressors and strains are present. I became interested in occupational stress while working as a graduate assistant in a research program on mental health in industry. While conducting this research, it soon became apparent that, in addition to mental health, physical health also might be affected by workplace events and characteristics. Like most people working in this area, I have focused on specific types of workplace stress. As an organizational psychologist, I have been more interested in social psychological events and characteristics related to work than in the physical aspects of work.

Tom Franz and I (Beehr and Franz, 1987) categorized approaches to understanding and treating occupational stress into four categories, giving them labels corresponding to professions that we thought were especially good at using each approach: medical; clinical/counseling psychology; engineering psychology; and organizational psychology approaches. The first approach, which we called medical because that profession seemed traditionally to be more focused on it and probably better at it than most other professions, is most likely to focus on stressors in the physical environment, on physical (physiological or biochemical) strains, and on treating the individual directly. The second approach, the clinical/counseling psychology approach, focuses more on stressors in the psychological work environment and on the psychological strain responses of the individual (e.g. depression or anxiety), but it also tends to treat the individual directly. The third approach to occupational stress, which we labeled engineering psychology, looks for stressors in the physical environment at work, examines changes in performance as an outcome as much or more often than employee strains, and prefers to change the organizational environment as a form of treatment. The organizational psychology approach, according to Beehr and Franz, looks for stressors in the psychological environment, focuses on psychological strain responses in the employee, and often recommends treatments that change something in the employees' organizational environment. The organizational psychology approach is the one I have used in my research. As discussed later in this chapter, seeking to understand the potentially harmful effects of the social psychological characteristics of the workplace on the person led to considering the concept of goal-directed behavior(s) in the face of uncertainty.

A Meta-Model of Facets of Occupational Stress

John Newman and I (Beehr and Newman, 1978; Newman and Beehr, 1979) conducted an early review of occupational stress research and developed a facet model outlining the relationships among stress- and non-stress-related variables found or assumed in the literature at that time (Figure 1.1). In this stress model, occupational stressors are located in the environmental facet, and the individual's strains are part of the human consequences facet. Stressors and strains are the two types of variables whose presence is necessary and sufficient to define an occupational stress situation.

The presence of other 'facets' indicates that other things may or may not also be occurring in relation to stressors and strains. The personal facet consists of relatively stable characteristics of the person (e.g. personality, ability, physical traits, and demographic traits). These can combine in some way with stressors (in the environmental facet) to produce the strains (in the human consequences facet). The process facet consists of intervening psychological or physical (physiological or biochemical) reactions of the person that are often assumed necessary for actual harm to occur to the person in the form of strains. The organizational consequences facet contains employee behaviors, in stressful situations, that have direct implications for the effectiveness of the organization (e.g. absenteeism, turnover, or changes in job performance). Adaptive responses are any responses, usually by the individual or the organization, but potentially also by third parties (e.g. government regulations or health insurance) that are an attempt to or successfully alleviate stressors, strains, or both. The time facet recognizes the importance of time in the occupational stress process, which is probably an under-recognized factor in such situations (McGrath and Beehr, 1990).

Overall, most research on occupational stress seems to fit quite well into this facet model. Rarely does any one study examine all these facets, but the assumptions behind and results from most studies usually fit into sections of the model quite well.

Fig. 1.1 Meta-model facets of occupational stress (Reprinted with permission from Beehr and Newman, 1978)

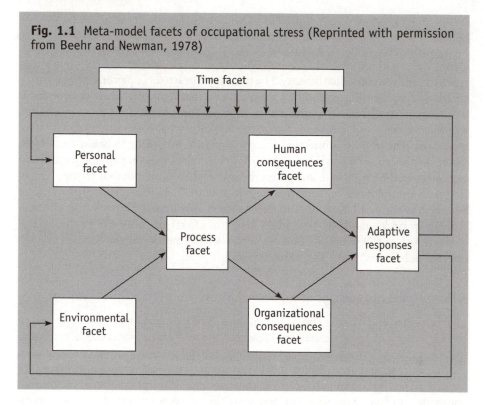

This should be the case, because the model was developed from pre-existing research and theory. In that sense, therefore, it is a 'meta-model', or a model that encompasses many others. This meta-model is the most basic model that seems to be consistent with nearly all stress research hypotheses and theories of occupational stress from the organizational psychology approach.

A More Specific Facet Model of Occupational Stress

Based on subsequent research and rethinking, Figure 1.2 illustrates a more refined or adjusted facet model that is more consistent with specific hypotheses found in current thinking about occupational stress. It is more specific, for example, by specifying moderator effects. It breaks the environmental facet into two parts, the workplace 'stressors' and other 'situational' characteristics. These other characteristics of the situation or work environment can moderate the relationship between stressors and processes (and therefore also moderate the relationship between stressors and strains). In addition, the model changes the role of personal characteristics to show them explicitly as moderators of these same stressor–response relationships. Personal characteristics (e.g. personality) might directly lead to or predict strain-type responses. When they do have direct effects on strains, however, there is no work stressor involved, and therefore it is not a condition of *occupational* stress. Instead, the nature of the person is directly leading to responses regardless of the presence of any sort of occupational situation. Therefore, there is no arrow from personal characteristics to strain responses. Time, now 'duration', is the other variable realigned as a moderator variable. This is consistent with the uncertainty theory of occupational stress by Beehr and Bhagat (1985a), in which the duration of the stressor is proposed as a factor causing stronger stress responses. The adaptive responses facet can be renamed 'coping and adaptation' to indicate its inclusiveness better. It consists of any actions taken to correct problems with the stressors, the strains, or the organizational outcomes. And finally, as noted in Beehr and Newman (1978), it is likely that strains to the individual person can lead to some of the behaviors that become organizational outcomes, e.g. too much strain might make the person quit his or her job.

Fig. 1.2 Refined facet model of occupational stress

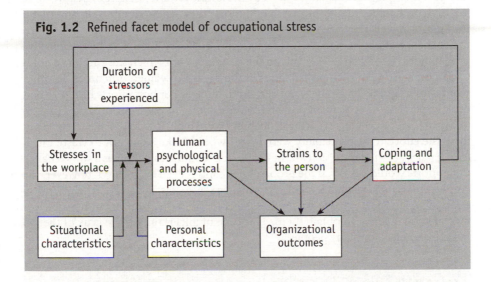

Uncertainty as a Key Element of the Process Facet of Occupational Stress

The psychological and physical processes have been one of the more mysterious parts of the stress model. It suggests that there are processes that are common to all stress experiences. Lazarus' (1966; Lazarus and Folkman, 1984) theory might suggest that cognitive appraisal processes are the common factor in experiences that are stressful; Selye (1956; 1975), based in the medical approach to stress, searched for physiological 'first mediators' during his career, but never found them; Mason (1975) has argued that psychological or emotional arousal responses are the initial response common to various stress situations; and various empirical articles, often from the engineering or medical approaches to stress, measure catecholamine secretion as if that is the initial stress response. Rabi Bhagat and I examined the nature of the typical stressors studied from the organizational psychology approach to stress, and concluded that uncertainty is likely to be a common initial response to many of them (Beehr and Bhagat, 1985b).

The uncertainty theory of occupational stress proposes that experienced stress is a multiplicative function of uncertainty, importance, and duration: $S = Uc \times I \times D$ (Figure 1.3). It assumes a proactive person. Rather than the image of a passive person being exposed to and reacting to environmental stressors, it proposes that people in the workplace are trying to perform certain (motivated) behaviors, and it uses the expectancy theory of motivation as a starting point for understanding the impact of occupational stressors. Employees' behaviors (e.g. job performance) are motivated by perceived links between their efforts (E) and performance (P) (E→P) and between their performance and some extrinsic or intrinsic outcomes (O) (P→O). In expectancy theory, it is the perception of (more specifically and formally, the perceived probability of) these links that motivates people—if they value the outcome. A simple example that is usually desired by the employer, is for people to believe there is a high probability that if they try hard (effort) they will perform well, and that if they perform well, they will receive valued rewards from their employer. The uncertainty theory of occupational stress focuses not on the strengths of these subjective probabilities (E→P and P→O), but on the certainty with which the employee holds or can even estimate such probabilities in the regard to valued outcomes. In other words, for example, he or she is not certain that his or her best efforts have a 10 percent, 50 percent, or 90 percent probability of resulting in good performance (uncertainty of E→P expectancies). If the probability were high, it would make sense to put forth the effort; if the probability were low, it would make sense not to waste much effort; if it were moderate, at least the employee would know there is a 50–50 chance their efforts would pay off. If the probabilities cannot even be guessed, however, the employee has no idea what level of effort makes sense. It is, in a sense, a helpless situation in which the proactive person has goals (desired outcomes), but has no clear way of knowing how to obtain them. This type of uncertainty is the crux of the job stress experience for many people.

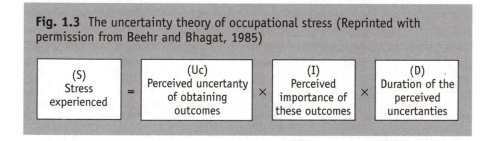

Fig. 1.3 The uncertainty theory of occupational stress (Reprinted with permission from Beehr and Bhagat, 1985)

(S) Stress experienced	=	(Uc) Perceived uncertainty of obtaining outcomes	×	(I) Perceived importance of these outcomes	×	(D) Duration of the perceived uncertanties

Three commonly studied stressors are role conflict, role ambiguity, and under-utilization of skills, and these can be analyzed in light of uncertainty theory. An employee experiencing role conflict has two or more sets of expectations placed on him or her that are in conflict in the sense that meeting one set of expectations seems to make it more difficult to meet the other. In this case, the employee is uncertain how to direct his or her efforts in order to have adequate job performance—in other words, uncertainty about the level of E→P expectancy. An employee experiencing under-utilization of skills, if the underutilization is not too severe, might experience P→O uncertainty, especially regarding an intrinsic outcome. Because the employees in such situations have plenty of ability to do the job, they should have little E→P uncertainty; they know it would be easy to perform the job well if they put forth the effort. There might be, however, some uncertainty regarding whether the employee would receive an intrinsic outcome such as a sense of achievement or pride as a result of accomplishing the work. If a job is too simple, the employee might be uncertain whether a feeling of accomplishment and resulting pride will occur. Even though we are often admonished in our culture to take pride in doing good work, it is not so clear that we will be especially proud of performing simple tasks well. The third example of a job stressor commonly studied from the organizational psychology point of view is role ambiguity, which is proposed to create uncertainty for both E→P and P→O expectancies. Role ambiguity sounds a good deal like uncertainty itself, but if it is truly a stressor, it must be a characteristic of the work environment rather than a reaction of the person such as inability to determine a perceived probability. Role ambiguity would occur when the situation lacks sufficient information or contains ambiguous information regarding what is expected of the employee (Katz and Kahn, 1978). Uncertainty is the employee's response or cognitive reaction to the environment (although she labels the terms differently, Pearce (1981) has discussed some of these distinctions). Ambiguous expectations can either be unclear regarding how to direct one's efforts in order to perform well (E→P) or how one's performance is or will be evaluated and rewarded (P→O), or both. Most of the types of social psychological occupational stressors commonly studied from the organizational psychology approach can result in these types of cognitive uncertainties for the person.

As noted earlier, uncertainty theory holds that such uncertainties combine with the importance of the potential outcome(s) and the duration of the uncertainty to result in a stress situation and therefore to cause harmful strains in the person. The three-variable combination is multiplicative ($S = Uc \times I \times D$). The uncertainty must exist for some duration, and the outcome must have at least some importance for any stress to result. Uc must exist for at least some duration, or else it does not exist at all, and the situation must include some potential outcome that has at least some importance, or the employee is not likely to be stressed by it. Therefore, a 'score' of zero on duration or importance results in a stress score of zero after multiplication. Furthermore, the longer the duration and the more important the potential outcome, the greater the resultant strain is likely to be.

In Figure 1.2, uncertainty is a human psychological (cognitive) process, and is an immediate reaction to the stressors in the workplace. Therefore, uncertainty theory proposes that the development of such uncertainties is frequently the common process underlying occupational stress situations. These uncertainties, therefore, are part of the solution to the mystery of the 'process' facet of the occupational stress model. Importance, on the other hand, is one of the personal characteristics of Figure 1.2, because it is the value or importance placed on an outcome by the person him or herself—which depends on individual preferences. And, of course, duration is represented in the model in Figure 1.2 by 'duration of the stressors experienced'.

Research on the Facet Model of Occupational Stress

Nearly all research on occupational stress conducted from an organizational psychology approach confirms one or more parts of the meta-model in Figure 1.1. Long ago, for example, studies found stressors in the work environment were related to human processes (e.g. piece rate jobs related to physiological processes such as secretion of the catecholamines, adrenaline, and noradrenaline; Timio and Gentili, 1976). The basic approach of much research has been to seek relationships between stressor measures and strain measures in non-experimental field studies, and there is nearly always such a relationship. As summaries of examples of research in this vein, two meta-analyses of role conflict and role ambiguity were published in the 1980s, both finding overall relationships between these two job stressors and strains such as tension or anxiety (Fisher and Gitelson, 1983; Jackson and Schuler, 1985). This sometimes means a link has been established between the environmental facet in Figure 1.1 and the human consequences facet, but because the majority of research on role conflict and role ambiguity has used self-reports (usually questionnaires and occasionally interviews) of role ambiguity and conflict, these perceptions can alternatively be considered part of the psychological processes of the process facet. Similarly, early field studies showed that stressors are related to organizational outcomes such as absenteeism and turnover (e.g. Gupta and Beehr, 1979). These are among the most basic types of research results that must be found if the general model in Figure 1.1 or the more specific model in Figure 1.2 are correct.

As noted earlier, compared to the general facet model in Figure 1.1, the more specific model in Figure 1.2 clarifies the roles of time (duration), environmental characteristics other than the stressors themselves ('situational characteristics'), and personal characteristics by specifying that they have moderator effects rather than main effects. In addition, it shows that coping or adaptation can directly affect strains and organizational outcomes as well as stressors, and that individual strains may lead to organizational outcomes. My colleagues and I have studied several parts of this model, and these parts are depicted in Figure 1.4 (Beehr, 1995). The large rectangle in the middle of the figure is the 'core relationship' in all models and theories of occupational stress in the sense that it comprises the very definition of an occupational stress situation: stressors in the work environment cause strain in the individual. If this relationship is not present in a situation, then there is no occupational stress in the situation. Occasionally in research purporting to be a study of occupational stress, this core relationship is not studied. That is, there may be a sample of executives who are studied to see if their personal characteristics (e.g. Type A behavior pattern) are related to potential strains (e.g. depression). In this type of research, there is actually no evidence that there is any occupational stress whatsoever! Just because people have jobs (executives), and some of their personal characteristics are linked to depression does not mean the job had anything to do with their situation. Similar to such research, in some applied treatments purporting to be occupational stress treatments, there is often no evidence that occupational stress exists. This occurs frequently when individual strains are treated (e.g. hypertension or depression) for

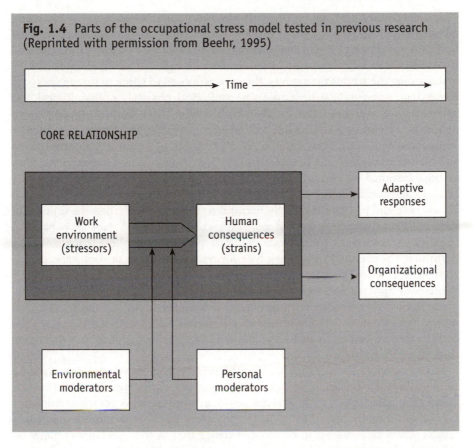

Fig. 1.4 Parts of the occupational stress model tested in previous research (Reprinted with permission from Beehr, 1995)

people who work in a single organization. Just because people have jobs does not mean that their jobs caused the strain. Therefore, if we explicitly wish to examine occupational stress, we would need to see if the core relationship exists—are stressors in the work environment at least related to strain reactions?

Evidence for the Core Relationship in Occupational Stress

The meta-analyses by Fisher and Gitelson (1983) and Jackson and Schuler (1985) indicated that role ambiguity and role conflict, two of the most-often studied stressors, were indeed usually related to strains, confirming the core, stressor–strain relationship. Other example stressors that have been shown related to one or more strains in research by my colleagues and myself include under-utilization of skills (e.g. Gupta and Beehr, 1979; Kaufmann and Beehr, 1986; 1989), role overload (e.g. Beehr *et al.*, 1976), interpersonal conflict (e.g. Beehr *et al.*, 1996; Beehr *et al.*, 1997*a*), lack of participation (e.g. Beehr *et al.*, 1976), daily events at work (e.g. Beehr *et al.*, 1997*b*), and job future ambiguity (e.g. Kaufmann and Beehr, 1986; 1989). In addition, research by others has implicated the following as occupational stressors: computer shutdowns

(Caplan and Jones, 1975), ethnic or gender discrimination (Sanchez and Brock, 1996), job activities involved in beginning a new job (Eden, 1982), and situational constraints (O'Connor *et al.*, 1984). There does seem adequate evidence that stressors might lead to strains.

Regarding the strains themselves, they are proposed to come in three types (e.g. Beehr, 1995; Kahn and Byosiere, 1992): psychological, physical or physiological, and behavioral. As noted in Kahn and Byosiere's review, there seems to be ample evidence that organizational stressors are linked to psychological strains (e.g. anxiety, depression) and probably to physiological strains (e.g. hypertension, catecholamine and cortisol secretions), but behavioral strains have been studied less often in relation to organizational stressors. Furthermore, there is a definition problem regarding behavioral strains. If strains are (1) responses to stressors and also (2) responses that are aversive and potentially directly harmful to the individual, then the domain of such behavioral strains is limited and somewhat value-laden. Not all behavioral responses to potential job stressors are strain responses—only those that are directly harmful to the person. Changes in job performance, therefore, are not strain behaviors, because, while they may be directly harmful (or helpful) to the organization, by themselves they are not necessarily harmful to the person. The same case can be made against absenteeism and turnover as behavioral strains. In the models presented here, these are organizational consequences rather than individual strains, because they more directly and immediately impact on the organization's well-being than on the individual's.

What behaviors, then, if they are in response to occupational stressors, are sufficiently harmful to the person to be judged strains? Potential examples would include illegal drug abuse and suicide. It is not obvious, however, whether these employee behaviors are really caused by occupational stress, due to a lack of clear research results. There does appear to be some evidence that smoking behaviors might be influenced by occupational stress, however (e.g. Caplan *et al.*, 1975). Behavioral strains are a topic in need of more investigation.

Evidence Regarding Uncertainty as a Psychological Process in Job Stress Situations

As noted earlier, the employees' uncertainty about their E→P and P→O expectancies are a common human process element in many occupational stress situations. This uncertainty is a somewhat difficult thing to study, because there are no handy measures of it in much of the prior research. It is probably easy to confuse such uncertainty with role ambiguity, and some role ambiguity measures seem to include one or more items whose content mixes environmental role ambiguity with the individual's uncertainty about performance or outcomes (Beehr, 1985). Four studies, however, have looked more explicitly at the uncertainty model than others. In the first study, of managers who were part-time evening students, Pardine (1987) showed that: (1) importance and uncertainty combined to predict four strains: anxiety, irritation, depression, and somatic complaints; (2) as predicted when the theory was developed (Beehr and Bhagat, 1985*b*), role ambiguity was related to both E→P and P→O uncertainties, while role conflict was related only to E→P uncertainty; and (3) the uncertainties showed some ability to mediate the relationship between the role stressors and the strains (as they should, since they are part of the process facet between stressors and strains in Figures 1.1 and 1.2). Pardine (1987) concluded that the results were generally supportive of the uncertainty model of occupational stress.

The second study (O'Driscoll and Beehr, 1994) examining the uncertainty model of occupational stress in two major accounting firms (one in the USA and one in New Zealand), was a path analytic study looking at leadership behaviors leading to stressors, which led to uncertainty, which in turn led to strains. As proposed in Figures 1.1 and 1.2, uncertainty (in the process facet) did seem to be an intermediate link between the stressors (role ambiguity and role conflict) and psychological strain. Unexpectedly, however, it was possible in the data that job satisfaction acted as a mediator variable in much the same way as the uncertainties did, and that the role stressors might have an additional independent effect on the strains.

The third study of uncertainty used uncertainty scales whose development was reported by Beehr (1987) in order to study occupational stress among hospital nurses (Beehr et al., 1986). The E→P and P→O uncertainties were generally related to role ambiguity and role conflict, and to psychological strains. In that study, the E→P uncertainties were more consistently related to stressors and strains than were the P→O uncertainties. It is not clear why this should be. One might speculate that the intrinsic rewards were especially important to these nurses, and the uncertainty regarding how to do a good job was especially distressing in that case. Role conflict, consistent with uncertainty theory and as found in the Pardine (1987) study, appeared to be more strongly related to E→P expectancies than to P→O expectancies, although the significance of this difference was not calculated.

The fourth study based explicitly on the uncertainty model focused on the proposed role of co-worker social support among a sample of human resource professionals in a large Midwestern city (Fenlason et al., 1997). In developing the uncertainty model of occupational stress, it was proposed that emotional support would have its effects on strains partially through affecting the importance of the outcomes, while instrumental social support would have most of its effect on strains through first affecting stressors and subsequently uncertainty. The model was tested via structural equation modeling comparing nested models, and the model most closely resembling the uncertainty model fit the data better than more simple, parsimonious models using the same variables.

Overall, therefore, the research on uncertainty as part of the process facet in the models in Figures 1.1 and 1.2 has so far been largely supportive.

Personal Characteristics as Moderators of Stressor–Strain Relationships

If there are individual differences or personal characteristics that moderate the relationship between occupational stressors and employees' strains (Figures 1.2 and 1.4), they would either strengthen or weaken the potential effects of stressors on strains. Many such differences have been proposed, but the research results have not often strongly confirmed them. One of the most popular is Type A Behavior Pattern, which is composed of several elements, such as employees' hostility, aggressiveness, competitiveness, and sense of time urgency (e.g. Friedman and Rosenman, 1974; Matthews, 1982). In recent years, however, empirical research has led to a narrowing of the concept of Type A to focus on the hostility component, because that part seems most consistently linked to strain-like health outcomes (Watkins and Eisler, 1988). The moderator hypothesis for Type A argues that Type A employees tend to have stronger relationships between occupational stressors and strains than non-Type A employees, who are sometimes labeled Type B (Ganster, 1987). Type A individuals are thus hyper-reactive to potentially stressful situations. Originally, however, Type A was simply considered to have a direct or main effect on people's health—specifically on coronary heart disease (Friedman and Rosenman, 1974), and it is still not clear how strongly it acts as a moderator. Kahn and Byosiere's (1992) review concluded that the moderating effect of Type A is likely to occur more for some stressors–strain combinations than others, although they did not offer specific proposals regarding which combinations, and they recommended continuing exploration of this relationship in future research.

Aside from Type A, other suggested personal characteristics that might act as moderators include gender, flexibility, and hardiness (a conglomerate of personality characteristics), self-esteem, and locus of control. Existing research on these in relation to occupational stress is, however, sparse. Few personal characteristics have been investigated for the moderating effect proposed here. Kahn and Byosiere (1992) noted a number of studies of self-esteem and locus of control that tested for moderator effects. According to their review, one of three studies on self-esteem found a moderating effect, and three of four studies on locus of control also found the same effect. One explanation for self-esteem having a moderating effect is that people with high self-esteem would have more confidence in themselves, including in their ability to cope, and therefore would appraise the situation as less threatening. This is saying that the personal characteristic influences the elements of the process facet in the models in Figures 1.1 and 1.2. Perception, appraisal, and evaluation are human processes that can occur when a potentially stressful situation is encountered. For locus of control, three of the four studies Kahn and Byosiere reviewed for moderator effects found one. The logic for locus of control as a moderator is similar to self-esteem. Internal people are more likely to have confidence in themselves (that they can affect their world in important ways) and are therefore more likely to control either their environment or their reactions to it. Current research on personal moderators is promising, and future research in this area seems warranted.

Environmental or Situational Characteristics as Moderators of Stressor–Strain Relationships

The models in Figures 1.2 and 1.4 propose that, in addition to personal characteristics, environmental characteristics can moderate the relationship between stressors and strains. The most frequently studied situational moderator is social support. Reviews of the research on the moderating or 'buffering' properties of social support generally conclude that social support is a potent variable, but part of its potency is due to its main effects, which are more consistently found than its moderating effects (Beehr, 1995; Kahn and Byosiere, 1992). Moderating effects of social support have been found too, but they are much more inconsistent. Furthermore, there are many instances of finding 'reverse buffering' effects, i.e. effects in which high levels of social support seem to strengthen the relationship between job stressors and strains instead of reducing it. More research is needed to figure out why this occurs. One problem with social support research is that social support is a very large number of 'things'. In the research, it has been operationalized as either structural (being in a social network, which almost everybody in an organization is) or functional (what functions does it provide for the person, usually emotional or instrumental). It can also have several sources (most commonly, in existing research, the supervisor, the co-workers, or organizational outsiders such as family and friends). For functional support, it would be useful to know exactly what behaviors the supportive people are doing that are helpful in reducing strains or that are deemed 'supportive' by the individual whether helpful or not. The inconsistent results regarding the moderating effects of social support may be due to the nature, type, and source of supportive behaviors. It is entirely possible that some sources of support and some supportive behaviors are more helpful than others, i.e. may result in more moderating effects than others (Beehr, 1995), and this should be a focus of future research. Regarding specific behaviors, some recent research by my colleagues and myself has focused on what people say to each other in potentially supportive situations in the workplace—in other words, the nature of the contents of their face-to-face communications (e.g. Beehr et al., 1990; Fenlason and Beehr, 1994; Fenlason et al., 1997).

Early research in stress and social support suggested that information exchange during supportive situations or episodes might constitute the crux of social support (e.g. Cobb, 1976), and this led us to examine what people say to each other as examples of social support. People can talk to each other, for example, about positive things about work, about negative things about work, or about non-work things. Co-workers, for example, can get together as friends and gripe to each other and agree about the poor working conditions, or they can be more positive, focusing their talk on the better things that have happened at work. Either of these may be seen as supportive of each other's views, but they may not be equally useful in alleviating the stressful effects of the workplace. Our research on these contents of potentially supportive communications indicates that they are likely to be important. Most basically, so far it looks as if positive communications are likely to have the most beneficial effects, and negative communications may not be very beneficial.

Aside from social support, the other environmental or situational characteristic that might moderate the stressor–strain relationship as depicted in Figures 1.2 and 1.4 is the control or autonomy the person has in his or her work situation. In organizational psychology, the job characteristic of autonomy has often been found related to good outcomes such as intrinsic job motivation and job satisfaction, and it is one of the characteristics of the most prominent model of job design (Hackman and Oldham, 1976; 1980). In some of my early research, I found that autonomy was a moderator of the relationship between one job stressor, role ambiguity, and some psychological strains (Beehr, 1976). Furthermore, there is an entire theory of job stress, sometimes labeled demand–control theory, that focuses on control of the situation as one of the major variables in occupational stress (Karasek, 1979), and control is usually described as a moderator. As in many other moderator research areas, however, research results have been mixed regarding control as a moderator. We may need to determine just what kind of control helps to moderate the situation; alternatively, it may turn out that control or autonomy moderates some stressor–strain relationships (i.e. some types of stressors or strains) more readily than others.

Evidence Regarding Organizational Consequences of Job Stress

As with social support and autonomy, some of my early research on job stress examined the organizational consequences of job stress. While organizational outcomes such as absenteeism, turnover, and changes in job performance are not necessarily part of the job stress process (i.e. job stress is defined by a situation in which stressors in the work environment lead to strains in the individual, regardless of whether or not they affect the organization), it does appear that the organization is also often affected by stress on the employees. This usually occurs through employee behaviors that have costs or benefits to the organization. Gupta and Beehr (1979) found, in a sample of five companies, employees who experienced more of the job stressors of role ambiguity, role overload, under-utilization of skills, and resource inadequacy were somewhat more likely to be absent during the subsequent month than other employees. Furthermore, for three of the four stressors, the correlation with the subsequent absenteeism was stronger than the correlation between these stressors and absenteeism prior to the measurement of the stressors. This comparison analysis was performed as a check on the potential confound that absenteeism was causing an increase in stressors rather than the other way around. Kaufmann and Beehr (1986), studying a sample of hospital nurses, found that one stressor, under-utilization of skills, was somewhat strongly related to absenteeism, while another (a combination of workload and ambiguity about the future) was not. Jackson and Schuler's (1985) meta-analysis found average effect sizes between role conflict and absenteeism to be near zero, and they reported negative but somewhat weak average relationships between role ambiguity and absenteeism.

Regarding another organizational outcome, turnover, Gupta and Beehr (1979) found that it was predicted by under-utilization of skills, but not by the other three stressors in the study. Turnover intentions have been studied more often than actual turnover in relation to job stress, however, and these intentions appear to be related to job stressors (reviews by Beehr, 1995; Jackson and Schuler, 1985).

A much less frequently studied organizational outcome, tardiness, may also be related to occupational stress. At least one study (Jamal, 1984) found evidence that tardiness might be related to job stressors or individual strains. It appears that this study used self-reported measures of the job stressors, role ambiguity, role overload, role conflict, and resource inadequacy that might have actually been a mixture of these stressors with some mild strain reactions (Beehr, 1995), and therefore it is not entirely clear whether the stressor or strain elements of the measures were responsible for the relationship with tardiness. It should be noted that the models in Figures 1.2 and 1.4 allow for either or both of these paths, however.

Regarding job performance, Kaufmann and Beehr (1986) found that nurses' job performance ratings (rated by their supervisors) were not related to the stressors, while Beehr *et al.* (1996) found that sales by booksellers were negatively predicted by three stressors: (1) workload variability and (2) chronic and (3) acute stressors specific to door-to-door booksellers. This job performance measure was not related to role overload, however. Jackson and Schuler's (1985) meta-analysis regarding role conflict and role ambiguity found average correlations between these two stressors and job performance to be generally weak.

Evidence for Duration or Time as a Factor in Occupational Stress

Time has been proposed as an important variable in occupational stress processes (e.g. McGrath and Beehr, 1990), but the study of it remains sketchy. It stands to reason that the longer one is exposed to a potentially noxious event, the stronger the consequences will be. In order to establish the duration of uncertainty, one would have to study the same uncertainty (i.e. uncertainty emanating from the same stressors) existing for different durations. No such studies have been conducted yet. There have been discussions, however, about acute, time-limited stressors versus chronic, long-term stressors (e.g. Beehr and Franz, 1987). In addition to the duration of the uncertainty specifically, it would also be relevant to see whether the same stressor over longer duration has greater effects on strains. Both acute, short-term occupational stressors (e.g. nurses dealing with patients for the first time; Eden, 1982) and chronic, long-term stressors (e.g. role ambiguity and role conflict) have been found individually to predict strains, although the bulk of the research has focused on chronic stressors. There is, in the popular literature, the notion that acute, dramatic, emotion-arousing events (traumatic events) at work might be especially stressful. In this case, the extreme arousal might be assumed to make up for the lack of duration of the event. Examples would be firefighters, police, and emergency medical technicians encountering severe injuries or death to others. Some of the better-controlled studies do not often find, however, that such events are strongly linked to strains among employees in such jobs (e.g. Allen, 1995; Barling *et al.*, 1987). It is not possible to evaluate the independent effects of duration from existing research, because the stressors are usually different when the duration is different. For one thing, measures of acute stressors tend to be occupation-specific, and while measures of chronic stressors could be occupation-specific, they usually are not. Instead, they are usually generic measures that could be used in a variety of occupations—perhaps in order to allow generalization across studies with different job samples. Beehr *et al.* (1996), however, were able to study chronic versus acute stressors among door-to-door book dealers using occupation-specific measures of both. In that study, they found that the chronic stressors had larger effect sizes on the strains than the acute stressors did. This provides some evidence consistent with the idea that duration is an important part of occupational stress, although more research on the time dimension is needed.

Treatments for Occupational Stress

Coping or adaptation in the stress models refer to ways in which people reduce, avoid, or alleviate the negative consequences of occupational stress. When consciously planned and implemented, such actions are often called 'treatments'. To understand the nature of such treatments, it is helpful to consider the types of primary targets that are the focus of a treatment. In all cases, the treatment is expected ultimately to affect the individual's strains, but the original or primary target might be something other than the strain itself. Two main categories of primary targets are the organization and the person (Ivancevich and Matteson, 1987; Murphy, 1987; Newman and Beehr, 1979).

The Individual as the Primary Target of Stress Treatments

The person or individual as the primary target is by far the most commonly used treatment category. In such treatments, there is an attempt to directly change something about the person him- or herself. Some of these treatments seem to aim directly at the strain. If an employee has hypertension, for example, medication may be prescribed. If he or she is tense and anxious, progressive muscle relaxation training may be undertaken so that the person can relax at will or remain relaxed in the face of otherwise stressful stimuli. These approaches, the most obvious examples of which are from the medical or clinical and counseling psychology approaches noted earlier, try to change the person directly, and to aim pretty close to the strain itself. It should be noted that this amounts to addressing the negative effects of stress (individual strains), while leaving the causes (organizational stressors) intact.

Other person-targeted approaches might focus more on changing the long-term nature of the person. If, for example, the individual's personality seems to play a part in the strain (e.g. a Type A person), one approach would be to try to alter the very nature of the person. Changing personality traits might be somewhat difficult and at best a slow process, because personality traits are considered relatively stable or semi-permanent. Long-term psychotherapy sometimes has this as a goal. Its use for the specific purpose of alleviating occupational stress, however, might seem misplaced. If there is indeed a situation with occupational stress, then by definition, a main cause is the nature of the work environment (it has stressors). Logically, treating the person as the initial target is leaving a primary cause of occupational stress untouched (the stressors in the workplace). If the stressors continue to exist, then the treatment must either have a permanent effect (e.g. if changing basic personality structures), or the treatment must continue forever (e.g. if treating the strains through medication or relaxation). This is because the environmental stressors, if chronic, will continue to exert pressure that tends to result in individual strains.

Individually targeted treatments for occupational stress seem to be mildly effective at best, according to the best, most objective evaluations of them (Beehr, 1995; Murphy, 1987). In one example of stress treatments among public agency employees, Ganster *et al.* (1982) reported a field experiment in which highly trained professionals used progressive relaxation to reduce tension and cognitive behavior modification to change the appraisal of the situation. These interventions appeared to reduce depression and urinary epinephrine levels compared to a randomly assigned control group, although they did not seem to affect norepinephrine, anxiety, irritation, or somatic complaints. The effects of the intervention were small, however, and they did not seem to replicate when the intervention was subsequently tried with the control group. These results seem fairly typical of reports of well-evaluated individually targeted stress treatments.

There are some common potential problems with the evaluations of many of these treatments, including small sample sizes, which make it difficult to find statistical significance (not a problem with the Ganster *et al.* study, however) and the need for people to follow through with their treatment plan (e.g. practising relaxation techniques). In addition philosophical, ethical, and logical problems with individually targeted treatments have also been voiced many times before (e.g. Beehr, 1995; Ganster *et al.*, 1982; Murphy, 1987), because it is placing the primary responsibility for treatment on the individual when the primary cause of the problem is in the organization.

The Organization as the Primary Target of Stress Treatments

Although few organizationally targeted treatments of occupational stress have been reported, they have their own set of problems. First, because they involve changing some ways in which the organization functions (e.g. rules, procedures, communication, supervisory styles), the actions or at least permission to undertake them must come from those in power in the organization—usually some level of management. Stress reduction is often not one of the major tasks managers believe they face in their jobs, and so it is likely to get less attention than other important matters in their work. This alone could account for the relative lack of organizational interventions for job stress. Second, diagnosis must be undertaken to determine the source (organizational stressor) that is likely to be causing the employee strains, because the stressors are to be the target of the treatment. One needs to know, for example, that role ambiguity is likely to be the stressor causing strains before developing a treatment program aimed at reducing ambiguity. It should be noted that the individually targeted treatments of job stress often do not make such a diagnosis. Instead, at most, the diagnosis of employee mental and/or physical health is usually the only one undertaken. When this happens, labeling the individual treatments as treatments of occupational stress has no evidence behind it. That is, if one finds ill people who have jobs, that does show that the jobs caused the illness, but labeling the treatments as occupational stress treatments asserts this. Therefore, it is unknown whether many of the occupational stress treatments have anything to do with job stress at all! When the organization is the primary target, however, this is not a problem, because stressors must be diagnosed before a treatment can logically be designed.

There are so few reports of organizationally targeted treatments that it is difficult at present to conclude anything about their effectiveness. One example is a study by Landisberger and Vivona-Vaughan (1995), in which they compared an intervention group with a matched control group among employees of a public agency. Because of some apparent employee strains, they set up an elected problem-solving committee of employee representatives who analyzed potential organizational stressors and recommended changes to management. At best, however, there were small and inconsistent effects on self-reported psychological and physical strains, or for that matter, on organizational targets such as group process, work demands, or other stressors. Apparently, management also underwent reorganization and personnel changes during this time, probably resulting in less commitment to the program; not all recommendations from the committees were implemented by management. More research is needed on organizationally targeted interventions, but the impact so far has been weak.

Occupational Stress Treatments and the Uncertainty Model

Most of the treatments reported in the literature, both organizationally and individually targeted, are just as sensible in the context of one occupational stress theory as another; they try to treat the employees' strains (usually) or the organization's stressors (occasionally), and stressors and strains are a basic part of every model or theory of occupational stress. Therefore, nearly all the stress treatments logically apply to the model presented here. One of the more unique things in this model, however, is the role of uncertainty. Occupational stress interventions are usually not aimed specifically at reducing uncertainty of how to direct one's efforts in order to perform the job well, nor do they usually try to clarify the relationships between performance levels and various outcomes. It does not make sense for a stress treatment to do *only* this, but this could be an additional aim of the intervention. There are surely situations in which employees can simply be provided with information that could reduce their uncertainties about E→P or P→O expectancies. If past company practices, current official policy, or other facts are pointed out to the employees, they might quickly become more clear about reward contingencies, thereby clarifying some P→O expectancies. Instruction and training might help clarify how they should direct their efforts in order to have better performance, thereby clarifying some E→P expectancies. In most organizations, however, these things are probably done fairly quickly for the employees, and therefore, these 'easy' solutions are probably not commonly useful. Instead, the best way to clarify these expectancies is probably to change the stressors, because they cause the uncertainty. Therefore, this again suggests the use of organizationally targeted treatments.

Social Support as a Treatment

There has been some disagreement about how social support might be useful in reducing the harmful effects of occupational stress, but most experts are agreed that it helps. As noted earlier, there are at least three major ways in which social support might be an effective treatment for job stress: it could reduce the stressors directly, reduce the strains directly, or reduce the strength of the effect of the stressors on the strains. While it is important in research and theory to examine each of these possibilities closely, in practice it probably matters little which is the stronger effect, so long as there is an effect. In each case, support would ultimately reduce the individual employees' strains, of course. Most research on social support and occupational stress has been non-experimental, and therefore has not tried explicitly to manipulate it, although many stress treatments probably include some increase in social support by accident if not by design (e.g. as in Caplan *et al.*, 1989). While providing any stress training in relaxation or cognitive restructuring, the trainer is probably also offering encouragement and support, and in situations in which there is a group of people receiving stress management training, the group members are likely to offer support in some form or other to each other.

Alternatively, if one is to offer support as the or one of the major treatments of occupational stress, it would be necessary to know more operationally what social support is. The research I have been conducting regarding the contents of oral communication to each other was aimed in part at providing such clues (e.g. Beehr *et al.*, 1990; Fenlason and Beehr, 1994; Fenlason *et al.*, 1997). For example, it appears that providing encouragement might be more helpful for reducing strain than commiserating about the stressors. This knowledge is a good start, but additional research, specifically on the nature of helpful social support, will aid in developing more useful programs of social support as an occupational stress treatment.

Two recent meta-analyses of social support and occupational stress concluded that its effects are small. Average published correlations between social support and job stressors might be about −.12 or −.13; average correlations between social support and strains might be between −.10 and −.21, perhaps depending on the type of strain; average effect size (usually an increase in R-square in moderated multiple regression) might .03 or less, again perhaps depending on the type of strain (Beehr, 1994; Sanchez *et al.*, 1997). These results indicate that the effectiveness of social support in reducing stressors directly, reducing strains directly, or in reducing the impact of stressors on strains, respectively, can only be modest but is probably worth trying. Research on the operational nature of social support (e.g. types of communication or other specific types of supportive behaviors) can help direct future applications in order to have the strongest possible effect.

Conclusion

Some advertising recently said that occupational stress has reached 'epidemic' proportions. While it is hard to find solid evidence for such statements, it does appear that stressors exist in the workplace, probably more in some places and types of work than in others, and that it can have serious harmful effects on the people working there. There is good evidence for models of job stress proposing that stressors in the work environment lead to some intermediate psychological or physiological processes that can result in harmful effects to the person. Furthermore, certain environmental and personal characteristics are probably able to moderate such effects. Some organizationally valued outcomes, such as absenteeism and turnover, are related to too much stress, but for others, such as job performance and productivity, the evidence is not so clear. While we have many good ideas about how to alleviate the deleterious effects of occupational stress on the person, in practice, the success of occupational stress treatments so far has been modest. More and better evaluation of stress treatment programs will eventually lead us to discover the most effective forms of treatment, however.

References

Allen, S. J. (1995) *An examination of the relationship between two types of occupational stressors: Chronic stressors and traumatic events*. Ph.D. dissertation, Central Michigan University, Mt. Pleasant, MI.

Barling, J., Bluen, S. D., and Fain, R. (1987) 'Psychological functioning following an acute disaster', *Journal of Applied Psychology*, 72, 683–690.

Beehr, T. A. (1976) 'Perceived situational moderators of the relationship between subjective role ambiguity and role strain', *Journal of Applied Psychology*, 61, 35–40.

Beehr, T. A. (1985) Organizational stress and employee effectiveness: A job characteristics approach. In T. A. Beehr and R. S. Bhagat (eds.), *Human Stress and Cognition in Organizations: An Integrated Perspective* (pp. 57–81). New York: John Wiley & Sons.

Beehr, T. A. (1987) The themes of social-psychological stress in work organizations: From roles to goals. In A. W. Riley and S. J. Zacarro (eds.), *Occupational Stress and Organizational Effectiveness* (pp. 71–102). New York: Praeger Press.

Beehr, T. A. (1994) Meta-analysis of Occupational Stress and Social Support. Paper presented at the annual meeting of the Midwestern Psychological Association, Chicago, April.

Beehr, T. A. (1995) *Psychological Stress in the Workplace*. London: Routledge.

Beehr, T. A. and Bhagat, R. S. (1985a) *Human Stress and Cognition in Organizations: An Integrated Perspective*. New York: John Wiley and Sons.

Beehr, T. A. and Bhagat, R. S. (1985b) Introduction to human stress and cognition in organizations. In T. A. Beehr and R. S. Bhagat (eds.), *Human Stress and Cognition in Organizations: An Integrated Perspective* (pp. 3–19). New York: John Wiley & Sons.

Beehr, T. A. and Franz, T. M. (1987) The current debate about the meaning of job stress. In J. M. Ivancevich and D. C. Ganster (eds.), *Job Stress: From Theory to Suggestion* (pp. 5–18). New York: Haworth Press.

Beehr, T. A. and McGrath, J. E. (1992) 'Social support, occupational stress, and anxiety', *Anxiety Research: An International Journal*, 5, 7–19.

Beehr, T. A. and McGrath, J. E. (1996) The methodology of research on coping: Conceptual, strategic, and operational-level issues. In M. Zeidner and N. S. Endler (eds.), *Handbook of Coping: Theory, Research, Applications*. New York: John Wiley & Sons, Inc.

Beehr, T. A. and Newman, J. E. (1978) 'Job stress, employee health, and organizational effectiveness: A facet analysis, model, and literature review', *Personnel Psychology*, 31, 365–399.

Beehr, T. A., Drexler, J. A. Jr., and Faulkner, S. (1997a) 'Working in small family businesses: Empirical comparisons to non-family businesses', *Journal of Organizational Behavior*, 18, 297–312.

Beehr, T. A., King, L. A., and King, D. W. (1986) Theoretical and empirical development of the function of uncertain expectancies in occupational stress. In D. J. Abramis (Chair), The Past, Present and Future of Job Stress Research: New Thoughts about Old Concepts. Symposium presented at the annual meeting of the Academy of Management, Chicago.

Beehr, T. A., King, L. A., and King, D. W. (1990) 'Social support and occupational stress: Talking to supervisors', *Journal of Vocational Behavior*, 36, 61–81.

Beehr, T. A., Stacy, B. A., Murray, M. A. and Jex, S. M. (1996) Work Stress and Coworker Support as Predictors of Individual Strain and Job Performance. Paper presented at the annual meeting of the Academy of Management, Cincinnati, OH, August.

Beehr, T. A., Walsh, J. T., and Taber, T. D. (1976) 'Relationships of stress to individually and organizationally valued states: Higher order needs as a moderator', *Journal of Applied Psychology*, 61, 35–40.

Caplan, R. D. and Jones, K. W. (1975) 'Effects of workload, role ambiguity, and Type A personality on anxiety, depression and heart rate', *Journal of Applied Psychology*, 60, 713–719.

Caplan, R. D., Cobb, S., and French, J. R. P. Jr. (1975) 'Relationships of cessation of smoking with job stress, personality, and social support', *Journal of Applied Psychology*, 60, 211–219.

Caplan, R. D., Vinokur, A. D., Price, R. H., and Van Ryn, M. (1989) 'Job seeking, reemployment, and mental health: A randomized field experiment in coping with job loss', *Journal of Applied Psychology*, 74, 759–769.

Cobb, S. (1976) 'Social support as a moderator of life stress', *Psychosomatic Medicine*, 38, 300–314.

Eden, D. (1982) 'Critical job events, acute stress, and strain: A multiple interrupted time series', *Organizational Behavior and Human Performance*, 30, 312–329.

Fenlason, K. J. and Beehr, T. A. (1994) 'Social support and occupational stress: Effects of talking to others', *Journal of Organizational Behavior*, 15, 157–175.

Fenlason, K. J., Johnson, J., and Beehr, T. A. (1997) Social support, stressors and strains: Support for a cognitive model of job stress. In J. I. Sanchez (Chair), Understanding the Role of Social Support in the Process of Work Stress: The Missing Links. Symposium presented at the annual meeting of the Society for Industrial and Organizational Psychology, Inc., St. Louis, MO, April.

Fisher, C. D. and Gitelson, R. (1983) 'A meta-analysis of the correlates of role conflict and ambiguity', *Journal of Applied Psychology*, 68, 320–333.

Friedman, M. and Rosenman, R. H. (1974) *Type A Behavior and your Heart*. New York: Alfred A. Knopf.

Ganster, D. C. (1987) Type A behavior and occupational stress. In J. M. Ivancevich and D. C. Ganster (eds.), *Job Stress: From Theory to Suggestion* (pp. 61–84). New York: Haworth Press.

Ganster, D. C., Mayes, B. T., Sime, W. E., and Tharp, G. D. (1982) 'Managing organizational stress: a field experiment', *Journal of Applied Psychology*, 67, 533–542.

Gupta, N. and Beehr, T. A. (1979) 'Job stress and employee behaviors'. *Organizational Behavior and Human Performance*, 23, 373–387.

Hackman, J. R. and Oldham, G. R. (1976) 'Motivation through the design of work: Test of a theory', *Organizational Behavior and Human Performance*, 16, 250–279.

Hackman, J. R. and Oldham, G. R. (1980) *Work Redesign*. Reading, MA: Addison-Wesley.

Ivancevich, J. M. and Matteson, M. T. (1987) Organizational level stress management interventions: A review and recommendations. In J. M. Ivancevich and D. C. Ganster (eds.), *Job Stress: From Theory to Suggestion* (pp. 229–248). New York: The Haworth Press.

Jackson, S. E. and Schuler, R. S. (1985) 'A meta-analysis and conceptual critique of research on role ambiguity and role conflict in work settings', *Organizational Behavior and Human Decision Processes*, 36, 16–78.

Jamal, M. (1984) 'Job stress and job performance controversy: an empirical assessment', *Organizational Behavior and Human Performance*, 33, 1–21.

Jex, S. M., Beehr, T. A., and Roberts, C. K. (1992) 'The meaning of "stress" items to survey respondents', *Journal of Applied Psychology*, 77, 623–628.

Kahn, R. L. and Byosiere, P. (1992) Stress in organizations. In M. D. Dunnette and L. M. Hough (eds.), *Handbook of industrial and organizational psychology, Vol. 3* (2nd edn.) (pp. 571–650). Palo Alto, CA: Consulting Psychologists Press, Inc.

Karasek, R. A. (1979) 'Job demands, job decision latitude, and mental strain: Implications of job redesign', *Administrative Science Quarterly*, 24, 285–308.

Katz, D. and Kahn, R. L. (1978) *The Social Psychology of Organizations* (2nd edn.), New York: John Wiley & Sons.

Kaufmann, G. M. and Beehr, T. A. (1986) 'Interactions between job stressors and social support: some counterintuitive results', *Journal of Applied Psychology*, 71, 522–526.

Kaufmann, G. M. and Beehr, T. A. (1989) 'Occupational stressors, individual strains, and social supports among police officers', *Human Relations*, 42, 185–197.

Landisberger, P. A. and Vivona-Vaughan, E. (1995) 'Evaluation of an occupational stress intervention in a public agency', *Journal of Organizational Behavior*, 16, 29–48.

Lazarus, R. S. (1966) *Psychological Stress and the Coping Process*. New York: McGraw-Hill.

Lazarus, R. S. and Folkman, S. (1984) *Stress, Coping and Adaptation*. New York: Springer.

McGrath, J. E. and Beehr, T. A. (1990) 'Some temporal issues in the conceptualization and measurement of stress', *Stress Medicine*, 6, 93–104.

Mason, J. W. (1975) 'A historical view of the stress field. Part I', *Journal of Human Stress*, 1, 6–12.

Matthews, K. A. (1982) 'Psychological perspectives on the Type A behavior pattern', *Psychological Bulletin*, 91, 293–323.

Murphy, L. R. (1987) A review of organizational stress management research: Methodological considerations. In J. M. Ivancevich and D. C. Ganster (eds.), *Job Stress: From Theory to Suggestion* (pp. 215–228). New York: The Haworth Press.

Newman, J. E. and Beehr, T. A. (1979) 'Personal and organizational strategies for handling job stress: A review of research and opinion', *Personnel Psychology*, 32, 1–43.

O'Connor, E. J., Peters, L. H., Pooyan, A., Weekley, J., Frank, B., and Erenkrantz, B. (1984) 'Situational constraint effects on performance, affective reactions, and turnover: A field replication and extension', *Journal of Applied Psychology*, 69, 663–672.

O'Driscoll, M. P. and Beehr, T. A. (1994) 'Supervisor behaviors, role stressors and uncertainty as predictors of personal outcomes for subordinates', *Journal of Organizational Behavior*, 15, 141–155.

Pardine, P. A., Jr. (1987) Empirical Test of a Cognitive Model of Work Stress. Paper presented at the annual meeting of the Eastern Psychological Association, April.

Pearce, J. L. (1981) 'Bringing some clarity to role ambiguity research', *Academy of Management Review*, 6, 665–674.

Sanchez, J. I. and Brock. P. (1996) 'Outcomes of perceived discrimination among Hispanic employees: Is diversity management a luxury or a necessity?' *Academy of Management Journal*, 39, 704–719.

Sanchez, J. I., Viswesvaran, C., and Fisher, J. (1997) A meta-analytic test of alternate models of the role of social support in the work stressor–strain relationship. In J. I. Sanchez (Chair), Understanding the Role of Social Support in the Process of Work Stress: The Missing Links. Symposium presented at the annual meeting of the Society for Industrial and Organizational Psychology, St. Louis, MO, April.

Selye, H. (1956) *The Stress of Life*. New York: McGraw-Hill.

Selye, H. (1975) 'Confusion and controversy in the stress field', *Journal of Human Stress*, (June), 37–44.

Timio, M. and Gentili, S. (1976) 'Adrenosympathetic overactivity under conditions of work stress', *British Journal of Preventive Sociology of Medicine*, 30, 262–265.

Watkins, P. L. and Eisler, R. M. (1988) 'The type A behavior pattern, hostility and interpersonal skill', *Behavior Modification*, 12, 315–334.

2

···

Person–Environment Fit Theory:
Conceptual Foundations, Empirical Evidence, and Directions for Future Research

Jeffrey R. Edwards, Robert D. Caplan and R. Van Harrison

Theories of stress have long recognized the importance of both the person and environment in understanding the nature and consequences of stress. Person constructs relevant to stress research include Type-A behavior (Friedman and Rosenman, 1959), locus of control (Rotter, 1966), hardiness (Kobasa, 1979), and coping styles (Menaghan, 1983). The environment has been construed as stressful life events (Rabkin and Struening, 1976), daily hassles (DeLongis *et al.*, 1982), and chronic stressors such as role conflict and ambiguity (Kahn *et al.*, 1964; Jackson and Schuler, 1985), role overload and underload (French and Caplan, 1972), and job demands and decision latitude (Karasek and Theorell, 1990). This dual emphasis on the person and environment in stress research is characteristic of the interactive perspective in psychology (Lewin, 1951; Magnusson and Endler, 1977; Murray, 1951; Pervin, 1989), which indicates that behavior, attitudes, and well-being are determined jointly by the person and environment.

The contributions of the person and environment to stress have been formalized in the person–environment (P–E) fit theory of stress (Caplan, 1983, 1987*a*, 1987*b*; Caplan and Harrison, 1993; French *et al.*, 1982; French *et al.*, 1974; Harrison, 1978, 1985). The core premise of P–E fit theory is that stress arises not from the person or environment separately, but rather by their fit or congruence with one another. This simple yet powerful notion is reflected in numerous theories of stress and well-being (Cummings and Cooper, 1979; Edwards, 1992; McGrath, 1976; Rice *et al.*, 1985; Schuler, 1980) and is largely responsible for the widespread impact of P–E fit theory in stress research (Edwards and Cooper, 1990; Eulberg *et al.*, 1988).

The purpose of this chapter is threefold. First, we provide a conceptual overview of P–E fit theory, defining its core constructs and examining its basic mechanisms. This overview encompasses presentations of P–E fit theory from the original work by French and colleagues (French and Kahn, 1962; French *et al.*, 1974) through later developments and refinements by Caplan (1983, 1987*a*, 1987*b*), Harrison (1978, 1985), and Edwards (1996; Edwards and Cooper, 1990). Second, we summarize empirical research relevant to P–E fit theory, including the original studies conducted at the Institute for Social Research at the University of Michigan (Caplan *et al.*, 1980; French *et al.*, 1982) and other studies relevant to the basic propositions of P–E fit theory (Assouline and Meir, 1987; Edwards, 1991; Michalos, 1986; Spokane, 1985). Third, we discuss conceptual and methodological issues pertaining to future research into P–E fit theory. As this discussion will show, existing research has addressed only the most basic propositions of P–E fit theory, and many unanswered questions regarding the meaning and consequences of P–E fit remain to be investigated. Collectively, these questions constitute an agenda for a second generation of P–E fit research that may substantially advance our knowledge of how the person and environment combine to influence stress and well-being.

Overview of P–E Fit Theory

Conceptual Foundations

Basic concepts and distinctions As noted previously, the fundamental premise of P–E fit theory is that stress arises from misfit between the person and the environment. The core elements of the theory are shown in Figure 2.1, which depicts three basic distinctions central to P–E fit theory. The first and most basic distinction is between

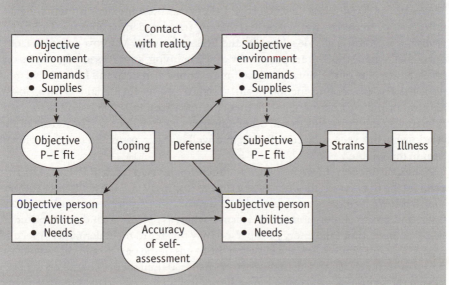

Fig. 2.1 A model of stress as person–environment fit. Concepts within circles are discrepancies between the two adjoining concepts. Solid lines indicate causal effects. Broken lines indicate contributions to person–environment comparisons (Adapted from Harrison, 1978)

the person and the environment. This distinction is a prerequisite for the conceptualization of P–E fit and provides the basis for examining reciprocal causation between
the person and environment. The second distinction is between objective and subjective representations of the person and environment. The *objective person* refers to
attributes of the person as they actually exist, whereas the *subjective person* signifies
the person's perception of his or her own attributes (i.e., the person's self-identity or
self-concept). Analogously, the *objective environment* includes physical and social situations and events as they exist independent of the person's perceptions, whereas the
subjective environment refers to situations and events as encountered and perceived by
the person. As shown in Figure 2.1, the objective person and environment are
causally related to their subjective counterparts (Harrison, 1978). These relationships
are imperfect due to perceptual distortions (e.g. repression, denial), cognitive construction processes (Weick, 1979), limited human information processing capacities
(March and Simon, 1958), and organizational structures that limit access to objective
information (Caplan, 1987b; Harrison, 1978).

The two distinctions described above combine to yield four types of correspondence between person and environment constructs: (1) *objective P–E fit*, which refers
to the fit between the objective person and the objective environment; (2) *subjective
P–E fit*, or the fit between the subjective person and the subjective environment; (3)
contact with reality, meaning the degree to which the subjective environment corresponds to the objective environment; and (4) *accuracy of self-assessment* (or accessibility of the self; French *et al.*, 1974), representing the match between the objective
person and the subjective person (Caplan, 1983; French *et al.*, 1974; Harrison, 1978).
Initial presentations of P–E fit theory (French *et al.*, 1974; Harrison, 1978) indicated
that good mental health is signified by minimal discrepancies on objective P–E fit,
subjective P–E fit, contact with reality, and accuracy of self-assessment. However,
subsequent refinements of the theory (Caplan, 1983, 1987a, 1987b; French *et al.*, 1982;
Harrison, 1985) point out that objective P–E fit has little impact on mental health
unless it is perceived by the person and thereby translated into subjective P–E fit (cf.
House, 1974; Kahn *et al.*, 1964; Lazarus and Folkman, 1984). Moreover, Caplan (1983)
notes that, when stressors are potentially overwhelming, some disengagement from
objective aspects of the situation or self may dampen anxiety and facilitate adaptation, thereby promoting mental health (Lazarus, 1983; Taylor and Brown, 1988).
Hence, current treatments of P–E fit theory emphasize subjective P–E fit as the critical pathway to mental health and other dimensions of well-being. The nature of the
relationship between subjective P–E fit and well-being is examined in greater detail
later in this chapter.

A third distinction shown in Figure 2.1 differentiates two types of P–E fit. The first
involves the fit between the demands of the environment and the abilities of the person. *Demands* include quantitative and qualitative job requirements, role expectations, and group and organizational norms, whereas *abilities* include the aptitudes,
skills, training, time, and energy the person may muster to meet demands. A second
type of P–E fit entails the match between the needs of the person and the supplies in
the environment that pertain to the person's needs. P–E fit theory characterizes *needs*
in general terms, encompassing innate biological and psychological requirements,

values acquired through learning and socialization, and motives to achieve desired ends (French and Kahn, 1962; Harrison, 1985). *Supplies* refer to extrinsic and intrinsic resources and rewards that may fulfill the person's needs, such as food, shelter, money, social involvement, and the opportunity to achieve (Harrison, 1978).

Commensurate person and environment constructs   For both needs–supplies fit and demands–abilities fit, P–E fit theory requires that person and environment constructs are commensurate, meaning they refer to the same content dimension. For example, needs–supplies fit regarding achievement should entail the comparison of need for achievement with opportunities for achievement in the environment. Likewise, demands–abilities fit regarding quantitative workload would involve comparing the amount of work to be done with the amount of work the person can do. Commensurate dimensions are required for the conceptualization and measurement of P–E fit, because the degree of fit between the person and the environment can be determined only if both refer to the same content dimension and can be measured on the same metric. Without commensurate dimensions, it is impossible to determine the proximity of the person and environment to one another, and the notion of P E fit becomes meaningless. The requirement of commensurate dimensions distinguishes P–E fit theory from more general interactionist models of the person and environment, such as those examining the moderating effects of personality on the relationship between environmental stressors and health (Cohen and Edwards, 1989; Parkes, 1994).

Definition of stress   Although P–E fit theory holds a central position in stress research (Eulberg *et al.*, 1988), the concept of stress is not explicitly depicted in Figure 2.1. The omission of stress does not threaten the internal validity of the theory, which is primarily concerned with the nature and consequences of P–E fit. Thus, some presentations of P–E fit theory have defined stress (Caplan *et al.*, 1980; French *et al.*, 1982; Harrison, 1978, 1985), whereas others have avoided the term (Caplan, 1983, 1987*a*, 1987*b*; French, 1973; French *et al.*, 1974). Although stress is ancillary to P–E fit theory, the meaning of stress has generated considerable debate in the stress literature (Lazarus and Folkman, 1984; Parker and DeCotiis, 1983; Schuler, 1980), and proposing a definition of stress consistent with P–E fit theory may help position the theory within the broader stress literature and facilitate its comparison with other theories.

For this chapter, we draw from the definition of stress proposed by Harrison (1978, 1985), who states that stress arises when: (1) the environment does not provide adequate supplies to meet the person's needs; or (2) the abilities of the person fall short of demands that are prerequisite to receiving supplies. Three features of this definition should be underscored. First, stress is defined not in terms of the person or the environment, but rather as their degree of misfit. This definition avoids problems with definitions of stress as a characteristic of the environment or as a psychological or physiological response by the person (for criticisms of such definitions, see Edwards, 1992; Lazarus and Folkman, 1984). Second, contrary to some definitions of stress (Shirom, 1982), this definition stipulates that a misfit between demands and abilities itself does not itself constitute stress. Rather, excess demands generate stress only if meeting demands is required to receive supplies, or if demands have been internalized as goals or motives of the person, as when norms or role expectations are accepted by the person as guidelines for his or her own behavior. Third, as noted previously, P–E fit theory views subjective misfit as the critical pathway from the person and environment to strain (see Figure 2.1). Therefore, we view stress as subjective rather than objective misfit between person and environment constructs. In sum, we define *stress* as *a subjective appraisal indicating that supplies are insufficient to fulfill the person's needs*, with the provision that insufficient supplies may occur as a consequence of unmet demands.

Outcomes of P–E misfit   According to P–E fit theory, subjective P–E misfit leads to two sets of outcomes. One set of outcomes comprises psychological, physical, and behavioral strains, defined as deviations from normal functioning (Caplan *et al.*, 1980; Harrison, 1978). Psychological strains include dissatisfaction, anxiety, dysphoria, or complaints of insomnia or restlessness. Physiological strains include elevated blood pressure, elevated serum cholesterol, and compromised immune system functioning. Behavioral symptoms of strain include smoking, overeating, absenteeism, and frequent utilization of health care services. When such responses constitute risk factors for disease, as in the case of smoking, overeating, and elevated blood pressure, the cumulative experience of strains over time can lead to mental and physical illnesses such as chronic depression, hypertension, coronary heart disease, peptic ulcer, and cancer. Conversely, a sustained good P–E fit can produce positive health outcomes (Edwards and Cooper, 1988; Harrison, 1978, 1985).

A second set of outcomes involves efforts to resolve P–E misfit, depicted in Figure 2.1 as coping and defense. *Coping* entails efforts to improve objective P–E fit, either by changing the objective person (i.e., adaptation) or the objective environment (i.e., environmental mastery) (French *et al.*, 1974). For example, a person experiencing excessive demands at work may seek training to enhance his or her abilities or attempt to negotiate a decreased workload with his or her supervisor (Harrison, 1978). *Defense* involves efforts to enhance subjective P–E fit through a cognitive distortion of the subjective person or environment (e.g. repression, projection, denial) without changing their objective counterparts (French *et al.*, 1974). For instance, a person may respond to role overload by overestimating his or her abilities or by downplaying or ignoring excess demands. Harrison (1978) notes that defense may also include the denial of experienced strain, such that the person acknowledges subjective P–E misfit but discounts its resulting negative impacts on health. Another form of defense is described by French *et al.* (1974), who indicate that a person may respond to subjective misfit by reducing the perceived importance of the dimension on which misfit occurs, as when a person disengages from unattainable goals (Klinger, 1975; Schuler, 1985). The terms coping and defense do not imply that defense is more primitive or undesirable than coping (Caplan, 1987a). Indeed, defense mechanisms such as denial can be adaptive, particularly when the objective person and environment cannot be changed (Lazarus, 1983). The choice from among these alternative methods of adjustment is influenced by various person and environment factors, such as stable preferences, coping styles, and environmental resources and constraints.

These two sets of P–E fit outcomes are likely to be interrelated. For example, coping may reduce or eliminate objective misfit, which may in turn resolve subjective misfit and reduce strain. Alternately, defense may attenuate the effects of objective misfit on subjective misfit, thereby influencing strain. In either case, coping and defense influence strain through their effects on subjective P–E fit. Conversely, strain may influence the choice or success of attempts to resolve P–E misfit via coping and defense. For instance, prolonged strain may lead to depression, which in turn may hinder social interactions and alienate potential sources of social support (Cole and Milstead, 1989). This withdrawal of social support may limit the person's options for resolving P–E misfit, forcing the person to rely on defensive reappraisals rather than instrumental coping efforts directed toward the objective person or environment (Valentiner *et al.*, 1994).

Relationships Between P–E Fit and Strain

Relationship of needs–supplies fit to strain   P–E fit theory specifies three basic relationships between fit and strain. These relationships are illustrated in Figure 2.2, which depicts the effects of needs–supplies fit on strain. The horizontal axis represents the comparison of needs to supplies, with positive scores indicating that supplies exceed needs, negative scores indicating that supplies fall short of needs, and a score of zero indicating perfect fit between supplies and needs. The vertical axis represents some form of strain (e.g. job dissatisfaction).

The solid line in Figure 2.2 depicts a decrease in strain as supplies increase toward needs. This relationship is hypothesized for all need–supply dimensions. Thus, insufficient food, money, love, social companionship, achievement, and opportunity for growth will produce strain, whereas increases in these supplies up to the point of perfect fit will decrease strain (Harrison, 1978).

The relationship between needs–supplies fit and strain becomes more complicated as supplies exceed needs. Three prototypical relationships between excess supplies and strain are shown in Figure 2.2. These three curves correspond to different hypothesized effects of excess supplies for needs on other dimensions. When excess supplies do not influence need fulfillment on other dimensions, strain should remain constant (curve A), yielding an overall *asymptotic relationship* between needs–supplies fit and strain. For example, food and water reduce strain until hunger and thirst are satiated, and additional consumption of these supplies will not further reduce strain (French, 1973; Harrison, 1978). Likewise, employee benefits such as health insurance reduce strain up to the point of covering health care costs but have little effect on strain beyond this point.

Curve B indicates that strain decreases as supplies exceed needs, yielding an overall *monotonic relationship* with strain. This relationship may occur when excess supplies for one dimension are used to satisfy needs on another dimension (French *et al.*, 1982; Harrison, 1978). For example, once a person's need for control is satisfied (Burger and Cooper, 1979), excess supplies for control may be used to bring about desired changes at work, thereby attaining needs–supplies fit on other dimensions. The relationship corresponding to curve B may also occur when excess supplies can

Fig. 2.2 Three hypothetical shapes of the relationship between needs–supplies fit and strain. Adapted from Harrison (1978)

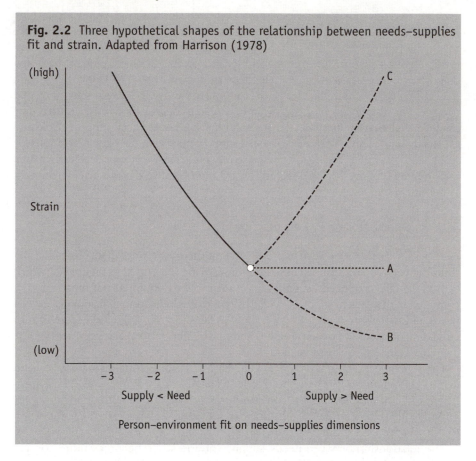

be preserved for later use, as when funds beyond one's current expenses are saved for later use (French *et al.*, 1982; Harrison, 1978). These two mechanisms by which excess supplies may reduce strain have been termed *carryover* and *conservation*, respectively (Edwards, 1996).

Finally, curve C shows that strain increases as supplies exceed needs, producing a *U-shaped relationship* between needs–supplies fit and strain. Excess supplies may increase strain when they inhibit the fulfillment of needs on other dimensions. For example, interaction with co-workers may fulfill one's need for companionship as supplies increase toward needs but then interfere with one's need for privacy as supplies exceed needs (Eidelson, 1980; French *et al.*, 1974; Harrison, 1978). French *et al.* (1982) note that the quality of the specific strain response may differ on either side of the U-shaped relationship corresponding to curve C. For example, too little contact with others may create feelings of loneliness and boredom, whereas too little privacy may lead to irritation. Nonetheless, both types of response would be associated with overall dissatisfaction. Excess supplies may also increase strain if they deplete supplies that could otherwise be used to satisfy needs in the future. For instance, obtaining excess financial resources from one's supervisor on one occasion may inhibit efforts to obtain needed resources on later occasions. These explanations for increased strain resulting from excess supplies have been labeled *interference* and *depletion*, respectively (Edwards, 1996).

Relationship of demands–abilities fit to strain Relationships between demands–abilities fit and strain are shown in Figure 2.3, in which the horizontal axis signifies the comparison of demands to abilities and the vertical axis represents strain. These relationships are analogous to those for needs–supplies fit, given that demands–abilities misfit influences strain by inducing needs–supplies misfit (French *et al.*, 1982; Harrison, 1978). Strain should increase as demands exceed abilities, assuming that excess demands inhibit the receipt of supplies required to fulfill needs (Harrison, 1978). In contrast, excess abilities may increase, decrease, or have no effect on strain. Excess abilities will not influence strain when they cannot be used to acquire supplies (curve A). For example, excess technical skills specific to a particular job demand may be of little use for meeting other demands or fulfilling other work needs or goals. Excess abilities may decrease strain (curve B) by providing supplies for needs, in the

Fig. 2.3 Three hypothetical shapes of the relationship between demands–abililies fit and strain. Adapted from Harrison (1978)

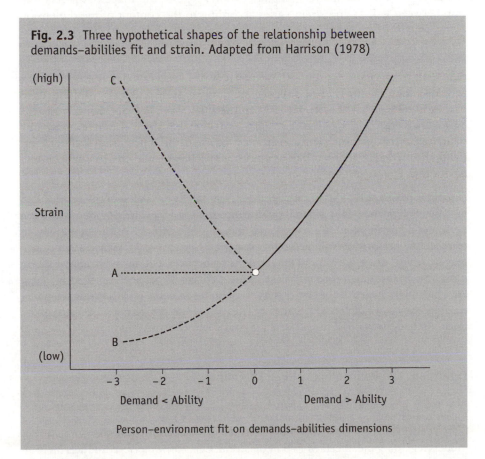

Person–environment fit on demands–abilities dimensions

way that being able to complete one's work more quickly than required creates time for reading, socializing, or other pleasurable activities (Harrison, 1978). Alternatively, excess abilities may decrease strain by allowing the person to conserve personal resources (e.g. time, energy) to apply toward future demands. These two mechanisms by which excess abilities may reduce strain represent carryover and conservation, as discussed with regard to the reduction of strain associated with excess supplies (Edwards, 1996). Finally, excess abilities may increase strain (curve C) by creating insufficient supplies for motives, as when the inability to utilize valued skills results in boredom and lowered self-esteem (Harrison, 1978). Excess abilities may also increase strain when they threaten the fulfillment of future demands. For example, unused knowledge or skills may be forgotten, making the person susceptible to task overload if demands increase in the future. These two processes correspond to interference and depletion respectively (Edwards, 1996).

Factors Affecting the Relationship Between P–E Fit and Strain

Dimension content   As the foregoing discussion suggests, the shape of the relationship between P–E fit and strain varies according to the content of the dimension along which the person and environment are conceptualized (French, 1973). The concepts of carryover, conservation, interference, and depletion constitute a set of principles that may be used to logically derive relationships between P–E fit and strain that apply to specific dimensions (Edwards, 1996). However, P–E fit theory does not provide a comprehensive taxonomy of content dimensions and their mappings onto particular relationships between P–E fit and strain. Rather, P–E fit theory represents a process theory (Campbell *et al.*, 1970), in that it articulates the mechanisms by which person and environment constructs combine to influence strain without specifying the particular content dimensions on which person and environment should be examined (Harrison, 1985).

Dimension importance   P–E fit theory also indicates that the shape of the relationship between P–E fit and strain depends on the importance of the dimension on which the person and environment are considered, meaning the priority of the dimension in terms of the person's overall hierarchy of needs (Harrison, 1985). Hence, importance may be viewed as a moderator of the relationship between P–E fit and strain. Misfit on more important dimensions will have greater effects on strain (French *et al.*, 1974; Harrison, 1985), such that the curves shown in Figures 2.2 and 2.3 will become steeper as the importance of a dimension increases. The use of importance as a moderator of the relationship between P–E fit and strain is consistent with theories of satisfaction and well-being (Locke, 1976; Mobley and Locke, 1970; Naylor *et al.*, 1980; Rice *et al.*, 1985).

Extensions and Refinements of P–E Fit Theory

Alternative relationships between P–E fit and strain   Since its initial development, several important extensions and refinements of P–E fit theory have been proposed. Building on the relationships shown in Figures 2.2 and 2.3, Kulka (1979) describes three sets of models regarding the effects of P–E fit on strain. *Cumulative difference* models indicate that the effects of P–E misfit are cumulative and continuous, such that strain varies gradually as misfit increases. Curve A in Figure 2.4 shows a cumulative difference model for a U-shaped relationship between P–E fit and strain.[1] Critical difference models specify a range of tolerance around perfect P–E fit, such that strain varies only when P–E misfit exceeds a certain threshold. A U-shaped critical difference model is illustrated by curve B, which shows that strain remains constant for small amounts of P–E misfit but then increases when P–E misfit exceeds a range of tolerance. Finally, *optimal congruence* models assume that strain results from P–E misfit *and* from perfect P–E fit (see curve C). For example, extreme misfit may exhaust adaptive resources, whereas perfect fit may result in stagnation and lack of stimulation. In either case, overall strain would increase. In contrast, small amounts of misfit may reduce strain, as when a slight excess for task complexity fulfills the person's desire for challenge. Kulka (1979) discusses variations of the curves shown in Figure 2.4 in which the effects of misfit may be curvilinear or linear and symmetric or asymmetric.

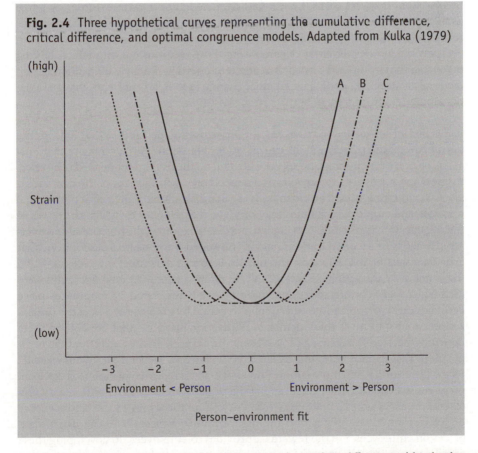

Fig. 2.4 Three hypothetical curves representing the cumulative difference, critical difference, and optimal congruence models. Adapted from Kulka (1979)

[1] The relationships shown in Figures 2.2 and 2.3 also represent the cumulative difference model, in that they depict gradual variation in strain as a function of needs–supplies fit and demands–abilities fit.

Past, present, and future P–E fit   Another noteworthy extension of P–E fit theory concerns the relationships among past, present, and future P–E fit and their combined effects on strain. These issues are examined by Caplan (1983), who explores various mechanisms by which past and anticipated P–E fit may influence present P–E fit and strain. According to Caplan (1983), past fit constitutes a standard by which current fit may be judged as an improvement, worsening, or continuation of previous fit. Consequently, current misfit may be experienced as benign if it was preceded by a substantially larger degree of misfit, whereas current misfit may be considered highly stressful if no misfit had been experienced in the past. Analogously, anticipated fit influences evaluations of current fit by indicating whether fit is expected to decrease, increase, or remain constant. Thus, current misfit may seem innocuous if conditions are expected to worsen but may be stressful if no misfit is expected in the future. Collectively, these effects of past and anticipated fit on current fit are termed *contrast effects*, because they assume that current fit is contrasted with or compared to fit in other time frames. A competing process discussed by Caplan (1983) and elaborated by Harrison (1985) concerns the *vicarious effects* of fit in other time frames, as when dwelling on past or anticipated misfit increases strain, analogous to the effects of current misfit (Edwards, 1992). Caplan (1983) elaborates the relationships between past, present, and anticipated fit by decomposing these relationships into effects linking person and environment constructs at different points in time, yielding different predictions for strain depending on whether change in P–E fit represents change in the person, the environment, or both.

P–E fit and organizational effectiveness   A third extension pertains to P–E fit from the perspective of the person and the organization. Harrison (1985) points out that, just as the person's functioning and survival depend on the fulfillment of needs, the effectiveness and survival of an organization depend on the fulfillment of the demands it places on its employees. These demands are manifestations of the needs of the organization, and employees' abilities may be viewed as supplies by which the needs of the organization can be fulfilled (Caplan, 1983). For example, the functional and operational needs of an organization may be translated into position descriptions that articulate specific job demands, and human resource personnel may seek to fulfill these needs by attracting, selecting, and retaining a supply of qualified employees (Schneider and Schmitt, 1992). Analogously, needs expressed by employees place demands on an organization, and supplies received by employees reflect the organization's ability to meet these demands. Thus, organizations that are able to meet demands that signify salient employee needs may experience less turnover than organizations that cannot meet these demands (Irving and Meyer, 1994; Wanous *et al.*, 1992). Harrison (1985) also examines objective and subjective person and environment constructs from the perspective of the organization. Contact with reality represents the accuracy of employee assessment and appraisal procedures, and accuracy of self-assessment translates into the organization's awareness of the demands it places on employees and the rewards it provides to employees. In developing these parallels regarding P–E fit for the person and organization, Harrison (1985) notes that the organization serves as a metaphor for organizational members, such as supervisors, co-workers, or staffing personnel. Thus, the principles developed by Harrison (1985) may be readily applied to the study of fit in dyadic relationships (Shumaker and Brownell, 1984).

Boundaries and Limitations of P–E Fit Theory

P–E fit theory provides a useful conceptual framework for understanding how person and environment constructs combine to produce strain and how coping and defense may resolve P–E misfit. Nonetheless, the theory has several boundaries and limitations.

Content of person and environment dimensions not specified   Although P–E fit theory describes the process by which person and environment jointly influence strain, it does not specify the content of person and environment dimensions. In this regard, P–E fit theory is a pure process theory (Campbell *et al.*, 1970), and the content of person and environment dimensions must be obtained from other theories. For example, the content of needs may be obtained from theories that specify taxonomies of needs (Maslow, 1954), preferences (Amabile *et al.*, 1994; Pryor, 1983), or values (Rokeach, 1973; Schwartz, 1994; Super, 1973), and the content of supplies may be derived from theories of job characteristics (Campion and Thayer, 1985; Hackman and Oldham, 1980) or activities (McCormick, 1979). Analogously, abilities may be obtained from conceptual frameworks of human aptitudes, abilities, and skills (Fleishman and Reilly, 1992; Lubinski and Dawis, 1990; Spenner, 1990), and demands may be based on theories of job requirements (Borman and Brush, 1993; Fleishman and Mumford, 1991).

Specific relationships with strain not predicted   P–E fit theory does not propose *a priori* hypotheses regarding the relationship between P–E fit and strain. Rather, the theory identifies a set of possible relationships, such as those shown in Figures 2.2, 2.3, and 2.4, but treats P–E fit relationships for specific content dimensions and indices of strain as an empirical matter. An initial foundation for hypothesizing specific relationships is provided by the concepts of carryover, conservation, interference, and depletion discussed by Edwards (1996). However, these concepts have been applied to only a limited set of content dimensions (Edwards, 1996; Livingstone *et al.*, 1997). Furthermore, evidence suggests that the relationship between P–E fit and strain may differ not only across content dimensions and indices of strain, but also across occupations (Caplan *et al.*, 1980). Developing hypotheses for major content dimensions, indices of strain, and occupations represents a significant, if not overwhelming, undertaking for future P–E fit research.

Specific coping and defense strategies not predicted   P–E fit theory devotes limited attention to coping and defense. For example, the theory does not specify the criteria by which the person will choose from among various methods for resolving P–E misfit. According to the theory, subjective P–E misfit may be resolved directly through cognitive distortion (i.e. defense) or indirectly by reducing objective misfit (i.e. coping), which in turn would reduce subjective misfit. The theory also indicates that subjective P–E misfit may be tolerated by reducing the importance of the dimension on

39

which misfit occurs. However, the theory does not articulate the conditions under which each of these various methods of adaptation will be used. Moreover, coping and defense may occur in an ordered progression, such that defensive adaptation strategies are implemented only after attempts to change the objective person and environment have failed. The selection and sequencing of these methods of adaptation are not addressed by P–E fit theory.

Summary of Empirical P–E Fit Research

Relevant Literature

As noted previously, numerous studies have examined the combined effects of the person and environment on strain. Results from these studies are relevant to P–E fit theory if they satisfy the following conditions:

Commensurate measures Person and environment measures must refer to commensurate dimensions. Hence, studies that combine non-commensurate person and environment variables, as when personality is viewed as a moderator of the effects of environmental stressors on strain (Cohen and Edwards, 1989; Parkes, 1994), are not relevant to P–E fit theory.

Needs–supplies fit or demands–abilities fit Person and environment variables must correspond to needs and supplies or abilities and demands, respectively. This criterion excludes studies of value congruence (Adkins *et al.*, 1994; Cable and Judge, 1996; Judge and Bretz, 1992; Lovelace and Rosen, 1996; Meglino *et al.*, 1989, 1992) and interpersonal similarity (e.g. Cable and Judge, 1996; Day and Bedeian, 1995; O'Reilly *et al.*, 1989; Tsui and O'Reilly, 1989; Turban and Jones, 1988; Zalesny and Kirsch, 1989), as these studies involve comparisons between persons rather than between the person and the environment.

Needs and demands as amount, frequency, or intensity For needs–supplies fit, needs should be measured as *desired amount, frequency,* or *intensity* of a dimension rather than the importance of a dimension. For example, needs–supplies fit regarding pay should compare actual pay to desired pay, *not* to the importance of pay. P–E fit theory views importance not as the standard by which supplies are evaluated, but rather as a moderator of the relationship between needs–supplies fit and strain (French *et al.*, 1974; Harrison, 1985; see also Locke, 1969; Mobley and Locke, 1970; Rice *et al.*, 1985). Thus, studies of the fit between supplies and need importance (e.g. Bizot and Goldman, 1993; Rounds *et al.*, 1987; Scarpello and Campbell, 1983; Vandenberg and Scarpello, 1990; Wood, 1981) are not relevant to P–E fit theory. Likewise, for demands–abilities fit, demands should be measured as the *required amount, frequency,* or *intensity* of a dimension, not as the importance of the dimension. Hence, studies that operationalize demands as the importance of job competencies (e.g. Caldwell and O'Reilly, 1990) are not relevant to P–E fit theory.

Analytical approach Studies must use a method of analysis that captures the fit, match, or similarity between the person and environment. Studies that use the interaction between person and environment to signify P–E fit (e.g. Chan, 1996; Joyce *et al.*, 1982; Moskowitz and Cote, 1995; O'Reilly, 1977; Ostroff, 1993; Puffer and Meindl, 1992; Rahim, 1981; Schein and Diamante, 1988) are therefore excluded, because the interaction between person and environment variables does not reflect their proximity to one another (Edwards and Cooper, 1990).

Strain, coping, or defense as outcomes   P–E fit should be used to predict strain, coping, or defense. Studies using P–E fit to predict task performance (e.g. McGrath, 1976; Westman and Eden, 1992, 1996) are not directly relevant to P–E fit theory, because task performance may result from coping efforts but does not itself represent coping efforts. Studies of the relationship between P–E fit and vocational choice (Meier, 1991) or job change (Breeden, 1993; Wilk and Sackett, 1996) are tangentially relevant to P–E fit theory, given that choosing or changing a vocation or job influences the objective environment, which is one method of coping with P–E misfit. However, these studies rarely examine changes in the person as a response to misfit and therefore provide a biased perspective on coping with P–E misfit. For this reason, these studies are not reviewed here.

Relevant Studies Prior to the Development of P–E Fit Theory

Empirical research on P–E fit theory began in the early 1970s, after the conceptual foundations of the theory were developed (Caplan *et al.*, 1980). However, earlier studies of concepts analogous to P–E fit provide evidence relevant to P–E fit theory. Many of these studies focused on need satisfaction, using the difference between needs and supplies to predict satisfaction with various aspects of work (Evans, 1969; Hulin and Smith, 1965; Katzell, 1964; Locke, 1969; Wanous and Lawler, 1972). Overall, these studies suggest that satisfaction increases as supplies increase toward needs. However, these studies provide limited evidence regarding the relationship of excess supplies with satisfaction, because few respondents in these studies reported excess supplies (Evans, 1969). Moreover, most of these studies operationalized needs–supplies fit using difference scores that imposed an *a priori* relationship between excess supplies and satisfaction (i.e. a positive relationship for an algebraic difference, a negative relationship for an absolute difference). An exception is Locke (1969), who plotted the relationship between needs–supplies fit and satisfaction and found a positive monotonic relationship for pay and an inverted-U relationship for length of work week.

Direct Tests of P–E Fit Theory

Of the studies explicitly designed to test P–E fit theory, the most comprehensive was conducted by French, Caplan, Harrison, and their colleagues (Caplan *et al.*, 1980; French *et al.*, 1982). Relationships between P–E fit and strain were examined using a random stratified sample of 318 workers in 23 occupations. Needs and supplies were measured for job complexity, role ambiguity, responsibility for persons, workload, income, and overtime, and demands and abilities were assessed in terms of education and length of service. P–E fit was operationalized using various difference scores between person and environment measures. Algebraic difference scores were used to test monotonic relationships between P–E fit and strain (curve B, Figures 2.2 and 2.3), right- and left-censored difference scores[2] were used for asymptotic relationships (curve A, Figures 2.2 and 2.3), and absolute and squared difference scores were used for U-shaped relationships (curve C, Figures 2.2 and 2.3). Data were also obtained on 18 psychological, physiological, and behavioral strains (e.g. job dissatisfaction, blood pressure, cigarette smoking). Relationships between P–E fit and strain were tested using bivariate correlations and by examining the increment in variance explained by P–E fit measures after controlling for E and P.[3]

Although the results of this study are too extensive to review fully here, several general findings may be summarized. First, P–E fit was related to psychological strains and, to a lesser extent, physiological and behavioral strains. These relationships were strongest for needs–supplies fit regarding job complexity, role ambiguity, responsibility for persons, and workload. Second, all three relationships predicted by P–E fit theory (i.e. monotonic, asymptotic, U-shaped) were detected. In general, relationship between psychological strains and needs–supplies fit on job complexity and role ambiguity were U-shaped, whereas relationships for responsibility for persons and workload were either U-shaped or asymptotic, with the latter indicating that strain increased for excess supplies but remained constant for deficient supplies (note that this relationship is the *opposite* of that shown in Figure 2.2). Third, difference scores used to depict non-linear relationships between P–E fit and strain (i.e. censored, absolute, and squared differences) often yielded statistically significant increments in explained variance after controlling for P and E, particularly for job complexity.

Evidence for a U-shaped relationship between P–E fit and strain is illustrated in Figures 2.5 and 2.6, which show the relationship between depression and needs, supplies, and needs–supplies fit regarding job complexity based on data from French *et al.* (1982; Caplan *et al.*, 1980). As Figure 2.5 shows, depression exhibits weak negative relationships with needs and supplies. In contrast, Figure 2.6 indicates that depression increases as supplies deviate from needs in either direction, yielding a U-shaped relationship between needs–supplies fit and strain. Moreover, the slope of the relationship is greater when supplies exceed needs than when supplies fall short of needs, suggesting that excess job complexity has a greater impact on depression than insufficient job complexity.

Subsequent Studies of the Relationship Between P–E Fit and Strain

Numerous studies relevant to P–E fit theory have been conducted since the early 1970s (Assouline and Meir, 1987; Michalos, 1986; Edwards, 1991; Spokane, 1985).

---

[2] Left-censored difference scores were created by setting all negative values of the P–E difference to zero, and right-censored difference scores were created by setting all positive values of the P–E difference to zero. Thus, left-censored scores were used to detect relationships between P–E fit and strain where E was greater than P, whereas right-censored scores were used to detect relationships where E was less than P.

[3] Tests of increments in explained variance were not performed for algebraic difference scores, as they represent linear combinations of E and P and therefore cannot explain variance beyond that accounted for by E and P (Edwards and Cooper, 1990).

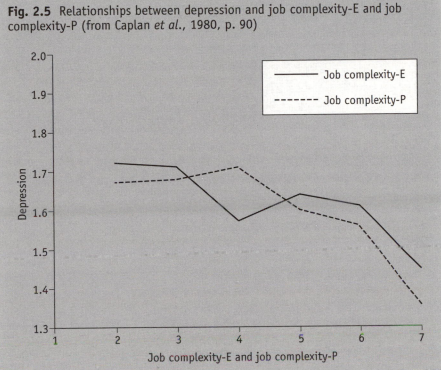

Fig. 2.5 Relationships between depression and job complexity-E and job complexity-P (from Caplan *et al.*, 1980, p. 90)

Edwards (1991) reviewed studies published from 1960 through 1989 and offered the following general conclusions regarding the relationship between P–E fit and strain. First, the vast majority of P–E fit studies have focused on needs–supplies fit rather than demands–abilities fit. Second, most of these studies have found significant relationships between needs–supplies fit and various indices of strain, including dissatisfaction, tension, fatigue, somatic complaints, and absenteeism. These relationships were found for algebraic, absolute, and squared differences between needs and supplies, suggesting that strain decreases as supplies increase towards needs (see Figure 2.2) but providing equivocal evidence regarding the relationship of excess supplies with strain.

Third, of the few studies examining demands–abilities fit, most have reported a U-shaped relationship between misfit and dissatisfaction. However, these studies used analytical techniques that imposed a U-shaped relationship between demands–abilities misfit and strain, making it impossible to detect monotonic or asymptotic relationships. Finally, virtually every study operationalized P–E fit by collapsing person and environment measures into a single score, most often an algebraic, absolute, or squared difference. Operationalizing P–E fit in this manner introduces numerous methodological problems, such as reduced reliability, ambiguous interpretation, and confounding of the effects of person and environment on strain (Cronbach, 1958;

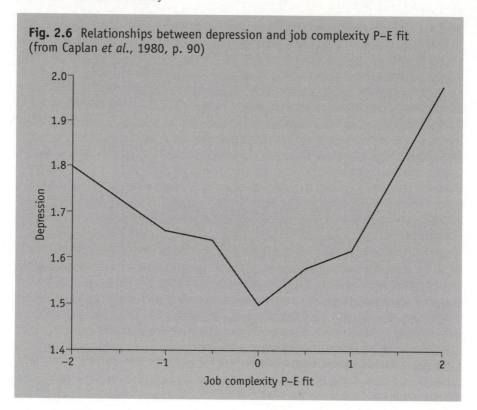

Fig. 2.6 Relationships between depression and job complexity P–E fit (from Caplan *et al.*, 1980, p. 90)

Edwards, 1994; Johns, 1981). These problems introduce serious ambiguities in the interpretation of relationships between P–E fit scores and strain. For example, a relationship between a P–E fit score and strain may simply reflect the influence of the person or the environment, not P–E fit. Furthermore, P–E fit scores force the relationship between P–E fit and strain to follow a particular functional form but provide no means of testing whether this functional form is, in fact, supported by the data. Because of these ambiguities, the results of most studies reviewed by Edwards (1991) are inconclusive.

Most P–E fit studies published since 1990 have operationalized fit using methods similar to those used in prior research. Results of these studies are consistent with prior research, suggesting that needs–supplies misfit is related to job dissatisfaction, low self-esteem, anxiety, and depression (Blau, 1994; Chatman, 1991; Conway *et al.*, 1992; Gati *et al.*, 1996; Kaldenberg and Becker, 1992; McFarlin and Rice, 1992; O'Reilly *et al.*, 1991; Tziner and Falbe, 1990), and that demands–abilities misfit is related to dissatisfaction, anxiety, and exhaustion (Chatman, 1991; Kahn and Morrow, 1991; Xie and Johns, 1993). However, like previous studies, the results of these studies are inconclusive, given the aforementioned problems created by collapsing person and environment measures into a single score.

Studies of the Joint Relationship of the Person and Environment with Strain

Problems created by collapsing person and environment measures into a single score are avoided when person and environment measures and their associated higher-order terms (e.g. their squares and product) are used as joint predictors of strain (Edwards, 1991, 1994). This approach reflects the premise that the person, the environment, and strain are three distinct constructs, and their relationship should therefore be conceived not as a two-dimensional function, but rather as a three-dimensional surface. Studies using this approach (Champoux, 1992; Edwards, 1993, 1994, 1996; Edwards and Harrison, 1993; Elsass and Veiga, 1997; Hesketh and Gardner, 1993; Livingstone *et al.*, 1997; Rice *et al.*, 1990; Sweeney *et al.*, 1990) have revealed a wide array of three-dimensional surfaces relating the person and environment to strain.

Collectively, the findings of these studies suggest several general conclusions. First, person and environment variables often exhibit relationships with strain that differ in form and magnitude. For example, tests of monotonic relationships between needs–supplies fit and dissatisfaction have found that the negative relationship for supplies is often larger in absolute magnitude than the positive relationship for needs (Edwards, 1993, 1994, 1996; Hesketh and Gardner, 1993; Livingstone *et al.*, 1997; Rice *et al.*, 1990). These relationships are presumed to be equal in absolute magnitude when P–E fit is operationalized using an algebraic difference score (Edwards and Cooper, 1990). Second, person and environment variables often exhibit curvilinear relationships with strain that deviate from the basic functional forms shown in Figures 2.2 and 2.3. For example, several studies have found that dissatisfaction increases more rapidly for insufficient supplies than for excess supplies, and that dissatisfaction is higher when needs and supplies are both low than when both are high (Edwards, 1996; Edwards and Harrison, 1993; Hesketh and Gardner, 1993; Livingstone *et al.*, 1997). Third, equations that capture three-dimensional surfaces relating the person and environment to strain usually explain significantly more variance than their two-dimensional counterparts, often doubling or tripling R^2 values (Edwards, 1991, 1993, 1994; Livingstone *et al.*, 1997).

An example of a three-dimensional relationship of the person and environment with strain is shown in Figure 2.7, based on a reanalysis of the French *et al.* (1982; Caplan *et al.*, 1980) data by Edwards and Harrison (1993). For comparative purposes, this surface depicts the relationship of needs and supplies for job complexity with depression, corresponding to the two-dimensional relationship shown in Figure 2.6. Consistent with the two-dimensional relationship, the three-dimensional surface indicates that depression increases as supplies deviate from needs, with a somewhat stronger relationship for excess supplies than for insufficient supplies. However, the surface is also rotated slightly counterclockwise such that, when supplies and values are both low, depression is lowest when supplies exceed values, whereas when supplies and values are both high, depression is lowest when supplies are less than values. This finding suggests that, for simple jobs, a slight excess of job complexity may reduce depression by providing stimulation and challenge, whereas for highly complex jobs, a slight deficiency of job complexity may reduce depression by avoiding

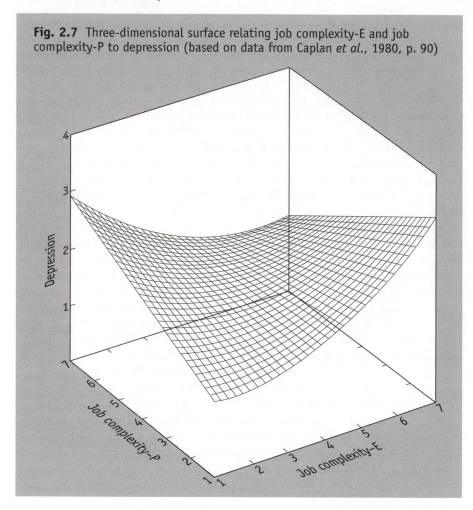

Fig. 2.7 Three-dimensional surface relating job complexity-E and job complexity-P to depression (based on data from Caplan *et al.*, 1980, p. 90)

overload and conserving adaptive resources. This finding is concealed when the relationship of needs and supplies with depression is viewed in two dimensions, as in Figure 2.6.

Summary of Empirical Findings

Numerous studies have reported evidence relevant to the basic tenets of P–E fit theory. These studies have consistently suggested that P–E misfit, particularly for needs and supplies, is related to strain. However, most of these studies have operationalized P–E fit by collapsing person and environment measures into a single score, such as an algebraic, absolute, or squared difference. This procedure introduces numerous methodological problems and renders results inconclusive. These problems have been avoided by recent studies that examine the three-dimensional relationship of the person and environment with strain. These studies indicate that strain often increases as the environment deviates from the person, as predicted by P–E fit theory. However, these studies also report complexities that are concealed by methods used in previous studies, such as asymmetric relationships between P–E misfit and strain, variation in strain along the line of perfect P–E fit, and minimum levels of strain at points other than perfect P–E fit. By applying three-dimensional procedures to existing data, conclusions of previous P–E fit studies may be clarified, revised, and elaborated (Edwards and Harrison, 1993).

Directions for Future P–E Fit Research

P–E fit theory has contributed to our understanding of the role of the person and environment in the stress process. Specifically, the theory has identified relevant person and environment constructs, described how and when misfit between these constructs signifies stress, generated a set of hypothetical relationships between P–E misfit and strain, and articulated how coping and defense may resolve objective and subjective P–E misfit and thereby reduce strain. However, P–E fit theory has conceptual boundaries that invite further theoretical development. Moreover, most studies of P–E fit suffer from important methodological flaws, and many key propositions of P–E fit theory have not been empirically investigated. The needs for conceptual elaboration, improved methodology, and further tests of propositions constitute the core elements of an agenda for future P–E fit research. In this section, we identify directions for future P–E fit research that we believe are particularly promising.

Relationships Between Objective and Subjective Person and Environment Constructs

P–E fit theory stipulates that objective person and environment constructs affect their subjective counterparts, and that these effects are influenced by perceptual and cognitive distortions and by personal and situational constraints on information access and processing. However, most studies of P–E fit have measured only subjective person and environment constructs (Edwards, 1991). Some studies have collected measures of the environment from sources other than the focal person (Assouline and Meir, 1987; Caldwell and O'Reilly, 1990; Chatman, 1991; Spokane, 1985), but these studies rarely include measures of the environment collected from the focal person. Consequently, these studies provide little evidence regarding the relationship between objective and subjective person and environment constructs or the mediating effects of subjective P–E fit in the relationship between objective P–E fit and outcomes. Moreover, measures of person and environment constructs are often treated as objective if they are obtained from respondents other than the focal person, such as supervisors or job analysts. It is unclear whether these measures should be considered objective, given that they are merely self-reports from another perspective.

The measurement of objective person and environment constructs raises both pragmatic and philosophical issues, and future P–E fit research should address not only how, but also whether objective person and environment measures can be developed (Caplan, 1987a, b; Starbuck and Mezias, 1996). If such measures can be developed and validated, studies should address the nature and magnitude of relationships between objective and subjective person and environment constructs and the mediating effects of subjective P–E fit postulated by P–E fit theory. These studies may also examine whether objective misfit, accuracy of self-assessment, and contact with reality have implications for mental health, as suggested by early presentations of P–E fit theory (French et al., 1974; Harrison, 1978).

Taxonomies for Person and Environment Content Dimensions

As noted previously, P–E fit theory does not specify content dimensions for the person and environment. Future P–E fit research may obtain content dimensions from theories that provide taxonomies for describing the person or the environment. Taxonomies based on the person may draw from theories of needs or abilities, depending on whether needs–supplies fit or demands–abilities fit is of interest. For example, studies of need satisfaction (e.g. Porter, 1964; Porter and Lawler, 1968) have used Maslow's need hierarchy to derive measures of desired and actual work experiences. Analogously, studies of demands–abilities fit (e.g. Barrett et al., 1980; Carlson, 1969) have adapted measures of skills and aptitudes to measure both abilities and demands.

Conversely, taxonomies that describe work environments (Borman and Brush, 1993; Campion and Thayer, 1985; Fleishman and Mumford, 1991; Hackman and Oldham, 1980; McCormick, 1979) may be used to identify supply and demand dimensions, and needs and abilities may be specified in commensurate terms. This approach was used by Edwards (1996), who measured job supplies and demands in terms of managerial task activities drawn from the Leader Observation System (LOS; Luthans and Lockwood, 1984) and derived corresponding measures of needs and abilities. By using existing person and environment taxonomies, future P–E fit research may avoid the ad hoc selection of content dimensions prevalent in previous studies of P–E fit, and dimensions relevant to the person or environment are less likely to be overlooked. Moreover, studies may use common taxonomies to determine whether the effects of P–E fit on a particular set of dimensions generalize across settings, occupations, and cultures.

Complexities in Relationships Between P–E Fit and Outcomes

Studies examining three-dimensional relationships between the person, the environment, and outcomes (e.g. Edwards, 1993, 1994, 1996; Edwards and Harrison, 1993; Elsass and Veiga, 1997; Hesketh and Gardner, 1993; Livingstone et al., 1997) have revealed complexities that were undetected in previous studies that focused on two-dimensional relationships between P–E fit and outcomes. Some of these complexities were anticipated during the initial development of P–E fit theory (e.g. Caplan, 1983; French, 1973; Harrison, 1978) but could not be examined using two-dimensional approaches to the study of P–E fit. Other complexities were identified empirically and suggest that P–E fit theory may require further elaboration and refinement. This interplay between theory and empiricism is central to the accumulation of knowledge (Runkel and McGrath, 1972) and is not, as some researchers have admonished, 'letting the empirical tail wag the theoretical dog' (Bedeian *et al.*, 1994, p. 695). Rather, the theory–empiricism interplay represents the use of theory to guide data collection, analysis, and interpretation, and the use of empirical findings to modify and refine theory. The following discussion focuses on complexities that have been replicated across studies and therefore hold promise for future conceptual and empirical P–E fit research.

Different effects for person and environment   As noted previously, several P–E studies have found that the person and environment exhibit relationships with strain that differ in absolute magnitude (Edwards, 1993, 1994, 1996; Hesketh and Gardner, 1993; Livingstone *et al.*, 1997; Rice *et al.*, 1990). One explanation for these differences draws from the distinction between strong and weak situations (Mischel, 1977). Strong situations provide uniform and clear cues regarding behavioral expectations and associated rewards, whereas in weak situations these cues are varied and ambiguous. Thus, in strong situations, environmental demands and supplies may be highly salient to the person, meaning the person is acutely aware of their amount, frequency, or intensity. If cues from the situation are stronger than those from the person (i.e. needs and abilities), then the effects of the environment may exceed those of the person. Conversely, in weak situations, cues from the person may be more salient than those from the environment and therefore may exert greater effects on strain.

Another explanation for the differential effects of the person and environment entails the variance of person and environment measures. Specifically, measures with greater variance are likely to exhibit stronger relationships with outcomes (Cooper and Richardson, 1986). Some studies of needs–supplies fit examine dimensions that are normatively desirable, meaning that most people would prefer a large amount of the dimension. Examples of such dimensions include pay, control, security, and achievement (Schwartz, 1994). For these dimensions, the variance in needs may be substantially smaller than the variance in supplies, thereby producing stronger effects for supplies than for needs. Conversely, studies of P–E fit occasionally use respondents from within a single job, organization, or occupation (e.g. Aranya *et al.*, 1981; Caldwell and O'Reilly, 1990; Doty and Betz, 1979; Wiggins, 1984). For these studies, the variance of environment measures is likely to be smaller than the variance in person measures, thereby producing stronger relationships for the person than for the environment.

Relationships between P–E fit on different dimensions   P–E fit theory posits that the effects of misfit on strain may differ inform and magnitude, depending on whether environmental levels exceed or fall short of personal levels (see Figures 2.2 and 2.3). These asymmetries were suggested by studies using censored algebraic difference scores between person and environment measures (Caplan *et al.*, 1980; French *et al.*, 1982) and have subsequently been demonstrated by studies examining three-dimensional surfaces relating the person and environment to strain (Edwards,

1996; Edwards and Harrison, 1993; Hesketh and Gardner, 1993; Livingstone *et al.*, 1997).

Explanations for these asymmetries are based on the premise that P–E fit on one dimension influences P–E fit on other dimensions through carryover and interference effects. For example, when monetary supplies fall short of needs, needs–supplies misfit is created for dimensions central to the person's welfare and survival, such as clothing, food, and shelter. In contrast, when monetary supplies exceed needs, needs–supplies misfit may occur on less important dimensions, such as feelings of entitlement or pay equity. Due to these differential effects of insufficient and excess pay, strain should be greater when monetary supplies fall short of needs than when they exceed needs (compare Pritchard, 1969). Alternately, an excessive workload may create needs–supplies misfit regarding performance and its attendant consequences (e.g. pay, recognition, job security), whereas an insufficient workload may create needs–supplies misfit regarding less threatening dimensions, such as skill utilization. In this case, an excessive workload would have greater effects on strain than an insufficient workload. Both of these examples rest on the assumption that needs–supplies misfit on one dimension creates needs–supplies misfit on other dimensions. To date, few studies have directly examined these effects, and explanations for asymmetries in the relationship between P–E fit and outcomes remain speculative.

Relationships between dimensions of P–E fit are also implicated by the hypothesized effects of demands–abilities misfit on strain. As argued by Harrison (1978, 1985), demands–abilities misfit will produce strain only if it induces needs–supplies misfit, as when work rewards are contingent upon meeting job demands. Although studies have found relationships between demands–abilities misfit and strain (Caplan *et al.*, 1980; French *et al.*, 1982; Edwards, 1996; Livingstone *et al.*, 1997), studies have not examined whether this relationship is mediated by needs–supplies fit. Edwards (1996) reported results indicating that demands–abilities misfit exhibits modest but statistically significant relationships with strain after controlling for needs–supplies misfit, suggesting that the effects of demands–abilities misfit are not fully mediated by needs–supplies misfit. However, this study was intended to compare the effects of demands–abilities fit and needs–supplies fit and therefore measured demands, abilities, needs, and supplies on commensurate dimensions. To explicitly test the mediating effects of needs–supplies fit, demands and abilities should be measured on dimensions that are instrumentally related to needs and supplies dimensions. For example, demands and abilities may refer to performance objectives, and needs and supplies may refer to rewards that are contingent upon meeting performance objectives. To our knowledge, no studies have examined the instrumental effects of demands–abilities fit on needs–supplies fit.

Variation in strain for perfect P–E fit   Relationships between P–E fit on different dimensions may affect the level of strain associated with perfect P–E fit. For example, studies of the three-dimensional relationship between needs, supplies, and strain have found that strain is often lower when needs and supplies are both high than when both are low (Edwards, 1994, 1996; Edwards and Harrison, 1993; Hesketh and

Gardner, 1993; Imparato, 1972; Livingstone *et al.*, 1997). These findings were foreshadowed by Harrison (1978) who noted that, although perfect fit exists when a person wants and has a job that is either simple or complex, more complex jobs often bring higher rewards such as pay, status, and recognition. Moreover, people who prefer complex jobs may also prefer high amounts of rewards associated with complex jobs (Edwards, 1996). Thus, high levels of actual and preferred job complexity may act as a surrogate for need fulfillment regarding pay, status, recognition, and related rewards. Although this explanation focuses on job complexity, its underlying logic generalizes to needs–supplies dimensions examined in recent studies, which include decision-making, authority, power, autonomy, prestige, and creativity (Edwards, 1994, 1996; Edwards and Harrison, 1993; Hesketh and Gardner, 1993; Livingstone *et al.*, 1997).

An alternative explanation for reduced strain when person and environment are both high concerns the sense of competence yielded by achieving high standards (White, 1959). High needs represent stringent standards emanating from the self, and fulfilling such standards may in itself constitute a supply for needs regarding self-actualization (Maslow, 1954; Rokeach, 1973; Schwartz, 1994). Analogously, high demands represent challenging standards set by others, and having abilities commensurate with such demands may constitute a supply for self-actualization needs. In either case, strain is reduced not only because fit is achieved, but also because an ambitious standard is met, thereby contributing to needs–supplies fit regarding self-actualization.

P–E misfit leading to minimum strain   Studies of P–E fit are typically based on the assumption that perfect fit reduces strain and enhances well-being. However, this assumption may not hold, for various reasons. First, as illustrated by curve B in Figures 2.2 and 2.3, excess supplies or abilities may decrease strain if they promote the fulfillment of needs on other dimensions. Although this possibility is noted in most discussions of P–E fit theory (e.g. French *et al.*, 1974; French *et al.*, 1982), it has received little attention in studies of P–E fit, which often employ methods that assume that perfect P–E fit is optimal and provide no means to verify this assumption (Assouline and Meir, 1987; Edwards, 1991; Michalos, 1986; Spokane, 1985).

Second, as shown by curve B in Figure 2.4, strain may be minimized not precisely at perfect P–E fit, but within an interval surrounding perfect P–E fit signifying a range of tolerance. Although few studies have employed analytical techniques that can detect a range of tolerance around perfect P–E fit (e.g. Locke, 1969; French, 1973), the piecewise linear model described by Edwards (1994) may be adapted for this purpose by specifying two changes in slope of the surface relating the person and environment to strain, each occurring where the environment exceeds or falls short of the person by some amount (e.g. one standard deviation).

Third, as indicated by curve C in Figure 2.4, perfect P–E fit may cause stagnation and produce strain, whereas small amounts of misfit may create challenge and provide opportunities to utilize valued skills, thereby reducing strain (Caplan, 1983; French, 1973; Harrison, 1978; Kulka, 1979). The scoring procedures used in most P–E fit studies prevent the detection of minimum strain at points other than perfect fit, although the three-dimensional procedure described earlier can readily determine whether strain is minimized at perfect P–E fit.

Finally, the point at which strain is minimized may depend not only on the proximity of person and environment to one another, but also on the absolute levels of person and environment. This phenomenon is illustrated in Figure 2.7, which shows that when needs and supplies for job complexity are low, depression is minimized when supplies slightly exceed needs, whereas when needs and supplies are both high, depression is minimized when supplies are somewhat less than needs (for further details and evidence, see Edwards and Harrison, 1993). Future P–E fit research should develop hypotheses regarding which combinations of person and environment minimize strain and employ analytical techniques that can substantiate or refute these hypotheses.

Summary of complexities in relationships between P–E fit and outcomes   As the preceding discussion indicates, relationships between P–E fit and outcomes may take a wide variety of forms. These relationships may depend on the type of P–E fit (i.e. needs–supplies fit versus demands–abilities fit), the content of person and environment dimensions, and the index of strain. To date, studies examining alternative relationships between P–E fit and strain (e.g. Edwards and Harrison, 1993; French *et al.*, 1982) have been largely exploratory. Studies hypothesizing specific functional forms relating P–E fit to strain (Edwards, 1996; Livingstone *et al.*, 1997) have focused on a limited set of content dimensions (i.e. managerial tasks, creativity), and only Livingstone *et al.* (1997) developed separate hypotheses for different indices of strain.

A major undertaking for future P–E fit research is to develop hypotheses regarding functional forms relating needs–supplies fit and demands–abilities fit on specific content dimensions to specific indices of strain. To initiate this undertaking, researchers may apply the principles of carryover, conservation, interference, and depletion to content dimensions obtained from relevant person or environment taxonomies. Researchers should also specify whether relationships are expected to differ across indices of strain that signify major dimensions of mental and physical well-being (Derogatis, 1977; Goldberg, 1978; Russell, 1980; Watson and Tellegen, 1985). Relationships for each combination of person, environment, and strain constructs may also be examined in different contexts (e.g. organizational settings, occupations, cultures) and in different demographic groups. Obviously, a comprehensive treatment of these relationships represents an enormous endeavor for future P–E fit research.

The immense variety of content dimensions, indices of strain, contexts, and populations may prohibit the discovery of relationships between P–E fit and strain that can be generalized. Rather, researchers may have to rely on the principles of carryover, conservation, interference, and depletion to derive hypotheses unique to each study. Although relationships between P–E fit and strain may vary considerably across studies, these relationships may ultimately converge into categories that represent theoretically meaningful prototypes. Moreover, relationships found in a particular context or population provide a knowledge base that may inform hypotheses derived for other contexts or populations. Thus, although the potential variety of relationships between P–E fit and strain may appear daunting, we believe these relationships will ultimately be placed in meaningful order by programmatic research that systematically varies content dimension, index of strain, context, and population.

P–E Fit and Coping

Studies of P–E fit have focused almost exclusively on the relationship of P–E fit with strain. Very few studies have examined the relationship of P–E fit with coping and defense or how coping and defense may influence the objective and subjective person and environment. One reason for this lack of research involves the absence of coping and defense measures relevant to P–E fit theory. Many available measures were derived using an inductive approach, in which respondents generate lists of strategies for dealing with stress and exploratory factor analysis is used to assign these strategies to dimensions (e.g. Amirkhan, 1990; Dewe and Guest, 1990; Folkman and Lazarus, 1988). This approach provides little assurance that the obtained dimensions will be relevant to any *a priori* theory, including P–E fit theory. Other measures have been derived deductively, with items generated to represent conceptual dimensions specified *a priori* (e.g. Carver *et al.*, 1989; Edwards and Baglioni, 1993; Stone and Neale, 1984). However, these measures were not intended to represent coping and defense as defined by P–E fit theory. Perhaps the measure most relevant to P–E fit theory is the Cybernetic Coping Scale (CCS; Edwards and Baglioni, 1993), which includes scales measuring efforts to change the environment, adjust preferences, and decrease perceived importance. However, the CCS does not measure efforts to change demands or abilities, nor does it differentiate efforts to change objective versus subjective person and environment constructs.

Measures of coping and defense as defined by P–E fit theory are clearly needed. The availability of such measures would create numerous opportunities for research into the interrelationships among the person, the environment, coping, and defense. Several fruitful directions for such research are suggested by Caplan (1983), who generated various hypotheses regarding the resolution of P–E misfit. For example, Caplan (1983) posits that resolving P–E misfit may yield different effects depending on whether misfit is resolved by changes in the person versus the environment and whether these changes are initiated by the self versus others. Caplan (1983) further suggests that the successful resolution of P–E misfit may itself improve well-being by satisfying the person's need for control. These hypotheses set a useful agenda for future research into the specific effects of coping and defense on P–E fit.

P–E fit Over Time

Most studies of P–E fit have relied on cross-sectional data. Consequently, very little evidence is available regarding the effects of P–E fit over time. P–E fit theory suggests two promising avenues for longitudinal P–E fit research.

First, P–E fit theory posits that misfit induces coping and defense, which in turn influence objective and subjective P–E fit, respectively. These relationships imply a cyclical recursive model, in which P–E misfit at time 1 affects coping and defense at time 2, which affect P–E fit at time 3, and so on (Billings and Wroten, 1978; Edwards, 1992). Studies of these sequential relationships would reveal the process by which

P–E fit causes and is caused by coping and defense and the time intervals required for the manifestation of these effects.

Second, Caplan's (1983) discussion of past, present, and future P–E fit provides numerous hypotheses regarding the effects of fit on strain over time and how retrospective and anticipated fit may influence current fit and strain. Available evidence indicates that current strain increases as retrospective and anticipated misfit increase (Caplan *et al.*, 1985; Sen, 1992), thereby suggesting that misfit from other time perspectives operates through vicarious experience rather than contrast effects (Caplan, 1983). This evidence also indicates that anticipated fit is more relevant than retrospective fit to the prediction of strain, implying that worries about the future have greater effects on strain than ruminations about the past. However, these studies treat P–E fit as a single variable and therefore provide no evidence regarding the relationships between specific person and environment constructs from different time perspectives. By examining these relationships, future research may uncover the underlying mechanisms by which retrospective and anticipated person and environment influence current P–E fit and strain.

P–E fit in Multiple Life Domains

As a process theory, P–E fit theory may be applied not only to different content dimensions, but also to different life domains, such as work, family, and leisure (Harrison, 1978; Rice *et al.*, 1985). Despite the generality of P–E fit theory, most P–E fit research has been conducted in work settings (Assouline and Meir, 1987; Edwards, 1991; Spokane, 1985). Studies in non-work settings (e.g. Campbell *et al.*, 1976; Michalos, 1985) have reported results similar to those found in work settings. However, these studies have collapsed the person and environment into a single P–E fit score, thereby introducing the methodological problems discussed earlier. Thus, future P–E fit research should examine three-dimensional relationships between the person, the environment, and outcomes in multiple life domains. Research on the combined effects of P–E fit in multiple life domains on strain is particularly important, given that strain refers to the overall well-being of the person and therefore depends on the person's total life experience, not just his or her experience in a single life domain (Rice *et al.*, 1985).

Methodological Issues

The preceding discussion has focused on major conceptual themes for future P–E fit research. However, these conceptual themes are intertwined with methodological issues regarding the measurement and analysis of P–E fit. The following discussion highlights measurement and analytical issues that are particularly relevant to P–E fit research.

Sampling the person and the environment   Complete tests of P–E fit relationships require the distribution of data throughout the two-dimensional space defined by the minima and maxima of person and environment measures. Scores must be distributed on either side of the line of perfect P–E fit to detect asymmetries in the relationship between P–E misfit and outcomes. Likewise, scores must be distributed throughout the range of person and environment measures to examine variation in outcomes along the line of perfect P–E fit.

The distribution of data throughout the two-dimensional person–environment space should be verified by plotting data, *not* by examining univariate statistics (e.g. the means, standard deviations, and ranges of person and environment scores). Focusing solely on univariate statistics can yield erroneous conclusions regarding the distribution of data within the two dimensional P–E space. For example, scores falling along the line of perfect P–E fit may cover the full range of person and environment measures, but because such scores only depict perfect fit, they cannot be used to analyze the effects of misfit on outcomes.

Typically, person and environment measures are positively correlated, given that people tend to select and remain in environments that provide P–E fit (Schneider *et al.*, 1995). Consequently, person and environment measures often yield an elliptical distribution with its primary axis running parallel to the line of perfect P–E fit. Although such distributions often yield reasonable tests of P–E fit relationships, they provide little information regarding the effects of extreme misfit due to the absence of data where person and environment scores are markedly different. A theory that predicts the conditions under which extreme P–E misfit occurs would help researchers obtain person and environment scores with distributions that permit complete tests of the effects of P–E misfit.

Commensurate measurement As emphasized earlier, P–E fit theory requires that the person and the environment are commensurate. Accordingly, person and environment measures must refer to the same content dimension and use the same response scale (Caplan, 1987b; French *et al.*, 1974). Commensurate measures may be derived from person and environment taxonomies, as suggested in the preceding discussion. These taxonomies may also be used to supplement person and environment measures with commensurate measures of strain, coping, and defense. For example, needs–supplies misfit regarding quantitative workload should influence satisfaction with workload, as opposed to satisfaction with other job facets (French *et al.*, 1982). Likewise, coping and defense directed toward needs–supplies misfit for quantitative workload should assess efforts to change objective and subjective needs and supplies concerning quantitative workload. Obviously, general indices of strain, such as chronic depression and coronary heart disease, cannot be commensurate with person and environment measures. However, the effects of P–E misfit on general indices of strain may be mediated by specific indices of strain that are commensurate with P–E fit dimensions, as in the relationship between job facet misfit, job facet satisfaction, and overall job satisfaction (Locke, 1976; Rice *et al.*, 1985).

Framing person and environment measures Previously, we emphasized that studies of needs–supplies fit should measure needs in terms of the desired amount, frequency, or intensity of a dimension rather than the importance of a dimension. However, desires may be framed in various terms, including preferences ('how much would you like?'), needs ('how much must you have?'), optima ('how much would be ideal?'), expectations derived from social norms ('how much should you have?'), or minimal acceptable levels ('how much would be adequate?'). Analogously, demands should refer to the required amount, frequency, or intensity of a dimension rather than its importance. However, like desires, requirements may refer to preferences ('how much would your boss like you to do?'), needs ('how much must you do?'), optima ('how much would your boss consider ideal?'), normative expectations ('how much does your boss think you should do?'), or minimal acceptable levels ('how much would your boss consider adequate?'). The consequences of these different framings of needs and demands measures have not been investigated.

Scale contamination　Person and environment measures are often implicitly framed in relative terms. For example, job demands may be measured using a response scale ranging from 'very low' to 'very high'. To assign meaning to the anchors on this scale, respondents may invoke some external or internal standard, such as demands placed on others, demands previously experienced by the respondent, or the ability of the respondent to meet the demands in question. When these standards are invoked, measures of demands will be partially confounded with the standard used by the respondent. Thus, if the respondent evaluates job demands by invoking his or her abilities as a standard, then reported demands will partially reflect demands relative to abilities. As a result, jobs with the same absolute level of demand may be described as highly demanding by a respondent with low abilities but may be considered not at all demanding by a respondent with high abilities. Likewise, measures of abilities may be contaminated if respondents describe their abilities relative to standards such as the abilities of others, the respondent's previous ability level, or demands pertaining to the ability in question. Hence, reported abilities may be biased upwards if the respondent is surrounded by people of lesser ability, has increased his or her abilities through training or experience, or is not experiencing demands that tax his or her abilities. Measures of needs and supplies may become contaminated in a similar manner.

Scale contamination may be reduced by using concrete response scales for person and environment measures (Caplan, 1983), as when job demands are measured in terms of the number of units the person must produce or the amount of time the person is given to complete a task or meet a performance objective. Concrete response scales are more difficult to develop for abstract dimensions, such as self-actualization. However, abstract dimensions can often be translated into specific dimensions that may be measured in relatively concrete terms. For example, self-actualization may be operationalized as the fulfillment of needs regarding specific, measurable career goals or milestones.

Scale equivalence　To examine P–E fit, person and environment measures must have equivalent scales, meaning they share the same zero point and have the same interval size (Edwards and Cooper, 1990; French *et al.*, 1974). Equivalent scales are required to quantify the direction and degree of misfit between the person and the environment. To our knowledge, no P–E fit studies have employed scaling techniques to determine the scale equivalence of person and environment measures (Bass *et al.*, 1974; Stevens, 1958). However, it may be reasonable to assume that person and environment scales are equivalent when they use the same metric and employ the same verbal anchors (Edwards and Cooper, 1990).

Some investigators suggest that equivalent scales may be created by standardizing person and environment measures (Rice *et al.*, 1985; Wilk and Sackett, 1996). However, standardization discards information regarding the absolute levels of person and environment scores, and this information is necessary to determine the direction and degree of P–E fit. Thus, scale equivalence must be achieved through the careful construction of person and environment measures, not by standardizing data collected using non-equivalent scales.

Analysis   A final set of methodological issues concerns the analysis of P–E fit relationships. As previously noted, most P–E fit studies have used analytical approaches that reduce the three-dimensional relationship between the person, the environment, and outcomes to two dimensions. Results of these studies are ambiguous and potentially misleading, as demonstrated by studies comparing two-dimensional relationships between P–E fit and outcomes to three-dimensional surfaces relating the person and environment to outcomes (Edwards, 1994, 1996; Edwards and Harrison, 1993). Most three-dimensional relationships relevant to P–E fit theory can be captured by a quadratic equation using measures of the person, the environment, their squares, and their product as predictors. Parameter estimates from these equations may be used to rigorously test features of three-dimensional surfaces that correspond to hypotheses derived from P–E fit theory (Edwards and Parry, 1993). Relationships with abrupt changes in slope, such as the three-dimensional analogs of curves B and C in Figure 2.4, can be analyzed by adapting the piecewise linear model described by Edwards (1994) to allow curvilinearity and multiple changes in slope.

P–E fit may also be treated as an outcome, as in studies of the effects of coping and defense on P–E fit or longitudinal investigations of relationships between P–E fit at different points in time. Methods for analyzing P–E fit as an outcome require the use of person and environment measures as dependent variables in a multivariate model (Edwards, 1995). These models can depict the joint effects of independent variables on the person and environment and can differentiate effects for cases where the environment exceeds the person from those where the environment falls short of the person. These models can also include quadratic person and environment terms, thereby permitting tests of three-dimensional surfaces relating the person and environment at one point in time to both the person and environment at later points in time.

The foregoing methods for analyzing P–E relationships have been implemented using regression analysis with ordinary least squares estimation (Edwards, 1994, 1995; Edwards and Parry, 1993). However, these methods may also be applied using structural equation modeling with latent variables (Bollen, 1989; Joreskog and Sorbom, 1993). Structural equation modeling typically relies on maximum likelihood estimation, which requires that the distribution of observed variables is multivariate normal. This assumption is almost certainly violated for quadratic structural equations required to depict three-dimensional surfaces relating latent person and environment constructs to outcomes. As an alternative, quadratic structural equations may be estimated using asymptotic distribution free estimation procedures (Browne, 1984). However, these procedures often require very large sample sizes to obtain stable parameter estimates. Further information regarding the specification and estimation of quadratic structural equation models may be obtained from Bollen (1989) and Jaccard and Wan (1996).

Practical Implications

Previous treatments of P–E fit theory have discussed its implications for reducing stress and strain at work (Caplan, 1983; Caplan *et al.*, 1980; French *et al.*, 1982; Harrison, 1978, 1985). These discussions emphasize several important themes, such as the relevance of both demands–abilities fit and needs–supplies fit to recruitment and selection decisions, the need to customize organizational interventions to suit the needs and abilities of the affected individuals, and the viability of resolving P–E misfit by targeting the person, the environment, or both. These general principles provide an overarching framework for stress management interventions. However, it is difficult to translate these principles into more detailed prescriptions, due to the limitations of available evidence regarding the exact nature of the relationship between P–E fit and strain.

Interventions to resolve P–E misfit require knowledge of the effects of P–E misfit for specific content dimensions. For example, employee involvement programs often change the responsibility, control, rewards, and contact with co-workers experienced by employees (Lawler *et al.*, 1995). To predict the effects of these changes, we must know the relationship between P–E fit and strain for these particular dimensions. Our current knowledge regarding these relationships is limited, and consequently we have little basis for asserting whether or how changes in P–E fit on specific dimensions will influence strain. Knowledge required to guide interventions might be gained through randomized field experiments that manipulate parameters hypothesized to improve P–E fit and track the effects of these manipulations on strain. These effects should be observed over time, as P–E fit theory views the relationship between the person and environment as dynamic, and changes in the environment may combine with changes in the person to influence P–E fit. In sum, although P–E fit theory identifies relevant person and environment constructs for interventions that may reduce stress and enhance well-being, specific prescriptions based on P–E fit theory await further research.

Summary and Conclusion

P–E fit theory provides a systematic, general framework for understanding how the person and environment combine to produce stress and influence strain. The basic postulates of P–E fit theory are pervasive in theories of stress, and P–E theory has stimulated numerous studies of the relationship between P–E fit and strain. However, available evidence relevant to P–E fit theory has important flaws and limitations, and much remains to be learned regarding the nature, causes, and consequences of P–E fit. Based on this overview of the past 25 years of P–E fit research, we believe the time has come to initiate a second generation of P–E fit research. We hope this generation of research will address the new and lingering conceptual questions pertaining to P–E fit theory and will avoid the methodological problems associated with much previous P–E fit research. We see important opportunities for identifying taxonomies of content dimensions relevant to P–E fit, for uncovering the mechanisms that generate complex three-dimensional relationships between the person, the environment, and outcomes, and for examining the interplay between P–E fit, strain, coping, and defense over time. By capitalizing on these opportunities, researchers will substantially advance our understanding of the joint effects of the person and environment in the stress process.

The authors thank Daniel M. Cable for his helpful comments on an earlier version of this chapter.

References

Adkins, C. L., Russell, C. J., and Werbel, J. D. (1994) 'Judgments of fit in the selection process: The role of work value congruence', *Personnel Psychology*, 47, 593–604.

Amabile, T. M., Hill, K. G., Hennessey, B. A., and Tighe, E. M. (1994) 'The work preference inventory: Assessing intrinsic and extrinsic motivational orientations', *Journal of Personality and Social Psychology*, 66, 950–967.

Amirkhan, J. H. (1990) 'A factor analytically derived measure of coping: The coping strategy indicator', *Journal of Personality and Social Psychology*, 59, 1066–1074.

Aranya, N., Barak, A., and Amernic, J. (1981) 'A test of Holland's theory in a population of accountants', *Journal of Vocational Behavior*, 19, 15–24.

Assouline, M. and Meir, E. I. (1987) 'Meta-analysis of the relationship between congruence and well-being measures', *Journal of Vocational Behavior*, 31, 319–332.

Barrett, G. V., Forbes, J. B., O'Connor, E. J., and Alexander, R. A. (1980) 'Ability–satisfaction relationships: Field and laboratory studies', *Academy of Management Journal*, 23, 550–555.

Bass, B. M., Cascio, W. F., and O'Connor, E. J. (1974) 'Magnitude estimations of expressions of frequency and amount', *Journal of Applied Psychology*, 59, 313–320.

Bedeian, A. G., Day, D. V., Edwards, J. R., Tisak, J., and Smith, C. S. (1994) 'Difference scores: Rationale, formulation, and interpretation', *Journal of Management*, 20, 673–698.

Billings, R. S. and Wroten, S. P. (1978) 'Use of path analysis in industrial/organizational psychology: Criticisms and suggestions', *Journal of Applied Psychology*, 63, 677–688.

Bizot, E. B. and Goldman, S. H. (1993) 'Prediction of satisfactoriness and satisfaction: An 8-year follow up', *Journal of Vocational Behavior*, 43, 19–29.

Blau, G. (1994) 'Testing the effect of level and importance of pay referents on pay level satisfaction', *Human Relations*, 47, 1251–1268.

Bollen, K. A. (1989) *Structural Equations with Latent Variables*. New York: Wiley.

Borman, W. C. and Brush, D. H. (1993) 'More progress toward a taxonomy of managerial performance requirements', *Human Performance*, 6, 1–21.

Breeden, S. A. (1993) 'Job and occupational change as a function of occupational correspondence and job satisfaction', *Journal of Vocational Behavior*, 43, 30–45.

Browne, M. W. (1984) 'Asymptotic distribution free methods in analysis of covariance structures', *British Journal of Mathematical and Statistical Psychology*, 37, 62–83.

Burger, J. M. and Cooper, H. M. (1979) 'The desirability of control', *Motivation and Emotion*, 3, 381–393.

Cable, D. M. and Judge, T. A. (1996) 'Person–organization fit, job choice decisions, and organizational entry', *Organizational Behavior and Human Decision Process*, 67, 294–311.

Caldwell, D. F. and O'Reilly, C. A. (1990) 'Measuring person-job fit with a profile comparison process', *Journal of Applied Psychology*, 75, 648–657.

Campbell, A., Converse, P. E., and Rodgers, W. L. (1976) *The Quality of American Life*. New York: Russell Sage Foundation.

Campbell, J. P., Dunnette, M. D., Lawler, E. E., III, and Weick, K. E. (1970) *Managerial Behavior, Performance, and Effectiveness*. New York: McGraw-Hill, Inc.

Campion, M. A. and Thayer, P. W. (1985) 'Development and field evaluation of an interdisciplinary measure of job design', *Journal of Applied Psychology*, 70, 29–43.

Caplan, R. D. (1983) Person–environment fit: Past, present, and future. In C. L. Cooper (ed.), *Stress Research* (pp. 35–78). New York: Wiley.

Caplan, R. D. (1987a) Person–environment fit in organizations: Theories, facts, and values. In A. W. Riley and S. J. Zaccaro (eds.), *Occupational Stress and Organizational Effectiveness* (pp. 103–140.). New York: Praeger.

Caplan, R. D. (1987b) 'Person–environment fit theory and organizations: Commensurate dimensions, time perspectives, and mechanisms', *Journal of Vocational Behavior*, 31, 248–267.

Caplan, R. D. and Harrison, R. V. (1993) 'Person–environment fit theory: Some history, recent developments, and future directions', *Journal of Social Issues*, 49, 253–275.

Caplan, R. D., Cobb, S., French, J. R. P., Jr., Harrison, R. V., and Pinneau, S. R. (1980) *Job Demands and Worker Health: Main Effects and Occupational Differences*. Ann Arbor, MN: Institute for Social Research.

Caplan, R. D., Tripathi, R. C., and Naidu, R. K. (1985) 'Subjective past, present, and future fit: Effects on anxiety, depression, and other indicators of well-being', *Journal of Personality and Social Psychology*, 8, 180–197.

Carlson, R. E. (1969) 'Degree of job fit as a moderator of the relationship between job performance and job satisfaction', *Personnel Psychology*, 22, 159–170.

Carver, C. S., Scheier, M. F., and Weintraub, J. K. (1989) 'Assessing coping strategies: A theoretically based approach', *Journal of Personality and Social Psychology*, 56, 267–283.

Champoux, J. E. (1992) 'A multivariate analysis of curvilinear relationships among job scope, work context satisfactions, and affective outcomes', *Human Relations*, 45, 87–111.

Chan, D. (1996) 'Cognitive misfit of problem-solving style at work: A facet of person–organization fit', *Organizational Behavior and Human Decision Process*, 68, 194–207.

Chatman, J. A. (1991) 'Matching people and organizations: Selection and socialization in public accounting firms', *Administrative Science Quarterly*, 36, 459–484.

Cohen, S. and Edwards, J. R. (1989) Personality characteristics as moderators of the relationship between stress and disorder. In W. J. Neufeld (ed.), *Advances in the Investigation of Psychological Stress* (pp. 235–283). New York: Wiley.

Cole, D. A. and Milstead, M. (1989) 'Behavioral correlates of depression: Antecedents or consequences?' *Journal of Counseling Psychology*, 36, 408–416.

Conway, T. L., Vickers, R. R., and French, J. R. P. (1992) 'An application of person–environment fit theory: Perceived versus desired control', *Journal of Social Issues*, 48, 95–107.

Cooper, W. H. and Richardson, A. J. (1986) 'Unfair comparisons', *Journal of Applied Psychology*, 71, 179–184.

Cronbach, L. J. (1958) Proposals leading to analytic treatment of social perception scores. In R. Tagiuri and L. Petrullo (eds.), *Person Perception and Interpersonal Behavior* (pp. 353–379). Stanford, CA: Stanford University Press.

Cummings, T. G. and Cooper, C. L. (1979) 'Cybernetic framework for studying occupational stress', *Human Relations*, 32, 395–418.

Day, D. V. and Bedeian, A. G. (1995) 'Personality similarity and work-related outcomes among African-American nursing personnel: A test of the supplementary model of person–environment congruence', *Journal of Vocational Behavior*, 46, 55–70.

DeLongis, A., Coyne, J. C., Dakof, G., Folkman, S., and Lazarus, R. S. (1982) 'Relationship of daily hassles, uplifts, and major life events to health status', *Health Psychology*, 1, 119–136.

Derogatis, L. R. (1977) *SCL-90-R Administration, Scoring, and Procedures Manual, Vol. 1*. Baltimore: Clinical Psychometric Research.

Dewe, P. J. and Guest, D. E. (1990) 'Methods of coping with stress at work: A conceptual analysis and empirical study of measurement issues', *Journal of Organizational Behavior*, 11, 135–150.

Doty, M. S. and Betz, N. E. (1979) 'Comparisons of the concurrent validity of Holland's theory for men and women in an enterprising occupation', *Journal of Vocational Behavior*, 15, 207–216.

Edwards, J. R. (1991) Person–job fit: A conceptual integration, literature review, and methodological critique. In C. L. Cooper and I. T. Robertson (eds.), *International Review of Industrial and Organizational Psychology* (Vol. 6, pp. 283–357). New York: Wiley.

Edwards, J. R. (1992) 'A cybernetic theory of stress, coping, and well-being in organizations', *Academy of Management Review*, 17, 238–274.

Edwards, J. R. (1993) 'Problems with the use of profile similarity indices in the study of congruence in organizational research', *Personnel Psychology*, 46, 641–665.

Edwards, J. R. (1994) 'The study of congruence in organizational behavior research: Critique and a proposed alternative', *Organizational Behavior and Human Decision Processes*, 58, 51–100 (erratum, 58, 323–325).

Edwards, J. R. (1995) 'Alternatives to difference scores as dependent variables in the study of congruence in organizational research', *Organizational Behavior and Human Decision Processes*, 64, 307–324.

Edwards, J. R. (1996) 'An examination of competing versions of the person–environment fit approach to stress', *Academy of Management Journal*, 39, 292–339.

Edwards, J. R. and Baglioni, A. J., Jr. (1993) 'The measurement of coping with stress: Construct validity of the Ways of Coping Checklist and the Cybernetic Coping Scale', *Work and Stress*, 7, 17–31.

Edwards, J. R. and Cooper, C. L. (1990) 'The person–environment fit approach to stress: Recurring problems and some suggested solutions', *Journal of Organizational Behavior*, 11, 293–307.

Edwards, J. R. and Cooper, C. L. (1988) 'The impacts of positive psychological states on physical health: A review and theoretical framework', *Social Science and Medicine*, 27, 1447–1459.

Edwards, J. R. and Harrison, R. V. (1993) 'Job demands and worker health: Three-dimensional re-examination of the relationship between person–environment fit and strain', *Journal of Applied Psychology*, 78, 628–648.

Edwards, J. R. and Parry, M. E. (1993) 'On the use of polynomial regression equations as an alternative to difference scores in organizational research', *Academy of Management Journal*, 36, 1577–1613.

Eidelson, R. J. (1980) 'Interpersonal satisfaction and level of involvement: A curvilinear relationship', *Journal of Personality and Social Psychology*, 39, 460–470.

Elsass, P. M. and Veiga, J. F. (1997) 'Job control and job strain: A test of three models', *Journal of Occupational Health Psychology*, 2, 195–211.

Eulberg, J. R., Weekley, J. A., and Bhagat, R. S. (1988) 'Models of stress in organizational research: A metatheoretical perspective', *Human Relations*, 41, 331–350.

Evans, M. G. (1969) 'Conceptual and operational problems in the measurement of various aspects of job satisfaction', *Journal of Applied Psychology*, 53, 93–101.

Fleishman, E. A. and Mumford, M. D. (1991) 'Evaluating classifications of job behavior: A construct validation of the ability requirements scales', *Personnel Psychology*, 44, 523–576.

Fleishman, E. A. and Reilly, M. E. (1992) *Handbook of Human Abilities: Definitions, Measurements, and Job Task Requirements*. Palo Alto, CA: Consulting Psychologists Press.

Folkman, S. and Lazarus, R. S. (1988) *Manual for the Ways of Coping Questionnaire*. Palo Alto, CA: Consulting Psychologists Press.

French, J. R. P., Jr. (1973) 'Person role fit', *Occupational Mental Health*, 3 (1), 15–20.

French, J. R. P., Jr. and Caplan, R. D. (1972) Organizational stress and individual strain. In A. J. Marrow (ed.), *The Failure of Success* (pp. 30–66). New York: Amacon.

French, J. R. P., Jr. and Kahn, R. L. (1962) 'A programmatic approach to studying the industrial environment and mental health', *Journal of Social Issues*, 18, 1–48.

French, J. R. P., Jr., Rodgers, W. L., and Cobb, S. (1974) Adjustment as person–environment fit. In G. Coelho, D. Hamburg, and J. Adams (eds.), *Coping and Adaptation* (pp. 316–333). New York: Basic Books.

French, J. R. P., Jr., Caplan, R. D., and Harrison, R. V. (1982) *The Mechanisms of Job Stress and Strain*. London: Wiley.

Friedman, M. and Rosenman, R. H. (1959) 'Association of specific overt behavior pattern with increases in blood cholesterol, blood clotting time, incidence of *arcus senilis* and clinical coronary artery disease', *Journal of the American Medical Association*, 169, 1286–1296.

Gati, I., Garty, Y. and Fassa, N. (1996) 'Using career-related aspects to assess person–environment fit', *Journal of Counseling Psychology*, 43, 196–206.

Goldberg, D. P. (1978) *Manual of the General Health Questionnaire*. Windsor: National Foundation for Educational Research.

Hackman, J. R. and Oldham, G. R. (1980) *Work Redesign*. Reading, Mass.: Addison-Wesley.

Harrison, R. V. (1978) Person–environment fit and job stress. In C. L. Cooper and R. Payne (eds.), *Stress at Work* (pp. 175–205). New York: Wiley.

Harrison, R. V. (1985) The person–environment fit model and the study of job stress. In T. A. Beehr and R. S. Bhagat (eds.), *Human Stress and Cognition in Organizations* (pp. 23–55). New York: Wiley.

Hesketh, B. and Gardner, D. (1993) 'Person–environment fit models: A reconceptualization and empirical test', *Journal of Vocational Behavior*, 42, 315–332.

House, J. S. (1974) 'Occupational stress and coronary heart disease: A review and theoretical integration', *Journal of Health and Social Behaviour*, 15, 12–27.

Hulin, C. L. and Smith, P. C. (1965) 'A linear model of job satisfaction', *Journal of Applied Psychology*, 49, 206–216.

Imparato, N. (1972) 'Relationship between Porter's Need Satisfaction Questionnaire and the Job Descriptive Index', *Journal of Applied Psychology*, 56, 397–405.

Irving, P. G. and Meyer, J. P. (1994) 'Reexamination of the met-expectations hypothesis: A longitudinal analysis', *Journal of Applied Psychology*, 79, 937–949.

Jaccard, J. and Wan, C. K. (1996) *LISREL Approaches to Interaction Effects in Multiple Regression*. Thousand Oaks, CA: Sage.

Jackson, S. E. and Schuler, R. S. (1985) 'A meta-analysis and conceptual critique of research on role ambiguity and role conflict in work settings', *Organizational Behavior and Human Decision Processes*, 36, 16–78.

Johns, G. (1981) 'Difference score measures of organizational behavior variables: A critique', *Organizational Behavior and Human Performance*, 27, 443–463.

Joreskog, K. G. and Sorbom, D. (1993) *LISREL 8: Structural Equation Modeling with the SIMPLIS Command Language*. Hillsdale, NJ: Erlbaum.

Joyce, W. F., Slocum, J. W., and von Glinow, M. A. (1982) 'Person–situation interaction: Competing models of fit', *Journal of Occupational Behavior*, 3, 265–280.

Judge, T. A. and Bretz, R. D., Jr. (1992) 'Effects of work values on job choice decisions', *Journal of Applied Psychology*, 77, 261–271.

Kahn, L. J. and Morrow, P. C. (1991) 'Objective and subjective underemployment relationships to job satisfaction', *Journal of Business Research*, 22, 211–218.

Kahn, R. L., Wolfe, D. M., Quinn, R. P., Snoek, J. D., and Rosenthal, R. A. (1964) *Organizational Stress: Studies in Role Conflict and Ambiguity*. New York: Wiley.

Kaldenberg, D. O. and Becker, B. W. (1992) 'Workload and psychological strain: A test of the French, Rodgers, and Cobb hypothesis', *Journal of Organizational Behavior*, 13, 617–624.

Karasek, R. A. and Theorell, T. (1990) *Healthy Work: Stress, Productivity, and the Reconstruction of Working Life*. New York: Basic Books.

Katzell, R. A. (1964) Personal values, job satisfaction, and job behavior. In H. Borow (ed.), *Man in a World of Work* (pp. 341–363). Boston: Houghton Mifflin Company.

Klinger, E. (1975) 'Consequences of commitment to and disengagement from incentives', *Psychological Review*, 82, 1–25.

Kobasa, S. C. (1979) 'Stressful life events, personality, and health: An inquiry into hardiness', *Journal of Personality and Social Psychology*, 37, 1–11.

Kulka, R. A. (1979) Interaction as person–environment fit. In L. R. Kahle (ed.), *New Directions for Methodology of Behavioral Science* (pp. 55–71). San Francisco: Jossey-Bass.

Lawler, E. E., III, Mohrman, S. A., and Ledford, G. E., Jr. (1995) *Creating High Performance Organizations*. San Francisco: Jossey-Bass.

Lazarus, R. S. (1983) The costs and benefits of denial. In S. Breznitz (ed.), *Denial of Stress* (pp. 1–30). New York: International Universities Press.

Lazarus, R. S. and Folkman, S. (1984) *Stress, Coping, and Adaptation*. New York: Springer.

Lewin, K. (1951) *Field Theory in Social Science*. New York: Harper.

Livingstone, L. P., Nelson, D. L., and Barr, S. H. (1997) 'Person–environment fit and creativity: An examination of supply–value and demand–ability versions of fit', *Journal of Management*, 23, 119–146.

Locke, E. A. (1969) 'What is job satisfaction?', *Organizational Behavior and Human Performance*, 4, 309–336.

Locke, E. A. (1976) The nature and causes of job satisfaction. In M. Dunnette (ed.), *Handbook of Industrial and Organizational Psychology* (pp. 1297–1350). Chicago: Rand McNally.

Lovelace, K. and Rosen, B. (1996) 'Differences in achieving person–organization fit among diverse groups of managers', *Journal of Management*, 22, 703–722.

Lubinski, D. and Dawis, R. V. (1990) Aptitudes, skills, and proficiencies. In M. D. Dunnette and L. M. Hough (eds.), *Handbook of Industrial and Organizational Psychology* (2nd edn., Vol. 3, pp. 1–60). Palo Alto, CA: Consulting Psychologists Press.

Luthans, F. and Lockwood, D. L. (1984) Toward an observation system for measuring leader behavior in natural settings. In J. G. Hunt, D. Hosking, C. Schriesheim, and R. Stewart (eds.), *Leaders and Managers: International Perspectives on Managerial Behavior and Leadership* (pp. 117–141). New York: Permagon Press.

McCormick, E. J. (1979) *Job Analysis: Methods and Applications*. New York: American Management Association.

McFarlin, D. B. and Rice, R. W. (1992) 'The role of facet importance as a moderator in job satisfaction processes', *Journal of Organizational Behavior*, 13, 41–54.

McGrath, J. E. (1976) Stress and behavior in organizations. In M. Dunnette (ed.), *Handbook of Industrial and Organizational Psychology* (pp. 1351–1395). Chicago: Rand McNally.

Magnusson, D. and Endler, N. S. (1977) Interactional psychology: Present status and future prospects. In D. Magnusson and N. S. Endler (eds.), *Personality at the Crossroads: Current Issues in Interactional Psychology* (pp. 3–31). New York: Erlbaum.

March, J. G. and Simon, H. A. (1958) *Organizations*. New York: Wiley.

Maslow, A. H. (1954) *Motivation and Personality*. New York: Harper.

Meglino, B. M., Ravlin, E. C., and Adkins, C. L. (1989) 'A work values approach to corporate culture: A field test of the value congruence process and its relationship to individual outcomes', *Journal of Applied Psychology*, 74, 424–434.

Meglino, B. M., Ravlin, E. C., and Adkins, C. L. (1992) 'The measurement of work value congruence: A field study comparison', *Journal of Management*, 18, 33–43.

Meier, S. T. (1991) 'Vocational behavior, 1988–1990: Vocational choice, decision-making, career development interventions, and assessment', *Journal of Vocational Behavior*, 39, 131–181.

Menaghan, E. G. (1983) Individual coping efforts: Moderators of the relationship between life stress and mental health outcomes. In H. B. Kaplan (ed.), *Psychosocial Stress: Trends in Theory and Research* (pp. 157–191). New York: Adacemic Press.

Michalos, A. C. (1985) 'Multiple discrepancies theory', *Social Indicators Research*, 16, 347–413.

Michalos, A. C. (1986) Job satisfaction, marital satisfaction, and the quality of life: A review and preview. In F. M. Andrews (ed.), *Research on the Quality of Life* (pp. 57–83). Ann Arbor: University of Michigan Institute for Social Research.

Mischel, W. (1977) The interaction of person and situation. In D. Magnusson and N. S. Endler (eds.), *Personality at the Crossroads: Current Issues in Interactional Psychology* (pp. 333–352). New York: Erlbaum.

Mobley, W. H. and Locke, E. A. (1970) 'The relationship of value importance to satisfaction', *Organizational Behavior and Human Performance*, 5, 463–483.

Moskowitz, D. S. and Cote, S. (1995) 'Do interpersonal traits predict affect? A comparison of three models', *Journal of Personality and Social Psychology*, 69, 915–924.

Murray, H. A. (1951) Toward a classification of interaction. In T. Parsons and E. A. Shils (eds.), *Toward a General Theory of Action* (pp. 434–464). Cambridge, MA: Harvard University Press.

Naylor, J. C., Pritchard, R. D., and Ilgen, D. R. (1980) *A Theory of Behavior in Organizations*. New York: Academic Press.

O'Reilly, C. A., III (1977) 'Personality–job fit: Implications for individual attitudes and performance', *Organizational Behavior and Human Performance*, 18, 36–46.

O'Reilly, C. A., III, Caldwell, D., and Barnett, W. (1989) 'Work group demography, social integration, and turnover', *Administrative Science Quarterly*, 34, 21–37.

O'Reilly, C. A., III, Chatman, J. A., and Caldwell, D. F. (1991) 'People and organizational culture: A Q-sort approach to assessing person–organization fit', *Academy of Management Journal*, 34, 487–516.

Ostroff, C. (1993) 'The effects of climate and personal influence on individual behavior and attitudes in organizations', *Organizational Behavior and Human Decision Process*, 56, 56–90.

Parker, D. F. and DeCotiis, T. A. (1983) 'Organizational determinants of job stress', *Organizational Behavior and Human Performance*, 32, 160–177.

Parkes, K. R. (1994) 'Personality and coping as moderators of work and stress processes: Models, methods, and measures', *Work & Stress*, 8, 110–129.

Pervin, L. A. (1989) 'Persons, situations, interactions: The history of a controversy and a discussion of theoretical models', *Academy of Management Review*, 14, 350–360.

Porter, L. W. (1964) *Organizational Patterns of Managerial Job Attitudes*. New York: American Foundation for Management Research.

Porter, L. W. and Lawler, E. E. (1968) *Managerial Attitudes and Performance*. Homewood, IL: Dorsey Press.

Pritchard, D. P. (1969) 'Equity theory: A review and critique', *Organizational Behavior and Human Performance*, 4, 176–211.

Pryor, R. G. L. (1983) *Manual for the Work Aspect Preference Scale*. Melbourne: Australian Council for Education Research.

Puffer, S. M. and Meindl, J. R. (1992) 'The congruence of motives and incentives in a voluntary organization', *Journal of Organizational Behavior*, 13, 425–434.

Rabkin, J. G. and Struening, E. L. (1976) 'Life Events, Stress, and Illness', *Science*, 194, 1013–1020.

Rahim, A. (1981) 'Job satisfaction as a function of personality–job congruence: A study with Jungian psychological types', *Psychological Reports*, 49, 496–498.

Rice, R. W., McFarlin, D. B., Hunt, R. G., and Near, J. P. (1985) 'Organizational work and the perceived quality of life: Toward a conceptual model', *Academy of Management Review*, 10, 296–310.

Rice, R. W., Phillips, S. M., and McFarlin, D. B. (1990) 'Multiple discrepancies and pay satisfaction', *Journal of Applied Psychology*, 75, 386–393.

Rokeach, M. (1973) *The Nature of Human Values*. New York: Free Press.

Rotter, J. B. (1966) 'Generalized expectancies for internal versus external control of reinforcement', *Psychological Monographs*, 80 (1, Whole No. 609).

Rounds, J. B., Dawis, R. W., and Lofquist, L. H. (1987) 'Measurement of person–environment fit and prediction of satisfaction in the Theory of Work Adjustment', *Journal of Vocational Behavior*, 31, 297–318.

Runkel, P. J. and McGrath, J. E. (1972) *Research on Human Behavior: A Systematic Guide to Method*. New York: Holt.

Russell, J. A. (1980) 'A circumplex model of affect', *Journal of Personality and Social Psychology*, 39, 1161–1178.

Scarpello, V. and Campbell, J. P. (1983) 'Job satisfaction and the fit between individual needs and organizational rewards', *Journal of Occupational Psychology*, 56, 315–328.

Schein, V. E. and Diamante, T. (1988) 'Organizational attraction and the person–environment fit', *Psychological Reports*, 62, 167–173.

Schneider, B. and Schmitt, N. (1992) *Staffing Organizations*. Prospect Heights, IL: Waveland Press.

Schneider, B., Goldstein, H. W., and Smith, D. B. (1995) 'The ASA framework: An update', *Personnel Psychology*, 48, 747–773.

Schuler, R. S. (1980) 'Definition and conceptualization of stress in organizations', *Organizational Behavior and Human Performance*, 25, 184–215.

Schuler, R. S. (1985) Integrative transactional process model of coping with stress in organizations. In T. A. Beehr and R. S. Bhagat (eds.), *Human Stress and Cognition in Organizations* (pp. 347–374). New York: Wiley.

Schwartz, S. H. (1994) 'Are there universal aspects in the structure and contents of human values?' *Journal of Social Issues*, 50, 19–45.

Sen, M. (1992) 'Retrospected and anticipated fits: An exploration into their differential effects in a sample of Indian managers', *Work and Stress*, 6, 153–162.

Shirom, A. (1982) 'What is organizational stress? A facet analytic conceptualization', *Journal of Occupational Behavior*, 3, 21–37.

Shumaker, S. A. and Brownell, A. (1984) 'Toward a theory of social support: Closing conceptual gaps', *Journal of Social Issues*, 40, 11–36.

Spenner, K. I. (1990) 'Skill: Meanings, methods, and measures', *Work and Occupations*, 17, 399–421.

Spokane, A. R. (1985) 'A review of research on person–environment congruence in Holland's theory of careers', *Journal of Vocational Behavior*, 26, 306–343.

Starbuck, W. H. and Mezias, J. M. (1996) 'Opening Pandora's box: Studying the accuracy of managers' perceptions', *Journal of Organizational Behavior*, 17, 99–118.

Stevens, S. S. (1958) Ratio scales, partition scales, and confusion scales. In H. Gulliksen and S. Messick (eds.), *Psychological Scaling: Theory and Application* (pp. 49–66). New York: John Wiley & Sons.

Stone, A. A. and Neale, J. M. (1984) 'New measure of daily coping: Development and preliminary results', *Journal of Personality and Social Psychology*, 46, 892–906.

Super, D. E. (1973) The Work Values Inventory. In D. G. Zytowski (ed.), *Contemporary Approaches to Interest Measurement* (pp. 189–205). Minneapolis: University of Minnesota Press.

Sweeney, P. D., McFarlin, D. B., and Inderrieden, E. J. (1990) 'Using relative deprivation theory to explain satisfaction with income and pay level: A multistudy examination', *Academy of Management Journal*, 33, 423–436.

Taylor, S. E. and Brown, J. D. (1988) 'Illusions and well-being: A social psychological perspective on mental health', *Psychological Bulletin*, 103, 193–210.

Tsui, A. S. and O'Reilly, C. A., III (1989) 'Beyond simple demographic effects: The importance of relational demography in superior–subordinate dyads', *Academy of Management Journal*, 32, 402–423.

Turban, D. B. and Jones, A. P. (1988) 'Supervisor–subordinate similarity: Types, effects, and mechanisms', *Journal of Applied Psychology*, 73, 228–234.

Tziner, A. and Falbe, C. M. (1990) 'Actual and preferred climates of achievement orientation and their congruency: An investigation of their relationships to work attitudes and performance in two occupational strata', *Journal of Organizational Behavior*, 11, 159–168.

Valentiner, D. P., Holahan, C. J., and Moos, R. H. (1994) 'Social support, appraisals of event controllability, and coping: An integrative model', *Journal of Personality and Social Psychology*, 66, 1094–1102.

Vandenberg, R. J. and Scarpello, V. (1990) 'The matching model: An examination of the processes underlying realistic job previews', *Journal of Applied Psychology*, 75, 60–67.

Wanous, J. P. and Lawler, E. E. III (1972) 'Measurement and meaning of job satisfaction', *Journal of Applied Psychology*, 56, 95–105.

Wanous, J. P., Poland, T. D., Premack, S. L., and Davis, K. S. (1992) 'The effects of met expectations on newcomer attitudes and behaviors: A review and meta-analysis', *Journal of Applied Psychology*, 77, 288–297.

Watson, D. and Tellegen, A. (1985) 'Toward a consensual structure of mood', *Psychological Bulletin*, 98, 219–235.

Weick, K. E. (1979) *The Social Psychology of Organizing* (2nd edn.). Reading, MA: Addison-Wesley.

Westman, M. and Eden, D. (1992) 'Excessive role demand and subsequent performance', *Journal of Organizational Behavior*, 13, 519–529.

Westman, M. and Eden, D. (1996) 'The inverted-U relationship between stress and performance: A field study', *Work & Stress*, 10, 165–173.

White, R. W. (1959) 'Motivation reconsidered: The concept of competence', *Psychological Review*, 66, 297–333.

Wiggins, J. D. (1984) 'Personality–environment factors related to job satisfaction of school counselors', *The Vocational Guidance Quarterly*, 33, 169–177.

Wilk, S. L. and Sackett, P. R. (1996) 'Longitudinal analysis of ability–job complexity fit and job change', *Personnel Psychology*, 49, 937–967.

Wood, D. A. (1981) 'The relation between work values and the perception of the work setting', *Journal of Social Psychology*, 115, 189–193.

Xie, J. L. and Johns, G. (1995) 'Job scope and stress: Can job scope be too high?', *Academy of Management Journal*, 38, 1288–1309.

Zalesny, M. D. and Kirsch, M. P. (1989) 'The effect of similarity on performance ratings and inter-rater agreement', *Human Relations*, 42, 81–96.

3

A Multidimensional Theory of Burnout

Christina Maslach

Introduction

Job burnout is a prolonged response to chronic interpersonal stressors on the job. The three key dimensions of this response are an overwhelming exhaustion; feelings of cynicism and detachment from the job; and a sense of ineffectiveness and failure (Maslach, 1982a; Maslach and Jackson, 1981b; Maslach and Leiter, 1997). The experience can impair both personal and social functioning. While some people may quit the job as a result of burnout, others will stay on, but will only do the bare minimum rather than their very best. This decline in the quality of work and in both physical and psychological health can be costly—not just for the individual worker, but for everyone affected by that person.

For many years, burnout has been recognized as an occupational hazard for various people-oriented professions, such as human services, education, and health care. The therapeutic or service relationships that such providers develop with recipients require an ongoing and intense level of personal, emotional contact. Although such relationships can be rewarding and engaging, they can also be quite stressful. Within such occupations, the prevailing norms are to be selfless and put others' needs first; to work long hours and do whatever it takes to help a client or patient or student; to go the extra mile and to give one's all. Moreover, the organizational environments for these jobs are shaped by various social, political, and economic factors (such as funding cutbacks or policy restrictions) that result in work settings that are high in demands and low in resources. Recently, as other occupations have become more oriented to 'high-touch' customer service, the phenomenon of burnout has become relevant for these jobs as well (Maslach and Leiter, 1997).

Despite the fact that practitioners had identified burnout as an important social problem in the workplace, it was a long time before it became a focus of systematic study by researchers (Maslach and Schaufeli, 1993). Thus, the development of a model of burnout was more of a grass-roots, 'bottom-up' process, grounded in the realities of people's experiences in the workplace, rather than a 'top-down' derivation from a scholarly theory. The term itself illustrates this point: 'burnout' had popular origins, not academic ones. However, despite its evocative imagery and popular usage, burnout was initially a very slippery concept—there was no standard definition of it, although there was a wide variety of opinions about what it was and what could be done about it. Different people used the term to mean very different things, and so there did not always exist a basis for constructive communication about the problem and solutions for it (Maslach, 1982*b*). However, there was actually an underlying consensus about three core dimensions of the burnout experience, and subsequent research on this issue led to the development of a multidimensional theory of burnout (Maslach and Jackson, 1981*b*; Maslach, 1993).

A Description of the Multidimensional Theory

Unlike unidimensional models of stress, the multidimensional theory conceptualizes burnout in terms of its three core components: emotional exhaustion, depersonalization, and reduced personal accomplishment (Maslach, 1993; Maslach and Jackson, 1981*a*, 1986). According to this theory, burnout is an individual stress experience embedded in a context of complex social relationships, and it involves the person's conception of both self and others.

Emotional exhaustion refers to feelings of being emotionally overextended and depleted of one's emotional resources. The major sources of this exhaustion are work overload and personal conflict at work. Workers feel drained and used up, without any source of replenishment. They lack enough energy to face another day or another person in need. The emotional exhaustion component represents the basic individual stress dimension of burnout.

Depersonalization refers to a negative, cynical, or excessively detached response to other people, which often includes a loss of idealism. It usually develops in response to the overload of emotional exhaustion, and is self-protective at first—an emotional buffer of 'detached concern'. But the risk is that the detachment can turn into dehumanization. The depersonalization component represents the interpersonal dimension of burnout.

Reduced personal accomplishment refers to a decline in feelings of competence and productivity at work. This lowered sense of self-efficacy has been linked to depression and an inability to cope with the demands of the job, and it can be exacerbated by a lack of social support and of opportunities to develop professionally. Workers experience a growing sense of inadequacy about their ability to help clients, and this may result in a self-imposed verdict of failure. The personal accomplishment component represents the self-evaluation dimension of burnout.

The significance of this three-dimensional model is that it clearly places the individual stress experience within a social context. What has been distinctive about burnout (as opposed to other kinds of stress reactions) is the interpersonal framework of the phenomenon. The centrality of relationships at work—whether it be relationships with clients, colleagues or supervisors—has always been at the heart of descriptions of burnout. These relationships are the source of both emotional strains and rewards, they can be a resource for coping with job stress, and they often bear the brunt of the negative effects of burnout. Thus, if one were to look at burnout out of context, and simply focus on the individual exhaustion component, one would lose sight of the phenomenon entirely.

In this regard, the multidimensional theory is a distinct improvement over prior uni-dimensional models of burnout (e.g. Freudenberger and Richelson, 1980; Pines *et al.*, 1981) because it both incorporates the single dimension (exhaustion), and extends it by adding two other dimensions: response toward others (depersonalization) and response toward self (reduced personal accomplishment). The inclusion of these two dimensions adds something over and above the notion of an individual stress response and makes burnout much broader than established ideas of occupational stress.

Interestingly, these three components have actually appeared within most of the various discussions of burnout, even if they have not been considered explicitly within a multidimensional framework. For example, exhaustion has also been described as wearing out, loss of energy, depletion, debilitation, and fatigue; deper-sonalization has been described as negative or inappropriate attitudes towards clients, loss of idealism, and irritability; and reduced personal accomplishment has been described as reduced productivity or capability, low morale, withdrawal, and an inability to cope (for a more extensive analysis of these definitional issues, see Maslach, 1982*b*).

Development of the Theory

The initial work on burnout did not begin with a clearly-defined phenomenon or a particular theoretical model. Indeed, the research did not even begin with a focus on burnout at all. Rather, it emerged out of a program of research on emotion—how people understand their feelings and how they cope with these when they become especially intense (Maslach, 1993). There was very little in the way of relevant theory for addressing these issues. However, two constructs in the medical literature seemed germane. One of these was 'detached concern' (Lief and Fox, 1963), which referred to the medical profession's ideal of blending compassion with emotional dis-tance. Although the practitioner is concerned about the patient's well-being, he or she recognizes that it is necessary to avoid over-involvement with the patient and to maintain a more detached objectivity. The second relevant concept was 'dehuman-ization in self-defense' (Zimbardo, 1970), which referred to the process of protecting oneself from overwhelming emotional feelings by responding to other people more as objects than as persons. For example, if a patient has a condition that is upsetting to see or otherwise difficult to work with, it may be easier for the practitioner to pro-vide the necessary care if he or she thinks of the patient as a particular 'case' or 'symp-tom' rather than as a human being who is suffering. Both of these concepts seemed to shed some theoretical light on the issue of how people cope with strong emotional arousal.

Given that the two guiding concepts had their origins in the medical professions, the initial, exploratory interviews were with physicians and nurses. Subsequent interviews were conducted with people working in the area of mental health, including psychiatrists, psychiatric nurses, and hospice counselors. As a result of various referrals and serendipitous events, the interviews were expanded to professions in the human services and education, including social workers, ministers, teachers, prison guards, probation officers, and poverty lawyers. It was the latter group that described the experience as 'burnout', as did staff members in alternative therapeutic institutions (Freudenberger, 1975).[1] What seemed to link all these occupations was the focus on providing aid and service to people in need—in other words, the core of the job was the relationship between provider and recipient.

Similar themes emerged from these interviews, although the specific content differed as a function of the type of occupation. This evidence of a parallel pattern suggested that burnout was not just some idiosyncratic response to stress, but was a syndrome with some identifiable regularities (Maslach, 1976). First, it was clear that the provision of service or care can be a very demanding and involving occupation, and that emotional exhaustion is not an uncommon response to such job overload. The second component of depersonalization also emerged from these interviews, as people described how they tried to cope with the emotional stresses of their work. Moderating one's compassion for clients by maintaining an emotional distance from them ('detached concern') was viewed as a way of protecting oneself from intense emotional arousal that could interfere with the ability to function effectively on the job. However, an imbalance of excessive detachment and little concern seemed to lead staff to respond to clients in negative, callous, and dehumanized ways. Thus, excessive detachment, or depersonalization, could impair performance and be detrimental to the quality of care.

In addition to the interviews, on-site field observations began to provide a better feel for the situational context of the provider–recipient relationship. It was possible to see first-hand some of the job factors that had been described in earlier interviews, such as the high number of clients (caseload), prevalence of negative client feedback, and scarcity of resources. It was also possible to observe other, unreported aspects of the interaction between provider and client, such as non-verbal 'distancing' behaviors. The focus on both sides of the helping relationship (as opposed to just the one perspective of the provider) led to the development of some ideas about the role of the client in the burnout process (Maslach, 1978).

The next phase of the research involved a series of questionnaire survey studies that were designed to be a more standardized assessment, with larger samples, of the ideas that had emerged from the interviews. The initial surveys, which were more exploratory in nature, were conducted with staff of mental health institutions (Pines and Maslach, 1978) and day-care centers (Maslach and Pines, 1977; Pines and Maslach, 1980). The surveys focused on providers' emotional states and reactions to their clients (the two burnout dimensions of emotional exhaustion and depersonalization) and investigated whether these dimensions were correlated with certain job factors.

[1] This was not the first mention of burnout in print, however. The most famous citation is Graham Greene's *A Burnt Out Case* (1960), in which a spiritually tormented and disillusioned architect quits his job and withdraws into the African jungle. There are earlier cases as well, both fictional and non-fictional, that did not use the term 'burnout' but are judged to be describing a similar phenomenon (Burisch, 1993; Maslach and Schaufeli, 1993).

The next set of survey studies was more systematic in its assessment of burnout because it was part of a psychometric research program to develop a standardized measurement tool. In addition to generating needed psychometric data, each study was designed to test some specific ideas about burnout. For example, a study of police officers and their spouses (Jackson and Maslach, 1982) obtained independent spouse ratings, which provided evidence of convergent validity for the measure; however, it also tested some hypotheses about the relationship between burnout and home life. Other studies combined useful psychometric data with investigations of how burnout is related to critical job factors, demographic variables, and coping strategies (Maslach and Jackson, 1982, 1984b, 1985).

At this point in the development of the theory, the key issues were to develop a more precise definition of burnout and to develop a standardized measure of it. The working definition of burnout, based on the interview data, consisted of two dimensions: emotional exhaustion and depersonalization. For the next few years, Susan Jackson and I conducted an extensive program of psychometric research, collecting systematic data from hundreds of people in a wide range of health, social service, and teaching occupations (Maslach and Jackson, 1981b). Our findings confirmed the dimensions of emotional exhaustion and depersonalization, but also revealed a third, separate dimension of feelings of reduced personal accomplishment. This empirically derived component was not inconsistent with the results of our earlier studies, but we had expected that such feelings would be one aspect of the other components and thus highly correlated with them. However, as a separate dimension, a feeling of reduced personal accomplishment is related conceptually to such phenomena as self-inefficacy (Bandura, 1977, 1982) and learned helplessness (Abramson et al., 1978).

This psychometric research led to the development of a measure called the Maslach Burnout Inventory (MBI), which assesses all three of the burnout dimensions (Maslach and Jackson, 1981a). The MBI is now considered to be the standard tool for research in this field. The three-dimensional structure has been found consistently across a wide range of occupational samples in many different countries (e.g. Enzmann et al., 1995; Leiter and Schaufeli, 1996). More psychometric research has been done on the MBI than on any other burnout measure, and its multidimensional conceptualization of burnout has made it particularly appropriate for theory-driven research.

There are now three versions of the MBI, designed for use with different occupations, which reflects the developing interest in this phenomenon (see Maslach et al., 1996 for information and relevant psychometric research on all three forms of the MBI). The original version of the MBI (now known as the MBI–Human Services Survey, or MBI–HSS) was designed for use with people working in the human services, as it was these occupations that had the greatest continuing concern about burnout. A second version of the MBI (the MBI–Educators Survey, or MBI–ES) was developed for use by people working in educational settings.

Given the increasing interest in burnout within occupations that are not so clearly people-oriented, a third, more generic version of the MBI (the MBI–General Survey, or the MBI–GS) has now been developed. Here, the three components of the burnout construct are conceptualized in slightly broader terms, with respect to the general job, and not just to the personal relationships that may be a part of that job. Thus, the three components are: Exhaustion, Cynicism (a distant attitude toward the job), and reduced Professional Efficacy.

New Theoretical Developments

At this stage of work on the phenomenon of burnout, there are two areas in which new theorizing, and subsequent empirical research, is taking place. The first of these areas is focusing on the contrasting, or opposite, state from burnout, namely *job engagement*. The second development involves a new framework for conceptualizing the key causal factors in burnout.

Engagement   Burnout is one end of a continuum in the relationship people establish with their jobs. As a syndrome of exhaustion, cynicism, and ineffectiveness, it stands in contrast to the energetic, involved, and effective state of engagement with work. Recently, the multidimensional theory of burnout has been expanded to this other end of the continuum (Leiter and Maslach, 1998). Engagement is defined in terms of the same three dimensions as burnout, but the positive end of those dimensions rather than the negative. Thus, engagement consists of a state of high *energy* (rather than exhaustion), strong *involvement* (rather than cynicism), and a sense of *efficacy* (rather than a reduced sense of accomplishment).

This state is distinct from established constructs in organizational psychology such as organizational commitment, job satisfaction, or job involvement. Organizational commitment focuses on an employee's allegiance to the organization that provides employment, while engagement focuses on the work itself. Job satisfaction is the extent to which the job is a source of need fulfillment and contentment, or a means of freeing employees from hassles or dissatisfiers; it does not encompass the person's relationship with the work itself. Job involvement is similar to the involvement aspect of engagement with work, but does not include the energy and effectiveness dimensions. Engagement with work provides a more complex and thorough perspective on an individual's relationship with work.

The extensive research on burnout has consistently found linear relationships of workplace conditions across the full range of the MBI subscales. Just as high levels of personal conflict are associated with high levels of emotional exhaustion, low levels of conflict are strong predictors of low exhaustion. Conversely, high personal accomplishment is associated with supportive personal relationships, the enhancement of sophisticated skills at work and active participation in shared decision making. These patterns indicate that the opposite of burnout is not a neutral state, but a definite state of mental health and social functioning within the occupational domain. While the burnout concept describes a syndrome of distress that may arise from enduring problems with work, engagement describes a positive state of fulfillment.

The concept of a burnout-to-engagement continuum enhances our understanding of how the organizational context of work can affect workers' well-being. It recognizes the variety of reactions that employees can have to the organizational environment, ranging from the intense involvement and satisfaction of engagement, through indifference to the exhausted, distant, and discouraged state of burnout.

One important implication of the burnout–engagement continuum is that strategies to promote engagement may be just as important for burnout prevention as strategies to reduce the risk of burnout. A work setting that is designed to support the positive development of the three core qualities of energy, involvement, and effectiveness should be successful in promoting the well-being and productivity of its employees.

Job–person Mismatches   Inherent to the fundamental concept of stress is the problematic relationship between the individual and the situation. In the case of job stress, the basic idea is that it is the result of a misfit between the person and the job. Some of the earliest models of organizational stress focused on this notion of job–person fit (French and Kahn, 1962; French *et al.*, 1982), and subsequent theorizing continues to highlight the importance of both individual and contextual factors (see Kahn and Byosiere, 1992). This basic approach would seem to be relevant for a theory of burnout, given that the research shows that burnout is largely a product of the organizational context, even if it is expressed on an individual level (Maslach and Leiter, 1997).

However, prior conceptualizations of job–person fit are limited in terms of their application to burnout. For example, the 'person' is usually framed in terms of personality or an accurate understanding of the job, rather than in terms of emotions or motivations or stress responses, and the 'job' is often defined in terms of specific tasks, and not the larger situation or organizational context. The notion of 'fit' is often presumed to predict such outcomes as choice of job/occupation or of organization (entry issues), or adjustment to the job (newcomer issues); in contrast, burnout involves a later point in the process, when the person has been working for a while and is experiencing a more chronic misfit between the self and the job. Thus, the theoretical challenge is to extend the job–person paradigm to a broader conceptualization of both person and job, and to combine that with models of job stress.

This challenge is beginning to be addressed by a new model of the causes of burnout (Maslach and Leiter, 1997). It proposes that the greater the gap, or mismatch, between the person and the job, the greater the likelihood of burnout. One new aspect of this approach is that the notion of mismatch (or misfit) is framed in terms of several constructs that are comparable between the worker and the workplace (e.g. values, job expectations) and thus allow a better evaluation of the individual within an organizational context. Secondly, whereas prior models of job–person fit predict that such fit produces certain outcomes (such as commitment, satisfaction, performance, and job tenure), this new model hypothesizes that burnout is an important mediator of this causal link. In other words, the mismatches lead to burnout, which in turn leads to various outcomes.

A third new aspect of this model is that it specifies not one, but six areas in which this mismatch can take place. In each area, the nature of the job is not in harmony with the nature of people, and the result is the increased exhaustion, cynicism, and inefficacy of burnout. On the other hand, when a better fit exists in these six areas, then engagement with work is the likely outcome. The six areas in which mismatches can occur are: workload, control, reward, community, fairness, and values

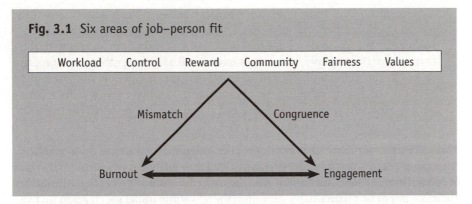

Fig. 3.1 Six areas of job–person fit

| Workload | Control | Reward | Community | Fairness | Values |

Mismatch — Congruence

Burnout ⟷ Engagement

(see Figure 3.1). Each area of mismatch has a distinct relationship with burnout and engagement, as reflected in the extant research literature.

A brief summary of these six mismatches follows (see Maslach and Leiter, 1997, for a more complete presentation):

- *Work overload* occurs when job demands exceed human limits. People have to do too much in too little time with too few resources. When overload is a chronic job condition, not an occasional emergency, there is little opportunity to rest, recover, and restore balance.

- *Lack of control* occurs when people have little control over the work they do, either because of rigid policies and tight monitoring, or because of chaotic job conditions. Such lack of control prevents people from being able to solve problems, make choices, and have some input into the achievement of the outcomes for which they will be held accountable.

- *Insufficient reward* involves a lack of appropriate rewards for the work people do. This lack of recognition devalues both the work and the workers. Prominent among these rewards are external ones such as salary and benefits, but the loss of internal rewards (such as pride in doing something of importance and doing it well) can also be a critical part of this mismatch.

- *Breakdown of community* occurs when people lose a sense of positive connection with others in the workplace. Some jobs isolate people from each other, or make social contact impersonal. However, what is most destructive of community is chronic and unresolved conflict with others on the job. Such conflict produces constant negative feelings of frustration and hostility, and reduces the likelihood of social support.

- *Absence of fairness* occurs when there is a lack of a system of justice and fair procedures which maintain mutual respect in the workplace. Unfairness can occur when there is inequity of workload or pay, or when there is cheating, or when evaluations and promotions are handled inappropriately. If procedures for grievance or dispute resolution do not allow for both parties to have voice, then those will be judged as unfair.

- *Value conflict* occurs when there is a mismatch between the requirements of the job and people's personal principles. In some cases, people might feel constrained by the job to do things that are unethical and not in accord with their own values. For example, they might have to tell a lie or be otherwise deceptive or not forthcoming with the truth. In other instances, people may be caught between conflicting values of the organization, as when there is a discrepancy between the lofty mission statement and actual practice, or when the organization undergoes major changes.

These six types of mismatches are not totally independent, but can be interrelated. For example, a mismatch in excessive workload may be linked to a mismatch in lack of control over the job. Currently, it is unclear whether some job–person mismatches are more important than others, although there is some initial speculation that values may be an important mediator of the relationship of the other five mismatches to burnout (Leiter and Maslach, in press). It is also an open question whether there is some minimum number of mismatches, or size of mismatch that will be more likely to produce burnout, and future research will need to address these and related issues.

The mismatches in these six critical areas of organizational life are not simply a list summarizing research findings from burnout studies. Rather, they provide a conceptual framework for the crises that disrupt the relationships people develop with their work. This approach emphasizes the social quality of burnout—it has more to do with the organizational context of the job than simply with the unique characteristics of an individual.

Research Linked to this General Theory

The empirical research on contributing factors has found that situational variables are more strongly predictive of burnout than are personal ones. In terms of antecedents of burnout, both job demands and a lack of key resources are particularly important. Work overload and personal conflict are the major demands, while the lack of such resources as control coping, social support, skill use, autonomy, and decision involvement seem to be especially critical. The consequences of burnout are seen most consistently in various forms of job withdrawal (decreased commitment, job dissatisfaction, turnover, and absenteeism), with the implication of a deterioration in the quality of care or service provided to clients or patients. Burnout is also linked to personal dysfunction, primarily in terms of impaired physical and mental health, although there is some evidence for increased substance abuse as well as marital and family conflicts. Figure 3.2 presents a diagrammatic summary of these major research findings, which have been discussed in a number of recent reviews (see Cordes and Dougherty, 1993; Lee and Ashforth, 1996; Leiter and Maslach, 1998; Maslach *et al.*, 1996; and Schaufeli *et al.*, 1993). Rather than repeat these reviews, this section will focus on a number of important themes within the research literature.

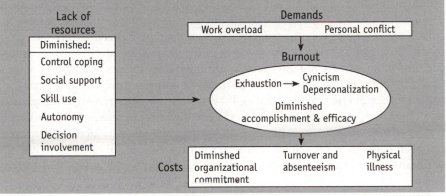

Fig. 3.2 Model of burnout. Modified and reproduced by special permission of the Publisher, Consulting Psychologists Press, Inc., Palo Alto, CA 94303 from Maslach Burnout Inventory by Chistina Maslach. Copyright 1996 by Consulting Psychologists Press, Inc. All rights reserved. Further reproduction is prohibited without the Publisher's written consent

Interrelationship of the Three Dimensions

The relative importance of the three dimensions of burnout, and their interrelationships, have been the subject of much theorizing and research. For example, in the early years of research using the newly-developed MBI, a common question had to do with whether MBI scores on the three dimensions could be combined to form a single overall index of burnout. This question was largely an attempt to simplify both the theory and the measure by reframing them in unidimensional terms. A related, but different question has focused on whether some dimensions are more important than others. Again, the thrust of this approach has been to argue for a unidimensional model, but this time in terms of the primacy of the exhaustion dimension, rather than an additive combination of the three. Such questions are no longer predominant in the field, as the superiority of the multidimensional theory has been well established. One of the main reasons for this is that the prior problems of analyzing a three-dimensional theory of burnout have been alleviated by the availability of statistical packages for structural analyses, such as LISREL (e.g. Joreskog and Sorbom, 1989). These analyses simultaneously consider distinct predictors for each of the three burnout dimensions in the context of the interrelationships among them.

Of the three aspects of burnout, exhaustion is the most widely reported and the most thoroughly analyzed. Exhaustion is the central quality of burnout and the most obvious manifestation of this complex syndrome. When people describe themselves or others as experiencing burnout, they are most often referring to the experience of exhaustion. In fact, nurses who responded to an advertisement about burnout scored much higher than the average on exhaustion but only moderately higher on the other two aspects of the syndrome (Pick and Leiter, 1991). The notion of exhaustion presupposes a prior state of high arousal or overload, rather than one of low arousal or underload. Thus, this definitional component of emotional exhaustion stands in contrast to some other conceptualizations, which have viewed burnout as a response to tedious, boring, and monotonous work.

The strong identification of exhaustion with burnout has led some to argue that the other two aspects of the syndrome are incidental or unnecessary (Shirom, 1989). However, the fact that exhaustion is a necessary criterion for burnout does not mean it is a *sufficient* one. Of the three burnout dimensions, emotional exhaustion is the closest to an orthodox stress variable. The factors hypothesized to relate to emotional exhaustion are very similar to those in the general literature on stress, and so the similar findings are not unexpected. Although this similarity validates the location of the burnout phenomenon within the stress domain, it can also be the cause for some skepticism (Jackson *et al.*, 1986). If burnout is simply a synonym for 'exhaustion', then nothing new has been learned from the burnout research—it has simply replicated what was previously known under the guise of a new label (a charge that has been made by some critics). Thus, to limit the concept of burnout to just the dimension of emotional exhaustion is to define it simply as exhaustion and nothing more.

Although exhaustion reflects the individual stress dimension of burnout, it fails to capture a critical aspect of the relationship people have with their work. Chronic exhaustion can lead people to distance themselves emotionally and cognitively from their work, so that they are less involved with, or responsive to, the needs of other people or the demands of the task. In various people-oriented professions, this distancing takes the form of depersonalizing others, while outside of the human services, it is reflected in a cynical attitude towards the job. Distancing is such an immediate reaction to exhaustion that a strong relationship from exhaustion to depersonalization or cynicism is found consistently in burnout research, across a wide range of organizational and occupational settings (Maslach *et al.*, 1996). This sequential relationship is indicated by the arrow from Exhaustion to Cynicism/Depersonalization in Figure 3.2. The relationship of reduced personal accomplishment to the other two aspects of burnout is somewhat more complex. In some instances, reduced personal accomplishment appears to be a function, to some degree, of either exhaustion, cynicism, or a combination of the two (Byrne, 1994; Lee and Ashforth, 1996). A work situation with chronic, overwhelming demands that contribute to exhaustion or cynicism is likely to erode one's sense of accomplishment or effectiveness. Further, the experience of exhaustion or depersonalization interferes with effectiveness: it is difficult to gain a sense of accomplishment when feeling exhausted or when helping people toward whom one is hostile. However, in other settings, reduced accomplishment appears to develop in parallel with the other two burnout aspects, rather than sequentially (Leiter, 1993). Here the lack of efficacy seems to arise more clearly from a lack of relevant resources, while exhaustion and cynicism emerge from the presence of work overload and social conflict.

This current model of the dimensional interrelationships succeeds prior theorizing about the developmental sequence of the burnout dimensions. One earlier proposal had been that the different dimensions developed simultaneously but independently, and thus could result in eight different patterns, or phases, of burnout

(Golembiewski *et al.*, 1986). Another proposal had argued for a sequential progression over time, in which the occurrence of one dimension precipitates the development of another. The phase model (Golembiewski and Munzenrider, 1988) hypothesized that depersonalization is the first phase of burnout, followed by reduced personal accomplishment, and finally by emotional exhaustion. An alternative model had been suggested by Leiter and Maslach (1988), in which emotional exhaustion occurs first, leading to the development of depersonalization, which leads subsequently to reduced personal accomplishment. The data currently support an amended version of the latter model, rather than the former. However, it should be noted that these data come from studies utilizing statistical causal models, and not from longitudinal studies that directly track the developmental progress of burnout.

Burnout and Related Concepts

Some of the early discussion about burnout focused on issues of discriminant validity—that is, was burnout truly a distinctly different phenomenon from other established constructs? A variety of such constructs were considered, but the primary focus was on two: depression and job satisfaction. Speculation on these issues was often more frequent than empirical data.

Research conducted during the development of the MBI found burnout to be distinct from, but related to, anxiety and depression (Maslach and Jackson, 1981*a*, 1986). A subsequent analysis (Leiter and Durup, 1994) demonstrated the distinction between burnout and depression in a confirmatory factor analysis of the MBI and the Beck Depression Inventory. This analysis established that burnout is a problem that is specific to the work context, in contrast to depression that tends to pervade every domain of a person's life. These findings lent empirical support to earlier claims that burnout is job-related and situation-specific, as opposed to depression which is general and context-free (Freudenberger, 1983; Warr, 1987).

Further support for this distinction comes from an analysis of various conceptualizations of burnout, which notes five common elements of the burnout phenomenon (Maslach and Schaufeli, 1993). First, there is a predominance of dysphoric symptoms such as mental or emotional exhaustion, fatigue, and depression. Second, the emphasis is on mental and behavioral symptoms more than physical ones. Third, burnout symptoms are work-related. Fourth, the symptoms manifest themselves in 'normal' persons who did not suffer from psychopathology before. Fifth, decreased effectiveness and work performance occur because of negative attitudes and behaviors.

In the case of job satisfaction and burnout, the issue concerns the interpretation of the commonly found negative correlation between these two constructs. Although the correlation is not large enough to conclude that the constructs are actually identical, the overall pattern of the research findings has led some researchers to conclude that burnout and job dissatisfaction are clearly linked (Zedeck *et al.*, 1988). However, the specific nature of that link is still a matter of speculation. Does burnout cause people to be dissatisfied with their job? Or does a drop in satisfaction serve as the precursor to burnout? Alternatively, both burnout and job dissatisfaction may be caused by another factor, such as poor working conditions.

Correlates and Causes

The issue of correlation and causality is as familiar for burnout as it is for other research literatures. Just because one interpretation is plausible does not mean that it is the correct one. This point is illustrated not only by the previous example on job satisfaction, but by the research on burnout and coping styles. These studies often find a correlation between the different components of burnout and specific coping techniques, such as problem-focused versus emotion-focused coping. But which comes first, coping or burnout? Is it that the experience of burnout or engagement causes one to cope differently with stressors? Or does the use of different coping styles lead one to be more or less burned out? Or is there some critical third variable that mediates this relationship? The implications of these alternative answers are important both theoretically and practically.

Related to the prior discussion about the relationship of burnout to depression has been the issue of the relation of mental dysfunction to burnout. It is often presumed that burnout precipitates negative effects in terms of mental health, such as anxiety, depression, drops in self-esteem, etc. But another possibility is that people who are mentally healthy are better able to cope with chronic stressors and thus less likely to experience burnout. Although not assessing burnout directly, one study addressed this question by analyzing archival longitudinal data of people who worked in interpersonally demanding jobs (Jenkins and Maslach, 1994). The results showed that people who were psychologically healthier in adolescence and early adulthood were more likely to enter, and remain in, such jobs, and they showed greater involvement and satisfaction with their work. Given this longitudinal data set, this study was better able to establish possible causal relationships than is true for the typical correlational studies.

Individual Factors in Burnout

Although there has been a long-standing interest in identifying some key individual predictors of burnout, so far no major ones have emerged. There are no critical personality variables that are predictive of burnout. Although there was considerable speculation about gender differences in burnout, the empirical data do not support that conclusion (Maslach and Jackson, 1985). Part of the reason for the discrepancy between the perception and the reality is that the variable of sex is often confounded with occupation and/or status. For example, if there were differences between female nurses and male doctors, would they be due to sex or to occupational position? When occupational differences are controlled for, any sex difference tends to diminish or disappear. Other demographic variables also do not show any strong relationship to burnout. In some instances the lack of effect may reflect the paucity of research on these issues. For example, there is not yet a good database on racial or ethnic differences in burnout, even though other studies suggest that cultural or cross-national differences may be important (see Maslach *et al.*, 1996).

However, another possible reason for the absence of definite associations between burnout and personal characteristics is a lack of relevant theory. Too often, there has been no a good conceptual model for hypothesizing which individual variables should be most predictive of burnout, and why. A notable exception is the approach taken by Buunk and Schaufeli (1993), because their integration of the multidimensional theory within a social comparison theory framework enables them to specify individual differences that are truly meaningful in terms of each of the burnout dimensions.

Another individual difference issue has centered around the potential clinical (as opposed to research) use of the MBI for diagnostic purposes. That is, is there a particular level or pattern of MBI scores that can serve as a meaningful cut-off score for problematic levels of burnout or for other dysfunctional patterns of response? Unfortunately, the necessary research to address this issue has not been done. The development of such a diagnostic tool is an important research goal for the near future.

Implications of the Theory for the Diagnosis and Management of Stress

The multidimensional theory provides a better understanding of burnout (and engagement) than does any kind of unidimensional 'stress' approach, because it more clearly recognizes the complexity of the phenomenon and its location within a situational context. Various levels of experience are not simply a function of individual variables but reflect the differential impact of organizational factors on the three dimensions. For example, certain job characteristics influence the sources of emotional stress—and thus emotional exhaustion or energy. Other job characteristics affect the resources available to handle the job successfully—and thus levels of personal accomplishment and efficacy. This implies that interventions should be planned and designed explicitly in terms of the three dimensions of burnout. That is, how will a particular strategy reduce the likelihood of emotional exhaustion, or prevent the tendency to depersonalize, or enhance one's sense of accomplishment? Framing an intervention in terms of these three dimensions will ensure that the proposed strategy is indeed addressing the phenomenon of burnout and establishing relevant criteria for determining its effectiveness. In other words, the theory provides a means for analyzing the more precise links between the job situation and personal experience. The advantage of such a framework is that it requires a clearer articulation of the sources of the problem and of the proposed solutions, and this may help in designing more effective intervention strategies.

The implication of the burnout–engagement continuum is that strategies to promote engagement may be just as important for burnout prevention as strategies to reduce the risk of burnout. A work setting that is designed to support the positive development of the three core qualities of energy, involvement, and effectiveness should be successful in promoting the well-being and productivity of its employees. A focus on what would constitute a more engaging workplace could be a better way of developing strategies to change the job situation, as opposed to a focus on reducing stress, which tends to lead to strategies of changing the person.

This general issue of the locus of intervention—the person or the situation—is a particularly important one in the literature on burnout prevention (Maslach and Goldberg, 1998). The emphasis is primarily on individual strategies to prevent burnout, rather than social or organizational ones. This is particularly paradoxical given that the vast bulk of the research has found that situational and organizational factors play a far bigger role in burnout than individual ones. Moreover, other research has found that individual strategies are relatively ineffective—and particularly in the workplace, where the person has much less control over stressors than in other domains of his or her life (Heaney and Van Ryn, 1990). There are both philosophical and pragmatic reasons underlying the predominant focus on the individual, including notions of individual causality and responsibility, and the assumption that it is easier and cheaper to change people instead of organizations. But the implication of the research is that this focus may be seriously in error—and that any progress in dealing with burnout will depend on the development of strategies that focus on the job context and its impact on the people who work within it.

All of this suggests that the six mismatch model may be a particularly useful framework for developing interventions, because it focuses attention on the *relationship* between the person and the situation, rather than either one or the other in isolation. It thus provides an alternative way of identifying the sources of burnout in any particular job context, and of designing interventions that will actually incorporate situational changes along with personal ones. Furthermore, the recognition of six areas of job–person mismatch expands the range of options for intervention. Rather than concentrating on the area of work overload for interventions (such as teaching people how to cope with overload, or how to cut back on work, or how to relax), a focus on some of the other mismatches may be more effective. For example, people may be able to tolerate greater workload if they value the work and feel they are doing something important, or if they feel well-rewarded for their efforts, and so interventions could target these areas of value and reward. The potential of this approach is very promising as a means of dealing with individual burnout in its situational context.

Conclusion

Significant progress in understanding burnout has been based on the development of new, rather than traditional, theoretical perspectives. What is unique about the burnout syndrome, and what distinguishes it from other types of job stress, is what has been, and needs to be, emphasized in theoretical formulations. Future progress will rest on the further elaboration of all three dimensions of burnout (rather than just the one of exhaustion) and on their relationship to the six areas of mismatch between worker and workplace. This theoretical elaboration should generate better hypotheses about the causes and consequences linked to each of these dimensions, and should guide a more informed search for solutions to this important social problem.

References

Abramson, L. Y., Seligman, M. E. P., and Teasdale, J. D. (1978) 'Learned helplessness in humans: Critique and reformulation', *Journal of Abnormal Psychology*, 87, 49–74.

Bandura, A. (1977) 'Self-efficacy', *Psychological Review*, 84, 191–215.

Bandura, A. (1982) 'Self-efficacy mechanism in human agency', *American Psychologist*, 37, 122–147.

Burisch, M. (1993) In search of theory: Some ruminations on the nature and etiology of burnout. In W. B. Schaufeli, C. Maslach, and T. Marek (eds.), *Professional Burnout: Recent Developments in Theory and Research* (pp. 75–93). Washington, DC: Taylor & Francis.

Buunk, B. P. and Schaufeli, W. B. (1993) Burnout: A perspective from social comparison theory. In W. B. Schaufeli, C. Maslach, and T. Marek (eds.), *Professional Burnout: Recent Developments in Theory and Research* (pp. 53–73). Washington, DC: Taylor & Francis.

Byrne, B. M. (1994) 'Burnout: Testing for the validity, replication, and invariance of causal structure across elementary, intermediate, and secondary teachers', *American Educational Research Journal*, 31, 645–673.

Cherniss, C. (1980) *Professional Burnout in Human Service Organizations*. New York: Praeger.

Cordes, C. L. and Dougherty, T. W. (1993) 'A review and an integration of research on job burnout', *Academy of Management Review*, 18, 621–656.

Enzmann, D., Schaufeli, W. B., and Girault, N. (1995) The validity of the Maslach Burnout Inventory in three national samples. In L. Bennett, D. Miller, and M. Ross (eds.), *Health Workers and AIDS: Research, Interventions and Current Issues in Burnout and Response* (pp. 131–150). London: Harwood.

French, J. R. P., Jr. and Kahn, R. L. (1962) 'A programmatic approach to studying the industrial environment and mental health', *Journal of Social Issues*, 18 (3), 1–47.

French, J. R. P., Jr., Caplan, R. D., and Harrison, R. V. (1982) *The Mechanisms of Job Stress and Strain*. Chichester, England: Wiley.

Freudenberger, H. J. (1975) 'The staff burnout syndrome in alternative institutions', *Psychotherapy: Theory, Research, & Practice*, 12, 72–83.

Freudenberger, H. J. (1983) Burnout: Contemporary issues, trends, and concerns. In B. A. Farber (ed.), *Stress and Burnout in the Human Service Professions* (pp. 23–28). New York: Pergamon Press.

Freudenberger, H. J. and Richelson, G. (1980) *Burnout: The High Cost of High Achievement*. Garden City, NY: Doubleday.

Golembiewski, R. T. and Munzenrider, R. F. (1988) *Phases of Burnout: Developments in Concepts and Applications*. New York: Praeger.

Golembiewski, R. T., Munzenrider, R. F., and Stevenson, J. G. (1986) *Stress in Organizations: Toward a Phase Model of Burnout*. New York: Praeger.

Greene, G. (1960) *A Burnt Out Case*. London: Heinemann.

Heaney, C. A. and Van Ryn, M. (1990) 'Broadening the scope of worksite stress programs: A guiding framework', *American Journal of Health Promotion*, 4, 413–420.

Jackson, S. E. and Maslach, C. (1982) 'After-effects of job-related stress: Families as victims', *Journal of Occupational Behaviour*, 3, 63–77.

Jackson, S. E., Schwab, R. L., and Schuler, R. S. (1986) 'Toward an understanding of the burnout phenomenon', *Journal of Applied Psychology*, 71, 630–640.

Jenkins, S. R. and Maslach, C. (1994) 'Psychological health and involvement in interpersonally demanding occupations: A longitudinal perspective', *Journal of Organizational Behavior*, 15, 101–127.

Joreskog, K. G. and Sorbom, D. (1989) *LISREL 7 User's Reference Guide*. Mooresville, IN: Scientific Software.

Kahn, R. L. and Byosiere, P. (1992) Stress in Organizations. In M. D. Dunnette and L. M. Hough (eds.), *Handbook of Industrial and Organizational Psychology*, Vol. 3 (pp. 571–650). Palo Alto, CA: Consulting Psychologists Press.

Lee, R. T. and Ashforth, B. E. (1996) 'A meta-analytic examination of the correlates of the three dimensions of job burnout', *Journal of Applied Psychology*, 81, 123–133.

Leiter, M. P. (1993) Burnout as a developmental process: Consideration of models. In W. B. Schaufeli, C. Maslach, and T. Marek (eds.), *Professional Burnout: Recent Developments in Theory and Research* (pp. 237–250). Washington, DC: Taylor & Francis.

Leiter, M. P. and Durup, J. (1994) 'The discriminant validity of burnout and depression: A confirmatory factor analytic study', *Anxiety, Stress, & Coping*, 7, 357–373.

Leiter, M. P. and Maslach, C. (1988) 'The impact of interpersonal environment on burnout and organizational commitment', *Journal of Organizational Behavior*, 9, 297–308.

Leiter, M. P. and Maslach, C. (1998) Burnout. In H. Friedman (ed.), *Encyclopedia of Mental Health*. San Diego, CA: Academic Press.

Leiter, M. P. and Maslach, C. (in press) Burnout and health. In A. Baum, T. Revenson, and J. Singer (eds.), *Handbook of Health Psychology*. Hillsdale, NJ: Lawrence Erlbaum.

Leiter, M. P. and Schaufeli, W. B. (1996) 'Consistency of the burnout construct across occupations', *Anxiety, Stress, and Coping*, 9, 229–243.

Lief, H. I. and Fox, R. C. (1963) Training for 'detached concern' in medical students. In H. I. Lief, V. F. Lief, and N. R. Lief (eds.), *The Psychological Basis of Medical Practice* (pp. 12–35). New York: Harper & Row.

Maslach, C. (1976) 'Burned-out', *Human Behavior*, 5, 16–22.

Maslach, C. (1978) 'The client role in staff burnout', *Journal of Social Issues*, 34 (4), 111–124.

Maslach, C. (1982a) *Burnout: The Cost of Caring*. Englewood Cliffs, NJ: Prentice-Hall.

Maslach, C. (1982b) Understanding burnout: Definitional issues in analyzing a complex phenomenon. In W. S. Paine (ed.), *Job Stress and Burnout* (pp. 29–40). Beverly Hills, CA: Sage.

Maslach, C. (1993) Burnout: A multidimensional perspective. In W. B. Schaufeli, C. Maslach, and T. Marek (eds.). *Professional Burnout: Recent Developments in Theory and Research* (pp. 19–32). Washington, DC: Taylor & Francis.

Maslach, C. and Goldberg, J. (1998) 'Prevention of burnout: New perspectives', *Applied and Preventive Psychology*, 7, 63–74.

Maslach, C. and Jackson, S. E. (1998) *The Maslach Burnout Inventory*. Research edition. Palo Alto, CA: Consulting Psychologists Press.

Maslach, C. and Jackson, S. E. (1981b) 'The measurement of experienced burnout', *Journal of Occupational Behavior*, 2, 99–113.

Maslach, C. and Jackson, S. E. (1982) Burnout in health professions: A social psychological analysis. In G. Sanders and J. Suls (eds.), *Social Psychology of Health and Illness* (pp. 227–251). Hillsdale, NJ: Erlbaum.

Maslach, C. and Jackson, S. E. (1984a) 'Burnout in organizational settings', *Applied Social Psychology Annual*, 5, 133–153.

Maslach, C. and Jackson, S. E. (1984*b*) 'Patterns of burnout among a national sample of public contact workers', *Journal of Health and Human Resources Administration*, 7 (2), 189–212.

Maslach, C. and Jackson, S. E. (1985) 'The role of sex and family variables in burnout', *Sex Roles*, 12, 837–851.

Maslach, C. and Jackson, S. E. (1986) *The Maslach Burnout Inventory*. 2nd edn. Palo Alto, CA: Consulting Psychologists Press.

Maslach, C. and Leiter, M. P. (1997) *The Truth about Burnout*. San Francisco, CA: Jossey-Bass.

Maslach, C. and Pines, A. (1977) 'The burnout syndrome in the day care setting', *Child Care Quarterly*, 6, 100–113.

Maslach, C. and Schaufeli, W. B. (1993) Historical and conceptual development of burnout. In W. B. Schaufeli, C. Maslach, and T. Marek (eds.), *Professional Burnout: Recent Developments in Theory and Research* (pp. 1–16). Washington, DC: Taylor & Francis.

Maslach, C., Jackson, S. E., and Leiter, M. P. (1996) *The Maslach Burnout Inventory*. 3rd edn. Palo Alto, CA: Consulting Psychologists Press.

Pick, D. and Leiter, M. P. (1991) 'Nurses' perceptions of the nature and causes of burnout: A comparison of self-reports and standardized measures', *The Canadian Journal of Nursing Research*, 23 (3), 33–48.

Pines, A., Aronson, E., and Kafry, D. (1981) *Burnout: From Tedium to Personal Growth*. New York: Free Press.

Pines, A. and Maslach, C. (1978) 'Characteristics of staff burnout in mental health settings', *Hospital and Community Psychiatry*, 29, 233–237.

Pines, A. and Maslach, C. (1980) 'Combatting staff burnout in a day care center: A case study', *Child Care Quarterly*, 9, 5–16.

Sauter, S. L. and Murphy, L. R. (eds.). (1995) *Organizational Risk Factors for Job Stress*. Washington, DC: American Psychological Association.

Schaufeli, W. B., Maslach, C., and Marek, T. (eds.) (1993) *Professional Burnout: Recent Developments in Theory and Research*. Washington, DC: Taylor & Francis.

Shirom, A. (1989) Burnout in work organizations. In C. L. Cooper and I. Robertson (eds.), *International Review of Industrial and Organizational Psychology* (pp. 25–48). New York: Wiley.

Warr, P. B. (1987) *Work, Unemployment and Mental Health*. Oxford: Clarendon Press.

Zedeck, S., Maslach, C., Mosier, K., and Skitka, L. (1988) 'Affective response to work and quality of family life: Employee and spouse perspectives', *Journal of Social Behavior & Personality*, 3, 135–157.

Zimbardo, P. G. (1970) The human choice: Individuation, reason, and order versus deindividuation, impulse, and chaos. In W. J. Arnold and D. Levine (eds.), *Nebraska Symposium on Motivation, 1969* (pp. 237–307). Lincoln: University of Nebraska Press.

4

Stress and the Sojourner

Ellen I. Shupe and Joseph E. McGrath

Introduction

This chapter presents a general theory of stress and coping, and a model of how that theory applies in the lives of sojourners—individuals living temporarily in a culture foreign to them. Sojourner stress is an important case because many aspects of the stress and coping cycle are intensified, or rendered more problematic, when the person experiencing the stress is from a different culture than the one in which the stressful situations are occurring. Stress among sojourners, therefore, is not only important in itself, especially given the increasing global interdependence; it is also an important topic of study in that it can give us new insights into the more general case of stress and the coping process.

We begin the chapter with a brief overview of our general theoretical conception of stress, then present a model of stress as it impinges upon the lives of sojourners. We summarize briefly some of the results of a study of sojourners which was conducted to help develop, test, and extend that model. Then, we present an analysis of stress as a dynamic, adaptive process.

A Theoretical Framework for the Study of Stress and Coping

An Individual 'Stress Event' as a Complex Cycle

We want to construe any given 'stress event' as a cycle consisting of:

- *a situation*: an event(s) or condition that occurs or is anticipated in the environment of some focal system (a focal system is an individual, group, organization, or other human system to which a stress researcher chooses to attend);
- *the perceived situation*: the focal system's interpretation of those events;
- *the response selection*: the system's choice of coping responses to those events;
- *the coping behavior*: those responses, the execution of which have consequences both for the focal system and for the external context within which all of this is taking place.

That cycle begins with some (actual or perceived) event or condition in the environment of a focal system. Elsewhere, we have called these *stress potential events* and *conditions*, or SPECs (McGrath and Beehr, 1990). Note that a SPEC is a *potential* stressor, depending on how it is interpreted or appraised by the focal system.

The four parts of the cycle are connected by four processes: the *appraisal process*, the *choice process*, the *performance process*, and the *outcome process*. The occurrence (or anticipated occurrence) of the SPEC is accompanied by an appraisal process by which the focal system interprets the 'meaning' of the event for the system—that is, the threat, demand, and/or opportunity, implied by its consequences—and the likelihood that the system can deal with the event effectively. Consequences of the SPEC may be either its potential harm if its threat is not guarded against, its potential for benefits if the opportunity is seized, or both harm and benefit. The probability of the system dealing effectively with the SPEC depends both on the difficulty of carrying out the necessary responses and on the system's available capabilities and resources at the time when it will need to make those required responses. The result of the appraisal process is the system's perceived situation, which includes the level of 'experienced stress' with regard to that event. In our view, level of experienced stress can be represented as a function of: (1) the (perceived) importance of the consequences of the SPEC, (2) the uncertainty surrounding the stressful situation, and (3) certain temporal features of the SPEC and its consequences.

Assuming that the appraisal process results in some denotable level of perceived stress, it is followed by a choice process in which the focal system selects one or more responses from its repertoire of potential responses, to deal with the SPEC and its consequences. These potential responses could include, for example, efforts to alleviate the SPEC itself, efforts to prevent the occurrence of a similar SPEC in the future, or attempts to modify the appraisal of the SPEC. The response choice depends on the nature of the SPEC and the focal system's interpretation of it, as well as on the array of potential responses that the focal system is aware of and has available for use. The latter, in turn, will depend not only on the past experiences of that focal system (hence the development of a repertoire of coping responses and strategies), but also upon the current status of the system (hence the degree to which it has available uncommitted resources to deal with the SPEC).

The choice of one or more coping responses is, presumably, followed by the execution of those responses, or the performance process. That execution may vary in quality and vigor, depending on the skills of the focal system, and its motivation with regard to those responses.

Note that observation of the focal system's coping responses poses some serious problems for the researcher. For one thing, some of the potential coping responses may be covert, hence only accessible to observation by the focal system itself. Moreover, one ever-potential coping response is 'do nothing'—and sometimes that is not only a deliberate, but also an effective, response. Furthermore, it is difficult (for anyone but the focal system) to distinguish which behaviors are being done in reaction to the perceived stressor, and which are simply behaviors that the focal system is doing in the 'normal' course of its ongoing life. Indeed, even if there is no perceived stress, the focal system will likely be carrying out some response (including the ubiquitous 'do nothing') at any given time (Beehr and McGrath, 1996). So the speci-fication by an 'outsider' (e.g. a researcher) that certain behaviors are coping responses is always, to some degree, arbitrary and/or subjective.

Whatever responses the focal system carries out will have consequences—both for the focal system itself and for portions of the system's embedding context. We refer to that as the outcome process. The focal system's responses may or may not serve to reduce or eliminate the negative consequences of the actual SPEC or change the appraisal of the threat posed by the SPEC. Thus, the cycle of appraisal, choice, per-formance, and outcome may or may not be a closed loop, because the responses may or may not alter the consequences of the SPEC. In fact, coping does not always work as a negative feedback loop, to reduce the level of stress. If ineffective, it can work as a 'positive feedback loop', amplifying the stressor or worsening the appraisal of it, thereby increasing the level of experienced stress.

All four stages of the stress cycle, and all four of the linking processes, involve sets of complex issues that depend on both the focal system involved, and the embedding context(s), as well as on the nature of the SPEC events themselves (see Figure 4.1). Later in this chapter, we will try to unpack some of those issues in relation to the experiences of sojourners. For now, though, we will try to connect this discussion of the dynamics of a single stress cycle to consideration of the overall level of stress expe-rienced by a given focal system at a given point in time.

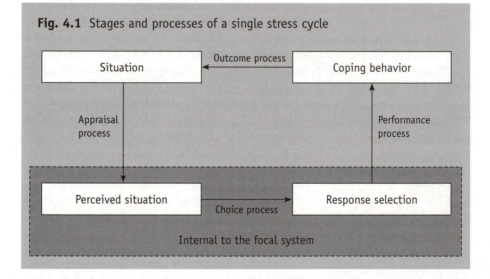

Fig. 4.1 Stages and processes of a single stress cycle

Overall Level of Stress

When we speak of a person or other focal system as experiencing 'a lot of stress', we ordinarily are not thinking about a single stress event (unless it is an event with vast and important consequences, such as the death of a loved one). More often, we are thinking about the cumulative level of stress that a given focal system has attained over some period of time. Stress in this sense is not simply the result of a single stress cycle. Rather, stress in this overall sense is the accumulation of residual stress from past stressors that were not completely eliminated, in combination with stress resulting from new events. To put the matter in this form invites us to consider both the negative 'residuals' and the positive effects—e.g. increased stress resistance or increased hardiness—that may accrue from past stress-and-coping experiences. So we can think about a focal system's overall level of stress, at any given time, as the algebraic total of all residual stress and acquired stress-resistance present for that focal system at that time.

That kind of definition has several problematic features embedded within it. For example, one consequence of unsuccessful coping efforts may be so-called burnout (e.g. Cherniss, 1980; Matteson, 1987; Vininga and Spradley, 1981). One part of burnout, however, is a decreased sensitivity to ambient conditions, hence a higher threshold for appraisal of stress, and this will lead to a lower level of residual stress as per the above definition. So 'burnout leads to reduced stress'—a logical implication that is not ordinarily a part of our conception of burnout. As a contrasting example: it is also probably the case that as a focal system gains experience in dealing with a given class of problems it will become more skilled at handling them. Thereafter, it will take more difficult problems of that class to reach the threshold at which they are appraised as 'stressful'. Therefore, that system will likely encounter fewer SPECs appraised as stressing if it remains in the same 'event context'. At the same time, the very success of such a system may lead to its undertaking, or being assigned, more difficult problems (with more negative consequences for failure). If that were the case, the system's coping success earlier might lead to increased levels of perceived stress for the range of tasks it actually tackles in the future—again, a logical implication that does not jibe with our ordinary conception of stress.

These problems arise largely because the definition given above is couched in terms implying that the actual level of stress is equal to the level of stress that that system *consciously experiences*. Conceptual perspectives that invoke repression, or other bases for non-awareness of one's level of stress, might argue that the focal system undergoing burnout in the illustration above would have very high levels of stress, which resulted in the decreased sensitivity and the consequent raising of the 'stress experience' threshold. However one stands on this specific issue, the discussion makes it clear that *all definitions of stress, and statements of consequences of coping, are intimately entwined with the conceptual perspective being applied*.

A Dynamic Systems View

How can we knit together a micro-level examination of 'the stress cycle' and a macro-level consideration of 'overall stress'? One way is to recognize that the focal systems whose stress we are studying are *complex, adaptive*, and *dynamic* systems (Baron *et al.*, 1994; Latane and Nowak, 1994; McGrath *et al.*, in press; Vallacher and Nowak, 1994). The focal systems, and consequently their accompanying processes, are complex in that their causal processes function in bi-directional, non-linear, and non-additive ways. Focal systems are adaptive in that they actively interact with their embedding contexts and their environments, adapting to one another. They are dynamic in that they develop and change over time, and their state at any given moment is a function of both their past and expected future states, as well as of their present states.

First, let's reconsider the dynamic nature of the stress cycle involved even in a single stressing event. Coping activity is seldom an all or nothing matter that either 'solves' the problem posed by the SPEC or fails to solve it. Nor is the coping response typically singular. Rather than a given appraisal leading to the selection of a single coping response, followed by performance of that response, followed by a definitive change in consequences (i.e. the idealized 'stress event cycle'), SPECs more often lead to the choice of a *response strategy*. So the coping response is itself an ongoing 'act–monitor–react' cycle: 'I will do A, and see how that works; depending on what happens I will then do B or C, and then do E, F, or G.' Moreover, not all actions going on at any given time are coping in relation to any given stressor. Many of them are attempts to take care of business as usual, in the midst of simultaneous attempts to deal with some not-so-usual stressor events. Furthermore, there is no reason to assume that only one SPEC is being reacted to (or anticipated) at any given time, or that some concurrent responses are not still carrying out the coping strategy undertaken for earlier SPECs. Therefore, although a micro-level examination of each individual stress cycle has analytic advantage, an understanding of the level of stress that a given focal system undergoes at any given time requires a more macro level consideration.

We can try to deal with the problem by borrowing some terms from dynamical systems and complexity theory (Vallacher and Nowak, 1994; McGrath *et al.*, in press). We can regard the stress cycle describing the course of any given SPEC as the 'local dynamics' of the system, which lead to emergent or 'global level dynamics' of the system. These global level dynamics, in turn, shape the subsequent local dynamics of the system. Moreover, the pattern of events occurring in the system's embedding context may change, and such changes will alter both the local and global dynamics of the system. This increases the complexity of the research questions that need to be considered immensely.

Stress and the Sojourner

Some Influences of Culture on Stress and Coping

We want to apply our theoretical framework to the special case of social and psychological stress as it is experienced in the lives of international sojourners—individuals who travel to a foreign country to work and live for an extended period of time. We think that sojourner stress is worthy of study both as a special case and as a means of elucidating the more general case of stress in individual lives.

The nature and course of a single stress cycle, and consequently the overall level of stress, is likely influenced by the national culture of the sojourner and by an interaction between the sojourner's culture and the host culture (Aldwin, 1994; Bhagat *et al.*,

1994). These cultural influences may occur in terms of one or more of the four parts of the stress cycle: situation, perceived situation, response selection, and coping behavior, and in terms of one or more of the four processes by which those parts are connected: appraisal process, choice process, performance process, and outcome process.

Due to differences in cultural norms and differences in perceptions and meanings, potentially stressful events are likely to be experienced qualitatively differently and at different frequencies by sojourners than by members of the host culture. For example, stressful situations involving communication problems are probably quite common for sojourners, who may not be entirely fluent in the verbal and non-verbal languages of the host culture. So are problems caused by negative stereotypes and prejudices.

As stated earlier, the appraisal of an event as personally relevant and threatening is a function of the perceived importance of the consequences of the SPEC, the perceived uncertainty of the system's ability to deal with the SPEC, and the duration and other temporal features of the SPEC. Culture likely interacts with each of these in influencing the appraisal of a potentially stressful event.

The importance of a given event depends largely on the values, beliefs, and attitudes of the individual, which are strongly influenced by his or her cultural background (e.g. Triandis, 1994). For example, loyalty to ingroups such as the family unit, workplace, or country, is highly valued by many East Asian cultures. Consequently, situations involving a perceived breech of loyalty are likely to be more important to sojourners from these countries than to sojourners or host nationals from other countries, for which in-group loyalty is not so highly valued.

Culture influences the uncertainty surrounding a potentially stressful event. In our thinking about uncertainty, we draw on Daft and colleagues' distinction between ambiguity involving uncertainty and ambiguity involving equivocality (e.g. Daft and Lengel, 1984). Ambiguity involving uncertainty results from lack of information, such as unfamiliar situations in which sojourners do not know where to go for certain services. Ambiguity involving equivocality, on the other hand, results when the meaning of a given situation or event is unclear, such as when a sojourner misinterprets or mis-appraises the actions of a colleague. It is easy to imagine many situations involving both types of ambiguity contributing to a sojourner's experiences.

The perceived situation, or the experienced stressfulness, is likely to be quite different for sojourners adapting to a new culture than for members of that host culture, for at least two reasons. First, the perceived situation is largely a result of the appraisal process, which itself is obviously influenced by culture as discussed above. Second, given that stress itself is typically conceptualized as an array of negative emotions, and given that emotions play different roles and have different meanings across cultures (e.g. Triandis, 1994), it seems likely that the actual experience of stress for a given event differs qualitatively for people from different cultures.

Few studies have explicitly compared coping responses used by people from diverse cultures (Aldwin, 1994; Slavin et al., 1991). However, because reactions to stressors are determined by interactions between individuals and their environment (e.g. Lazarus, 1993), which in turn are influenced by culture (e.g. Triandis, 1980, 1994), it is likely that sojourners make different response choices and perform those responses differently, than do host nationals.

Interpersonal conflicts based on intercultural factors are given special emphasis in the model to be discussed later in this chapter. Results of the limited research on conflict management across cultures suggest that there are cultural differences (e.g. Leung, 1988; Trubinsky *et al.*, 1991). More generally, researchers have proposed cultural differences in coping responses, including the expression versus the control of emotion (Aldwin, 1994), active versus passive coping styles (e.g. Diaz-Guerrero, 1977; Holtzman *et al.*, 1975), and problem-solving versus emotion focused coping (Bhagat *et al.*, 1994).

As mentioned above, the actual performance of a given coping response is primarily determined by the skills, resources, and motivations of the system. Thus, to the extent that sojourners bring different coping skills, resources, and motivations to the stressful situation, the performance process is also likely to be influenced by culture.

Finally, the outcome process of any given coping behavior potentially interacts with culture in several ways. First, the response–outcome contingency (i.e. the effectiveness of a chosen response alternative in modifying the situation) depends on the host culture setting. Second, the meaning of the outcomes may be different for sojourners, since the perceptions and meaning of events and behaviors are culturally determined. Finally, some of the important outcomes occur in the system's embedding context, such as the responses of co-workers; these are likely influenced by culture.

Before we conclude our discussion of cultural influences on the stress and coping process, we note that although it is likely that sojourners experience more frequent and more intense individual stressors and therefore more overall stress as they move to a new culture, it is also possible that some sojourners experience less overall stress, due to more favorable conditions in the new culture. Even though many sojourners may find some aspects of their experience in the new culture less stressful, we believe that the overall level of stress is likely to be higher, at least in the initial months of stay, for the large majority of sojourners.

A Model of Stress and Coping by Sojourners

The model to be presented below was developed, tested, and modified based on a study, by the first author, of international graduate students who had recently sojourned to a large midwestern US university to carry out their graduate studies (Shupe, 1997). That study was done in three phases. The first phase consisted of in-depth interviews of twenty-five sojourners from a variety of countries and fields of study. Those interview data were then used to develop measures of intercultural work-related conflicts and coping responses. The second phase of the study consisted of a survey of all international graduate students who had been enrolled at that university for one semester (somewhat over 500). A total of 206 completed surveys were obtained. The model focuses on a particular class of stressors, namely: interpersonal conflicts related to intercultural factors encountered in the workplace. Shupe (1997) developed a two-part model of sojourner stress and coping and tested the model on these data. The third phase consisted of follow-up interviews of some of those respondents.

Like our general theoretical framework, the model conceptualizes sojourner stress as a phenomenon important at both the level of a single stress cycle and the level of overall stress on the system. The model assumes that cycles from past stress and coping situations can contribute to an overall level of stress, by adding both incremental benefits (based on successful handling of past SPECs and increased understanding of the host culture) and incremental damages (resulting from past stress and coping cycles that were less than perfectly successful). We believe that during a sojourner's initial months in a foreign culture, the residual damages of SPECs from an onslaught of culture-related stressors (e.g. interpersonal conflicts), will typically outweigh the benefits accrued through successful stress and coping cycles. However, as time passes, the sojourner who is able to withstand the high level of overall stress early on, may increasingly reap the benefits. Most importantly, the level of uncertainty, both in terms of the lack of necessary information and in terms of the misunderstanding of meaning in a situation, will begin to diminish as the sojourner gains experience in the host culture. We call this experience-based increase in understanding of the host culture *adaptation*—a term we adopted from the intercultural communication literature, which conceptualizes adaptation as the process of adjustment to another culture (e.g. Hammer, 1987; Hawes and Kealey, 1981; Searle and Ward, 1990).

One part of the model, cast at the level of the individual stress cycle, is a stressor–appraisal–coping model. That model links sets of features of the person and of a single conflict event to the stressfulness of that conflict event; and it then links that experienced stressfulness of the conflict event to coping responses. The main constructs of that part of the model are: uncertainty (including indices of predictability, controllability, social support, and cultural distance), importance (including indices reflecting what is at stake, status of the other party, and duration), incident stressfulness, and coping behaviors.

The other part of the model, dealing with the individual's overall level of stress, is the intercultural conflict model. That model focuses on the cumulative effects of all intercultural conflicts on the individual's level of adaptation. The main constructs of that part of the model are: intercultural conflict experiences, psychological well-being, health, job satisfaction, sociocultural adaptation, and job stress. The two parts of the model are shown in Figures 4.2 and 4.3.

Path analyses of the survey data suggested substantial support for both the stress–appraisal–coping model and the intercultural conflict model (Shupe, 1997). Results for the stress–appraisal–coping model suggest that the uncertainty and the importance of intercultural, work-related conflicts predict the experienced stressfulness of those conflicts. As sojourners experience more stressful conflicts, they engage more frequently in attempts to manage the conflicts and the stressfulness associated with the conflicts, using both direct and indirect coping responses. Thus, different coping responses do not appear to be alternative ways of handling stress, but rather complementary responses to be used in patterned sequences over time. We will comment further on this point in a later section of this chapter, where we examine some data from sojourners about dealing with stress over time.

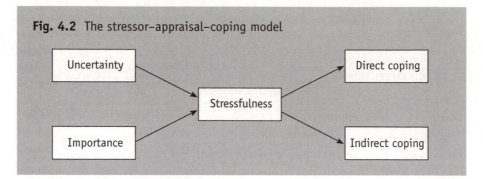

Fig. 4.2 The stressor–appraisal–coping model

With regard to the intercultural conflict model: intercultural conflict occurring between graduate students and the people they work with is directly related to work dissatisfaction. This relation is consistent with a large body of research indicating that a variety of occupational stressors have a negative impact on work satisfaction and other work-related outcome variables (Kahn and Byosiere, 1992). In addition, there is a strong relation between intercultural conflicts and the distress experienced from non-work hassles, such as living away from family and friends and adjusting to the weather and pace of life in a new culture. This relation suggests that the stress experienced by sojourners at work can spill over to, and intensify, potentially distressing situations encountered outside of the workplace. Moreover, the model suggests that intercultural conflict contributes to poor adaptation over and above the baseline effects of job stress. Finally, the model suggests that the effects of intercultural conflicts on work satisfaction and sociocultural distress lead to a degradation in psychological well-being, which in turn mediates the effects of intercultural conflicts on health conditions.

The Shupe (1997) study represents an examination of the experience of intercultural conflict as a workplace stressor, and an explicit test of our theory of stress and

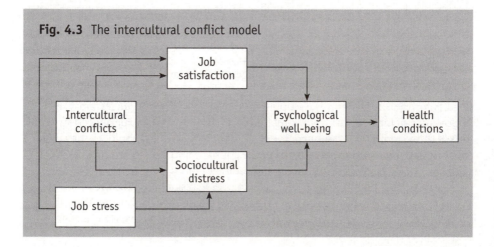

Fig. 4.3 The intercultural conflict model

coping for sojourners. Results of the study provide insight into the stress and coping experience of a culturally diverse group of sojourners in their initial months in a new country. At the same time, they may offer insights into the more general case of stress and coping.

Stress as a Dynamic, Adaptive Process

We argued above that the stressful impact of any given SPEC is a dynamic process that unfolds over time, and that combines with the effects of the system's reaction to other SPECs.

In order to model the dynamics of the stress and coping process and to capture temporal features of the stress and coping resulting from a single stressor, we conducted follow-up interviews with a sample of the participants from the Shupe study. Participants were asked detailed questions about the entire course of the single stressful experience they had responded about in the survey. While results of those interviews cannot be reported in full here since their analysis is still ongoing, a qualitative examination of illustrative samples is instructive for our consideration of stress as an unfolding dynamic process.

Interview participants were given their surveys and asked to recall the stressful incidents about which they had answered the follow-up coping questions in the survey. They were then asked to describe in detail the incident as it unfolded over time and all of the ways in which they responded to it. Although they had completed the survey several months earlier, a large majority of the participants readily recalled the incidents in detail and were able to describe the course of the coping process with a great deal of certainty. They gave articulate descriptions of the events themselves and the context surrounding the events, such as the reactions of uninvolved parties and other concurrent stressors, and they exhibited an unexpected degree of insight into their choices of responses and the bases for these choices. Participants were then given a list of eight major types of coping responses (such as 'seek social support') and specific examples of each (such as 'talk to a friend'). Based on the participants' descriptions of the stressor–coping process, the interviewer helped them identify which of the eight major types of responses they had used in coping with their stressful situations. Participants then indicated the approximate times the stressor–coping process began and ended on a timeline instrument. Using these beginning and ending times as anchors, they then indicated on the timeline the period of time during which they had engaged in each type of coping response. Finally, participants indicated whether each type of response made the situation better or worse, in terms of the objectives of both problem-focused coping (alleviating the stressor itself) and emotion-focused coping (alleviating the stress experienced). The entire interview lasted approximately forty minutes.

The interview data clearly indicated that the participants' experiences were not simple, static events but rather complex, unfolding processes with multiple determinants, including for example the perceived availability of resources and their history with other stressors and coping responses. Regardless of the magnitude of the stressors, participants consistently engaged in multiple types of coping responses. In fact, they used an average of six of the eight categories of coping responses, and rarely used fewer than four.

In many cases, their use of one or more types of coping responses was contingent on the effectiveness (or more accurately, the ineffectiveness) of previously used responses. A woman from an Eastern European country, for example, had difficulties in that her advisor did not provide the kind of hands-on academic guidance to which she was accustomed and which she obviously needed in order to understand the nuances of the unfamiliar education system. The advisor's lack of appropriate guidance was largely responsible for the student's enrollment in twice as many courses as other graduate students in her program. Over a period of several months, the woman dealt with the situation using many types of coping responses. Her first response was to confront her advisor and ask for more direct guidance concerning her course load. When this confrontational response did not result in the desired outcome, she began to distance herself from the tensions with her advisor, and at the same time attempted to keep others from realizing how miserable and upset she was by using self-control. Although these strategies helped the situation in terms of keeping the tensions from surfacing, they did not totally alleviate the problem. She subsequently coped using social support from a fellow graduate student, and in the end made an effort to understand the difficult situation and to use it as an opportunity to learn and grow (i.e. re-appraisal).

This approach of using an initial coping response and later either replacing or supplementing it with one or more other coping responses was extremely common among participants. In many cases, though, the pattern of responses was even more complex. In addition to responding to the stressors with a set of sequential responses, nearly all of the participants used two or more coping responses concurrently. Consider for example, a Chinese participant who experienced what he described as constant problems understanding and communicating with his advisor and other professors, during his initial months in the USA. He assumed personal responsibility for these communication problems and accepted them as part of the cultural adaptation process, as illustrated by his statement, 'Whenever you go into a new culture it takes time to adapt.' For the entire course of these difficult months he tried to distance himself from the communication problems by ignoring them and focusing more determinedly on his studies and work. At the same time, he engaged in planful problem-solving by working diligently on his English-speaking abilities and tried to re-appraise and learn from the situation. Although responses such as 'ignoring the situation' and 'planful problem-solving' may seem incompatible to an outside observer, they actually played complementary roles by allowing him to ignore his own pain and embarrassment from not being able to communicate effectively, while at the same time helping him to attenuate future difficulties.

As we noted above, the participants' use of a given coping response was determined in part by the ineffectiveness of previous responses used in coping with that stressor. Consistent with our theory, the choice was apparently also determined by participants' experience with particular coping responses in relation to other stressors, and by the perseverance of residual effects from previous and concurrent stressors. Consider a male participant from Canada. He had repeated difficulties dealing with bureaucracy at the university and with a few key individuals in the administration who, he believed, made deliberate efforts to discourage international students from successfully applying to and remaining in graduate programs at the university. He described experiencing a heightened sensitivity to being an international student and to the differences between his own culture and the culture of the USA; and he believed that his worries about such things as being a victim of crime in the unfamiliar culture contributed to this increased sensitivity and anxiety. The participant attributed his fear, that one of the administrators who had been particularly rude to him would have him expelled from the university, to this high level of anxiety. To prevent a possible expulsion, the man chose to cope not by confronting the administrator or reporting the inappropriate behavior to her superiors, but rather sought social support and used self-control.

The experiences of a participant from India illustrate the influence of one's history in coping with similar stressors. The participant reported experiencing interpersonal tensions with a fellow graduate student after he jokingly made a comment that apparently offended the other student. He initially thought about apologizing to the other student, but upon consideration of their previous interactions, the participant realized that it would be more appropriate and effective to distance himself from the problem and to 'wait for it to pass', so as to allow both parties to save face. This response, along with his attempt to understand the situation so as to prevent future incidents, was effective in alleviating the tensions in a period of about two days.

Although these few examples by themselves do not provide conclusive evidence for our theory, they do clearly illustrate the dynamics and complexities inherent in the coping responses to stressors such as those experienced by sojourners adapting to a new culture. In order to more fully understand such responses we must explore the stressor–coping response relation not as a single 'stimulus–response' event, but as a dynamic system. We must also recognize the likelihood of the system using multiple complementary responses, simultaneously or in sequence, and the important role that a system's own history and context can play in the appraisal, choice, and execution of a coping response at any given time.

Conclusion

The complexity of the stress and coping process makes it both a challenge to conceptualize and a challenge to measure. We conceptualize a single stressful encounter as a cycle that consists of the event, or SPEC, the interpretation or appraisal of the SPEC, and performance of those responses, the execution of which has consequences for the SPEC and its embedding context. Thus, a single stress cycle is a complex process in and of itself. Ordinarily, however, examination of such a single cycle tells us little about the system's overall level of stress, which is determined by the totality of the stressful encounters experienced and results of the system's reactions to them, together with contextual influences. There is an accumulation of effects from all past stress cycles that constitutes the sojourners' overall adaptation, as manifested in job satisfaction, distress resulting from non-work related hassles, psychological well-being, and health conditions. We therefore represent the effects of a single stressor, and the overall level of stress as separate parts of the overall model.

One major insight resulting from the follow-up interview data, that is consistent both with the sojourner models and with our more general theory, is that a focal system's encounter with a stressor is not a simple, static event. Rather, it is a complex, adaptive, dynamic interaction. A given SPEC combines with the system's other stressful encounters in a non-linear rather than simple additive way, and must therefore be understood in relation to the totality of the system's circumstances at a given time. An encounter with a stressor is not a simple transitory occurrence with a specifiable beginning and end; rather, it is an unfolding process that changes over time and is defined in part by the system's past and anticipated future. Moreover, such a stress event occurs not in a vacuum but rather in a rich embedding context with which the system interacts, and that interaction influences the meaning and course of events.

Although we chose to focus on intercultural conflicts as a stressor, and the data presented here are limited to sojourners of a particular kind (students doing graduate work in a culture foreign to them), our theory and our model may well provide a template useful for study of the stress process much more generally. What applies in the case of intercultural conflicts experienced by international sojourners is likely to be close kin to the stress and coping processes that operate for many other kinds of workplace situations. For example: workgroups that are demographically diverse in racial, ethnic, and/or gender terms can be regarded as undergoing multicultural conflicts (McGrath *et al.*, 1995). Similar processes may play out in instances where organizational cultures clash. Aspects of it may apply even outside the workplace context; for example, members of so-called 'blended families' may experience stress–appraisal–coping challenges similar to those experienced by the sojourners in our study.

All of these are speculations, of course. Our model's strict applicability is limited to the impact of intercultural conflicts experienced by international graduate student sojourners. Nonetheless, these considerations suggest that our theory will need a rich and wide ranging research program to explore it fully. We hope this chapter will encourage other researchers to join in that exploration.

References

Aldwin, C. M. (1994) *Stress, Coping and Development: An Integrated Perspective*. New York: The Guilford Press.

Baron, R. M., Amazeen, P. G., and Beek, P. J. (1994) Local and global dynamics of social relations. In R. R. Vallacher and A. Nowak, *Dynamical Systems in Social Psychology* (pp. 111–138). New York: Academic Press, Inc.

Beehr, T. A. and McGrath, J. E. (1996) The methodology of research on coping: Conceptual, strategic, and operational level issues. In M. Zeidner and N. Endler (eds.) *Handbook of Coping: Theory, Research and Applications*. New York: Wiley.

Bhagat, R. S., O'Driscoll, M. P., Babakus, E., Frey, L., Chokkar, J., Ninokumar, H., Pate, L. E., Ryder, P. A., Fernandez, M. J. G., Ford, D. L., and Mahanyele, M. (1994) Organizational stress and coping in seven national contexts: A cross-cultural investigation. In G. P. Keita and J. J.

Hurrell, Jr. (eds.) *Job Stress in a Changing Workforce*. Washington, DC: American Psychological Association.

Cherniss, C. (1980) *Professional Burnout in Human Service Organizations*. New York: Praeger.

Daft, R. L. and Lengel, R. H. (1984) Information richness: A new approach to managerial behavior and organizational design. In B. M. Staw and L. L. Cummings (eds.) *Research in Organizational Behavior, 6*, (pp. 191–233).

Diaz-Guerrero, R. (1977) 'A Mexican psychology', *American Psychologist*, November: 934–944.

Hammer, M. R. (1987) 'Behavioral dimensions of intercultural effectiveness: A replication and extension', *International Journal of Intercultural Relations*, 11, 65–88.

Hawes, F. and Kealey, D. J. (1981) 'An empirical study of Canadian technical assistance: Adaptation and effectiveness on overseas assignment', *International Journal of Intercultural Relations*, 5, 239–258.

Holtzman, W. H., Diaz-Guerrero, R., and Swartz, J. D. (1975) *Personality Development in Two Cultures: A Cross-cultural Longitudinal Study of School Children in Mexico and the United States*. Austin: University of Texas Press.

Kahn, R. L. and Byosiere, P. (1992) Stress in organizations. In H. C. Triandis, M. D. Dunnette, and L. M. Hough (eds.), *Handbook of Industrial and Organizational Psychology* (2nd edn.) (Vol. 3, pp. 571–650). Palo Alto, CA: Consulting Psychologists Press.

Latane, B. and Nowack, A. (1994) Attitudes as catastrophes: From dimensions to categories with increasing involvement. In R. R. Valacher and A. Nowack (eds.). *Dynamical Systems in Social Psychology*. New York: Academic Press.

Lazarus, R. S. (1993) 'Coping theory and research: Past, present, and future', *Psychosomatic Medicine*, 55, 234–247.

Leung, K. (1988) 'Some determinants of conflict avoidance', *Journal of Cross-Cultural Psychology*, 19, 125–136.

McGrath, J. E. and Beehr, T. A. (1990) 'Time and the stress process: Some temporal issues in the conceptualization and measurement of stress', *Stress Medicine*, 6, 93–104.

McGrath, J. E., Arrow, H., and Berdahl, J. L. (in press) *A Theory of Groups as Complex, Adaptive, Dynamic Systems*. Newbury Park, CA: Sage Publishing Co.

McGrath, J. E., Berdahl, J. L., and Arrow, H. (1995) Traits, expectations, culture and clout: The dynamics of diversity in work groups. In S. E. Jackson and M. M. Ruderman (eds.), *Diversity in Work Teams: Research Paradigms for a Changing Workplace*. Washington DC: American Psychological Association.

Matteson, M. T. (1987) Individual–organizational relationships: implications for preventing job stress and burnout. In J. C. Quick, R. S. Bhagat, J. E. Dalton, and J. D. Quick. *Work Stress: Health Care Systems in the Workplace* (pp. 156–209). New York: Praeger.

Searle, W. and Ward, C. (1990) 'The prediction of psychological and sociocultural adjustment during cross-cultural transitions', *International Journal of Intercultural Relations*, 14, 449–464.

Shupe, E. I. (1997) Cultures clashing in the workplace: A model of intercultural conflict as a stressor. Unpublished doctoral dissertation, University of Illinois at Urbana-Champaign.

Slavin, L. A., Rainer, K. L., McCreary, M. L., and Gowda, K. K. (1991) 'Toward a multicultural model of the stress process', *Journal of Counseling and Development*, 70, 156–163.

Triandis, H. C. (1980) Values, attitudes, and interpersonal behavior. In H. E. Howe and M. M. Page (eds.), *Nebraska Symposium on Motivation* (pp. 195–260). Lincoln: University of Nebraska Press.

Triandis, H. C. (1994) *Culture and Social Behavior*. New York: McGraw Hill.

Trubinsky, P., Ting-Toomey, S., and Lin, S. (1991) 'The influence of individualism–collectivism and self-monitoring on conflict styles', *International Journal of Intercultural Relations*, 15, 65–84.

Vallacher, R. R. and Nowak, A. (1994) *Dynamical Systems in Social Psychology*. New York: Academic Press, Inc.

Vininga, R. L. and Spradley, J. P. (1981) *The Work–Stress Connection: How to Cope with Job Burnout*. New York: Ballantine Books.

5

··

A Cybernetic Theory of Organizational Stress

Thomas G. Cummings and Cary L. Cooper

There is a growing body of evidence from studies in the workplace (Cooper and Marshall, 1976; Sauter *et al.*, 1989; Cooper, 1996) to suggest that occupational stress (OS) is an important causal factor in cardiovascular disease, mental ill-health and other health behaviors. The empirical work in this field has expanded so rapidly (Cooper and Payne, 1988) that we have been unable to put these developments into a coherent theoretical framework. Cartwright and Zander (1960) have argued that all scientific endeavor moves progressively through the stages of armchair speculation, to data collection to theory building. Osler (1910), Selye (1946), and others (Ryle and Russell, 1949) provided the early speculative notions of the dynamics underlying occupational stressors and the general adaptation syndrome. Our intention here is to continue the process of theory-building in the OS field by presenting a cybernetic theory of stress, drawn from our earlier model (Cummings and Cooper, 1979).

Overview of Cybernetic Theory

The theory of stress used here is derived from the framework and concepts of cybernetics or systems control (Weiner, 1948, 1954; Ashby, 1954, 1966). Briefly, cybernetics is concerned with the use of information and feedback to control purposeful behavior. The basic premise of this theory is that behavior is directed at reducing deviations from a specific goal-state: 'it is the deviations from the goal-state itself that direct the behavior of the system, rather than some predetermined internal mechanism that aims blindly' (Buckley, 1967: 53). This perspective has been used widely in the biological, physical, and social sciences to explain how systems (i.e. organisms, plants, things) adjust or adapt their actions to cope with disturbances from goal achievement.

The idea of people adapting to disturbances is not new in the stress field. Starting with the pioneering work of Cannon (1932) into the homeostatic processes operating to maintain the organism's equilibrium, much of the theory and research related to stress has followed (often implicitly) a cybernetic framework (Basowitz *et al.*, 1958; Cofer and Appley, 1964; McGrath, 1976). Although this has drawn attention to the organism–environment interaction, or the person–environment (P–E) fit, the systematic application of cybernetic concepts has been relatively uneven among the disciplines studying stress (i.e. medicine, psychology, management, and sociology). This makes it difficult to compare the different concepts of stress, or to integrate the variety of research findings into a coherent theory. This latter difficulty is especially troublesome in the OS field, where empiricism has far outstripped theory building (Cooper and Payne, 1988, 1991).

A more formal application of cybernetic theory would greatly help theorizing and research in OS. Considerable research has shown that individuals must cope with a variety of potential stresses in the work environment (Cooper and Payne, 1991; Sauter and Murphy, 1995). Cybernetic theory provides a comprehensive portrayal of this person–environment interaction. It emphasizes time, information, and feedback (Shibutani, 1968). The temporal dimension provides a dynamic view of stress frequently missing in OS research. The focus on information underscores the key notion that information mediates the person–environment relationship. The idea of feedback recognizes that coping behavior is purposeful, directed by knowledge of its previous effects. These factors are central to an understanding of stress. Moreover, they are equally applicable to the stress phenomena studied both by physiologists and social scientists.

For purposes of explanation, Miller's (1965) application of cybernetics to living systems is used here. It explains how living systems (i.e. plants and animals) maintain themselves in steady states or homeostasis by keeping a variety of variables in balance. These variables having to do with the import, transformation, and export of matter/energy and information represent those conditions the system must maintain if it is to survive. Forces that tend to disrupt these conditions, whether from inside or outside the system, are counteracted to restore as nearly as possible the original balance. Hence, individual behavior is directed toward maintaining a steady state both within the organism and with respect to its environment.

The concept of stress is related to this drive toward homeostasis. Each of the numerous variables in an organism has a specific range of stability. When a variable is within this range, it is in steady state and the person has no need for corrective action. Conversely, when forces disrupt a variable beyond its range of stability, the organism must act (or cope) to restore its steady state. A *stress* is any force displacing a variable beyond its range of stability. This produces a *strain* within the organism. Strains may or may not be capable of being reduced, depending upon their intensity and the resources of the individual.

Organisms may also anticipate a stress. Knowledge that a stress is likely to occur constitutes a *threat* to the individual. A threat can cause a strain because of its meaning to the person: a pattern of information is a threat when it is capable of eliciting responses that can counteract the stress it presages. Thus, either a stress or a threat can create a strain within the individual.

The totality of strains within the organism represents its *values*, and the relative urgency of reducing each of these strains denotes the individual's *hierarchy of values*.

Each person develops, through genetic makeup, experience, and reinforcements, a preferential hierarchy of values. This gives rise to decision-making rules which determine the individual's preference for a particular steady state. It is this preferred steady state which determines the range of stability for each of the variables the person attempts to maintain in balance.

Individual behavior directed at maintaining a steady state represents the person's *adjustment processes*. These processes are aimed at reducing deviations from the individual's preferred state. Since separate adjustment processes are interrelated, the organism may be considered ultrastable (Ashby, 1954); if initial behavior cannot cope with a stress or threat, related responses are implemented, and so on. Eventually, the entire adjustment processes of the individual may be directed at coping with stress.

Adjustment processes are guided by information feedback. Information about the state of a person's variables is fed back to the individual, thus enabling her or him to detect strain and to direct subsequent coping behavior to reduce it. If the information increases deviation from the preferred steady state, *positive feedback* exists. Conversely, when information decreases (or negates) deviations from the steady state, it is *negative feedback*. Because the latter kind of feedback is needed to restore the individual's steady state, it is the minimum requirement for coping with stress.

Feedback processes have three major properties that determine their effectiveness: (1) *probability of error*; (2) *lag* or time which they require to affect the individual; and (3) *gain* or extent of corrective effect. Negative feedback with a low probability of error, or a short lag time, or a large gain is generally more effective than feedback with dissimilar characteristics.

Miller's (1965) conception of stress may be summarized as follows:

- Based on genetic makeup, experience, and reinforcements, a person develops a preferential hierarchy of values. This determines the individual's preference for one steady state rather than another, and hence, the range of stability for each of the variables he or she attempts to maintain in balance.

- A stress or threat creates a strain within the individual when it pushes a steady state variable beyond its range of stability.

- The individual experiences this strain through an information feedback process where the actual state of the variable is compared to its preferred state. A discrepancy between the actual and the preferred informs the individual of the presence of strain and the need to cope with it.

- Depending upon the probability of error, lag, and gain of the feedback, the individual may synthesize and enact effective adjustment processes. This feedback–adjustment cycle continues until the person reduces the strain, or alters the preferred steady state, or perishes from inability to cope with the stress or threat situation.

Concept of Stress

Cybernetic theory provides a number of precise concepts that may help to reduce the ambiguity frequently associated with the generic use of the term stress. Typically, OS researchers have used the term stress to denote: the environmental factors imping-ing upon the individual; their immediate effects; and the person's reactions (Appley and Trumbull, 1986). This confusion of independent, intervening, and dependent variables makes it difficult to compare the results of different studies or to understand the causal relationships reported in the research. Starting with the environment, the terms 'stress' and 'threat' refer to those external conditions that disturb the individ-ual's normal functioning. The former signifies those external factors that are cur-rently affecting the person, while the latter represents those conditions that the individual perceives are likely to affect him or her in the future. This temporal dis-tinction is not often made in the OS literature. Researchers traditionally focus on the relationship between current conditions at work (e.g. work overload, role conflict, overpromotion) and individual coping behavior (e.g. escapist drinking, smoking, reduced aspiration). Although this accounts for existing stresses at work, it ignores the possibility that certain factors not currently in the work situation (i.e. threats) may also affect the individual. Thus, for example, a person's present employment sta-tus may not affect his or her behavior adversely; yet the rumor that company down-sizing is likely to occur and may result in job loss can be quite stressful.

Whereas stresses and threats are environmental conditions that disturb the per-son, the immediate effect or disruption constitutes a 'strain' within the individual. Subsequent behavior directed at reducing these strains represents the individual's 'adjustment processes'. This distinction between strains (immediate effects) and adjustment processes (the person's response) is also not often made in the OS litera-ture. Researchers frequently group these two distinct concepts or stages of the stress cycle into one category termed 'symptoms of occupational ill health' (Cooper and Payne, 1988). These symptoms include such variables as raised blood pressure, increased cholesterol level, rapid pulse rate, smoking, escapist drinking, job dissatis-faction, and reduced aspiration. A close inspection of these items suggests, however, that some are probably indicators of strain (e.g. rapid pulse rate, job dissatisfaction), others of adjustment processes (e.g. smoking, escapist drinking, reduced aspiration), and still others of the secondary or long-term results of ineffective coping (e.g. raised blood pressure, high cholesterol level).

These conceptual distinctions among the terms stress, threat, strain, and adjust-ment processes refine considerably the generic concept of stress. They suggest a clas-sification of variables—stress or threat (independent variable), strain (intervening variable), and adjustment processes (dependent variable)—which can serve as a start-ing point for defining and operationalizing the empirical referents of these distinct aspects of the P–E fit.

Stress Cycle

Cybernetic theory depicts stress as an information–feedback cycle. The underlying characteristics of this process are the person's detection of strain and translation of this knowledge into adjustment processes to cope with the stress or threat situation. Information and feedback are central to this conception of stress. The individual must receive information as to whether his or her steady state variables are beyond their ranges of stability, and if so, use it to select appropriate adjustment behavior. The outcomes of this behavior are fed back to the person to inform subsequent coping, and so on.

Until now, the information and feedback aspects of the P–E fit have received only cursory attention in the OS field. The tendency is to uncover potential sources of stress in the work environment (e.g. work overload, role conflict) and to link these to individual characteristics (e.g. tolerance for ambiguity, Type A behavioral pattern) and to symptoms of ineffective coping (e.g. mental ill-health, coronary heart disease). Although there is often recognition given to the feedback aspect of the P–E interaction and to the information needed to appraise the environment and to choose a coping response (McGrath, 1976), there have been few attempts to apply these cybernetic concepts systematically to the stress cycle. This requires attention to four distinct phases of the stress cycle: (1) detection of strain; (2) choice of adjustment processes; (3) implementation of adjustment processes; and (4) affects of adjustment processes on the stress or threat situation. Each is discussed below in reference to OS and the implications of studying it from a cybernetic perspective.

Detection of Strain

Traditionally, OS researchers have studied stress from a subjective or psychological perspective. The detection or experience of stress rests on a 'cognitive appraisal' of the environment (Lazarus, 1966). If the individual appraises the situation as stressful, then it is experienced as such, regardless of its objective characteristics. From a cybernetic view, the detection process is based on a comparison between the person's actual and preferred states. A disparity between the two yields a mismatch signal which informs the individual of the presence of strain and of the need to cope with a stress or threat situation.

Detection of strain through the feedback of mismatch signals presupposes that individuals have: (1) a preference for one state rather than another; (2) knowledge of the actual state; and (3) an ability to compare the two. Most biological researchers are relatively successful in explaining how these conditions operate physiologically—e.g. maintenance of the bodily water balance (Elkinton and Danowski, 1955). Here, the preferred state of the organism is genetically determined. This provides reasonable assurance that organisms with similar genetic codes are trying to maintain similar physiological conditions, at least over their individual life spans. Similarly, knowledge of the actual state of the organism is usually found in the numerous physiological or chemical processes governing the organism's preferred variables. This tends to make comparison of the preferred and actual a relatively straightforward physiological process. Conversely, OS researchers find it more difficult to explain the detection of subjective or psychological strain. Examination of the conditions for detection sheds light on this problem.

Preferred State The preferred state of the individual represents that condition he or she is trying to achieve or maintain. This is analogous to the temperature setting on a thermostat. Since detection of strain rests on a disparity between the preferred and the actual, knowledge of the individual's preferred state is a necessary starting point for identifying which environmental variables are likely to affect or disturb those preferences, thus resulting in strain.

OS researchers have uncovered a broad array of work conditions that are possible sources of stress—e.g. work overload, time pressures, role ambiguity, etc. The relationships between these variables and indicators of strain, however, are generally quite modest with correlation coefficients in the range of .06 to .50 (Cooper and Marshall, 1976). Failure to account for different preferences among individuals can contribute to this low association between environmental and stress variables. Differences in people's values, experience, and personality make it axiomatic that one person's heaven may be another's hell. This variability in people and their preferences makes it difficult to determine *a priori* which work conditions will result in strain.

A promising path for identifying employees' work preferences derives from research on individual differences. OS researchers have discovered several individual-difference factors that contribute to people's reactions to stresses and threats. These individual differences include personality traits (e.g. locus of control) and behavioral characteristics (e.g. Type A behavior pattern) that can affect which work conditions are likely to be seen as stressful or threatening. They provide insight about people's preferred work situation. For example, the Type A behavior pattern consists of predisposition to competitive behavior, time urgency, and hostility. Research suggests that Type A individuals tend to have high needs to control their environment, and thus conditions that threaten such control evoke Type A behaviors. Many work conditions that have been identified as possible stresses, such as work overload, role conflict, and role ambiguity, present employees with high amounts of uncertainty. For Type A people, these work conditions are likely to result in a disparity between the amount of control that is preferred and that which the situation affords, thus resulting in experienced strain. Similar research in work design has identified individual differences that can affect how people react to the workplace. For example, people with high growth needs tend to prefer enriched forms of work; individuals with high social needs prefer team-based work (Cummings and Worley, 1997). These employees are likely to experience strain when encountering work designs that are highly routinized or that require working alone.

This research suggests that employees differ widely in their work preferences. Since these differences are likely to determine which work stresses are actually experienced as strain, further research along these lines is needed to refine understanding of the linkage between the work context and the detection of strain. Specifically, it is necessary to sort out from among the totality of work preferences that exist simultaneously, which ones the person is actually trying to maintain in a given situation. This requires knowledge of individuals' preferred hierarchy of values, the ordering of preferences in terms of the relative urgency of reducing deviations from their desired states. Presumably, people attend to disruptions from the highest-ranked preference; depending on the amount of deviation and the coping success of the person, a decreasing level of attention is given to strain associated with the next lower ranked preference, and so on.

Assessing employees' hierarchy of work values provides a preliminary indication of which work stresses the person is attending to—i.e. work stresses that disturb a higher-ranked preference are likely to receive more attention than those that disturb a lower-ranked preference. Lowe and McGrath (1971) suggested a method for evaluating individuals' preferential hierarchy of values. It is based on two perceptual factors that are likely to affect stress arousal: the perceived consequences of the situation, and the uncertainty of meeting its demands effectively. Lowe and McGrath presented evidence that arousal is high when both perceived consequences and uncertainty are high. Application of this research to work preferences can reveal their hierarchical ordering in terms of potential for strain arousal. This can provide an indirect measure of employees' preferential hierarchy of work values. It would be possible, for example, to assess work preferences in regard to their consequence on the person's work life—i.e. the potential gain or loss that is expected from maintaining them effectively versus ineffectively. A further evaluation of work preferences would include individuals' expected certainty/uncertainty in maintaining them effectively. The combination of the consequence and uncertainty measures would provide an ordering of work preferences in terms of their potential for strain arousal, and hence an indication of employees' preferential hierarchy of work values. This ranking of work preferences would be a promising start toward understanding which work stresses are operative or relevant to the person in a particular work context.

Actual State   Detection of strain requires, in addition to a preferred state, knowledge of the actual state. Subjective assessment of the actual state is inherently prone to error. Information about actual conditions at work is rarely complete, exact, or direct. Further, individuals are able to attend to only limited parts of the work environment at a time. These factors present certain problems for the subjective detection of strain. Foremost among these are the clarity and accessibility of environmental cues. Many of the possible work stresses appear to be both ambiguous and inaccessible: role demands; promotion requirements; relationships with superiors, subordinates and peers; amount of participation in decision making, etc. These conditions frequently present employees with a myriad of subtle and contradictory signals, making it difficult to interpret what is real or imaginary. Direct knowledge of the states of these situations is also rarely available. Indeed, the very concepts of role ambiguity (inadequate information about the work role) and role conflict (contradictory job demands) point to the distortions and omissions that are likely to arise in role-relevant information. Similarly, the ideas of quantitative work overload (too much to do) and qualitative overload (too difficult) suggest a rate, timing, and intensity of task-related information beyond (or below in the case of work underload) that which individuals can process effectively.

Forces in the person that affect the detection process include both the quantity and quality of information required for detection and identification of strain. Notterman and Trumbull (1950) suggested that individuals differ on both dimensions. They presented preliminary evidence that people who score high on anxiety (as measured by the question mark section of the MMPI) emit more inquiries, or 'feelers', to bring structure or meaning to an unidentified disturbance than those who are less anxious. This excessive need for feedback may explain why such personality factors as emotional instability, anxiety, and neuroticism have been shown to relate to symptoms of stress (Cooper and Payne, 1991). Perhaps such individuals suffer from inability to select environmental cues appropriate to the detection of strain. This is likely to lead to a search for feedback in excess of that normally required. The implications for such individuals working in an environment with ambiguous and inaccessible stimuli are ominous. In addition to differing needs for feedback, a number of perceptual studies (Vernon, 1962) point to the innumerable ways that people selectively distort their perceptions. Although much of this research is not derived from the workplace, there is sufficient evidence to suggest that employees often distort or limit their views of actual work conditions (Buck, 1972; Arnold et al., 1995).

The preceding discussion points to both environmental and individual variables that make assessment of actual work conditions problematical. Because the ability to choose appropriate adjustment processes is determined, in part, by the accuracy of the detection process, a better understanding of the forces that either facilitate or thwart knowledge of the actual work situation is needed: the clarity and accessibility of different sources of stress; the individual factors that affect both the need for feedback and perceptions of work conditions. Integration of this research is needed to provide clearer insight into how specific features of the work environment interact with certain individual characteristics to affect knowledge of the actual state. Perhaps much of what is now termed ineffective coping is caused by faulty detection of the actual work situation; coping is likely to be ineffective if assessment of the actual environment is inaccurate.

Comparison of Preferred and Actual   The final condition for detection of strain is the ability to match the preferred state to the actual. Assuming that people know their preferences and have sufficient and accurate knowledge of the actual, the essential issue is whether these two streams of information are comparable. Because subjective information is represented in a code, such as symbols, writing, and figures, the actual must register in the same code as the preferred, otherwise the two could not be compared. Although this may seem rudimentary at the physiological level of stress, it is less straightforward at the psychological level. Here, people transform information into symbolic codes that serve as hypothetical constructs of ideas and reality. Since there may be wide variation both among codes and in how well a particular code maps the conditions it represents, there is considerable scope for incongruity among coded information. An employee, for instance, may have a mental image of his or her preferred social relationships at work. The actual state of these relationships may not register well on this code, however, making comparison of the actual with the preferred image difficult if not impossible. This leaves the person with little knowledge of whether his or her relationships at work are matching (or mismatching) the preferred.

Research on work motivation provides clues about employees' ability to compare work preferences and actual work conditions. Studies have measured employees' perceptions of how much of a particular work characteristic (e.g. task variety) they would like and how much of the condition is actually present (Locke *et al.*, 1996). The assumption is that the greater the disparity between the two measures, the greater the perceived dissatisfaction. Although it can be argued that the comparison between the 'would like' and 'is now' indices is done by the researchers rather than the subjects, the discrepancy (or dissatisfaction) scores have been shown to relate to behavioral variables (e.g. higher absenteeism and labor turnover) consistent with what would be expected from dissatisfied workers. This suggests that individuals are able to make such comparisons and the results can affect their behavior. It should be noted, however, that the strength of the relationships between discrepancy scores and the behavioral variables are usually moderate, suggesting that the comparison process is less than ideal.

A second area of motivational research focuses on employees' perceptions of equity at work (Cropamzomo and Greenberg, 1997). Here, researchers have measured workers' perceptions of whether their job provides equitable outcomes (e.g. pay) for the inputs (e.g. performance) it requires. Again, there is evidence to suggest that individuals are able to make equity comparisons, and that the results relate to their behavior. For instance, Arthur and Gunderson (1965) found that promotional lag was significantly related to psychiatric illness in the US Navy. Later, Erikson *et al.* (1972) found that naval personnel experienced greater job satisfaction when their rates of advancement exceeded their expectation; dissatisfaction increased as advancement rates were retarded.

The above-mentioned research suggests that for certain work conditions (e.g. job characteristics, rewards, workloads), individual preferences and actual conditions register in codes similar enough to permit comparison. Further research is needed, however, about the environmental and personal factors that affect the coding process, and how this, in turn, affects an individual's ability to compare different streams of preferred and actual data. It is likely that certain features of the environment are more easily and accurately codifiable than others; that individuals differ in the limits or distortions inherent in the codes they employ; and that specific codes and coding processes are more accurate and comparable than others.

Choice of Adjustment Processes

The second phase of the stress cycle involves people's choice of adjustment processes to reduce strain. OS researchers have typically neglected this decision-making process. The tendency is to relate potential work stresses to indicators of ineffective coping, ignoring the choices that initially led to such behavior. Knowledge of the decision-making process starts with an understanding of how experiences of strain affect ability to choose relevant responses; a subsequent issue is whether an individual's repertoire of available responses matches the variety of stresses actually encountered.

Cybernetic theory provides an understanding of the relationship between detection of strain and choice of adjustment process. The underlying premise is that coping behavior is guided by information feedback. This feedback, inherent in the detection process, informs the individual of the need to cope with strain; it is the basis for the subjective assessment of strain. Given this essential linkage between detection and choice of adjustment process, three key properties of feedback affect the decision-making process: error, lag, and gain.

Feedback Error Choice of appropriate coping behavior depends, in part, on the accuracy of information the individual receives about the presence and causes of strain. If there is feedback error, the person may fail either to experience strain subjectively (even though it may exist physiologically) or to identify its source correctly. The former may cause the individual to delay the decision-making process inadvertently allowing physiological strain to persist unabated; the latter may result in adjustment processes inappropriate to the situation.

The previous discussion of the detection process identified several possible sources of feedback error: the clarity and accessibility of environmental cues; differences in the quantity and quality of information needed to detect strain; perceptual distortion; and inability to compare actual and preferred states. The presence of such factors, in either the individual or the workplace, can force employees to choose adjustment responses based on insufficient or inaccurate data. The extent to which this affects the decision-making process adversely, however, is currently unknown. It is likely that work stresses differ in the clarity of information that is needed to respond to them. Similarly, employees are likely to vary in the amount of feedback error that can be tolerated before decision-making becomes untenable.

Feedback Lag The time lag of feedback concerns how long feedback takes to affect the individual. Physiologically, there is always some time lag because of the slowness of transmission in the nervous system. At the subjective level of stress, the time lag is invariably longer. Employees may have difficulty obtaining relevant information and interpreting it correctly; they may experience problems comparing actual and preferred data; simultaneous stresses in the work environment may overload the employee's information-processing capacity, delaying the rate at which strains are processed or experienced. Regardless of the exact causes of time lag, the critical issue is how this temporal dimension of feedback affects the individual's capacity to choose adjustment processes.

Generally, the longer the time lag of feedback, the slower the detection of strain. The speed of detection, in turn, influences how fast a person can decide to cope. Although OS researchers have devoted little attention to the timing of feedback, it is likely that employees have a limited range of how fast they can process feedback effectively. Feedback that falls outside of this range, either too quickly or too slowly, presents certain difficulties. Feedback with too short a time lag may overload the person's ability to process data—e.g. rapid knowledge of role ambiguity may be interpreted simply as 'noise'. Conversely, feedback with too long a time lag may not allow the person to make relevant and timely choices—e.g. slow identification of role ambiguity may limit a person's choices to those that have more drastic consequences. Research on how people's level of anxiety affects their need for information suggests that this individual factor may determine the optimal time lag for feedback (Notterman and Trumbull, 1950). Individuals who score high on anxiety may require a shorter time lag than those who are less anxious. Similarly, Miller (1965) identified a number of strategies that living systems employ to cope with lacks and excesses of information—e.g. generalization, substitution, filtering, chunking, etc. Research into these factors is needed to understand how the timing of feedback affects the speed and accuracy of detection, and how these, in turn, affect the choice of response.

Feedback Gain   Feedback gain involves the extent to which adjustment processes reduce strain; high gain connotes a high corrective effect. This dimension of feedback influences choice of coping behavior by informing the individual of both the rate and intensity at which the strain is changing, either positively or negatively. This suggests that strains are either gradually or discretely changed by successive responses   i.e. both the strain and the response are variable, such that the strain decreases in proportion to some changing aspect of the response (e.g. its force and duration), and the response, in turn, varies according to some changing aspect of the strain (e.g. its rate of decrease or increase). Thus, adjustment processes are more dynamic and complex than simple binary responses to the presence or absence of a strain.

The presence of time-variant strain suggests that adjustment processes are chosen to cope with the rate at which strain is changing. This raises the possibility that the extent of feedback gain not only affects which responses are chosen, but their force, duration, and timing. If so, it is necessary to account for this factor in explaining why individuals choose specific coping behaviors and vary their choices accordingly. Moreover, knowledge of feedback gain can provide a more thorough understanding of coping behavior. Because we are dealing primarily with psychological stress, a person's ability to judge feedback gain accurately may determine whether he or she chooses an appropriate response and enacts it properly. Again, the possibilities for perceptual distortion seem considerable. If people are to fine tune their coping responses to achieve maximum positive effect, accurate information about feedback gain is critical.

Variety of Adjustment Processes   Whereas the previous discussion concerned the effects of information feedback on choice of adjustment process, it is also necessary to consider the subsequent issue of whether the actual repertoire of responses available to the employee is adequate for the stresses and threats encountered in the work environment. Because effective coping requires some match between stresses and responses, a person's array of adjustment processes affects his or her capacity to cope with different sources of stress.

McGrath (1976) conceived of an individual's adjustment processes as representing a probability or frequency distribution. Different sources of stress affect the probability (or frequency) of choosing particular behaviors—e.g. a task-related stress would be expected to increase the probability of choosing a task-relevant response. This conception of the stress-response linkage suggests that people have an array of adjustment processes, each geared, more or less, to a specific set of conditions. Moreover, the variety of available responses may limit the number of different stresses that a person can cope with effectively.

Ashby (1966) has developed this idea into a formalized cybernetic law: Ashby's Law of Requisite Variety. He proposed that a system regulator (e.g. an employee) is effective only to the extent that it possesses the requisite number of responses (e.g. coping behaviors) to match the number of distinct disturbances (e.g. work stresses) it must face. Further, the regulator must have within its response set the appropriate responses for reducing the actual disturbance (Hare, 1967). Hence, an employee can cope with only that number of different work stresses for which he or she has a requisite number of relevant responses.

Ashby's law provides a useful method for studying the linkage between work stresses and employees' coping behaviors. Starting with the environmental side of the relationship, determination of the variety of stresses in a particular work context provides a preliminary measure of its 'stress complexity'. Hare (1967) suggested that environmental complexity refers to the variety of distinctions the controller must make to obtain adequate control. In our case, this means the number of different sources of work stress employees must attend to if they are to cope effectively. Because the objective work environment and individuals' perceptions of it may differ, it is necessary to examine stress complexity both objectively (i.e. in terms of the variety of stresses individuals *must* attend to) and subjectively (i.e. in terms of the variety of distinctions employees *actually* make) and to compare the two. This indicates the fit between the work environment's actual stress demands and employees' ability to recognize them. A poor fit between the two measures identifies those situations where the work environment has too much or too little stress variety for the detection capability of it occupants. Variety overload may adversely affect feedback error, lag, and gain; hence the quantity, quality, and timing of information needed to choose adjustment processes. This seems particularly pertinent to knowledge workers. It has been found, for example, that qualitative overload was significantly related to lower self-esteem (and consequently, to less adaptive behavior) among professors (French et al., 1965), and to higher cholesterol levels among tax accountants (Friedman et al., 1958). Conversely, variety underload may not provide sufficient challenge to the person's decision-making capacity, leading to boredom or atrophy of the choice process. Heller's (1975) fictional but highly illuminating account of a stressed manager aptly illustrates: 'I am bored with my work very often now. Everything routine that comes in I pass along to somebody else. This makes my boredom worse. It's a real problem to decide whether it's more boring to do something boring than to pass along everything boring that comes in to somebody else and then have nothing to do at all.'

Turning to the response side of the relationship, determination of the variety of the individual's adjustment processes provides a measure of his or her 'response complexity'. Here, we are concerned with both the number of possible coping behaviors and their appropriateness for reducing strain. The former requires some method for categorizing and counting responses; the latter, for assessing their relevance to specific work stresses. This is a pertinent point, for response complexity is meaningful only if it represents the variety of responses appropriate to a given situation. Measurement of response complexity is likely to show that people differ in their behavioral repertoires. Indeed, Hartston and Mottram (1975) found distinct behavioral characteristics for a variety of different managerial jobs among a sample of 603 UK middle managers. Bank managers were people oriented, more conservative and conscientious than the norm; accountants were precise and objective; salesmen were outgoing, adaptable, and competitive. Moreover, it draws attention to the appropriateness of specific adjustment processes to particular sources of stress. For example, an employee may have a large variety of responses, yet few that are suited to the work stresses he or she encounters.

The foregoing discussion suggests that employee response complexity must match workplace stress complexity if strain is to be reduced effectively. Failure to match variety with variety may lead to either stress overload or underload. It is open to question how much of either condition people can tolerate. Further, Ashby's law underscores the need to map the objective work environment onto both employees' detection capabilities and repertoires of available responses. This would provide a preliminary indication of individuals' capacity to detect different sources of stress and to respond to them appropriately.

Ashby's law also directs attention to two major strategies for personal stress management: increase the person's response complexity or reduce the environment's stress complexity. The former requires learning new coping behaviors; the latter, simplifying the environment to more manageable levels of complexity. Examination of both methods is needed to provide a fuller account of employees' coping decisions, including the personal and situational factors that affect each strategy; the actual methods whereby employees acquire new behavior and simplify their environment; the effects of each strategy on subsequent stress reduction. For example, habitual responses to stress (e.g. escapist drinking, excessive smoking, reduced aspiration, etc.) can reduce the probability of learning new behaviors (Zajonc, 1966). Similarly, certain simplification methods (e.g. selective perception, grouping common stresses, abstraction, etc.) may neglect important sources of work stress.

Implementation of Adjustment Processes

The third phase of the stress cycle involves performance of coping behavior. OS researchers tend to focus on the effects of situational demand (or arousal) on task performance, investigating the shape of the relationship (e.g. linear or curvilinear) and the personal and situational factors (e.g. ability and task difficulty) that modify it (Scott, 1966; Lowe, 1971; Lowe and McGrath, 1971). Although this research provides considerable knowledge of how demand affects performance, it is limited primarily to the statics of the relationship; the relationship between different magnitudes of demand and performance. Cybernetic theory, on the other hand, extends this analysis to include an essential time dimension. Based on the premise that successive responses either gradually or discretely change successive strains (and vice-versa), cybernetics focuses on the time variant aspects of the relationship—i.e. the relationship between the rate at which the response changes (i.e. its first and second time derivatives) and the rate at which the strain changes (i.e. its first and second time derivatives). This is necessary because successive responses and strains both take place in time.

Consideration of time is needed to understand the dynamics of the strain–adjustment process relationship. It is likely, for example, that people adjust the rate at which their behavior changes (e.g. its intensity and speed) to match the rate at which strain changes (i.e. the magnitude of difference between the preferred and actual). Moreover, ability and task difficulty are likely to affect this matching process (McGrath, 1976). The more able or experienced the person, the better she or he should be able to vary the rate of behavioral change to account for variation in the rate at which strain changes. Conversely, the more difficult the stress situation, the harder it is likely to be to match variations in behavioral and stimulus rates of change.

Cooper and Marshall (1976) presented a hypothetical example of work stress and coping behavior that clearly shows the need to study adjustment processes dynamically. They discussed a manager who received a hazily worded request from a superior; his reactions to the ambiguous message might take one of two forms: maladaptive (e.g. delay in recognizing the ambiguity), or adaptive (e.g. seek clarity). Although Cooper and Marshall (1976) analyzed the choice of adjustment behavior and its likely consequences on the stress situation, they failed to consider the time variants of each. A more dynamic analysis might have revealed how changes in the rate at which the manager's response varies affect changes in the rate at which the ambiguous request varies. The manager, for instance, may seek to clarify the request with his or her superior. If the rate at which the ambiguity diminishes is slow, the manager may intensify the rate at which he or she seeks clarity, and so on. Perhaps this process may reach a point of diminishing returns, where increasing rates of clarity seeking reap decreasing rates of request clarity. The major point of this illustration is that dynamic analysis of the demand–performance relationship accounts for temporal variability in coping behavior.

Although measurement and analysis of time-variant variables seem formidable in the OS field, research along these lines is needed to more fully understand the dynamic quality of adjustment processes. Most of the research in OS has been done retrospectively or at a single point in time. Relatively little research has been designed on either a long-term basis or prospectively by collecting data on a representative sample and following that group over time. Because most of our current OS knowledge is based on cross-sectional studies, we have limited capacity to make strong causal inferences. Longitudinal research is needed to assess accurately the nature of the interrelationships between employees and workplace stressors, and to develop clearer epidemiological pictures of both the stressed and non-stressed person.

Affects of Adjustment Processes on Stress or Threat Situation

The final stage of the stress cycle concerns the impact of coping behavior on the stress situation. McGrath (1976) suggested that stress researchers tend to overlook this relationship because either the effect takes place outside of the person or the behavior-to-situation link is assumed to be perfect in the laboratory settings where much of this research takes place. This apparent oversight impedes knowledge of OS. Work environments are sufficiently complex and uncertain to render the situational effects of coping behavior problematical. Here, exogenous factors, such as the task behavior of interdependent co-workers and the structural features of the wider organization, interact with employee adjustment processes to affect their consequences. A fuller account of these interactions is needed to understand the actual versus intended effects of adjustment processes.

Cybernetic theory draws attention to the cumulative effects of adjustment processes. Based on the premise that information about the outcome of behavior affects subsequent behavior, it raises the essential issue of whether such feedback is actually reducing strain (negative feedback) or increasing it (positive feedback). The concepts of negative and positive feedback may make possible more precise descriptions of the cumulative development of both adaptive and maladaptive stress cycles. A negative feedback (or adaptive) cycle implies that successive coping behaviors interact favorably with the situation to decrease strain; conversely, a positive feedback (or maladaptive) cycle suggests that a succession of response–situation interactions amplifies strain.

Much of the OS research focuses on the relationship between work stresses and symptoms of occupational ill-health. Although this static analysis suggests that specific work characteristics (e.g. work overload, role ambiguity, overpromotion, etc.) may lead to cardiovascular disease and mental ill-health, it fails to account for the progressive development of such adverse effects of work. The concept of positive feedback provides a framework for addressing this issue. It raises the possibility that successive adjustment processes may amplify strain inadvertently; the cumulative effects of this vicious cycle may eventually result in heart disease or mental illness. An employee, for instance, may respond to an overpromotion by devoting longer hours to work; this may lead to a still higher promotion which, in turn, elicits longer work hours, and so on. Eventually, the employee may collapse from mental and physical exhaustion. This example points to the need to trace more fully the succession of behavioral and situational interactions that result in occupational ill-health. This may lead to the identification of particular stress syndromes—i.e. vicious cycles of stress amplification. Similarly, study of response–environment linkages that result in reduced strain (i.e. negative feedback cycles) may result in a clearer knowledge of the behavioral and situational factors that reduce strain.

The above discussion points out the pitfalls of studying stress from either an individual or situational perspective alone. Because the actual effects of coping behavior are in part determined by the environment, the interaction of both must be considered. This suggests the need for a contingency approach to understanding the response–situation linkage: how specific individual differences interact with particular situational variables to affect strain. Cybernetic theory suggests that such interaction effects take place over time; hence the need to study the cumulative (short- and long-term) effects of a succession of response–situation linkages.

Organization Implications

The cybernetic theory of occupational stress presented here has significant implications for how organizations can ameliorate work stresses and help employees better cope with them. It draws attention to three key aspects of OS that can inform how organizations design and implement stress interventions: (1) the P–E interaction; (2) the information feedback that is needed to detect strain in the workplace and to devise and implement effective coping strategies; and (3) the temporal process underlying the stress cycle. Each is discussed more fully below.

P–E Interaction

Cybernetic theory suggests that both the person and the environment (and the interaction between them) are essential referents for understanding and resolving OS. Following a medical model, organizations have traditionally addressed OS from the person side of the relationship (Murphy, 1995). They have implemented a number of practices aimed at helping employees understand stress–health relationships and gain the skills to manage workplace stresses. These individual-oriented interventions include relaxation techniques such as meditation and biofeedback; health facilities for physical exercise; time-management practices; wellness programs; and stress-inoculation training which helps employees identify stress indicators and devise personal coping behaviors. Evidence suggests that these personal approaches can provide employees with better coping skills and reduce indicators of strain such as anxiety, depression, and blood pressure (Ivancevich *et al.*, 1990). These positive effects are typically short-term, however, pointing to the need to address the environmental conditions giving rise to experienced strain. Unless organizations also improve the workplace side of the relationship, the underlying causes of OS are likely to persist.

Researchers have identified a diversity of organizational conditions as potential stresses and threats to employees (Cooper and Marshall, 1976; Hurrell and Murphy, 1992). These include factors having to do with job design such as workload and autonomy; role in the organization such as role conflict and ambiguity; relationships with supervisors and peers; career development such as over- or underpromotion; rewards such as pay inequity; and structure such as bureaucratic practices and communication patterns. Examination of these conditions suggests that a large number of management and organization innovations not typically associated with OS can have applicability in this area. In the field of organization development, for example, interventions have been developed for improving many of the workplace factors that can be stresses and threats (Cummings and Worley, 1997). Job enrichment, employee involvement, and self-managing work teams can provide employees with the autonomy and social support needed to reduce strain. Role clarification interventions can help supervisors and employees reduce role ambiguity and conflict. Skill-based pay and gainsharing can help organizations create equitable reward systems. Career development interventions can help employees choose appropriate career paths and develop themselves accordingly. Decentralized structures and reengineering can facilitate effective communication and workflows.

In sum, a cybernetic perspective greatly expands the kinds of interventions that organizations typically consider for addressing OS. It directs attention to both sides of the P–E relationship and to designing comprehensive OS interventions. Person-oriented programs can help employees gain the knowledge and skills to detect and cope with stresses and threats more effectively. Environment-oriented interventions can help to improve the workplace conditions giving rise to experienced strain in the first place. Both types of changes are needed to reduce workplace strains and to assure that those results persist long-term.

Information Feedback

Cybernetic theory points to the information that is needed to detect strain in the workplace and to devise and implement effective coping strategies. Despite researchers' admonitions to the contrary (Newman and Beehr, 1979; Latack and Havlovic, 1992), organizations have tended to design stress interventions based on limited information of workplace stresses and threats, of individual differences in employees' reactions to them, and of intervention effects. Lack of information about stresses and individual differences can lead to poor choices of stress interventions. Insufficient knowledge of effects can make it difficult or impossible to adjust or modify the interventions if necessary.

From a cybernetic perspective, assessing stresses and threats in the workplace requires information about employees' preferred and actual working conditions, so a comparison can be made between the two. The greater the discrepancy between the preferred and the actual, the greater the likelihood of experienced strain. Moreover, because not all strains require equal attention, information is needed about the relative importance of working conditions for employees' well-being. Stress interventions would have the greatest effect by focusing on the most important working conditions showing the greatest discrepancy between the preferred and the actual.

Organizations can collect information on workplace stresses through a variety of methods, from informal discussions with workers to standardized questionnaires administered to large groups of employees (Murphy, 1995). These data-collection techniques can be designed to elicit employee responses about what working conditions are important to their well-being, what the preferred state of those conditions should be, and what the actual state is. For example, a focus group composed of employees from different organization levels and functions could be asked to discuss the importance of various working conditions, such as job design, supervisor and peer relationships, reward systems, career opportunities, communication, and the like. The discussion could also address participants' preferences about these conditions as well as their actual state. This information could then be used to design appropriate stress interventions. In settings involving large numbers of employees, questionnaires could be used to collect similar information on working conditions. Motivational researchers have developed instruments to assess employees' perceptions of the importance of working conditions including preferences and actual conditions (Locke, 1969). These methods could be applied to creating stress questionnaires or to modifying existing standardized instruments, such as the occupational stress indicator (Cooper *et al.*, 1988) or the occupational stress inventory (Osipow and Davis, 1988).

In addition to information about work stresses, organizations need knowledge of intervention effects to guide change programs and to modify them if necessary. As suggested by Cummings and Worley (1997), such information feedback should provide indicators both of whether the stress-management program is being implemented properly (implementation feedback) and whether it is having the intended results (evaluation feedback). Researchers have long called for conceptual models specifying how particular OS interventions can be expected to affect specific workplace stresses and indicators of strain (Newman and Beehr, 1979; Latack and Havlovic, 1992). In addition to guiding stress diagnosis and intervention design, these models can be used to develop measures of the interventions themselves and of their expected effects. For example, an organization might create an on-site health facility based on the belief that it will improve employees' coping behaviors and reduce indictors of strain such as high blood pressure, anxiety, and somatic complaints. In light of this conception, measures of health facility usage and of strain indicators could inform the organization how well the intervention is being implemented and whether it is having the intended effects.

To be effective, cybernetic theory suggests that such information feedback must be accurate, timely, and descriptive of intervention gains or losses. This means that the measures described above need to be valid indicators of OS interventions and effects; they need to be collected repeatedly and at relatively short time intervals; they need to be compared to preferred baselines or targets. Such measures would provide a series of snapshots of how the OS intervention is progressing.

Temporal Process

Cybernetic theory emphasizes the need to consider OS temporally. It directs attention to the sequential stages of the stress cycle, from detection of strain to affects of adjustment processes on the stress situation. Because these stages occur over time, both the person and the environment (and their interaction) are likely to be undergoing change as the stress cycle unfolds. This suggests that OS is an ongoing process, not a periodic episode occurring between employees and their work environment. Thus, stress management needs to be a continuous process for addressing and resolving workplace stresses, not a discrete program with temporal boundaries.

This dynamic perspective has important implications for how organizations design and implement stress-management interventions. It points to the need to build stress management into the organization like other approaches to continuous improvement, such as total quality management (Deming, 1982; Juran, 1989), self-design (Mohrman and Cummings, 1989), and organization learning (Senge, 1990). These approaches rely heavily on continual measurement, problem solving, and employee involvement. Based on organization values and strategic objectives

(Cooper and Jackson, 1997), improvement goals are set, progress is measured against them, and necessary changes are made. This feedback–change process seeks to improve the organization continually. It involves employees directly in the process to gain their valuable input and commitment to change.

These continuous change and improvement practices can be applied to stress management. They can help organizations address the temporal aspects of OS as well as the P–E interaction and the information feedback needed to manage workplace stress. For example, organizations could involve employees in setting preferences for how the workplace should be designed and managed. These preferences would guide the stress-management process; they would provide the values against which the workplace is measured and improved. Based on these preferences, instruments could be designed to measure the workplace including individual differences among employees and indicators of OS. These data could be fed back to employees, so they can analyze them and devise appropriate improvements. This process could be repeated periodically throughout the organization. Although it is aimed at continuously improving the OS of the workplace, stress management could readily be integrated with similar processes geared to quality and performance improvements.

This theory is drawn from the authors' paper 'A cybernetic theory of occupational stress', published in the journal *Human Relations* 1979, 32 (5), 395–418.

References

Appley, M. H. and Trumbull, R. (1986) *Dynamics of Stress*. New York: Plenum.

Arnold, J., Cooper, C. L., and Robertson, I. R. (1995) *Work Psychology*. London: FT-Pitman.

Arthur, R. J. and Gunderson, E. K. (1965) 'Promotion and mental illness in the navy', *Journal of Occupational Medicine*, 7, 452–456.

Ashby, W. R. (1954) *Design for a Brain*. London: Chapman & Hall.

Ashby, W. R. (1966) *An Introduction to Cybernetics*. New York: Wiley.

Basowitz, H., Korchin, S. I., and Grinker, R. R. (1958) 'Anxiety in life stress', *Journal of Psychology*, 38 (2), 503–510.

Buck, V. (1972) *Working under Pressure*. London: Staple Press.

Buckley, W. (1967) *Sociology and Modern Systems Theory*. Englewood Cliffs, NJ: Prentice-Hall.

Cannon, W. (1932) *The Wisdom of the Body*. New York: Norton.

Cartwright, D. and Zander, A. (1960) *Group Dynamics*. Evanston, IL: Row Peterson.

Cofer, C. N. and Appley, M. H. (1964) *Motivation: Theory and Research*. New York: Wiley.

Cooper, C. L. (1996) *Handbook of Stress, Medicine and Health*. Florida: CRC Press.

Cooper, C. L. and Jackson, S. (1997) *Creating Tomorrow's Organizations: A Handbook for Future Research in Organizational Behavior*. Chichester: John Wiley and Sons.

Cooper, C. L. and Marshall, J. (1976) 'Occupational sources of stress: A review of the literature relating to coronary heart disease and mental ill health', *Journal of Occupational Psychology*, 49, 11–28.

Cooper, C. L. and Payne, R. (1988) *Causes, Coping and Consequences of Stress at Work*. New York: Wiley.

Cooper, C. L. and Payne, R. (1991) *Personality and Stress*. New York: Wiley.

Cooper, C. L., Sloan, S. J., and Williams, S. (1988) *Occupational Stress Indicator: Management Guide*. Windsor: NFER-Nelson.

Cropamzomo, R. and Greenberg, J. (1997) Progress in organizational justice. In C. L. Cooper and I. R. Robertson, *International Review of Industrial and Organizational Psychology*, vol. 12, pp. 317–372.

Cummings, T. and Cooper, C. L. (1979) 'A cybernetic theory of occupational stress', *Human Relations*, 32, 395–418.

Cummings, T. and Worley, C. (1997) *Organization Development and Change*, 6th edn. Cincinnati: South-Western.

Deming, W. (1982) *Quality, Productivity, and Competitive Advantage*. Cambridge: MIT Center for Advanced Engineering Study.

Elkinton, J. R. and Danowski, T. S. (1955) *The Body Fluids: Basic Physiology and Practical Therapeutics*. Baltimore: William and Wilkins.

Erikson, J., Pugh, W., and Gunderson, A. (1972) 'Status congruence as a predictor of job satisfaction', *Journal of Applied Psychology*, 56, 523–525.

French, J. R. P., Tupper, C. J., and Mueller, E. I. (1965) *Workload of University Professors*. Unpublished research report, University of Michigan, Ann Arbor.

Friedman, M., Rosenman, R. H., and Carrol, V. (1958) 'Changes in serum cholesterol and blood clotting time in men subjected to cyclic variations of occupational stress', *Circulation*, 17, 852–861.

Hare, V. (1967) *Systems Analysis: A Diagnostic Approach*. New York: Harcourt, Brace, and World.

Hartston, W. R. and Mottram. R. D. (1975) 'Personality profiles of managers: A study of occupational differences', *ITRU Publication SL9* (Cambridge).

Heller, J. (1975) *Something Happened*. New York: Ballantine Books.

Hurrell, J. J. and Murphy, L. R. (1992) An overview of occupational stress and health. In W. M. Rom (ed.) *Environmental and Occupational Medicine*, 2nd edn. (pp. 675–684). Boston: Little, Brown.

Ivancevich, J. M., Matteson, M. T., Freedman, S. M., and Phillips, J. (1990) 'Worksite stress management interventions', *American Psychologist*, 45, 225–261.

Juran, J. (1989) *Juran on Leadership for Quality: An Executive Handbook*. New York: Free Press.

Latack, J. C. and Havlovic, S. J. (1992) 'Coping with job stress: A conceptual evaluation framework for coping measures', *Journal of Organizational Behavior*, 13, 479–508.

Lazarus, R. S. (1966) *Psychological Stress and the Coping Process*. New York: McGraw-Hill.

Locke, E. (1969) 'What is job satisfaction?' *Organizational Behavior and Human Performance*, 4, 309–336.

Locke, E., McClear, K., and Knight, D. (1996) Self esteem and work. In C. L. Cooper and I. R. Robertson, *International Review of Industrial and Organizational Psychology*, vol. 11, (pp. 1–32).

Lowe, R. (1971) Stress, arousal and task performance of little league baseball players. Unpublished doctoral dissertation, University of Illinois, Urbana.

Lowe, R. and McGrath, J. (1971) *Stress, Arousal and Performance: Some Findings Calling for a New Theory*. Project report, AF 1161-1167, AFOSR.

McGrath, J. (1976) Stress and behavior in organizations. In M. Dunnette (ed.), *Handbook of Industrial and Organizational Psychology*. Chicago: Rand McNally.

Miller, J. (1965) 'Living systems: Basic concepts', *Behavioral Science*, 10, 193–237.

Mohrman, S. and Cummings, T. (1989) *Self-designing Organizations: Learning How to Create High Performance*. Reading, MA: Addison Wesley.

Murphy, L. R. (1995) Occupational stress management: Current status and future directions. In C. Cooper and D. Rousseau (eds.), *Trends in Organizational Behavior*, Vol. 2. (pp. 1–14). Chichester: John Wiley and Sons.

Newman, J. D. and Beehr, T. (1979) 'Personal and organizational strategies for handling job stress: A review of research and opinion', *Personnel Psychology*, 32, 1–43.

Notterman J. and Trumbull, R. (1950) 'Note on self-regulating systems and stress', *Behavioral Science*, 4, 324–327.

Osipow, S. H. and Davis, A. S. (1988) 'The relationship of coping resources to occupational stress and strain', *Journal of Vocational Behavior*, 32, 1–15.

Osler, W. (1910) 'The umleian lectures on angina pectoris', *The Lancet*, 1, 696–700, 839–844, 947–977.

Ryle, J. A. and Russell, W. T. (1949) 'The natural history of coronary disease: A clinical and epidemiological study', *British Heart Journal*, 11, 370–389.

Sauter, S. and Murphy, L. (1995) *Organizational Risk Factors for Job Stress*. Washington, DC: APA.

Sauter, S., Hurrell, J., and Cooper, C. L. (1989) *Job Control and Health*. Chichester: John Wiley and Sons.

Scott, W. E. (1966) 'Activation theory and task design', *Organizational Behavior and Human Performance*, 1, 1–30.

Selye, H. (1946) 'The general adaptation syndrome and the diseases of adaptation', *Journal of Clinical Endocrinology*, 6, 117.

Senge, P. (1990) *The Fifth Discipline: The Art and Practice of the Learning Organization*. New York: Doubleday.

Shibutani, T. (1968) A cybernetic approach to motivation. In W. Buckley (ed.), *Modern Systems Research for the Behavioral Scientist*. Chicago: Aldine.

Vernon, M. D. (1962) *The Psychology of Perception*. London: Penguin.

Weiner, N. (1948) *Cybernetics*. Cambridge, MA: MIT Press.

Weiner, N. (1954) *The Human Use of Human Beings*. New York: Doubleday Anchor.

Zajonc, R. B. (1966) *Social Psychology: An Experimental Approach*. Belmont, CA: Wadsworth.

6

....

Cybernetic Theory of Stress, Coping, and Well-Being:
Review and Extension to Work and Family

Jeffrey R. Edwards

Cybernetic theory provides a useful general framework for understanding human behavior. Cybernetic theory was originally developed to describe the functioning of self-regulating systems (Ashby, 1966, Wiener, 1948). According to cybernetic theory, the purpose of self-regulating systems is to minimize discrepancies between environmental inputs and internal standards that serve as reference criteria. This purpose is achieved through the negative feedback loop, which assesses discrepancies between environmental input and internal standards and attempts to minimize these discrepancies by changing the environment, adjusting standards, or both. Cybernetic theory has been adapted to explain human behavior, often under the rubric of control theory (Carver and Scheier, 1981; Miller *et al.*, 1960; Powers, 1973), and has been further elaborated to explain specific psychological and behavioral phenomena, such as motivation (Hyland, 1988; Klein, 1989; Lord and Hanges, 1987; Taylor *et al.*, 1984), goal-setting (Campion and Lord, 1982), impression management (Bozeman and Kacmar, 1997), and mental and physical health (Hyland, 1987; Pyszczynski and Greenberg, 1987; Seeman, 1989).

Principles of cybernetic theory have also been applied to theories of stress and coping (Carver and Scheier, 1985; Cummings and Cooper, 1979; Edwards, 1992; Latack *et al.*, 1995; McGrath, 1976; Tapp, 1985). Drawing from cybernetic theory, Edwards (1992) developed an integrative theory of stress, coping, and well-being in organizations. This theory views stress, coping, and well-being as critical elements of a negative feedback loop, in which discrepancies between environmental inputs and internal standards induce stress, which damages well-being and stimulates coping efforts intended to resolve discrepancies between the environment and standards. This theory integrates other theories that define stress in terms of person–environment congruence and incorporate feedback relationships linking coping to the sources of stress (e.g. Beehr and Newman, 1978; Cummings and Cooper, 1979; French *et al.*, 1982; Kahn *et al.*, 1964; Lazarus and Folkman, 1984; McGrath, 1976; Newman and Beehr, 1979; Schuler, 1980).

This chapter reviews and extends the cybernetic theory of stress, coping, and well-being presented by Edwards (1992). First, basic principles of cybernetic theory are summarized, and recent criticisms of the application of cybernetic theory to human behavior are addressed. Second, definitions and core mechanisms of the theory proposed by Edwards (1992) are discussed. Third, empirical evidence relevant to cybernetic stress theory is summarized. Fourth, the theory is extended to encompass stress, coping, and well-being associated with work and family. The chapter concludes by discussing implications of the extended theory to stress and coping research.

Overview of Cybernetic Theory

Basic Principles

A basic model of the cybernetic control process is shown in Figure 6.1 (Carver and Scheier, 1982). Starting at the bottom, the model shows that the environment is sensed by the input function, which then feeds information regarding the environment into the comparator. The comparator evaluates environmental input relative to internal standards, which are provided by the reference criterion. If this comparison indicates a discrepancy between the environment and standards, the output function is engaged, which attempts to resolve the discrepancy by changing the environment. The model shows that the environment may also be influenced by a disturbance emanating from outside the control system. This basic model represents a negative feedback loop, given that its purpose is to minimize (i.e. negate) discrepancies between environmental input and internal standards.

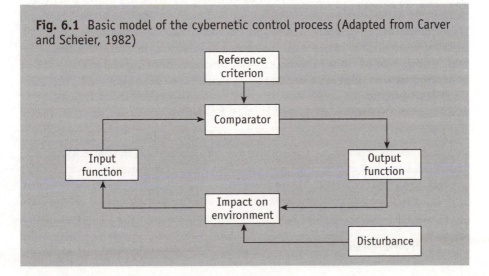

Fig. 6.1 Basic model of the cybernetic control process (Adapted from Carver and Scheier, 1982)

Applications to Human Behavior

Applications of the basic cybernetic model to human behavior (e.g. Carver and Scheier, 1981; Miller *et al.*, 1960; Powers, 1973) have translated the components of the model into perceptual, cognitive, and behavioral constructs. Specifically, the input function represents the person's perception of the environment, and the reference criterion corresponds to the desires, values, or goals of the person. The comparator signifies the cognitive comparison of the perceived environment to the person's desires, values, or goals. The output function refers to behavioral attempts by the person to influence the environment, and the disturbance represents forces other than the person (e.g. powerful others, social structures, chance events) that may impact the environment.

Most applications of the basic model in Figure 6.1 to human behavior include two important elaborations. First, a path is often added from the output function to the reference criterion, thereby indicating that the person can resolve discrepancies by adjusting standards to conform with the environment (e.g. Campion and Lord, 1982; Klein, 1989; Lord and Hanges, 1987; Taylor *et al.*, 1984). Second, the single feedback loop in Figure 6.1 is viewed as one element in a system of multiple feedback loops (Carver and Scheier, 1981; Powers, 1973). These loops are arranged hierarchically, with each level of the hierarchy representing feedback and regulation with respect to standards at a particular level of abstraction. Standards at higher levels of abstraction signify superordinate goals, whereas standards at low levels represent subordinate goals. Throughout this goal hierarchy, feedback loops at higher levels act by specifying standards for one or more feedback loops at lower levels. For example, a salesperson with an ambitious superordinate goal regarding sales performance may set high subordinate goals regarding new accounts, repeat business, and customer satisfaction. These subordinate goals invoke feedback processes that specify goals at even lower levels, such as making calls, providing samples, and offering discounts to potential customers. The fulfillment of subordinate goals creates changes in the environment that provide input to feedback loops throughout the hierarchy. This input is interpreted at a level of abstraction appropriate for each feedback loop. Thus, calling a targeted number of potential customers in a day not only provides input relevant to the goal of calling customers, but also generates input for the goals of generating new accounts and meeting overall sales targets.

Criticisms of Cybernetic Models of Human Behavior

Applications of cybernetic theory to human behavior capture the dynamic process by which people appraise the environment relative to internal standards, how these appraisals stimulate efforts to change or adapt to the environment, and how this process operates at different levels of abstraction to guide behavior. Despite the general utility of cybernetic theory, applications of the theory to human behavior have generated criticism (e.g. Bandura, 1989; Locke, 1991, 1994; Locke and Latham, 1990). Most of these criticisms fall into four areas. First, critics argue that, although cybernetic theory may describe the behavior of mechanical systems, it cannot describe the conscious, self-motivated behavior of humans. Adaptations of the theory to human behavior have borrowed concepts from other theories and, according to critics, these adaptations leave little that is unique to cybernetic theory. Second, critics have asserted that the sole purpose of cybernetic systems is discrepancy reduction. Given this assertion, the easiest way to reduce discrepancies is merely to lower standards, thereby obviating the need to change the environment. This narrow view of discrepancy reduction is obviously at odds with the behavior of humans, who create discrepancies by setting goals and resolve discrepancies by striving to attain goals, often by changing the environment rather than by lowering goals. Third, cybernetic models have been characterized as reactive, meaning they predict behavior in response to feedback but do not account for behavior arising from forethought regarding future goals and potential discrepancies. Finally, critics have noted that cybernetic theories of human behavior were derived deductively, arguing that this approach to theory development is inferior to an inductive, grounded theory approach. Based on these criticisms, some critics recommend that we abandon all cybernetic theories of human behavior (Locke, 1994).

Closer examination of cybernetic theories of human behavior indicate that these criticisms are specious and unwarranted. First, cybernetic theories of human behavior have indeed elaborated basic cybernetic principles to reflect the complexity of human cognition and action. However, these elaborations have left intact the core mechanism of cybernetic theory, i.e. the negative feedback loop (Klein, 1989). Moreover, these elaborations address the very criticisms of cybernetic theory as mechanistic, thereby rendering the theory appropriate for human behavior. Furthermore, Powers (1978) has pointed out that cybernetic theory was originally developed to facilitate the design of control systems that mimic human behavior, such as automated servomechanisms that control production processes. Thus, cybernetic theory has not been adapted to describe human behavior, but rather was initially developed to characterize human behavior as it naturally occurred.

Second, cybernetic theories of behavior involve not only discrepancy reduction, but also discrepancy creation (Klein, 1989; Lord and Levy, 1994). Cybernetic control begins with the selection of a standard. Unless this standard happens to match environmental input, a discrepancy is created. Moreover, cybernetic theories of behavior emphasize that feedback loops are arranged hierarchically, such that loops at higher levels set standards for loops at lower levels (Carver and Scheier, 1981; Powers, 1973). Through this mechanism, higher-level loops create discrepancies for lower-level loops, and efforts to resolve discrepancies at lower levels serve to resolve discrepancies at higher levels. Resolving discrepancies by simply lowering their standards is unlikely, because doing so would fail to resolve discrepancies at higher levels. One could argue that all discrepancies could be resolved by simply lowering the standard for the loop at the highest level. However, the standard at this level represents basic conditions for survival (Powers, 1973), and lowering this standard would be tantamount to giving up on life.

Third, cybernetic models of behavior do not rule out forethought. Standards at higher levels, such as the system level described by Powers (1973), entail long-term goals (e.g. live a full, healthy life) that may take years to achieve. These higher-level goals engage control processes at lower levels that, in combination, are expected to facilitate ongoing progress toward long-term higher-level goals. Setting standards at lower levels requires forethought as to which standards are likely to generate behavior that will ultimately fulfill long-term goals. Moreover, control processes at lower levels occur more rapidly than those at higher levels (Campion and Lord, 1982; Carver and Scheier, 1982; Lord and Levy, 1994), and as these processes unfold, the person may shift attention between lower and higher levels to ensure that current efforts to resolve short-term discrepancies facilitate the gradual fulfillment of long-term discrepancies. Thus, forethought is integral to the selection and setting of lower-level standards to achieve higher-level goals.

Finally, theory development may occur both inductively and deductively (Dubin, 1976), and neither approach is inherently superior. Indeed, many recent cybernetic theories of behavior were derived deductively, tracing their core ideas to classic sources such as Ashby (1966), Miller (1965), Wiener (1948), and von Bertalanffy (1968). However, these sources contain cybernetic models with inductive origins, in that they attempted to account for the observed behavior of living systems. In any case, cybernetic theories of human behavior should be judged on their inherent merits, not their origins (Klein, 1989). Moreover, debates regarding the internal logic of cybernetic theories must be supplemented with empirical research. Of particular value are studies that compare predictions from cybernetic theory with those from competing models, such as goal-setting theory (Phillips *et al.*, 1996). Due to the paucity of such studies, the utility of cybernetic theories relative to other theories of human behavior has yet to be determined.

Cybernetic Theory of Stress, Coping, and Well-Being

Definitions of Core Constructs

This section provides an overview of the cybernetic theory of stress, coping, and well-being developed by Edwards (1992). According to this theory, stress refers to a discrepancy between the perceptions and desires of the person, provided this discrepancy is viewed as important by the person (Cummings and Cooper, 1979; Harrison, 1978; Schuler, 1980). Perceptions are non-evaluative subjective representations of events, situations, and conditions, including the physical and social environment surrounding the person and the person's own characteristics (e.g. gender, social status, competence, physical appearance). Perceptions are not limited to the present, but may entail recollections of the past or anticipations of the future. Desires represent what the person consciously wants and encompass goals, values, and interests (Cummings and Cooper, 1979; Locke, 1976; Schuler, 1980). Importance is the degree to which the person considers a discrepancy central to his or her overall well-being (Beehr and Bhagat, 1985; Schuler, 1980).

Some investigators define stress as a situational condition or event (e.g. Cooper and Marshall, 1976; Kahn and Quinn, 1970; Matteson and Ivancevich, 1979) or as a psychological or physiological response of the person (e.g. Ivancevich and Matteson, 1980; Martin and Schermerhorn, 1983; Parker and DeCotiis, 1983; Selye, 1956).

Situational definitions overlook individual differences in how situations are cognitively appraised. Moreover, situational definitions usually denote a situation as stressful only if it damages well-being, thereby confounding stress with one of its primary outcomes. Response definitions ignore differences in the subjective meaning of situations that may generate the same psychophysiological outcome (Lazarus and Folkman, 1984), as when danger and exercise both produce physiological arousal. Response definitions also exclude episodes in which coping successfully avoids or ameliorates stress, thereby preventing damage to well-being. The definition of stress employed here avoids these problems by incorporating cognitive appraisal as the subjective comparison of perceptions to desires and by defining stress independent of its hypothesized outcomes (i.e. well-being, coping).

Several theories define stress as a discrepancy between environmental demands and the abilities of the person, indicating that stress arises when demands exceed abilities and failure to meet demands has important consequences (Beehr and Bhagat, 1985; Cox, 1987; Lazarus and Folkman, 1984; Shirom, 1982). This definition of stress is consistent with the demands–control model, which posits that strain results when demands exceed decision latitude, a situational determinant of ability (Karasek and Theorell, 1990). The view of stress as excess demands has been challenged by Harrison (1978), who contends that excess demands are stressful only when: (1) failure to meet demands prevents the receipt of desired outcomes (e.g. rewards, approval); or (2) demands are internalized by the person as desired goals, motives, or rules of behavior. In either case, excess demands generate stress only if they create discrepancies between perceptions and desires. Hence, excess demands do not constitute stress itself, but rather are a potential cause of stress. Discrepancies between demands and abilities may also influence coping efficacy, in that coping strategies are more likely to succeed when the demands of the strategy are within the person's abilities (Edwards, 1988, 1992).

Three other key constructs in Edwards' (1992) theory are duration, well-being, and coping. Duration refers to the amount of time the person spends thinking about a discrepancy (Beehr and Bhagat, 1985; Gardner *et al.*, 1989). Duration captures the person's awareness of a discrepancy, which is a necessary condition for the experience of psychological stress (Lazarus and Folkman, 1984; McGrath, 1976). Well-being refers to psychological and physical health, including short-term affective and physiological outcomes and chronic, long-term mental and physical functioning. Unlike strain, which focuses on dysfunction (French *et al.*, 1982), well-being ranges from mental and physical illness to positive mental health and physiological growth and regeneration (Edwards and Cooper, 1988; Karasek *et al.*, 1982; Seeman, 1989). Coping represents efforts to prevent or reduce the negative effects of stress on well-being. To avoid confounding coping with its outcomes, coping is defined as *efforts* to influence stress and well-being, *not* as the successful implementation of these efforts (Edwards, 1988; Lazarus and Folkman, 1984).[1] Coping involves a decision-making process in which

---

[1] Latack *et al.* (1995, p. 328) incorrectly state that Edwards (1992) defines coping as the successful implementation of coping efforts. This statement is incorrect. Quoting directly from Edwards (1992), coping is defined as '*efforts to prevent or reduce the negative effects of stress on well-being*' (emphasis in original) (p. 253). Latack *et al.* (1995) omitted the word 'efforts' from their quotation of this definition.

coping strategies are selected and implemented. This process may range from a careful generation, evaluation, and selection of coping strategies to an intuitive or preconscious coping response (Edwards, 1988). Each coping strategy signifies a causal pathway by which coping may affect stress and well-being. These pathways are described later when the effects of coping are discussed.

Relationships Among Core Constructs

Interrelationships among the core constructs of Edwards' (1992) cybernetic theory are depicted in Figure 6.2.[2] Starting at the left-hand side, perceptions are influenced by the objective characteristics of the person (i.e. self-perception) and the physical and social environment. Perceptions of the self and the environment are filtered, modified, and supplemented by cognitive construction processes (Weick, 1979) and social information (Salancik and Pfeffer, 1978). Social information also affects desires

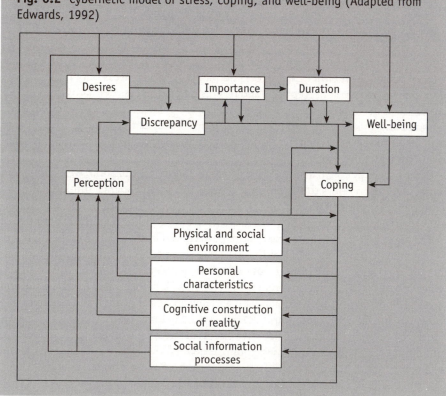

Fig. 6.2 Cybernetic model of stress, coping, and well-being (Adapted from Edwards, 1992)

[2] Although Edwards (1992) proposed that duration moderates the effects of discrepancies on well-being and coping, he did not include duration in the figure depicting the cybernetic model (Edwards, 1992: 248 Figure 3). For clarity, the present chapter depicts the moderating effects of duration in Figure 6.2.

and importance through cues from others regarding the relevance and significance of evaluative standards (Kahn *et al.*, 1964; Salancik and Pfeffer, 1978). Perceptions are cognitively compared to desires, yielding a subjective representation of the magnitude and direction of their discrepancy. This comparison may range from a conscious evaluation to a nearly automatic assessment (Klein, 1989; Lord and Hanges, 1987; Lord and Levy, 1994; Taylor *et al.*, 1984).

Discrepancies between perceptions and desires affect well-being and coping. These effects may take various functional forms, depending on the type of desire involved in the discrepancy (French *et al.*, 1982; Klein, 1989; Naylor *et al.*, 1980; Rice *et al.*, 1985). For desires that represent optima or ideal amounts, either positive or negative discrepancies will damage well-being and stimulate coping. Similar effects will be produced by desires that signify a range of tolerance, provided that perceptions deviate beyond the tolerable range. For desires that represent minimum thresholds, negative discrepancies will damage well-being and evoke coping, whereas positive discrepancies will slightly improve well-being. In contrast, for desires that represent maximum limits, positive discrepancies will damage well-being and produce coping, whereas negative discrepancies will slightly improve well-being. In Figure 6.2, the direct effect of discrepancies on coping indicates that the person may attempt to avoid or reduce stress before well-being is damaged. The indirect effect of discrepancies on coping through well-being signifies that coping may occur after well-being has been damaged.

Figure 6.2 shows that the effects of discrepancies on well-being and coping are moderated by importance and duration. Importance intensifies the effects of discrepancies on well-being and coping (Hyland, 1988; Mobley and Locke, 1970; Rice *et al.*, 1985; Taylor *et al.*, 1984). Likewise, the effects of discrepancies on well-being and coping are intensified by duration, such that well-being and coping are influenced more by those discrepancies upon which the person focuses his or her attention (Beehr and Bhagat, 1985; Carver and Scheier, 1981; Gardner *et al.*, 1989; Hollenbeck, 1989). Importance and duration are affected by discrepancy size, such that larger discrepancies are considered more significant and draw more attention (Lord and Hanges, 1987; Lord and Levy, 1994). Importance also affects duration, with greater attention devoted to discrepancies considered more consequential to the person's overall well-being (Carver, 1994; Klein, 1989; Lord and Hanges, 1987; Lord and Levy, 1994).

As shown in Figure 6.2, coping may influence well-being both directly and indirectly through the determinants and moderators of stress. Coping targeted directly at well-being has been labeled emotion-focused coping (Billings and Moos, 1981; Lazarus and Folkman, 1984) and includes relaxation, catharsis, alcohol and drug use, and other efforts to dampen symptoms without influencing their causes. Coping may affect perception by altering personal characteristics or the physical and social environment, representing problem-focused coping directed toward the self and situation, respectively (Lazarus and Folkman, 1984). Coping may also influence perception through cognitive reconstruction or the selection, reinterpretation, or rejection of social information. Additionally, coping may align desires with perceptions or devalue the importance of stressful discrepancies, both of which represent forms of cognitive reappraisal (Billings and Moos, 1981; Latack, 1986; Lazarus and Folkman,

129

1984). Finally, coping may reduce duration by diverting attention from discrepancies, signifying avoidant coping (Lazarus, 1983).

Figure 6.2 shows that the effects of discrepancies on coping are moderated by environmental and personal factors. Environmental factors include opportunities or constraints regarding coping strategy choice (Mattlin *et al.*, 1990; Terry, 1994) and access to coping resources, such as social support (Cohen, 1988; House *et al.*, 1988). Personal factors refer to coping styles that arise from personality traits (e.g. locus of control, Type A behavior) and cognitive schema that elicit scripted coping strategies (Edwards, 1988; Lord and Hanges, 1987; Menaghan, 1983). Environmental and personal factors also moderate the effects of coping on the sources and moderators of stress. For example, as noted previously, coping efforts are more likely to succeed when the demands of the chosen coping strategy are within the abilities of the person. Likewise, physical constraints and powerful others may impact coping strategy success (Edwards, 1992).

Hierarchy of Multiple Feedback Loops

The basic feedback loop shown in Figure 6.2 is a component of a hierarchy of feedback loops. Powers (1973) classifies this hierarchy into nine levels. At the top of the hierarchy is the system level, which regulates discrepancies involving self-esteem and survival (Carver and Scheier, 1981; Powers, 1973). Next is the principle level, which comprises discrepancies regarding guiding principles or rules such as being a reliable employee or a conscientious boss. Below is the program level, where sequences of behaviors analogous to scripts (Schank and Abelson, 1977) are enacted (e.g. arrive at work on time, provide feedback to subordinates). Lower levels, which primarily involve sensory and motor control, rarely require conscious attention (Powers, 1973) and therefore do not directly influence psychological stress (Edwards, 1992).

The present theory specifies three mechanisms by which higher-level loops activate lower-level loops. First, higher loops may shift desires in lower loops to create discrepancies (Carver and Scheier, 1981; Powers, 1973). For example, a discrepancy regarding progress toward tenure may prompt a professor to increase goals for publication, teaching, and service. Second, higher loops may raise the importance of lower loops. For instance, the desire for job security may heighten the importance of meeting specific performance objectives, such that even small discrepancies regarding these objectives are not tolerated. Third, higher loops may affect duration by directing attention to lower loops, focusing on those loops that are most instrumental to resolving discrepancies at higher levels (Lord and Levy, 1994). These mechanisms may operate concurrently, such that discrepancies created by shifting desires may be assigned greater importance and command more attention.

Higher-level loops may also deactivate loops at lower levels through these three mechanisms. Thus, a lower loop may be deactivated by adjusting its desires to align with perceptual input. Alternately, the importance of a lower loop may be decreased through a reprioritization of desires, values, or goals. Finally, duration may be reduced by ignoring or denying a lower loop. Deactivation of a lower loop is likely when ongoing attempts to resolve its discrepancy fail (Klinger, 1975). Once a lower loop is deactivated, other lower loops linked to the same higher loop may be activated in an attempt to find alternative means for resolving the discrepancy of the higher loop (Hyland, 1988). If all lower loops are exhausted, the higher loop itself may be deactivated, meaning that the desire or goal associated with the higher loop is forsaken (Abramson *et al.*, 1978).

Loops at lower levels may resolve discrepancies in loops at higher levels through two mechanisms. First, environmental factors regulated at lower levels may influence environmental factors at higher levels. This is illustrated by the tenure example cited earlier, in which publishing articles, earning high teaching ratings, and performing service activities lead to the receipt of tenure. Second, loops at different levels may monitor the same feature of the environment but interpret it at different levels of abstraction (Powers, 1973; Carver and Scheier, 1981). For example, carrying out the program of arriving at work on time may be interpreted as being a reliable employee at the principle level and as enhancing one's overall self-esteem at the system level.

Summary

Edwards' (1992) cybernetic theory views stress, coping, and well-being as critical elements of a negative feedback loop. Stress refers to a discrepancy between perceptions and desires, and the effects of this discrepancy intensify as its importance and duration increase. Stress damages well-being and stimulates coping, which signifies efforts to improve well-being either directly or by altering the determinants and moderators of stress. These basic feedback processes are embedded in a hierarchy of feedback loops, in which loops at higher levels activate loops at lower levels, and efforts to resolve discrepancies at lower levels help resolve discrepancies at higher levels. Thus, this theory depicts the dynamic, ongoing process by which people appraise the environment as stressful or benign and attempt to alter or adapt to the environment to reduce stress and improve well-being.

Empirical Studies of Cybernetic Stress Processes

To date, few studies have explicitly tested propositions derived from Edwards' (1992) cybernetic theory. However, evidence regarding certain aspects of the theory is available from studies in the stress, satisfaction, motivation, and control theory literatures. These studies are briefly reviewed in this section, with an emphasis on studies that provide evidence relevant to the core processes underlying Edwards' (1992) theory. This review is intended to provide a general overview of relevant evidence rather than an exhaustive description of individual studies, and more detailed reviews are cited as appropriate.

Determinants of Perceptions

Studies of stress typically measure environmental stressors and perceived stress using self-report measures (Burke *et al.*, 1993). Because of this, very little evidence is available regarding the effects of the objective physical and social environment on perceptions. Evidence across various domains of organizational research indicates that the relationship between objective and self-report measures is modest (Starbuck and Mezias, 1996). However, these studies often construct objective measures based on descriptions from key informants, such as supervisors, job analysts, or the researchers themselves. It is questionable whether these descriptions should be considered objective, given that they are essentially self-reports from alternative perspectives. Despite the shortcomings of available evidence, it appears that perceptions may depend on input from sources other than the objective environment. Two sources indicated by the model in Figure 6.2 are social information and cognitive construction processes, and research supports the contention that perceptions are influenced by these two sources (Thomas and Griffin, 1983; Weick, 1979). However, the relative effects on perceptions of the objective environment, social information, and cognitive construction have yet to be examined.

Effects of Discrepancies Between Perceptions and Desires on Well-Being and Coping

Numerous studies have examined how discrepancies between perceptions and desires relate to various indices of well-being (Assouline and Meir, 1987; Edwards, 1991; Michalos, 1986). Most of these studies have operationalized well-being as self-reported affect, such as job satisfaction. Overall, these studies suggest that satisfaction is related to the discrepancy between perceptions and desires. However, the functional form of this relationship is unclear, because most studies have operationalized the discrepancy between perceptions and desires using either an algebraic, absolute, or squared difference score (Edwards, 1991). Studies using all three of these scores have shown that, for a given data set, each score may yield a significant relationship with well-being (French *et al.*, 1982). Moreover, studies using difference scores to operationalize discrepancies between perceptions and desires suffer from numerous methodological problems that render their results inconclusive (Edwards, 1994; Johns, 1981).

Problems created by using difference scores to represent the discrepancy between perceptions and desires are avoided by studies using polynomial regression analysis to examine the joint relationship of perceptions and desires with well-being (Edwards, 1993, 1994, 1996; Edwards and Harrison, 1993; Elsass and Veiga, 1997; Hesketh and Gardner, 1993; Livingstone *et al.*, 1997). This procedure is based on the premise that perceptions, desires, and well-being are distinct constructs, and their relationship should therefore be viewed as a three-dimensional surface in which perceptions and desires constitute two horizontal axes and well-being represents the vertical axis (Edwards, 1994; Edwards and Parry, 1993). Studies using this procedure have revealed that well-being often decreases as perceptions deviate from desires, although the decrease in well-being is sometimes more pronounced when perceptions fall short of desires than when perceptions exceed desires. These studies have also indicated that, when perceptions match desires, well-being is often higher when perceptions and desires are both high than when both are low. Further generalizations are difficult to draw, however, because surfaces relating perceptions and desires to well-being vary according to the content dimension on which perceptions and desires are assessed (e.g. Edwards, 1993, 1994; Edwards and Harrison, 1993; Hesketh and Gardner, 1993).

Although numerous studies have examined how discrepancies between perceptions and desires relate to well-being, few studies have examined the effects of discrepancies on coping. According to Edwards (1992), these effects should mirror those for well-being, such that discrepancies simultaneously reduce well-being and increase coping efforts. Available evidence suggests that coping efforts intensify as discrepancies increase (Caplan *et al.*, 1984; Mayes and Ganster, 1988) and that the choice of coping strategies may depend on personal characteristics such as gender (Eagan and Walsh, 1995). Relevant evidence is also provided by studies of the effects of goal–performance discrepancies on subsequent performance and goals (e.g. Bandura and Cervone, 1986; Campion and Lord, 1982; Kernan and Lord, 1989; Wood and Bandura, 1989). These studies suggest that, when goals are appraised as attainable, people attempt to resolve goal–performance discrepancies by raising performance. However, when goals seem unattainable, people tend to resolve discrepancies by lowering goals. Goals may seem unattainable if discrepancies are particularly large (Bandura and Cervone, 1986; Kernan and Lord, 1989) or if repeated attempts to achieve goals have failed (Campion and Lord, 1982; Carver *et al.*, 1979). In terms of the cybernetic model, these studies suggest that the decision to focus coping efforts on changing the environment or adjusting desires depends in part on whether the discrepancy is appraised as resolvable. However, these studies focused on task performance, and it is unclear whether their findings generalize to other types of discrepancies regarding the situation or self. Furthermore, none of the studies reviewed included measures that encompass the full range of coping strategies specified by the cybernetic theory. Edwards and Baglioni (1993) developed measures of coping as efforts to change perceptions, desires, importance, duration, and well-being, but their study focused on the inherent psychometric properties of these measures rather than their relationships with other constructs.

Moderating Effects of Importance and Duration

Several studies have examined whether the effects of discrepancies between perceptions and desires on well-being are moderated by importance (Edwards, 1996; Locke, 1969; McFarlin and Rice, 1992; Mobley and Locke, 1970). Most of these studies have focused on affective dimensions of well-being, such as job satisfaction. Overall, these studies support the contention that, as importance increases, discrepancies between perceptions and desires have greater effects on satisfaction. However, the magnitude of the moderating effect of importance is typically small, explaining much less variance in satisfaction than the discrepancy itself. In addition, most of these studies have used difference scores to operationalize the discrepancy between perceptions and desires, thereby obscuring the form of the moderating effect of importance. One exception is Edwards (1996), who used moderated polynomial regression analysis. This study found that, when importance was low, well-being increased as perceptions exceeded desires and decreased as perceptions fell short of desires. When importance was at its mean, well-being was greatest when perceptions matched desires and decreased as perceptions deviated from desires in either direction. Finally, when importance was high, well-being not only increased when perceptions matched desires, but also increased when perceptions and desires were both high. These findings did not emerge when well-being was operationalized as self-reported tension.

Studies also provide indirect evidence regarding the moderating effects of duration on the relationship between discrepancies and well-being. For example, studies have shown that reactions to perceived work conditions are stronger when employees focus their attention on work (Gardner et al., 1989; Siegall and McDonald, 1995). Although these studies did not examine both perceptions and desires regarding work conditions, their findings are consistent with the assertion that, as duration increases, appraisals of the environment have stronger effects on well-being. Relevant evidence is also reported by studies of private self-consciousness (PSC; Fenigstein et al., 1975). Some studies have found that PSC dampened the relationship between stressful life events and symptoms of ill-health (Mullen and Suls, 1982; Suls and Fletcher, 1985), suggesting that PSC facilitates the detection and resolution of discrepancies (Scheier and Carver, 1983). In contrast, other studies have found that the relationship between chronic work stressors and ill-health is stronger among persons high in PSC (Frone and McFarlin, 1989). One resolution to these conflicting findings involves the person's beliefs regarding coping efficacy (Carver et al., 1979; Hollenbeck, 1989). Specifically, if the person believes a discrepancy cannot be resolved, self-focus merely draws attention to experienced stress, and well-being should decrease. However, if the discrepancy is considered resolvable, decreases in well-being caused by self-focus may be offset by its beneficial effects on self-regulation and discrepancy reduction. This line of reasoning is consistent with available evidence (Carver et al., 1979; Hollenbeck, 1989; Kivimaki and Lindstrom, 1995).

Effects of Coping on Stress and Well-Being

Numerous studies have investigated strategies by which people cope with stress (Dewe et al., 1993; Menaghan, 1983; Silver and Wortman, 1980). Most of these studies have examined the direct effect of coping on well-being or the moderating effects of coping on the relationship between stressors and well-being (Edwards et al., 1990). Studies of the direct effect of coping on well-being are relevant to the present discussion, as this effect is included in the cybernetic model (see Figure 6.2). Although coping strategies investigated in these studies vary widely, most can be classified as problem-focused coping (e.g. instrumental action, negotiation), cognitive reappraisal (e.g. minimization, emphasizing the positive), attention deployment (e.g. escapism, denial), or symptom management (e.g. relaxation, exercise, venting emotions). Overall, these studies suggest that well-being is positively related to problem-focused coping and negatively related to attention deployment and symptom management, whereas findings for cognitive reappraisal have been mixed. However, most of these studies are cross-sectional, making it impossible to determine whether well-being stimulated coping, coping influenced well-being, or both. This ambiguity is critical, as the effects of well-being on coping should be negative (i.e. as well-being worsens, coping intensifies), whereas the effects of coping on well-being should be positive (i.e. as coping efforts increase, well-being improves). Because a cross-sectional design cannot disentangle the causal ordering of coping and well-being, it provides no basis for predicting *a priori* whether their relationship should be positive or negative.

In contrast to the numerous studies of the relationship between coping and well-being, few studies have examined the relationship between coping and stress. Anderson *et al.* (1977) studied coping among small business owners following damage from a flood and found that economic recovery was positively related to problem-focused coping and negatively related to symptom management. Similarly, Folkman *et al.* (1986) found that problem-focused coping was related to reports that a stressful situation had been resolved, whereas attention deployment was related to reports that the situation had not been adequately resolved or had worsened. In contrast, Menaghan and Merves (1984) found that problem-focused coping, cognitive reappraisal, and selective attention were unrelated to subsequent occupational problems. Unfortunately, the stressful situations examined in these studies cannot be differentiated into perceptions, desires, importance, and duration. Therefore, results from these studies provide only suggestive evidence regarding the effects of coping on stress as specified by the cybernetic theory.

Summary

Studies from diverse areas of research provide evidence relevant to the cybernetic theory of stress. However, this evidence pertains primarily to individual effects embedded in the theory. To date, no study has employed a longitudinal design to assess the cyclical relationships among the major constructs specified by the theory. Therefore, we have little evidence regarding the ongoing process by which discrepancies between perceptions and desires affect well-being and coping, how these effects are moderated by importance and duration, or how coping contributes to the resolution of discrepancies and the improvement of well-being. Moreover, no studies have examined the hierarchical relationships among feedback loops central to the cybernetic theory. Thus, although available evidence provides general support for selected aspects of the cybernetic theory, a comprehensive test of the theory awaits future research.

Extension to Stress, Coping, and Well-Being in Multiple Life Domains

The cybernetic theory developed by Edwards (1992) focuses on stress, coping, and well-being at work, and evidence pertaining to the theory was drawn primarily from studies conducted in work settings. However, the principles underlying the cybernetic theory may be applied to other life domains. In this section, the theory is extended to the family domain. Focusing on stress, coping, and well-being in the work and family domains is important, for three reasons. First, work and family have been identified as the two most central domains of human life (Burke and Greenglass, 1987; Zedeck, 1992). Therefore, experiences in these domains have great potential for generating stress and influencing well-being. Second, work–family research emphasizes constructs subsumed within stress research, such as role stressors, inter-role conflict, satisfaction, coping, and mental and physical health (Burke and Greenglass, 1987; Eckenrode and Gore, 1990; Greenhaus and Parasuraman, 1986; Gutek *et al.*, 1988; Voydanoff, 1989). Therefore, work–family research would benefit from an integrative theory of stress, coping, and well-being that encompasses the work and family domains. Third, many indices of well-being, such as depression, anxiety, and physical illness, are not specific to a single life domain, but instead reflect the overall health of the person. These indices of well-being would be better understood by considering stress and coping in multiple life domains, such as work and family.

To establish a foundation for the extended theory, it is necessary to define work and family. For this discussion, work is defined as instrumental activity intended to provide goods and services to support life (Piotrkowski *et al.*, 1987). This definition does not characterize work as a physical location, because many instrumental activities that qualify as work are not confined to the workplace, particularly with the advent of advanced communications technology. Rather than implying a location, work signifies membership in a market or organization that gives the worker rewards (e.g. compensation, goods, services) in exchange for his or her contributions (Burke and Greenglass, 1987; Kabanoff, 1980). Family is defined as persons related by biological ties, marriage, social custom, or adoption (Burke and Greenglass, 1987; Piotrkowski *et al.*, 1987). Like work, family implies membership in a social organization to which the person contributes (Zedeck, 1992). However, these contributions are not intended to gain extrinsic rewards, but rather are intended to promote the well-being and stability of the family itself.

Hierarchy Spanning Work and Family Domains

The hierarchy of feedback loops described earlier provides the architecture for developing a cybernetic theory of stress that encompasses the work and family domains. The present discussion will focus on the top three levels of Powers' (1973) hierarchy, i.e. the system, principle, program levels. These levels dominate the conscious attention of the person and are therefore particularly relevant for understanding psychological stress associated with work and family. As indicated previously, the system level is concerned with overall self-esteem and survival. These concerns are not specific to work or family, but instead pertain to life as a whole. The principle level entails rules that govern behavior in service of the person's overall self-esteem and survival. At this level, rules that pertain to work and family may be distinguished. In the work domain, these rules may be differentiated according to the various roles occupied by the person, such as supervisor, co-worker, and subordinate. Likewise, rules in the family domain may be differentiated according to roles such as parent, spouse, sibling, and offspring. Finally, the program level guides behaviors that, in combination, help the person live according to work and family rules specified at the principle level.

Figure 6.3 provides a heuristic representation of a three-level hierarchy of feedback loops spanning the work and family domains. Each loop in this hierarchy is a shorthand representation of the detailed feedback loop shown in Figure 6.2. For simplicity, this hierarchy includes a single loop at the system level devoted to the maintenance and enhancement of overall self-esteem. The principle level is limited to one loop each in the work and family domains, with the former focused on fulfilling the role of subordinate and the latter focused on fulfilling the role of parent. The program level contains three loops each in the work and family domains. In the work domain, these loops guide behaviors regarding work quantity, work quality, and attendance, representing typical components of subordinate role performance. In the family domain, the loops are characterized in terms of the support a parent may provide to a child, including teaching, advice, and instruction (i.e. informational support), displays of warmth and caring (i.e. emotional support), and providing food, shelter, and clothing (i.e. material support). These dimensions represent common distinctions in models of social support (Cohen, 1988; House *et al.*, 1988).

Figure 6.3 shows three types of relationships between the feedback loops contained within the hierarchy. First, arrows labeled 'a' correspond to mechanisms by which higher loops may active lower loops. For example, a discrepancy regarding the subordinate role (e.g. falling short of one's general desire to be a good subordinate) may prompt the person to raise standards, increase importance, and focus attention on work quantity, work quality, and attendance. Likewise, a discrepancy regarding the parent role may lead the person to increase desires, importance, and attention with regard to the informational, emotional, and material support provided to a child. Second, arrows labeled 'b' represent the process by which behaviors at lower levels facilitate the resolution of discrepancies at higher levels. Thus, by engaging in behaviors that resolve discrepancies regarding work quality, work quantity, and attendance, a person may reduce a general discrepancy regarding his or her role as a subordinate. Similarly, behaviors that resolve discrepancies regarding the informational, emotional, and material support provided to a child may help resolve a general discrepancy regarding the person's role as a parent. Reducing discrepancies for the subordinate and parent roles, in turn, may contribute to the attainment of the ideal self, thereby enhancing the person's overall self-esteem (Brook, 1991; Pelham and Swann, 1989).

Figure 6.3 also indicates that arrows linking higher and lower loops may span life domains. For example, a parent may wish to model responsible behavior for his or her children. This desire may activate a lower loop in the work domain regarding attendance, and maintaining regular work attendance would then contribute to the higher loop of parental role fulfillment. These sequential effects are represented by the 'a' and 'b' arrows linking the parent role to work attendance in Figure 6.3. Analogously, to manage impressions with his or her boss, a subordinate may want to display the image of a conscientious parent (Bozeman and Kacmar, 1997). This desire may activate a lower loop in the family domain regarding informational support, manifested by sending children to prestigious schools. These effects are shown by the 'a' and 'b' arrows linking the subordinate role to informational support in Figure 6.3.

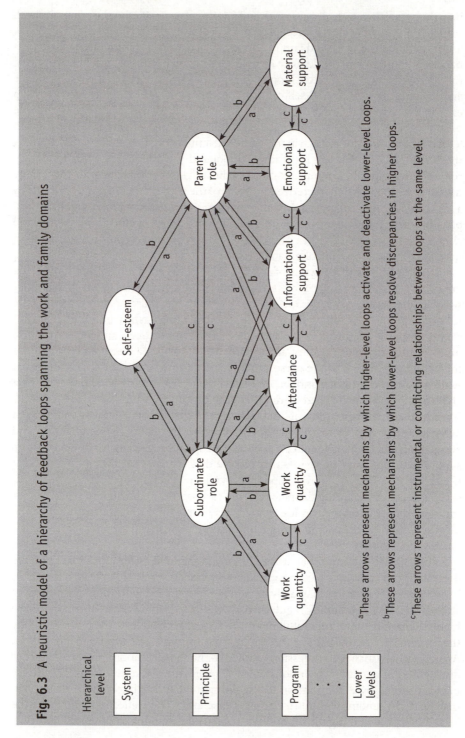

Fig. 6.3 A heuristic model of a hierarchy of feedback loops spanning the work and family domains

[a]These arrows represent mechanisms by which higher-level loops activate and deactivate lower-level loops.

[b]These arrows represent mechanisms by which lower-level loops resolve discrepancies in higher loops.

[c]These arrows represent instrumental or conflicting relationships between loops at the same level.

Of course, these examples are merely illustrative and do not preclude other relationships between higher loops in one domain and lower loops in the other domain.

Third, Figure 6.3 shows that loops at the same hierarchical level may be related, as indicated by arrows labeled 'c'. For example, loops may be instrumentally related, such that resolving a discrepancy in one loop helps resolve a discrepancy in another loop. Thus, achieving work goals regarding performance quantity and quality may generate financial rewards that provide material support for the family (Burke and Greenglass, 1987; Evans and Bartolome, 1986; Kanter, 1977). Instrumental linkages such as these imply positive relationships between the environmental characteristics controlled by loops at the same level. Alternately, loops may be in conflict, such that resolving a discrepancy in one loop exacerbates discrepancies in other loops. Within the work domain, this conflict is exemplified by the familiar tradeoff between performance quantity and quality (Erez, 1990). Within the family domain, this conflict is illustrated by the tension between disciplining children and encouraging their autonomy and independence. Between the work and family domains, conflict is epitomized by the tradeoff between time devoted to work and family (Eckenrode and Gore, 1990; Greenhaus and Beutell, 1985; Small and Riley, 1990; Staines, 1980). In cybernetic terms, this conflict represents a negative relationship between the attention (i.e. duration) associated with work and family loops, such that attending to discrepancies in one domain consumes attention needed to resolve discrepancies in the other domain (Carver and Scheier, 1981; Lord and Levy, 1994; Simon, 1967). In Figure 6.3, work–family conflict is symbolized at the principle level by the arrows connecting the subordinate and parent roles (e.g. committing time to satisfying one's boss takes time away from one's children) and at the program level by the arrows connecting attendance and informational support (e.g. rigidly adhering to a work schedule makes one unavailable to answer spontaneous questions from an inquisitive child). Additional horizontal linkages may be added to Figure 6.3 to depict other forms of work–family conflict.

Clarifying Work–Family Linking Mechanisms

The extended cybernetic model may be used to explain mechanisms that link the work and family domains. Three linking mechanisms that have received extensive attention in work–family research are spillover, compensation, and segmentation (Burke and Greenglass, 1987; Evans and Bartolome, 1986; Lambert, 1990; Staines, 1980; Voydanoff, 1989; Zedeck, 1992). Although these linking mechanisms are central to work-family research, they have not been incorporated into models of work and family stress (e.g. Eckenrode and Gore, 1990; Frone *et al.*, 1997; Greenhaus and Parasuraman, 1986; Higgins *et al.*, 1992; Kopelman *et al.*, 1983; Martin and Schermerhorn, 1983). Incorporating these linking mechanisms into the present model integrates two major streams of work–family research, one focusing on how work and family experiences influence stress and well-being, and the other concerning mechanisms that link these two life domains. This integration provides a foundation for studying such important phenomena as the transfer of stress between work and family (Bolger *et al.*, 1989; Eckenrode and Gore, 1990), the dynamic allocation of coping efforts between work and family (Beutell and Greenhaus, 1983; Fondacaro and Moos, 1987; Pearlin and Schooler, 1978), and the cumulative effects of work and family stress on overall well-being (Bhagat et al., 1985; Rice et al., 1985).

Spillover Spillover refers to the transfer of attitudes, feelings, and behaviors from one domain to the other (Burke and Greenglass, 1987; Lambert, 1990; Staines, 1980; Zedeck, 1992). Two versions of spillover prevalent in work–family research are mood spillover (Gutek et al., 1988; Piotrkowski, 1979; Repetti, 1987; Rice et al., 1980; Staines, 1980) and skill transfer (Crouter, 1984; Payton-Miyazaki and Brayfield, 1976). The following discussion elucidates the process underlying these two versions of spillover using the extended cybernetic model of work and family stress.

Mood is represented in the cybernetic model as an affective dimension of well-being (Edwards, 1992; Watson and Tellegen, 1985). Therefore, mood spillover may be viewed as a positive relationship between work and family well-being (Tenbrunsel et al., 1995). The cybernetic model suggests two processes by which work and family well-being may be positively related. First, this relationship may arise from instrumental linkages connecting feedback loops in the work and family domains. For example, financial rewards from work may not only increase work satisfaction, but may also meet material needs for the family, thereby enhancing family satisfaction (Burke and Greenglass, 1987; Evans and Bartolome, 1986; Kanter, 1977). Second, personal characteristics at the system level may generate a spurious positive relationship between work and family well-being. For example, generalized coping skills (Spivack et al., 1976) may facilitate the resolution of discrepancies for both work and family, thereby enhancing well-being in both domains. Analogously, affective dispositions such as negative affectivity (NA) may prompt people to experience low levels of well-being across life domains, including work and family (Frone et al., 1994; Watson and Pennebaker, 1989). The effects of NA on work and family well-being may reflect the maintenance of unreasonably high standards (i.e. desires) for work and family, such that experiences in both life domains are rarely appraised as satisfactory (Parkes, 1990). Alternately, NA may inhibit effective coping by reducing perceived coping efficacy or by alienating potential sources of social support (Burke et al., 1993), thereby exacerbating stress and damaging well-being for both work and family.

Some investigators characterize mood spillover as the expression of emotion generated in one domain while physically present in the other domain, such as venting work frustrations while at home or worrying about family matters while at work (Eckenrode and Gore, 1990; Evans and Bartolome, 1986; Piotrkowski, 1979; Voydanoff, 1989). Unlike the aforementioned version of mood spillover, this phenomenon does not represent a relationship between work and family well-being. Instead, it signifies that, while physically present in one domain, the person may attend to discrepancies associated with the other domain and express emotions corresponding to those discrepancies (Edwards, 1992). Attention to discrepancies associated with another domain may occur when the discrepancies in that domain are larger or more important than discrepancies in the domain in which the person is physically present (Lord and Hanges, 1987; Lord and Levy, 1994).

The extended cybernetic model may also be used to capture spillover as the transfer of skills between work and family. Skills are represented in the model as personal characteristics that act as coping resources to enhance the success of coping efforts. Coping skills may be intentionally transferred between domains (Crouter, 1984; Eckenrode and Gore, 1990) or may become embedded in scripts and applied across life domains without conscious evaluation of their suitability (Greenhaus and Beutell, 1985; Lord and Hanges, 1987; Repetti, 1987; Schank and Abelson, 1977). In either case, the transfer of coping skills is more likely when stressful experiences in work and family entail similar coping requirements or convey similar situational cues, thereby eliciting similar coping strategies. Work and family coping skills may also be similar due to the effects of personal characteristics at the system level, such as general coping skills (e.g. analytical ability; Spivack *et al.*, 1976) and coping styles that represent habitual ways of coping with stress (Menaghan, 1983).

Compensation Compensation represents efforts to offset dissatisfaction in one domain by seeking satisfaction in another domain (Burke and Greenglass, 1987; Lambert, 1990; Zedeck, 1992). Compensation is achieved by decreasing involvement in the dissatisfying domain and increasing involvement in another potentially satisfying domain, yielding a negative relationship between involvement in the two domains (Lambert, 1990). Although compensation is often described in these general terms, it implies different processes depending on whether involvement is conceptualized as the perceived importance of a domain (Champoux, 1978; Frone *et al.*, 1997; Lambert, 1990; Lobel, 1991), psychological absorption with a domain (Kanter, 1977; Small and Riley, 1990; Voydanoff, 1987), or time devoted to a domain (Lobel, 1991). The following discussion is organized in terms of these three conceptualizations of involvement.

The extended cybernetic model suggests two forces that may generate a negative relationship between work and family importance. First, the person may cope with large irresolvable discrepancies in a domain by reducing the importance of that domain (Edwards, 1992; Schuler, 1985). The person might then assign greater importance to the other domain, provided discrepancies in that domain are tolerable or more manageable than those in the initial domain. This reprioritization of life domains signifies the operation of a superordinate coping strategy at the system level in which overall well-being is enhanced by shifting importance between work and family, deactivating the domain with large irresolvable discrepancies and activating the domain with discrepancies that are tolerable or can be resolved (Champoux, 1978; Evans and Bartolome, 1986). Second, work and family importance may be negatively related due to life stage or socialization forces that influence the prioritization of work and family. For example, work is often a top priority in early adulthood, whereas family often becomes more important in later years (Evans and Bartolome, 1986; Piotrkowski, 1979). Analogously, a subscription to traditional gender roles may increase the importance of work relative to family for men and the importance of family relative to work for women (Aryee and Luk, 1996; Gutek *et al.*, 1991; Voydanoff, 1988).

Psychological absorption refers to focusing attention on a domain (Small and Riley, 1990; Voydanoff, 1987) and therefore corresponds to duration in the cybernetic model. As noted previously, if a discrepancy cannot be resolved, the person may cope by attempting to ignore or deny the discrepancy (Lazarus, 1983). This reasoning can be generalized to discrepancies in an entire life domain. That is, if the majority of discrepancies in a domain are appraised as irresolvable, the person may attempt to divert attention from that domain. Attention diverted from the dissatisfying domain will presumably shift to domains that require monitoring and regulation (Carver and Scheier, 1981; Lord and Levy, 1994). If discrepancies in those domains can be successfully managed or are considered tolerable, overall well-being will be enhanced (Carver et al., 1979; Bhagat et al., 1985; Hollenbeck, 1989; Rice et al., 1985).

Time devoted to a domain exposes the person to the physical and social environment in that domain, which in turn increases time spent thinking about the domain, or duration. These effects are imperfect, given that the person may dwell on a domain removed in place and time from his or her surroundings (Edwards, 1992; Gardner et al., 1989; Siegall and McDonald, 1995). Nonetheless, if the person spends less time in one domain and more time in another, duration is likely to decrease for the former domain and increase for the latter domain. Hence, reallocating time devoted to work and family may be viewed as one method for shifting duration associated with the two domains. Beyond its effects on duration, time devoted to a domain should not generate stress or influence coping or well-being, given that a domain cannot elicit stress unless the person is consciously aware of events and circumstances in the domain (Lazarus and Folkman, 1984; McGrath, 1976).

Segmentation Segmentation refers to the separation of work and family, such that experiences in the two domains do not influence one another (Lambert, 1990; Zedeck, 1992). Although segmentation was originally viewed as a natural division between the work and family domains (Blood and Wolfe, 1960; Dubin, 1973), subsequent research debunked the view that work and family are inherently separate (Burke and Greenglass, 1987; Kanter, 1977; Voydanoff, 1987). Thus, recent research characterizes segmentation as active attempts to maintain a boundary between work and family (Lambert, 1990; Piotrkowski, 1979).

The extended cybernetic model suggests two processes by which active segmentation may occur. First, segmentation may operate through duration, such that attention is focused solely on the domain in which the person is physically present (Piotrkowski, 1979). The person is likely to devote attention to the physically present domain when discrepancies in that domain are large or important, particularly when compared to discrepancies in the other domain (Carver, 1994; Crouter, 1984; Klein, 1989; Lord and Hanges, 1987; Lord and Levy, 1994). Alternately, if discrepancies in another domain are irresolvable, the person may avoid thinking about that domain and focus attention on the physically present domain (Carver et al., 1989; Folkman et al., 1986; Lazarus, 1983). Either of these mechanisms would cause the person to focus his or her attention on the domain in which he or she is physically present, mentally segmenting the work and family domains.

Second, segmentation may be manifested as the conscious utilization of different coping strategies in the work and family domains (Kabanoff, 1980). The use of different coping strategies for work and family stress may arise from the recognition of different coping requirements in the two domains. For example, coping at work may require problem-focused strategies such as direct confrontation, but these strategies may be ineffective or counterproductive in the family domain (Folkman and Lazarus, 1980; Eckenrode and Gore, 1990; Greenhaus and Beutell, 1985; Pearlin and Schooler, 1978). Differentiation of work and family coping requirements is more likely when the person consciously evaluates the suitability of alternative coping strategies, which may occur when discrepancies are large, important, novel, or persistent (Edwards, 1992).

Work, Family, and Total Life Stress and Well-Being

Based on the extended cybernetic model, stress and well-being may be conceptualized separately for work, family, and life as a whole. Specifically, overall work stress can be viewed as the sum of all discrepancies between perceptions and desires within the work domain. The contribution of each discrepancy to overall work stress depends on its importance and duration, such that important discrepancies that command much attention would contribute greatly to overall work stress. Given that attention is rarely focused below the program level (Powers, 1973), most discrepancies contributing to overall work stress occur at the program and principle levels. Likewise, overall family stress refers to the sum of all discrepancies between perceptions and desires in the family domain, with each discrepancy weighted by its importance and duration. It follows that total life stress is the sum of stress associated with all life domains, including work, family, and other relevant domains (e.g. leisure). The logic underlying these conceptualizations of work and family stress is consistent with definitions of stress that encompass multiple life domains (Bhagat *et al.*, 1985; Rice *et al.*, 1985).

Well-being may also be conceptualized for work, family, and life as a whole. Some dimensions of well-being, such as satisfaction, may be differentiated between work and family and at different hierarchical levels within these domains. Returning to the model in Figure 6.3, satisfaction may refer to work quantity, work quality, attendance, or work as a whole (Ironson *et al.*, 1989). Moving up in the hierarchy, satisfaction may refer to work, family, or life as a whole (Kelly and Kelly, 1994). Other dimensions of well-being, including many symptoms of mental and physical illness (e.g. depression, hypertension, peptic ulcer), refer to the person's overall well-being and therefore cannot be differentiated according to specific life domains. Naturally, the *causes* of these symptoms may emanate from different life domains, but the symptoms themselves are not specific to a domain.

The foregoing discussion may tempt researchers to create aggregate measures of work, family, and overall stress and well-being by summing measures of their components. This approach should be avoided. In empirical research, work, family, and overall stress should be examined not by using summated weighted discrepancy scores, but rather by using multivariate methods for testing discrepancy and moderation effects (Edwards, 1993, 1994; Edwards and Parry, 1993; Evans, 1991). To examine stress at a particular hierarchical level, researchers should measure perceptions, desires, importance, and duration at that level, as opposed to measuring these constructs at lower levels and aggregating the resulting measures. Likewise, measures of well-being should be specified at the hierarchical level of interest, rather than aggregating measures of well-being at lower levels. For example, overall satisfaction with work should be measured with multiple indicators of one's general affective response to work, not as the sum of indicators representing satisfaction with different facets of work (Ferratt, 1981; Scarpello and Campbell, 1983).

Summary

The extended cybernetic model of work and family stress, coping, and well-being operates through a hierarchy of feedback loops that encompasses the work and family domains. This hierarchy traces the mechanisms by which feedback loops are related vertically and horizontally, and how these relationships may span the work and family domains. The extended cybernetic model provides a foundation for translating work-family linking mechanisms, such as spillover, compensation, and segmentation, into relationships between constructs embedded in feedback loops in the work and family domains. Thus, the model permits the integration of research on work and family stress, coping, and well-being with research into mechanisms that link the work and family domains. The model also provides a basis for conceptualizing stress and well-being for the work domain, the family domain, and life as a whole.

Implications for Practice

The cybernetic theory discussed in this chapter suggests several implications for the management of stress. First, stress results from the appraisal of environmental conditions relative to the desires of the person. Given that people hold different desires, it follows that stress management interventions must be individualized, representing a clinical rather than an epidemiological approach to the reduction of stress. Second, people are continually engaged in coping efforts intended to resolve stressful discrepancies, reduce their importance or duration, improve well-being directly, or some combination thereof. These different methods of coping signify different avenues of intervention for stress management efforts. For example, when stress management interventions cannot alleviate environmental stressors, such as an impending plant closing, they may focus on other methods to help employees cope with stress. For example, displaced employees may be counseled to lower their financial aspirations or reprioritize work relative to family until they are reemployed (Leana and Feldman, 1988). Third, the extended cybernetic model suggests that interventions intended to help employees manage family stress may also help reduce work stress, and vice-versa. Further suggestions for stress management interventions are unwarranted, however, due to the paucity of empirical studies based on the cybernetic theory. Future research may yield specific guidelines linking stress management interventions to the ongoing self-regulation processes posited by the theory.

Summary and Conclusion

This chapter reviewed the fundamental constructs and processes of the cybernetic theory of stress, coping, and well-being proposed by Edwards (1992). This theory integrates other theories in the stress literature and holds promise for understanding the dynamic, reciprocal relationships between stress, coping, and well-being. Although few studies have directly examined the theory, available evidence provides tentative support for several of its core propositions. The theory also provides a general foundation for examining stress and coping processes in multiple life domains, as illustrated by the extension of the theory to work and family. This extended model was also used to explain mechanisms linking work and family (i.e. spillover, compensation, segmentation) and to conceptualize stress and well-being regarding work, family, and life as a whole. Additional research is needed to test cybernetic stress and coping processes within and between the work and family domains and their ultimate effects on individual well-being.

The author thanks Nancy P. Rothbard for her helpful comments on an earlier version of this chapter.

References

Abramson, L. Y., Seligman, M. E. P., and Teasdale, J. D. (1978) 'Learned helplessness in humans: Critique and reformulation', *Journal of Abnormal Psychology*, 87, 49–74.

Anderson, C. R., Hellriegel, D., and Slocum, J. W., Jr. (1977) 'Managerial response to environmentally induced stress', *Academy of Management Journal*, 20, 260–272.

Aryee, S. and Luk, V. (1996) 'Balancing two major parts of adult life experience: Work and family identity among dual-earner couples', *Human Relations*, 49, 465–487.

Ashby, W. R. (1966) *An Introduction to Cybernetics*. New York: Wiley.

Assouline, M. and Meir, E. I. (1987) 'Meta-analysis of the relationship between congruence and well-being measures', *Journal of Vocational Behavior*, 31, 319–332.

Bandura, A. (1989) 'Human agency in social cognitive theory', *American Psychologist*, 44, 1175–1184.

Bandura, A. and Cervone, D. (1986) 'Differential engagement of self-reactive influences in cognitive motivation', *Organizational Behavior and Human Decision Process*, 38, 92–113.

Beehr, T. A. and Bhagat, R. S. (1985) Introduction to human stress and cognition in organizations. In T. A. Beehr and R. S. Bhagat (eds.), *Human Stress and Cognition in Organizations* (pp. 3–19). New York: Wiley.

Beehr, T. A., and Newman, J. E. (1978) 'Job stress, employee health, and organizational effectiveness: A facet analysis, model and literature review', *Personnel Psychology*, 31, 665–699.

Beutell, N. J. and Greenhaus, J. H. (1983) 'Integration of home and nonhome roles: Women's conflict and coping behavior', *Journal of Applied Psychology*, 68, 43–48.

Bhagat, R. S., McQuaid, S. J., Lindholm, H., and Segovis, J. (1985) 'Total life stress: A multimethod validation of the construct and its effects on organizationally valued outcomes and withdrawal behaviors', *Journal of Applied Psychology*, 70, 202–214.

Billings, A. G. and Moos, R. H. (1981) 'The role of coping responses and social resources in attenu-ating the stress of life events', *Journal of Behavioral Medicine*, 4, 139–157.

Blood, R. O. and Wolfe, D. M. (1960) *Husbands and Wives*. New York: Macmillan.

Bolger, N., DeLongis, A., Kessler, R. C., and Wethington, E. (1989) 'The contagion of stress across multiple roles', *Journal of Marriage and the Family*, 51, 175–183.

Bozeman, D. P. and Kacmar, K. M. (1997) 'A cybernetic model of impression management processes in organizations', *Organizational Behavior and Human Decision Process*, 69, 9–30.

Brook, J. A. (1991) 'The link between self-esteem and work/nonwork perceptions and attitudes', *Applied Psychology: An International Review*, 40, 269–280.

Burke, M. J., Brief, A. P., and George, J. M. (1993) 'The role of negative affectivity in understanding relations between self-reports of stressors and strains: A comment on the applied psychology lit-erature', *Journal of Applied Psychology*, 78, 402–412.

Burke, R. J., and Greenglass, E. (1987) Work and family. In C. L. Cooper and I. T. Robertson (eds.), *International Review of Industrial and Organizational Psychology* (pp. 273–320). New York: Wiley.

Campion, M. and Lord, R. (1982) 'A control system conceptualization of the goal-setting and chang-ing process', *Organizational Behavior and Human Performance*, 30, 265–287.

Caplan, R. D., Naidu, R. K., and Tripathi, R. C. (1984) 'Coping and defense: Constellations vs. com-ponents', *Journal of Health and Social Behavior*, 25, 303–320.

Carver, C. S. (1979) 'A cybernetic model of self-attention', *Journal of Personality and Social Psychology*, 37, 1251–1281.

Carver, C. S. (1994) 'Cognitive processes and self-regulation: Determinants of concentration and distraction', *Applied Psychology: An International Review*, 43, 387–391.

Carver, C. S. and Scheier, M. F. (1981) *Attention and Self-regulation: A Control-theory Approach to Human Behavior*. New York: Springer-Verlag.

Carver, C. S. and Scheier, M. F. (1982) 'Control theory: A useful conceptual framework for person-ality–social, clinical, and health psychology', *Psychological Bulletin*, 92, 111–135.

Carver, C. S. and Scheier, M. F. (1985) Self-consciousness, expectancies, and the coping process. In T. M. Field, P. M. McCabe, and N. Schniederman (eds.), *Stress and Coping* (pp. 305–330). Hillsdale, NJ: Erlbaum.

Carver, C. S., Blaney, P. H., and Scheier, M. F. (1979) 'Focus of attention, chronic expectancy, and responses to a feared stimulus', *Journal of Personality and Social Psychology*, 37, 1186–1195.

Carver, C. S., Scheier, M. F., and Weintraub, J. K. (1989) 'Assessing coping strategies: A theoreti-cally based approach', *Journal of Personality and Social Psychology*, 56, 267–283.

Champoux, J. E. (1978) 'Perceptions of work and nonwork: A reexamination of the compensatory and spillover models', *Sociology of Work and Occupations*, 5, 402–422.

Cohen, S. (1988) 'Psychosocial models of the role of social support in the etiology of physical dis-ease', *Health Psychology*, 7, 269–297.

Cooper, C. L. and Marshall, J. (1976) 'Occupational sources of stress: Review of literature relating to coronary heart disease and mental ill health', *Journal of Occupational Psychology*, 49, 11–28.

Cox, T. (1987) 'Stress, coping, and problem solving', *Work & Stress*, 1, 5–14.

Crouter, A. C. (1984) 'Spillover from family to work: The neglected side of the work–family inter-face', *Human Relations*, 37, 425–441.

Cummings, T. G. and Cooper, C. L. (1979) 'Cybernetic framework for studying occupational stress', *Human Relations*, 32, 395–418.

Dewe, P., Cox, T., and Ferguson, E. (1993) 'Individual strategies for coping with stress at work: A review', *Work & Stress*, 7, 5–15.

Dubin, R. (1973) Work and non-work: Institutional perspectives. In M. D. Dunnette (ed.), *Work and Non-Work in the Year 2001* (pp. 53–68). Monterey, CA: Brooks/Cole.

Dubin, R. (1976) Theory building in applied areas. In M. Dunnette (ed.), *Handbook of Industrial and Organizational Psychology* (pp. 17–39). Chicago: Rand McNally.

Eagan, A. E. and Walsh, W. B. (1995) 'Person–environment congruence and coping strategies', *Career Development Quarterly*, 43, 246–256.

Eckenrode, J. and Gore, S. (1990) Stress and coping at the boundary of work and family. In J. Eckenrode and S. Gore (eds.), *Stress between Work and Family* (pp. 1–16). New York: Plenum Press.

Edwards, J. R. (1988) The determinants and consequences of coping with stress. In C. L. Cooper and R. Payne (eds.), *Causes, Coping, and Consequences of Stress at Work* (pp. 233–263). New York: Wiley.

Edwards, J. R. (1991) Person–job fit: A conceptual integration, literature review, and methodological critique. In C. L. Cooper and I. T. Robertson (eds.), *International Review of Industrial and Organizational Psychology* (Vol. 6, pp. 283–357). New York: Wiley.

Edwards, J. R. (1992) 'A cybernetic theory of stress, coping, and well-being in organizations', *Academy of Management Review*, 17, 238–274.

Edwards, J. R. (1993) 'Problems with the use of profile similarity indices in the study of congruence in organizational research', *Personnel Psychology*, 46, 641–665.

Edwards, J. R. (1994) 'The study of congruence in organizational behavior research: Critique and a proposed alternative', *Organizational Behavior and Human Decision Processes*, 58, 51–100 (erratum, 58, 323–325).

Edwards, J. R. (1996) 'An examination of competing versions of the person–environment fit approach to stress', *Academy of Management Journal*, 39, 292–339.

Edwards, J. R. and Baglioni, A. J., Jr. (1993) 'The measurement of coping with stress: Construct validity of the Ways of Coping Checklist and the Cybernetic Coping Scale', *Work & Stress*, 7, 17–31.

Edwards, J. R. and Cooper, C. L. (1988) 'The impacts of positive psychological states on physical health: A review and theoretical framework', *Social Science & Medicine*, 27, 1447–1459.

Edwards, J. R. and Harrison, R. V. (1993) 'Job demands and worker health: Three-dimensional reexamination of the relationship between person–environment fit and strain', *Journal of Applied Psychology*, 78, 628–648.

Edwards, J. R. and Parry, M. E. (1993) 'On the use of polynomial regression equations as an alternative to difference scores in organizational research', *Academy of Management Journal*, 36, 1577–1613.

Edwards, J. R., Baglioni, A. J., and Cooper, C. L. (1990) 'Stress, Type-A, coping, and psychological and physical symptoms: A multi-sample test of alternative models', *Human Relations*, 43, 919–956.

Elsass, P. M. and Veiga, J. F. (1997) 'Job control and job strain: A test of three models', *Journal of Occupational Health Psychology*, 2, 195–211.

Erez, M. (1990) Performance quality and work motivation. In U. Kleinbeck, H. H. Quast, H. Thierry, and H. Hacker (eds.), *Work Motivation* (pp. 53–65). Hillsdale, NJ: Erlbaum.

Evans, M. G. (1991) 'The problem of analyzing multiplicative composites: Interactions revisited', *American Psychologist*, 46, 6–15.

Evans, P. and Bartolome, F. (1986) 'The dynamics of work–family relationships in managerial lives', *International Review of Applied Psychology*, 35, 371–395.

Fenigstein, A., Scheier, M. F., and Buss, A. H. (1975) 'Public and private self-consciousness: Assessment and theory', *Journal of Consulting and Clinical Psychology*, 43, 522–527.

Ferratt, T. W. (1981) 'Overall job satisfaction: Is it a linear function of facet satisfaction?' *Human Relations*, 34, 463–473.

Folkman, S. and Lazarus, R. S. (1980) 'An analysis of coping in a middle-aged community sample', *Journal of Health and Social Behaviour*, 21, 219–239.

Folkman, S., Lazarus, R. S., Dunkel-Schetter, C., DeLongis, A., and Gruen, R. J. (1986) 'Dynamics of a stressful encounter: Cognitive appraisal, coping, and encounter outcomes', *Journal of Personality and Social Psychology*, 50, 992–1003.

Fondacaro, M. R. and Moos, R. H. (1987) 'Social support and coping: A longitudinal analysis', *American Journal of Community Psychology*, 15, 653–673.

French, J. R. P., Jr., Caplan, R. D., and Harrison, R. V. (1982) *The Mechanisms of Job Stress and Strain*. New York: Wiley.

Frone, M. R. and McFarlin, D. B. (1989) 'Chronic occupational stressors, self-focused attention, and well-being: Testing a cybernetic model of stress', *Journal of Applied Psychology*, 74, 876–883.

Frone, M. R., Russell, M., and Cooper, M. L. (1994) 'Relationship between job and family satisfaction: Causal or noncausal covariation?' *Journal of Management*, 20, 565–579.

Frone, M. R., Yardley, J. K., and Markel, K. S. (1997) 'Developing and testing an integrative model of the work–family interface', *Journal of Vocational Behavior*, 50, 145–167.

Gardner, D. G., Dunham, R. B., Cummings, L. L., and Pierce, J. L. (1989) 'Focus of attention at work: Construct definition and empirical validation', *Journal of Occupational Psychology*, 62, 61–77.

Greenhaus, J. H. and Beutell, N. J. (1985) 'Sources of conflict between work and family roles', *Academy of Management Review*, 10, 76–88.

Greenhaus, J. H. and Parasuraman, S. (1986) 'A work–nonwork interactive perspective of stress and its consequences', *Journal of Organizational Behavior Management*, 8, 37–60.

Gutek, B. A., Repetti, R., and Silver, D. (1988) Nonwork roles and stress at work. In C. L. Cooper and R. Payne (eds.), *Causes, Coping, and Consequences of Stress at Work* (pp. 141–174). New York: Wiley.

Gutek, B. A., Searle, S., and Klepa, L. (1991) 'Rational versus gender role explanations for work–family conflict', *Journal of Applied Psychology*, 76, 560–568.

Harrison, R. V. (1978) Person–environment fit and job stress. In C. L. Cooper and R. Payne (eds.), *Stress at Work* (pp. 175–205). New York: Wiley.

Hesketh, B. and Gardner, D. (1993) 'Person–environment fit models: A reconceptualization and empirical test', *Journal of Vocational Behavior*, 42, 315–332.

Higgins, C. A., Duxbury, L. E., and Irving, R. H. (1992) 'Work–family conflict in the dual-career family', *Organizational Behavior and Human Decision Process*, 51, 51–75.

Hollenbeck, J. R. (1989) 'Control theory and the perception of work environments: The effects of focus of attention on affective and behavioral reactions to work', *Organizational Behavior and Human Decision Process*, 43, 406–430.

House, J. C., Umberson, D., and Landis, K. R. (1988) 'Structures and processes of social support', *Annual Review of Sociology*, 14, 293–318.

Hyland, M. E. (1987) 'Control theory interpretation of psychological mechanisms of depression: Comparison and integration of several theories', *Psychological Bulletin*, 102, 109–121.

Hyland, M. E. (1988) 'Motivational control theory: An integrative framework', *Journal of Personality and Social Psychology*, 55, 642–651.

Ironson, G. H., Smith, P. C., Brannick, M. T., Gibson, W. M., and Paul, K. B. (1989) 'Construction of a job in general scale: A comparison of global, composite, and specific measures', *Journal of Applied Psychology*, 74, 193–200.

Ivancevich, J. M. and Matteson, M. T. (1980) *Stress and Work*. Glenview, IL: Scott, Foresman.

Johns, G. (1981) 'Difference score measures of organizational behavior variables: A critique', *Organizational Behavior and Human Performance*, 27, 443–463.

Kabanoff, B. (1980) 'Work and nonwork: A review of models, methods, and findings', *Psychological Bulletin*, 88, 60–77.

Kahn, R. L. and Quinn, R. P. (1970) Role stress: A framework for analysis. In A. McLean (ed.), *Occupational Mental Health* (pp. 50–115). New York: Rand McNally.

Kahn, R. L., Wolfe, D. M., Quinn, R. P., Snoek, J. D., and Rosenthal, R. A. (1964) *Organizational Stress: Studies in Role Conflict and Ambiguity*. New York: Wiley.

Kanter, R. M. (1977) *Work and Family in the United States: A Critical Review and Agenda for Research and Policy*. New York: Russell Sage.

Karasek, R. A., Jr. and Theorell, T. (1990) *Healthy Work: Stress, Productivity, and the Reconstruction of Working Life*. New York: Basic Books.

Karasek, R. A., Jr., Russell, R. S., and Theorell, T. (1982) 'Physiology of stress and regeneration in job related cardiovascular illness', *Journal of Human Stress*, 8 (1), 29–42.

Kelly, J. R. and Kelly, J. R. (1994) 'Multiple dimensions of meaning in the domains of work, family, and leisure', *Journal of Leisure Research*, 26, 250–274.

Kernan, M. C. and Lord, R. G. (1989) 'The effects of explicit goals and specific feedback on escalation processes', *Journal of Applied Social Psychology*, 19, 1125–1143.

Kivimaki, M. and Lindstrom, K. (1995) 'Effects of private self-consciousness and control on the occupational stress–strain relationship', *Stress Medicine*, 11, 7–16.

Klein, H. J. (1989) 'An integrated control theory model of work motivation', *Academy of Management Review*, 14, 150–172.

Klinger, E. (1975) 'Consequences of commitment to and disengagement from incentives', *Psychological Review*, 82, 1–25.

Kopelman, R. E., Greenhaus, J. J., and Connolly, T. F. (1983) 'A model of work, family, and interrole conflict: A construct validation study', *Organizational Behavior and Human Performance*, 32, 198–215.

Lambert, S. J. (1990) 'Processes linking work and family: A critical review and research agenda', *Human Relations*, 43, 239–257.

Latack, J. C. (1986) 'Coping with job stress: Measures and future directions for scale development', *Journal of Applied Psychology*, 71, 377–385.

Latack, J. C., Kinicki, A. J., and Prussia, G. E. (1995) 'An integrative process model of coping with job loss', *Academy of Management Review*, 20, 311–342.

Lazarus, R. S. (1983) The costs and benefits of denial. In S. Breznitz (ed.), *Denial of Stress* (pp. 1–30). New York: International Universities Press.

Lazarus, R. S. and Folkman, S. (1984) *Stress, Coping, and Adaptation*. New York: Springer.

Leana, C. R. and Feldman, D. C. (1988) 'Individual responses to job loss: Perceptions, reactions, and coping behaviors', *Journal of Management*, 14, 375–389.

Livingstone, L. P., Nelson, D. L., and Barr, S. H. (1997) 'Person–environment fit and creativity: An examination of supply–value and demand–ability versions of fit', *Journal of Management*, 23, 119–146.

Lobel, S. A. (1991) 'Allocation of investment in work and family roles: Alternative theories and implications for research', *Academy of Management Review*, 16, 507–521.

Locke, E. A. (1969) 'What is job satisfaction?' *Organizational Behavior and Human Performance*, 4, 309–336.

Locke, E. A. (1976) The nature and causes of job satisfaction. In M. Dunnette (ed.), *Handbook of Industrial and Organizational Psychology* (pp. 1297–1350). Chicago: Rand McNally.

Locke, E. A. (1991) 'Goal theory vs. control theory: Contrasting approaches to understanding work motivation', *Motivation and Emotion*, 15, 9–28.

Locke, E. A. (1994) 'The emperor is naked', *Applied Psychology: An International Review*, 43, 367–370.

Locke, E. A. and Latham, G. P. (1990) *A Theory of Goal Setting and Task Performance*. Englewood Cliffs, NJ: Prentice Hall.

Lord, R. G. and Hanges, P. J. (1987) 'A control systems model of organizational motivation: Theoretical development and applied implications', *Behavioral Science*, 32, 161–178.

Lord, R. G. and Levy, P. E. (1994) 'Moving from cognition to action: A control theory perspective', *Applied Psychology: An International Review*, 43, 335–367.

Maccoby, M. (1976) *The Gamesman*. New York: Simon & Schuster.

McFarlin, D. B. and Rice, R. W. (1992) 'The role of facet importance as a moderator in job satisfaction processes', *Journal of Organizational Behavior*, 13, 41–54.

McGrath, J. E. (1976) Stress and behavior in organizations. In M. Dunnette (ed.), *Handbook of Industrial and Organizational Psychology* (pp. 1351–1395). Chicago: Rand McNally.

Martin, T. N. and Schermerhorn, J. R., Jr. (1983) 'Work and nonwork influences on health: A research agenda using inability to leave as a critical variable', *Academy of Management Review*, 8, 650–659.

Matteson, M. T. and Ivancevich, J. M. (1979) 'Organizational stressors and heart disease: A research model', *Academy of Management Review*, 4, 347–357.

Mattlin, J. A., Wethington, E., and Kessler, R. C. (1990) 'Situational determinants of coping and coping effectiveness', *Journal of Health and Social Behavior*, 31, 103–122.

Mayes, B. T. and Ganster, D. C. (1988) 'Exit and voice: A test of hypotheses based on fight/flight responses to job stress', *Journal of Organizational Behavior*, 9, 199–216.

Menaghan, E. G. (1983) Individual coping efforts: Moderators of the relationship between life stress and mental health outcomes. In H. B. Kaplan (ed.), *Psychosocial Stress: Trends in Theory and Research* (pp. 157–191). New York: Academic Press.

Menaghan, E. G. and Merves, E. S. (1984) 'Coping with occupational problems: The limits of individual efforts', *Journal of Health and Social Behavior*, 25, 406–423.

Michalos, A. C. (1986) Job satisfaction, marital satisfaction, and the quality of life: A review and preview. In F. M. Andrews (ed.), *Research on the Quality of Life* (pp. 57–83). Ann Arbor: University of Michigan Institute for Social Research.

Miller, G. A., Galanter, E., and Pribrum, K. H. (1960) *Plans and the Structure of Behavior*. New York: Holt, Rinehart, and Winston.

Miller, J. G. (1965) 'Living systems: Basic concepts', *Behavioral Science*, 10, 193–237.

Mobley, W. H. and Locke, E. A. (1970) 'The relationship of value importance to satisfaction', *Organizational Behavior and Human Performance*, 5, 463–483.

Mullen, B. and Suls, J. (1982) ' "Know thyself": Stressful life changes and the ameliorative effect of private self-consciousness', *Journal of Experimental Social Psychology*, 18, 43–55.

Naylor, J. C., Pritchard, R. D., and Ilgen, D. R. (1980) *A Theory of Behavior in Organizations*. New York: Academic Press.

Newman, J. E. and Beehr, T. A. (1979) 'Personal and organizational strategies for handling job stress: A review of research and opinion', *Personnel Psychology*, 32, 1–43.

Parker, D. F. and DeCotiis, T. A. (1983) 'Organizational determinants of job stress', *Organizational Behavior and Human Performance*, 32, 160–177.

Parkes, K. R. (1990) 'Coping, negative affectivity, and the work environment: Additive and interactive predictors of mental health', *Journal of Applied Psychology*, 75, 399–409.

Payton-Miyazaki, M. and Brayfield, A. H. (1976) The good job and the good life: Relationship of characteristics of employment to general well-being. In A. D. Biderman and T. F. Drury (eds.), *Measuring Work Quality for Social Reporting* (pp. 125–150). New York: Sage Publications.

Pearlin, L. I. and Schooler, C. (1978) 'The structure of coping', *Journal of Health and Social Behavior*, 19, 2–21.

Pelham, B. W. and Swann, W. B. (1989) 'From self-conceptions to self-worth: On the sources and structure of global self-esteem', *Journal of Personality and Social Psychology*, 57, 672–680.

Phillips, J. M., Hollenbeck, J. R., and Ilgen, D. R. (1996) 'Prevalence and prediction of positive discrepancy creation: Examining a discrepancy between two self-regulation theories', *Journal of Applied Psychology*, 81, 498–511.

Piotrkowski, C. S. (1979) *Work and the Family System*. New York: Free Press.

Piotrkowski, C. S., Rapoport, R. N., and Rapoport, R. (1987) Families and work. In M. Sussman and S. Steinmetz (eds.), *Handbook of Marriage and the Family* (pp. 251–283). New York: Plenum.

Powers, W. T. (1973) *Behavior: The Control of Perception*. Chicago: Aldine.

Powers, W. T. (1978) 'Quantitative analysis of purposive systems: Some spadework at the foundations of scientific psychology', *Psychological Review*, 85, 417–435.

Pyszczynski, T. and Greenberg, J. (1987) 'Self-regulatory preservation and the depressive self-focusing style: A self-awareness theory of reactive depression', *Psychological Bulletin*, 102, 122–138.

Repetti, R. L. (1987) 'Linkages between work and family roles', *Applied Social Psychology Annual*, 7, 98–127.

Rice, R. W., Near, J. P., and Hunt, R. G. (1980) 'The job-satisfaction/life-satisfaction relationship: A review of empirical research', *Basic and Applied Social Psychology*, 1, 37–64.

Rice, R. W., McFarlin, D. B., Hunt, R. G., and Near, J. P. (1985) 'Organizational work and the perceived quality of life: Toward a conceptual model', *Academy of Management Review*, 10, 296–310.

Salancik, G. R. and Pfeffer, J. (1978) 'A social information processing approach to job attitudes and task design', *Administrative Science Quarterly*, 23, 224–253.

Scarpello, V. and Campbell, J. P. (1983) 'Job satisfaction: Are all the parts there?', *Personnel Psychology*, 36, 577–600.

Schank, R. C. and Abelson, R. P. (1977) *Scripts, Plans, Goals, and Understanding: An Inquiry into Human Knowledge Structures*. New York: Wiley.

Scheier, M. F. and Carver, C. S. (1983) 'Self-directed attention and the comparison of self with standards', *Journal of Experimental Social Psychology*, 19, 205–222.

Schuler, R. S. (1980) 'Definition and conceptualization of stress in organizations', *Organizational Behavior and Human Performance*, 25, 184–215.

Schuler, R. S. (1985) Integrative transactional process model of coping with stress in organizations. In T. A. Beehr and R. S. Bhagat (eds.), *Human Stress and Cognition in Organizations* (pp. 347–374). New York: Wiley.

Seeman, J. (1989) 'Toward a model of positive health', *American Psychologist*, 44, 1099–1109.

Selye, H. (1956) *The Stress of Life*. New York: McGraw-Hill.

Shirom, A. (1982) 'What is organizational stress? A facet analytic conceptualization', *Journal of Occupational Behavior*, 3, 21–37.

Siegall, M. and McDonald, T. (1995) 'Focus of attention and employee reactions to job change', *Journal of Applied Social Psychology*, 25, 1121–1141.

Silver, R. L. and Wortman, C. B. (1980) Coping with undesirable life events. In J. Garber and M. E. P. Seligman (eds.), *Human Helplessness: Theory and Application* (pp. 279–340). New York: Academic Press.

Simon, H. A. (1967) 'Motivational and emotional controls of cognition', *Psychological Review*, 74, 29–39.

Small, S. A. and Riley, D. (1990) 'Toward a multidimensional assessment of work spillover', *Journal of Marriage and the Family*, 52, 51–61.

Spivack, G., Platt, J. J., and Shure, M. B. (1976) *The Problem-solving Approach to Adjustment*. San Francisco: Jossey-Bass.

Staines, G. L. (1980) 'Spillover versus compensation: A review of the literature on the relationship between work and nonwork', *Human Relations*, 33, 111–129.

Starbuck, W. H. and Mezias, J. M. (1996) 'Opening Pandora's box: Studying the accuracy of managers' perceptions', *Journal of Organizational Behavior*, 17, 99–118.

Suls, J. and Fletcher, B. (1985) 'Self-attention, life stress and illness: A prospective study', *Psychosomatic Medicine*, 47, 465–481.

Tapp, J. T. (1985) Multisystems holistic model of health, stress and coping. In T. M. Field, P. M. McCabe, and N. Schniederman (eds.), *Stress and Coping* (pp. 285–304). Hillsdale, NJ: Erlbaum.

Taylor, M. S., Fisher, C. D., and Ilgen, D. R. (1984) Individuals' reactions to performance feedback in organizations: A control theory perspective. In K. Rowland and J. Ferris (eds.), *Research in Personnel and Human Resources Management* (pp. 81–124). Greenwich, CT: JAI Press.

Tenbrunsel, A. E., Brett, J. M., Maoz, E., Stroh, L. K., and Reilly, A. H. (1995) 'Dynamic and static work–family relationships', *Organizational Behavior and Human Decision Process*, 63, 233–246.

Terry, D. J. (1994) 'Determinants of coping: The role of stable and situational factors', *Journal of Personality and Social Psychology*, 66, 895–910.

Thomas, J. and Griffin, R. (1983) 'The social information processing model of task design: A review of the literature', *Academy of Management Review*, 8, 672–682.

von Bertalanffy, L. (1968) *General Systems Theory*. New York: Brazeller.

Voydanoff, P. (1987) *Work and Family Life*. Newbury Park, CA: Sage.

Voydanoff, P. (1988) 'Work role characteristics, family structure demands and work/family conflict', *Journal of Marriage and the Family*, 50, 749–762.

Voydanoff, P. (1989) Work and family: A review and expanded conceptualization. In E. B. Goldsmith (ed.), *Work and Family: Theory, Research, and Applications* (pp. 1–22). Newbury Park, CA: Sage.

Watson, D. and Pennebaker, J. W. (1989) 'Health complaints, stress, and distress: Exploring the central role of negative affectivity', *Psychological Review*, 96, 234–254.

Watson, D. and Tellegen, A. (1985) 'Toward a consensual structure of mood', *Psychological Bulletin*, 98, 219–235.

Weick, K. E. (1979) *The Social Psychology of Organizing* (2nd edn.). Reading, MA: Addison-Wesley.

Wiener, N. (1948) *Cybernetics: Control and Communication in the Animal and the Machine*. New York: Wiley.

Wood, R. and Bandura, A. (1989) 'Impact of conceptions of ability on self-regulatory mechanisms and complex decision making', *Journal of Personality and Social Psychology*, 56, 407–415.

Zedeck, S. (1992) Introduction: Exploring the domain of work and family concerns. In S. Zedeck (ed.), *Work, Families, and Organizations* (pp. 1–32). San Francisco: Jossey-Bass.

7

A Control Theory of the Job Stress Process

Paul E. Spector

Control has served a central role in many theories of job stress, as well as other areas of organizational research (Ganster and Fusilier, 1989). It has been implicated as a potential cause of both physical health and psychological well-being (e.g., Evans and Carrére, 1991; Ganster and Fusilier, 1989). A more complex moderator role has also been suggested in the control/demands model (Karasek, 1979), whereby control buffers the negative effects of job stressors. Although the relation of control with health and well-being has been well established (see Ganster and Fusilier, 1989; Spector, 1986), the moderator role has not received consistent support. Furthermore, in much of the job stress literature, the exact mechanisms by which control affects people has not been completely delineated. It is the purpose of this chapter to help clarify these issues by presenting a model of the job stress process that includes control as a central variable.

A complex role for control will be discussed whereby it has both direct and moderating effects on the job stress process. It will be argued that control can act as a job stressor, as well as a factor that influences how the work environment is perceived. Thus it helps determine how an individual will appraise objective work conditions as job stressors. Furthermore, the role of negative emotions will be emphasized as an important aspect of the stress process. A careful distinction between the objective environment and perceptions of that environment will be made, as this may help explain why the (Karasek, 1979) control/demands model has had such inconsistent empirical support.

The Job Stress Model

Definitions

The two major classes of variables in the job stress process are job stressors and job strains. A stressor has been typically defined as a condition or situation that requires an adaptive response from a person (e.g. Beehr and Newman, 1978). However, it is not totally clear in this definition exactly what is meant by the adaptive response, and how it differs from a non-adaptive response. Any situation that results in any response might be classified as a job stressor, which fails to distinguish job stressors from other situations. In the present model a job stressor is considered to be a condition or situation that elicits a negative emotional response, such as anger/frustration or anxiety/tension. Although more restrictive, this definition limits job stressors to a more specific subset of all organizational conditions or situations.

It is also imperative that a distinction is made between environmental conditions and their perception (Parasuraman and Alutto, 1981). At the environmental level a particular condition might be perceived as a job stressor by some individuals and not others. The concept of appraisal (Lazarus, 1991; 1995) is relevant here, as it underscores the importance of perception and interpretation of conditions. For the most part, job conditions or situations that go unnoticed cannot be perceived as stressors, and will not have a psychological impact. Environmental stressors are conditions that tend to be perceived as such by individuals. It is indeed likely that what are considered environmental stressors by researchers are not always viewed in the same way by all job incumbents. In the research in our field we have identified specific job conditions that are likely environmental stressors (e.g. Evans *et al.*, 1994; Parker and DeCotiis, 1983).

It has been quite difficult to operationalize environmental job stressors in practice. Efforts have involved using sources other than incumbents, such as observers or supervisors, often completing the same scales. This approach removes the subject's appraisal from the assessment and is considered objective from this perspective (Frese and Zapf, 1988). However, such procedures are less than ideal in that the alternative sources might not be very knowledgeable about job stressors. Furthermore, many job stressors involve rather abstract concepts, such as role ambiguity, which are not easily assessed with methods other than human judgment. By contrast the stressor of workload can be assessed with physical measures, such as caloric expenditure or time spent.

Perceived stressor refers to the appraisal and interpretation made by an individual of a potential environmental stressor. They lead to negative emotional reactions, such as anxiety or anger, which can vary in intensity (Parasuraman and Alutto, 1981; Spielberger, 1975). Some perceived stressors can be powerful and lead to immediate reactions, while others might be quite mild and have a cumulative effect over time. Being fired would be an example of the former, as the individual is likely to experience immediate anger and anxiety. Workload is an example of the latter, as over time an individual might begin to feel increased fatigue and pressure which would lead to escalating emotion, perhaps starting with mild irritation and ending in strong anger and/or anxiety. These emotional reactions do not at any time have to be extreme, as the individual might merely experience mild discomfort or uneasiness.

Researchers have identified classes of conditions that are classified as job stressors. Conditions such as role conflict and role overload have been hypothesized to have particular effects on individuals. However, empirical evidence is required to establish that any potential variables are in fact environmental job stressors. This requires demonstrating a connection between those conditions and perceptions.

Furthermore, those perceptions must be shown to lead to emotional reactions. This does not require that subjects interpret the environmental condition in the same way as the researcher, and it is quite possible that interpretations are different. For example, we as researchers might classify a heated exchange with a supervisor as interpersonal conflict, while the incumbent sees it as a threat to autonomy. However, the exchange is likely to result in an emotional reaction regardless of which interpretation the incumbent chooses.

A job strain is the reaction to the job stressor. Jex and Beehr (1991) classified the major job strains as behavioral, physical, or psychological. In the present model, the psychological job strains occur first. This is the emotional reaction to the job stressor, which happens in many cases immediately. Also included as psychological strains are attitudinal reactions, such as job dissatisfaction. Such reactions typically require more time to develop than emotional states and are often quite stable (e.g. Staw and Ross, 1985).

Behavioral strains are instances of behavior elicited in response to the job stressor. They can range from the quite immediate and impulsive act, such as hitting someone who does something annoying, to long-term, well thought out strategies, such as seeking alternative employment. Many of these behaviors can be considered coping responses, which are acts done to handle the job stressor. These can be classified as emotion-focused versus problem-focused (Lazarus and Folkman, 1984). Emotion-focused coping is a behavior designed to reduce the emotional response without dealing directly with the job stressor, such as drinking alcohol or staying home from work. Problem-focused directly addresses the job stressor and might involve discussing the situation with the supervisor to find a resolution, or engaging in activities to reduce the job stressor.

From the organization's perspective, behavioral strains can be considered counterproductive or productive. A counterproductive act is one that interferes with organizational efficiency and functioning. Both absence and sabotage are examples. Productive acts contribute to the organization's goals and objectives though both required job performance and extra-role behaviors such as organizational citizenship behavior or OCB (Organ and Konovsky, 1989). Much of the emotion-focused coping is counterproductive, although it does not have to be. Escape behavior both physically through absence or psychologically through alcohol or drug use can have detrimental effects on organization functioning. Problem focused approaches are often productive, in that employees might successfully solve organizational problems by taking direct action to reduce job stressors. For example, an employee might choose to handle an increase in workload by staying home from work (counterproductive and emotion-focused) or by suggesting a more efficient procedure to save time (productive and problem-focused). Of course, emotion-focused approaches of avoiding work might in some cases be productive by providing needed rest in the short run so the person could be more effective in the long run, and a problem-focused approach might be to find a new job, which would not typically be productive for the organization.

Physical strain is a physiological reaction, which can be divided into long-term and short-term (Frese and Zapf, 1988). A long-term strain is a physical illness, such as heart disease, which has been suggested as an outcome of the stress process (Greenglass, 1996; Julkunen, 1996). Short-term strains are physiological reactions, such as increased blood pressure or suppression of the immune response. Many of the short-term physical strains are associated with emotional reactions (O'Leary, 1990), and they may in fact be mechanisms by which long-term physical strains occur.

Control is the ability of the individual to choose his or her own actions from two or more options (Ganster and Fusilier, 1989). The focus here is on behavioral control as opposed to cognitive control (Averill, 1973) which might also reduce the impact of job stressors (Thompson, 1981). Behavioral control in the workplace ranges from autonomy, which is control over the individual's own immediate scheduling and tasks, to participation in more global decision making that might not affect the person directly. For the job stress process, it is control over the immediate and specific job stressors that is important. This implies that merely having autonomy or being able to participate in decisions may or may not have any effect on job stressors. To be effective, control must be over the job stressor itself. Having autonomy over job tasks is not likely to have any impact on a poor relation with co-workers, but on the other hand, having the autonomy to work at home and avoid them, is likely to be helpful.

Control must also be divided into environmental and perceived. The former is the degree of choice an individual is given, either by the situation or by superiors, while the latter is the amount of choice the individual believes he or she has. An individual who is given control does not necessarily perceive that control. He or she might not feel capable of using the control. For example, self-efficacy (Bandura, 1982) is the belief a person has in his or her ability to accomplish something. Low self-efficacy is a form of low perceived control in which someone does not believe he or she can do something successfully. It is also likely in many circumstances that incumbents do not trust superiors, and do not believe that the control they are given is real. Even though an individual is given autonomy to work on a project, he or she might perceive that superiors will require that things be done in a particular way, which negates their feeling of control.

The Job Stress Process

This model, illustrated in Figure 7.1, posits that perceived stressors lead to emotional reactions, which lead to job strains. Although emotions have been classified as a form of job strain (Jex and Beehr, 1991), it is here distinguished from longer term psychological strains, such as job dissatisfaction (see also Parker and DeCotiis, 1983). Emotions mediate, at least in part, the effects of job stressors on behavioral and physical strains, as well as longer term psychological strains such as job dissatisfaction. On the behavioral side, emotions play an important role in that they can induce powerful motivations to reduce them. Both anger and anxiety help direct behavior in a general way, although there are typically many choices available to the individual. These choices can involve emotion- or problem-focused approaches, which can be counterproductive or productive.

Although this chain of events seems on one level to be quite simple, there are many complicating factors. Perceptions of job stressors are due to many things, including

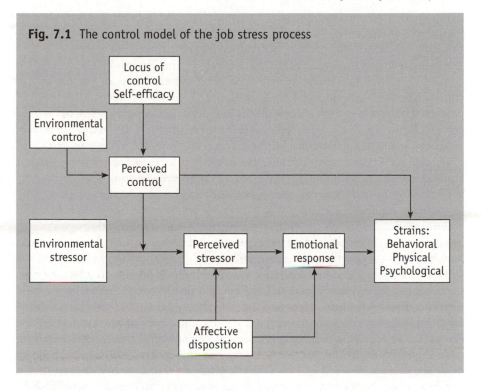

Fig. 7.1 The control model of the job stress process

both personal and situational factors. Given a particular perception, there are considerable individual differences in response at both the affective and behavioral levels. Control is one very important component in both of these points in the model. Furthermore, the correspondence between environmental control and perceived control is imperfect, further complicating this process.

Perceived control is posited to moderate the relation between environmental and perceived job stressor. Specifically, when control is high, the strength of relation between environmental and perceived stressor should be low. The individual is not likely to interpret the condition/situation as a job stressor and will not exhibit an emotional reaction. Conversely, when perceived control is low, the relation between environmental and perceived job stressor will be strong. An individual is likely to interpret the condition/situation as being a job stressor and will exhibit an emotional reaction. Note that the control must be over the specific job stressor itself. More general control is not going to have an effect unless it is perceived to be effective against the job stressor. Being able to determine one's work schedule is not going to reduce the perceived job stressor of being fired. Having two attractive job offers in hand will greatly reduce the impact, however.

Frankenhaeuser and Lundberg (1982) describe jobs and situations that produce effort and distress, which can be distinguished physiologically. Effort leads to a rise in catecholamines such as adrenaline and noradrenaline, and a decrease in cortisol. Distress leads to a rise in all three. These so called stress hormones are associated with experienced emotions (Frankenhaeuser, 1979), and help explain how psychological strains result in physical strains. An individual who feels in control of a situation may experience effort, but lack of control is likely to result in distress.

Beyond reducing the impact of environmental job stressors on perceived stressors, control also helps determine an individual's behavioral reactions particularly in choosing between emotion- and problem-focused coping approaches. High levels of perceived control over a situation leads the individual to attempt a problem-focused and productive approach, intended to overcome the situation. Often this can be successful in managing job strains, but at the cost of increased effort and workload (Tattersall and Farmer, 1995). The job stressor likely induces minor irritation which is easily channeled into something constructive. Low perceived control leaves the person believing that nothing constructive can be done to overcome the situation, so he or she must cope with it another way. This more emotion-focused approach can be counterproductive, which can mean avoiding the situation entirely through absence or engaging in covert or overt acts of aggression and other antisocial behaviors that have been associated with anger and frustration at work (Spector, 1997).

There are many individual difference variables that can potentially affect the connection between environmental and perceived control. Two in particular are relevant to control itself—locus of control and self-efficacy. Locus of control is a tendency for an individual to believe he or she can control rewards and punishments in life. The external is an individual who believes that fate or powerful others are controlling rewards and punishments, and that he or she has little control. The internal believes he or she is in control. Self-efficacy is the belief, limited to a specific domain, that a person is able to be effective in accomplishing something. An employee might have a high level of self-efficacy in his or her ability to do the job, for example. Self-efficacy is undoubtedly more malleable than most personality variables in that it can change with experience, but it can be considered for our purposes as a disposition.

Locus of control is expected to relate to perceived control in that externals should be lower than internals. This has been found in most studies (e.g. Spector, 1987), although the magnitude of correlations found is often surprisingly low. Part of this is due to the general nature of locus of control measures, and in fact correlations of control at work tend to be higher with the work domain work locus of control scale (Spector, 1987) than with more general scales. Furthermore, the personality variable of locus of control is a dispositional tendency which can be overshadowed by clear situational conditions. An internal person who may believe he or she can achieve desired outcomes may be quite aware of the fact that the job requires strict compliance with specific procedures to accomplish tasks.

Locus of control has also been shown to relate, perhaps more strongly, with job strains. Thus by feeling more in control in general, an internal might have a lessened emotional reaction. Even given the same emotional response, internals might respond more constructively. Research, to be discussed later, has shown that locus of control relates to counterproductive and productive behavior (e.g. Perlow and Latham, 1993; Spector, 1982).

Control has so far been discussed mainly in terms of its buffering effects on the perception of stressors and on job strains. However, under some conditions control itself can function as a stressor. There are two ways in which this can occur. First, control typically comes with responsibility, and enhanced responsibility can be perceived as a job stressor by many individuals. Second, an individual who feels in control will often respond to job stressors with actions designed to overcome them. If those actions are unsuccessful, the situation can become a job stressor. Houston (1972) found that actual control was associated with greater physiological arousal in response to physical stressors than lack of control. His explanation was that control resulted in an effort to use it, which itself resulted in greater strain. If efforts are unsuccessful, the individual might experience even higher levels of emotional reaction. These results fit well with the aforementioned study by Frankenhaeuser and Lundberg (1982) which found an increase in catecholamines associated with effort. Control then can be counterproductive in leading to increased strains if the situation is one in which it is unlikely to be effective.

Self-efficacy is another dispositional control variable that is more specific than locus of control. It also moderates the relation between certain types of environmental job stressors and perceived job stressors. Individuals who believe that they are capable of handling a situation will be unlikely to perceive it as a job stressor. Nelson and Sutton (1990), for example, found that individuals who were high in mastery at work (self-efficacy) reported lower levels of job stressors than their counterparts who were low in mastery. For self-efficacy to be an effective buffer, the job stressor must be something relevant to the domain in which the individual feels capable. An individual who has high self-efficacy for doing job tasks, for example, is not likely to perceive a challenging new assignment as a job stressor. Such a person is also likely to respond to situations constructively, with efforts made to overcome potential job stressors rather than merely survive them. Nelson and Sutton (1990) also found that mastery correlated positively with the use of problem-focused coping.

Individual differences in affective dispositions, such as negative affectivity (Watson et al., 1988) or trait anxiety (Spielberger, 1972), are also important. People may differ in their tendency to perceive the world as threatening, as well as in their tendency to respond emotionally. This can be considered a threshold difference among people, whereby some individuals have bigger reactions than others to the same situation. Such dispositions act independently of control, i.e. it is not that high anxious people respond more strongly because they perceive themselves to have less control. Rather they respond more strongly because they have a lower threshold for anxiety. For example, Spielberger (1972) discussed how individuals high in trait anxiety showed greater state anxiety increases in response to certain stressors than low anxious counterparts. These stressors were characterized as representing threats to self-esteem rather than physical danger. Affective dispositions have also been associated with reports of somatic symptoms (Watson and Pennebaker, 1989).

Certainly there are many other personality variables which are possibly important in the job stress process. For example, Hogan and Hogan (1989) developed the delinquent personality profile to help explain counterproductive behavior at work. This is a cluster of specific traits that predict what are here classified as behavioral strains. Work in the integrity test area has also identified personality traits associated with counterproductive behavior (see Ones *et al.*, 1993), which in many cases may be a reaction to job stressors.

In summary, this model of the job stress process posits that the connection between job stressors and strains is mediated by emotional reactions. This makes the model more restrictive than most job stress models in eliminating situations that do not involve emotions. It is possible that some reactions classified here as job strains occur without emotions. However, it may be useful to restrict the model to avoid being so general that literally every situation becomes a job stressor.

This model also includes counterproductive behavior as a form of behavioral job strain. These behaviors are often associated with negative emotions, specifically anger/frustration (Spector, 1997). Furthermore, anger and frustration have been found to be more common reactions to job stressors than anxiety (Narayanan *et al.*, in press). These behaviors are not typically considered in a job stress context, but they may occur in response to the same situations that induce other job strains.

Empirical Support for the Model

Some of the linkages in the model are very well supported empirically, while others are somewhat more speculative. For the most part the direct links have support, but evidence for the moderators is not so readily available. One reason for this is that most job stress studies have limited assessment of job stressors to incumbent reports, which measure perceptions. The moderator tests require assessment of the work environment, independent of the incumbent's perception of it. However, operationally distinguishing the environmental job stressor from the perception of it is essential to this model.

The control/demands model also hypothesizes an interaction of control with job stressors (Karasek, 1979). Many empirical tests of this model have failed to support it. The reason, if the present model is correct, is that it does not distinguish environmental job demands from their perception. Most empirical tests have used incumbent reports of control and demands, and have not found significant moderator effects on a variety of job strains. However, if control affects the person's interpretation of the environment, its effect has already occurred when the moderator tests have been done in these studies. In the few tests that have been positive, different procedures were used, as will be discussed later in this chapter.

Relations of Job Stressors and Job Strains

The model posits a chain of events from environmental to perceptual job stressors to emotional reactions and then to various job strains. Empirical evidence exists showing relations among all of these variables. Most studies have used incumbent reports of job stressors and job strains, so that it is very well established that these variables are related. Less research has used alternative methods which are independent of incumbent perception. In addition few studies used designs that will allow causal conclusions.

A handful of studies used multiple methods to assess job stressors to investigate relations among environmental conditions and perceptions. Such studies have provided evidence that, at least for some variables, there is convergence. For example, Frese (1985) compared incumbents with observers and peers on composite measures of job stressors. He found significant correlations in all cases, ranging from .30 to .61. Kirmeyer (1988) found that an incumbent measure of workload correlated .59 with an objective measure of the amount of work done.

Not all measures of job stressors find good convergence among methods, however. Spector *et al.* (1988) reported correlations between incumbents and supervisors on six job stressors. There was considerable variability in magnitude of correlations, ranging from a non-signficant .08 for role ambiguity to .83 for hours worked per week. However, taken as a whole these studies indicate that perceptions of job stressors are very much reflective of the work environment. It should be kept in mind that some of these alternative methods are not necessarily accurate (Frese and Zapf, 1988), making these correlations underestimates of how strongly environmental and perceptual job stressors are related.

Consistent support has also been found for relations between perceived job stressors and emotional reactions (Jex and Beehr, 1991). For example, Jackson and Schuler (1985) found mean correlations of role ambiguity and role conflict with affective reactions generally in the .30s. Compiling results across four of our own studies (Chen and Spector, 1991; Spector, 1987; Spector *et al.*, 1988; Spector and O'Connell, 1994), there was a median correlation of five job stressors (interpersonal conflict, organizational constraints, role ambiguity, role conflict, and workload) with an anxiety score of .37, and frustration of .39. Although correlations were similar for four job stressors with job satisfaction, workload had a considerably smaller median correlation of −.17. For example, in Spector and O'Connell (1994) frustration and workload were correlated at .61, while job satisfaction and workload were correlated at .00.

The next step in the model is that emotions should relate to behavioral and physical job strains. Support for such a connection is provided in the four studies by the present author noted in the above paragraph. The median correlation was .44 between anxiety and physical symptoms and .24 between frustration and physical symptoms. Counterproductive behavior has been shown to significantly correlate with anger and frustration at work (Chen and Spector, 1992; see Spector, 1997 for a review).

According to the present model, emotions mediate the relations between job stressors and job strains. Therefore, we would expect to find larger correlations of emotions with job stressors than other job strains with job stressors. The aforementioned four studies by the present author addresses this question for somatic symptoms. Although the median correlations of job stressors with the two affect variables of anxiety and frustration were .37 and .39, respectively, median correlations with physical symptoms was .21. This occurred even in Spector *et al.* (1988) despite a strong .51 correlation between anxiety and physical symptoms. Although not formal tests for mediation, these patterns of results are supportive of the contention that emotions mediate the relation between job stressors and physical job strains. A more complete mediation test is provided by Fox and Spector (in press) who used structural equation modeling to support a model in which frustration mediated the relation of organizational constraints with counterproductive behavior, providing a link with behavioral job strains.

Role of Perceived Control

Far less evidence is available to support the hypothesized moderator effects of control. There have been several tests of the Karasek (1979) control/demands model, many of which have failed to find support for it (Fletcher and Jones, 1993; Wall *et al.*, 1996). Most of the failed tests have used perceptual measures of job stressors. As noted by Wall *et al.*, those tests that have found support for the moderator effect tended to use more objective measures, which were indicators of the environment. In their study a descriptive job characteristics measure was used, that the authors argued reflected the objective job better than most perceptual measures used in this domain. Results supported the control/demand model in that there was a significant moderator effect for the job strains of anxiety, depression, and job dissatisfaction. Landsbergis *et al.* (1995) note support for the model in the majority of studies that used more objective measures.

Although the present model hypothesizes a moderator effect on relations between environmental and perceptual job stressors, it would be expected that this would also produce a moderator effect for job strains that were the result of perceptual job stressors. In other words if control moderated the relation between environmental and perceptual job stressors which in turn caused job strains, control should also moderate to some extent the relation between environmental job stressors and job strains.

Indirect tests of the moderator effect of control come from a series of studies relating job conditions to physiological measures. Johansson *et al.* (1978) showed that jobs requiring high attention under conditions of machine pacing (low control) resulted in increased levels of physical and psychological job strains, including catecholamines, cortisol, health symptoms, illnesses, job dissatisfaction and tension. Jobs characterized as allowing confident task involvement with high control were found to lead only to increases in catecholamines (Frankenhaeuser, 1979) associated with effort. The elevation of both catecholamines and cortisol have been linked to heart disease (Johansson, 1989).

The present model also hypothesizes a role for control in the choice of coping strategy made by an individual. Research on this topic tends to support this contention, although much of it involves the personality variable locus of control rather than perceived control itself. Storms and Spector (1987) found that locus of control moderated the relation between experienced frustration and counterproductive behavior, with externals being more likely to engage in such behavior. Perlow and Latham (1993) reported that externals were more likely to abuse residents of a state facility for the developmentally disabled than were internals. In a more general sense, Hurrell and Murphy (1991) summarized research showing that internals use more constructive problem-focused coping approaches than externals.

The final part of the model that will be discussed is the evidence concerning influences on perceived control. First, there are several studies that have compared different measures of autonomy, which is one aspect of control at work. Spector (1992) reported a mean correlation of .30 across seven studies that compared commonly used autonomy measures completed by job incumbents with other sources, such as supervisors. However, these measures tend to be rather general and have been criticized for being vulnerable to affective bias (Spector, 1992; Taber and Taylor, 1990). Thus they might underestimate how strongly environmental control affects perceptual control. In fact measures that are more descriptive and fact based have been shown to have better convergent validity between incumbents and other sources. For example, Fox, Spector, and Van Katwyk (1997) developed a fact based autonomy scale that had a correlation between incumbents and their supervisors of .52. Thus it seems likely that the environment has a big influence on perceived control.

As noted earlier, personality traits such as locus of control also play a role in perceptions of control. It should be noted, however, that this personality construct concerns the individual's belief in being able to acquire rewards, rather than the belief in being able to control all situations. Correlations of autonomy with locus of control have in some cases been rather modest (e.g. Spector, 1988). Spector and O'Connell (1994) found a correlation of –.31 between autonomy and work locus of control in a longitudinal study. In this study of recent college graduates, personality might have played a bigger role in perceptions than would have been true with an older sample. Note that Spector (1988) reported a significant correlation of only –.10 with the same measures in a sample of municipal managers where the median age was 45. Perhaps for those well experienced individuals environmental control far overshadowed the influence of personality. After a while on the job, an individual learns how much control is available, despite the predisposition to believe he or she has or does not have control. Thus it seems likely that personality plays a bigger role in determining perceptions of control, as well as other job conditions, when situations are new, such as early in the working career.

Overall there is considerable evidence to support some of the proposed connections hypothesized. Most of it is from cross-sectional designs which only establish relations rather than causation. Some of the moderators have yet to be directly tested. This is because the role of control here is far more specific than has been considered in most research. At the present time, this model seems feasible based on existing evidence, but additional research is needed for it to be more directly tested.

Implications of the Model for the Control of Job Stress

The present model clearly suggests a complex interplay of dispositional and environmental factors in the job stress process. Although environmental factors are important, experiences are filtered through individual personality and other individual difference variables. Control of job strains must involve both aspects of the job and aspects of the person. Most interventions conducted in organizations to deal with job stress, at least in the USA, have taken a definite employee focus. Counterproductive behavior has been combated with the use of integrity tests that help screen out individuals who are likely to engage in such acts (Ones *et al.*, 1993). Physical and psychological health interventions have focused on stress management training designed to enhance an individual's ability to deal with job stressors. Little attention has been given to environmental interventions.

Perhaps the most important implication of the present model is that control can reduce the effect of environmental job stressors. Control must be over the job stressor itself, as merely increasing control in general will often make matters worse. The individual who finds a situation to be a job stressor will likely benefit from being given more control over the particular aspects that are perceived as job stressors. For example, if an individual finds the amount of work is difficult to handle, being given control over work assignments and work pace will be helpful. Being given the opportunity to participate in organizational decisions could be counterproductive because it produces yet another demand that increases workload.

There are many organizational techniques that might potentially enhance perceived control. Job redesign has as one objective increasing control and responsibility over tasks. Autonomous work groups allow more control than traditional working arrangements. Survey feedback is intended to give input to employees over issues that concern them. Team building could be used for much the same objective by allowing discussions of work problems.

Another more specific intervention that is directly targeted to control over job stressors would be to train supervisors to conduct special problem-solving sessions with subordinates. Supervisors would help subordinates identify their job stressors, and implement strategies designed to enhance perceived control over those situations. This can be done by having meetings during which work problems are discussed and solutions to those problems developed. Clearly to be successful it is essential that there be trust between subordinates and supervisors. A focus on work problems affecting performance rather than job stress and personal problems is likely to produce more candor and less defensiveness. However, what is likely to result is a discussion of things that are by definition job stressors, such as conflicts with other employees or organizational conditions that interfere with the employee in doing his or her job.

One solution to work problems is likely to be enhanced control over the situation by the employee. If discussions happen regularly and they provide an opportunity for the individual to have input, control is already enhanced. The focus on control over the specific problem discussed limits it to an area in which it will likely reduce perceived job stressors. It is also essential that the person has control over their control. In other words control should be something that an individual is free to accept or decline. Not everyone wishes to have control (Xie, 1996), and it can produce additional job strain as the individual perceives more job stressors from the responsibility of unwanted control.

It is also likely that through such discussions, effective strategies will be undertaken that will reduce environmental job stressors. For example, an individual who feels overworked might suggest ways to make their work more efficient. The person who is experiencing the situation might be in the best position to come up with an effective solution, which is suggested quite clearly in research on principles of sociotechnical systems theory (e.g. Wall *et al.*, 1992). In addition to remediating the problem of job stress, this approach is likely to have beneficial effects on job performance and organizational efficiency.

Specific solutions to problems of job stressors must be directed to their particular nature. What might help for one environmental condition or situation might be counterproductive in another. For example, an individual might perceive high workload for a variety of reasons. If the person lacks skills to do a task efficiently, additional training would be appropriate. If the problem was defective equipment, a different solution would be required.

Although this discussion has suggested an individual approach to identifying job stressors, it is not necessarily the case that reactions are always unique to the individual. For example, most people would respond negatively to being fired. However, each individual typically has unique experiences at work since people's responsibilities and tasks differ. The focus of an intervention for a person should be on job stressors he or she actually encounters. Thus individualized interventions would seem most appropriate.

Future Directions

As noted earlier, most research in the job stress domain has viewed control in rather general terms. Although autonomy is distinguished from other forms of control, such as participation in decision making, there has been little attempt to further divide control. One exception is Breaugh (1985) who developed a scale to assess three types of autonomy. Clearly measures are needed of specific control over job stressors. For example, since workload has been identified as an important variable, it would be worthwhile assessing control of it. This is to some extent covered by Breaugh's (1985) schedule autonomy subscale, but even more specific measures are needed. It might be helpful to develop parallel control scales for the commonly used job stressor scales to assess such variables as interpersonal conflict or role ambiguity. It would be expected that control would be negatively associated with reports of these corresponding job stressors, although not necessarily with objective measures of them. Of course it is possible that if an individual has control, he or she will reduce the environmental job stressor itself.

A parallel has been shown here between counterproductive behavior and job stress. It is argued that emotion is an important mediator in the relation between the job environment and behavior. At least some of this behavior occurs in response to conditions or situations defined here as perceived job stressors. Far more research is needed to help us understand the causes of this important phenomenon in organizations.

The job stress field has often failed to completely distinguish environmental from perceived control and job stressors. Much of the work which used alternative measures to incumbent reports has tended to use the former to validate the latter. Although most researchers undoubtedly recognize the limitations and subjectivity of incumbent reports, these factors are often considered biases in the assessment of job conditions. It would be instructive to treat these reports as perceptions which are only somewhat related to the work environment. Our research questions might then be rephrased to ask which conditions or situations will be perceived as job stressors. It has been clearly established that reports of job stressors correlate with all three types of job strains. What is less clear are the environmental conditions at work that lead individuals to perceive particular job stressors.

The model presented here is discussed in static terms, with the causal flow running from environment to job strains. This is admittedly an oversimplification as the process is undoubtedly a dynamic interplay of all variables, with causal flows running in many directions. There is evidence that job satisfaction impacts perceptions, for example (Spector, 1992). One way control can affect job strains is by allowing the individual to reduce environmental job stressors directly (Karasek *et al.*, 1981). Although it can be very difficult, research is needed that addresses more complex causal relations among these variables. Longitudinal designs will be necessary to help us fully explore such complex situations.

The job stress process is a complex interaction among people and the work environment. Research should investigate both sets of factors simultaneously. A full understanding of relations between the work environment and job strains must take into account individual differences in response and the reasons for those differences. A variety of approaches and methodologies will be required to accomplish the difficult task that studying a complex process entails.

The author thanks Steve M. Jex for his comments on an earlier version of this chapter.

References

Averill, J. (1973) 'Personal control over aversive stimuli and its relationship to stress', *Psychological Bulletin*, 80, 286–303.

Bandura, A. (1982) 'Self-efficacy mechanism in human agency', *American Psychologist*, 37, 122–147.

Beehr, T. A. and Newman, J. E. (1978) 'Job stress, employee health, and organizational effectiveness: A facet analysis, model and literature review', *Personnel Psychology*, 31, 665–699.

Breaugh, J. A. (1985) 'The measurement of work autonomy', *Human Relations*, 38, 551–570.

Chen, P. Y. and Spector, P. E. (1991) 'Negative affectivity as the underlying cause of correlations between stressors and strains', *Journal of Applied Psychology*, 76, 398–407.

Chen, P. Y. and Spector, P. E. (1992) 'Relationships of work stressors with aggression, withdrawal, theft and substance use: An exploratory study', *Journal of Occupational and Organizational Psychology*, 65, 177–184.

Evans, G. W. and Carrére, S. (1991) 'Traffic congestion, perceived control, and psychophysiological stress among urban bus drivers', *Journal of Applied Psychology*, 76, 658–663.

Evans, G. W., Johansson, G., and Carrére, S. (1994) Psychosocial factors and the physical environment: Inter-relations in the workplace. In C. L. Cooper and I. T. Robertson (eds.) *International Review of Industrial and Organizational Psychology: 1994* (pp. 1–29). Chichester, UK: John Wiley.

Fletcher, B. C. and Jones, F. (1993) 'A refutation of Karasek's demand–discretion model of occupational stress with a range of dependent measures', *Journal of Organizational Behavior*, 14, 319–330.

Fox, S. and Spector, P. E. (in press) 'A model of work frustration–aggression', *Journal of Organizational Behavior*.

Fox, S., Spector, P. E., and Van Katwyk, P. T. (1997) Objectivity in the assessment of control at work. Paper presented at the Society for Industrial and Organizational Psychology Convention, St. Louis, April.

Frankenhaeuser, M. (1979) Psychoneuroendocrine approaches to the study of emotion as related to stress and coping. In H. E. Howe and R. A. Diensbier (eds.). *Nebraska Symposium on Motivation* (pp. 123–161). Lincoln: University of Nebraska Press.

Frankenhaeuser, M. and Lundberg, U. (1982) Psychoneuroendocrine aspects of effort and distress as modified by personal control. In W. Bachmann and I. Udris (eds.). *Mental Load and Stress in Activity* (pp. 97–103). Amsterdam: North-Holland.

Frese, M. (1985) 'Stress at work and psychosomatic complaints: A causal interpretation', *Journal of Applied Psychology*, 70, 314–328.

Frese, M. and Zapf, D. (1988) Methodological issues in the study of work stress: objective vs. subjective measurement of work stress and the question of longitudinal studies. In C. L. Cooper and R. Payne (eds.). *Causes, Coping and Consequences of Stress at Work* (pp. 375–410). Chichester, UK: John Wiley.

Ganster, D. C. and Fusilier, M. R. (1989) Control in the workplace. In C. L. Cooper and I. T. Robertson (eds.). *International Review of Industrial and Organizational Psychology 1989* (pp. 235–280). Chichester, UK: John Wiley.

Greenglass, E. R. (1996) Anger suppression, cynical distrust, and hostility: Implications for coronary heart disease. In C. D. Spielberger, I. G. Sarason, J. M. T. Brebner, E. Greenglass, P. Laungani, and A. M. O'Roark (eds.). *Stress and Emotion: Anxiety, Anger, and Curiosity* (Vol. 16, pp. 205–225). Washington, DC: Taylor & Francis.

Hogan, J. and Hogan, R. (1989) 'How to measure employee reliability', *Journal of Applied Psychology*, 74, 273–279.

Houston, B. K. (1972) 'Control over stress, locus of control, and response to stress', *Journal of Personality and Social Psychology*, 21, 249–255.

Hurrell, J. J., Jr. and Murphy, L. R. (1991) Locus of control, job demands, and health. In C. L. Cooper and R. Payne (eds.). *Personality and Stress: Individual Differences in the Stress Process* (pp. 133–149). Chichester, UK: John Wiley.

Jackson, S. E. and Schuler, R. S. (1985) 'A meta-analysis and conceptual critique of research on role ambiguity and role conflict in work settings', *Organizational Behavior and Human Decision Processes*, 36, 16–78.

Jex, S. M. and Beehr, T. A. (1991) 'Emerging theoretical and methodological issues in the study of work-related stress', *Research in Personnel and Human Resources Management*, 9, 311–365.

Johansson, G. (1989) 'Stress, autonomy, and the maintenance of skill in supervisory control of automated systems', *Applied Psychology: An International Review*, 38, 45–56.

Johansson, G., Aronsson, G., and Lindstrom, B. O. (1978) 'Social psychological and neuroendocrine stress reactions in highly mechanized work', *Ergonomics*, 21, 583–599.

Julkunen, J. (1996) Suppressing your anger: Good manners, bad health? In C. D. Spielberger, I. G. Sarason, J. M. T. Brebner, E. Greenglass, P. Laungani, and A. M. O'Roark (eds.). *Stress and Emotion: Anxiety, Anger, and Curiosity* (Vol. 16, pp. 227–240). Washington, DC: Taylor & Francis.

Karasek, R. A. (1979) 'Job demands, job decision latitude, and mental strain: Implications for job redesign', *Administrative Science Quarterly*, 24, 285–308.

Karasek, R., Baker, D., Marxer, F., Ahlbom, A., and Theorell, T. (1981) 'Job decision latitude, job demands, and cardiovascular disease: A prospective study of Swedish men', *American Journal of Public Health*, 71, 694–705.

Kirmeyer, S. L. (1988) 'Coping with competing demands: Interruption and the Type A pattern', *Journal of Applied Psychology*, 73, 621–629.

Landsbergis, P. A., Schnall, P. L., Schwartz, J. E., Warren, K., and Pickering, T. G. (1995) Job strain, hypertension, and cardiovascular disease: Empirical evidence, methodological issues, and recommendations for future research. In S. L. Sauter and L. R. Murphy (eds.). *Organizational Risk Factors for Job Stress* (pp. 97–112). Washington, DC: American Psychological Association.

Lazarus, R. S. (1991) 'Cognition and motivation in emotion', *American Psychologist*, 46, 352–367.

Lazarus, R. S. (1995) Psychological stress in the workplace. In R. Crandall and P. L. Perrewe (eds.), *Occupational Stress* (pp. 3–14). Washington, DC: Taylor & Francis.

Lazarus, R. S. and Folkman, S. (1984) *Stress, Appraisal and Coping*. New York: Springer.

Narayanan, L., Menon, S., and Spector, P. E. (in press) 'Stress in the workplace: A comparison of gender and occupations', *Journal of Organizational Behavior*.

Nelson, D. L. and Sutton, C. (1990) 'Chronic work stress and coping: A longitudinal study and suggested new directions', *Academy of Management Journal*, 33, 859–869.

O'Leary, A. (1990) 'Stress, emotion, and human immune function', *Psychological Bulletin*, 108, 363–382.

Ones, D. S., Viswesvaran, C., and Schmidt, F. L. (1993) 'Comprehensive meta-analysis of integrity test validities: Findings and implications for personnel selection and theories of job performance', *Journal of Applied Psychology*, 78, 679–703.

Organ, D. W. and Konovsky, M. (1989) 'Cognitive versus affective determinants of organizational citizenship behavior', *Journal of Applied Psychology*, 74, 157–164.

Parasuraman, S. and Alutto, J. A. (1981) 'An examination of the organizational antecedents of stressors at work', *Academy of Management Journal*, 24, 48–67.

Parker, D. F. and DeCotiis, T. A. (1983) 'Organizational determinants of job stress', *Organizational Behavior and Human Performance*, 32, 160–177.

Perlow, R. and Latham, L. L. (1993) 'Relationship of client abuse with locus of control and gender: A longitudinal study', *Journal of Applied Psychology*, 78, 831–834.

Spector, P. E. (1982) 'Behavior in organizations as a function of employee locus of control', *Psychological Bulletin*, 91, 482–497.

Spector, P. E. (1986) 'Perceived control by employees: A meta-analysis of studies concerning autonomy and participation at work', *Human Relations*, 39, 1005–1016.

Spector, P. E. (1987) 'Interactive effects of perceived control and job stressors on affective reactions and health outcomes for clerical workers', *Work & Stress*, 1, 155–162.

Spector, P. E. (1988) 'Development of the work locus of control scale', *Journal of Occupational Psychology*, 61, 335–340.

Spector, P. E. (1992) A consideration of the validity and meaning of self-report measures of job conditions. In C. L. Cooper and I. T. Robertson (eds.) *International Review of Industrial and Organizational Psychology: 1992*. West Sussex, England: John Wiley.

Spector, P. E. (1997) The role of frustration in anti-social behavior at work. In R. A. Giacalone and J. Greenberg (eds.) *Anti-social Behavior in the Workplace* (pp. 1–17). Newbury Park, CA: Sage.

Spector, P. E. and O'Connell, B. J. (1994) 'The contribution of individual dispositions to the subsequent perceptions of job stressors and job strains', *Journal of Occupational and Organizational Psychology*, 67, 1–11.

Spector, P. E., Dwyer, D. J., and Jex, S. M. (1988) 'The relationship of job stressors to affective, health, and performance outcomes: A comparison of multiple data sources', *Journal of Applied Psychology*, 73, 11–19.

Spielberger, C. D. (1972) Anxiety as an emotional state. In C. D. Spielberger (ed.), *Anxiety: Current Trends in Theory and Research* (Vol. 1, pp. 23–49). New York: Academic Press.

Spielberger, C. D. (1975) Anxiety: State-trait-process. In C. D. Spielberger and I. G. Sarason (eds.), *Stress and Anxiety* (pp. 115–142). Washington: Hemisphere/Wiley.

Staw, B. M. and Ross, J. (1985) 'Stability in the midst of change: A dispositional approach to job attitudes', *Journal of Applied Psychology*, 70, 469–480.

Storms, P. L. and Spector, P. E. (1987) 'Relationships of organizational frustration with reported behavioral reactions: The moderating effect of perceived control', *Journal of Occupational Psychology*, 60, 227–234.

Taber, T. D. and Taylor, E. (1990) 'A review and evaluation of the psychometric properties of the Job Diagnostic Survey', *Personnel Psychology*, 43, 467–500.

Tattersall, A. J. and Farmer, E. W. (1995) The regulation of work demands and strain. In S. L. Sauter and L. R. Murphy (eds.). *Organizational Risk Factors for Job Stress* (pp. 139–156). Washington, DC: American Psychological Association.

Thompson, S. C. (1981) 'Will it hurt less if I can control it? A complex answer to a simple question', *Psychological Bulletin*, 90, 89–101.

Wall, T. D., Jackson, P. R, and Davids, K. (1992) 'Operator work design and robotics system performance: A serendipitous field study', *Journal of Applied Psychology*, 77, 353–362.

Wall, T. D., Jackson, P. R., Mullarkey, S., and Parker, S. K. (1996) 'The demands–control model of job strain: A more specific test', *Journal of Occupational and Organizational Psychology*, 69, 153–166.

Watson, D., Clark, L. A., and Tellegen, A. (1988) 'Development and validation of brief measures of positive and negative affect: The PANAS scales', *Journal of Personality and Social Psychology*, 54, 1063–1070.

Watson, D. and Pennebaker, J. W. (1989) 'Health complaints, stress, and distress: Exploring the central role of negative affectivity', *Psychological Review*, 96, 234–254.

Xie, J. L. (1996) 'Karasek's model in the People's Republic of China: Effects of job demands, control, and individual differences', *Academy of Management Journal*, 39, 1594–1618.

8

Stressors, Innovation, and Personal Initiative:
Are Stressors Always Detrimental?

Doris Fay, Sabine Sonnentag and Michael Frese

Introduction

This chapter will focus on the relationship between stressors, innovation, and personal initiative. Both innovation and initiative are theoretically and practically important concepts. Personal initiative can be conceptualized to be part of the general research area of contextual performance (Organ, 1997), which has received much attention due to its relevance for organizational effectiveness and improvement of production procedures or services (Frese *et al.*, 1997; Podsakoff and Mackenzie, 1997). Likewise, with increasing global competition the pressure to innovate is becoming stronger. Research on stressors has consistently proved their negative effects on health, performance, and satisfaction (Kahn and Byosiere, 1991; Zapf *et al.*, 1996).

In this chapter we want to establish a link between the separate lines of research on innovation and personal initiative on the one hand and stressors on the other. The relationship of stressors, innovation, and personal initiative will be discussed from various perspectives: we shall consider the negative effects of stressors on both activities and we shall also explore the potential positive effects of stressors. Literature will be reviewed for both approaches.

Central Concepts

Innovation and Personal Initiative

Innovation Innovation is a rather broad term that may refer to a product, to an outcome or to a process (Anderson and King, 1993). West and Farr (1990) defined innovation as 'the intentional introduction and application within a role, group, or organisation of ideas, processes, products or procedures, new to the relevant unit of adoption, designed to significantly benefit the individual, group, organisation or wider society' (p. 9). Amabile and her co-workers conceptualized innovation as the successful implementation of creative, i.e. novel and useful ideas within an organization, even though these creative ideas do not necessarily come from within that organization but may also include ideas produced elsewhere (Amabile, 1988; Amabile *et al.*, 1996).

Innovation has to be differentiated from creativity. Creativity is related to generating novel ideas for the individual while innovation refers to ideas that are new for the organization, the work group or work role, but not necessarily for the individual putting these ideas forward. Furthermore, creativity comprises only the production while innovation requires also the implementation of novel ideas (Amabile, 1988; Anderson and King, 1993; West and Farr, 1990). This implies that innovation always affects others directly or indirectly; thus, innovation has been conceptualized as a social process, while creativity is an intraindividual cognitive process (West and Farr, 1990).

In general, individual, group, and organizational level innovations can be differentiated (Staw, 1984). Here, we will focus on the individual level view and will mainly concentrate on individuals as innovators. One important type of innovation at the individual level is work role innovation. Role innovation is characterized by 'the intentional introduction within one's work role of new and useful ideas, processes, products, or procedures' (Farr and Ford, 1990: 63; cf. also Nicholson, 1984). It is crucial that such an 'innovation must be brought about by the role incumbent and not from a mandate from others' (Farr and Ford, 1990: 63). Role innovation has often been examined in the context of organizational socialization of newcomers (Allen and Meyer, 1990; Ashforth and Saks, 1996; Nicholson, 1984). However, role innovation is also possible for persons who have already been working a longer time within their jobs (West, 1987a).

Personal Initiative 'Personal initiative is a behavior syndrome resulting in an individual's taking an active and self-starting approach to work and going beyond what is formally required in a given job' (Frese *et al.*, 1996: 38). This implies that a person pursues self-set extra-role goals, which are consistent with the organization's overall mission; those goals are pursued persistently in spite of barriers and setbacks, and have a long-term focus on work.

At work, people do not usually self-start their actions. Job holders carry out the tasks demanded in their job descriptions, follow additional assignments given by the supervisor, or complete favors asked by colleagues. These activities are not self-started as they are carried out on the basis of external requests and of expectations to fulfill the work role. If, however, an individual develops an additional goal and executes it without being asked to do so, this is an act of initiative. Imagine, for example, the computer expert of a department, who is formally responsible for error-free functioning of personal computers and printers. If this expert implements a method for saving paper for printing (e.g. by installing a gadget that allows the printing of drafts on used paper), he or she has developed an extra-role goal whose execution was self-started—this is an act of initiative.

A further important feature of initiative is that the action is characterized by a long-term focus: initiative often aims at removing and preventing re-occurring problems, anticipating future demands, or increasing efficiency.

The definition of personal initiative makes no specific assumptions on the content of initiative—with one exception: personal initiative comprises only actions that are in accordance with the company's goals. Harmful activities such as stealing the company's resources are self-started, but deliberately excluded from the category 'personal initiative'; this is not the focus of our interest here.

Although the organization profits from initiative, not all organizational members may support initiative unconditionally and immediately: colleagues and supervisors may fear the changes because of initiative. Additional obstacles may appear because of technical problems. These social and physical barriers make achievement of the self-set goal difficult. Thus, persistence is crucial for initiative.

Pursuing a self-set goal can—for some time—be in conflict with assigned goals. Thus, when taking initiative, an employee might act against an order of the supervisor or violate company rules to eventually reach a pro-company goal. Hence, initiative can include an element of disobedience and rebellion.

Differentiation Between Innovation and Personal Initiative

In the past, creativity and innovation have been successfully differentiated (Amabile, 1988; Anderson and King, 1993; West and Farr, 1990). Personal initiative has been differentiated from other, related concepts such as organizational citizenship behavior or achievement motivation (Fay *et al.*, 1998; Frese *et al.*, 1997). The question arises whether and how innovation and personal initiative are different from each other. In a first step, the differentiation between innovation and personal initiative will be discussed; in a second step we will focus on the special case of role innovation.

Both innovation and personal initiative are actions that refer to the implementation of ideas within a given work setting. Therefore, a wide range of events or phenomena can be subsumed under both terms. Imagine a catering service confronted with customer complaints. Within the normal work procedure, there is no way of dealing with those complaints except sending a letter of apology. If a member of the catering team suggests and organizes regular meetings in which customer complaints are to be discussed and when this person insists in finding solutions to typical complaints—this activity is both innovation and personal initiative. The idea of complaint meetings is both new to the catering team and it is a self-started activity aimed at improving the service in the long run.

However, innovation and personal initiative do not overlap completely. First, innovation implies that the idea, procedure, or process is new to the context in which it is to be implemented. In contrast, personal initiative does not need to be novel. Second, a crucial characteristic of personal initiative is that it is self-started and that it goes beyond the formal requirements of the job. This does not necessarily apply to innovation: innovation can be both self-started or part of an assigned task. The latter, for example, is the case when designing new products (Ancona and Caldwell, 1992).

Role innovation refers to the implementation of new ideas, behaviors, or procedures in one's *work role*. Therefore, there is some overlap between personal initiative and role innovation, but again, both concepts should not be equated as they differ in two aspects. First, role innovation refers to innovating some aspects of one's role by fulfilling *role requirements differently*; for example by choosing other methods for achieving work targets or by rearranging the order in which different parts of the job are done (West, 1987*a*). In contrast, personal initiative pursues *extra-role* goals. Second, role innovation is a rather descriptive concept focusing on *doing* one's job *differently* from others (West, 1987*a*), irrespective of the time-frame or goals associated with these innovative behaviors. Role innovation does not necessarily include features crucial for personal initiative such as a long-term focus and persistence when confronted with barriers and setbacks. Imagine a newcomer in an organization who adjusts some features of her job so that they fit her personal working style better. This is clearly role innovation but—in the absence of a long-term goal—no act of personal initiative.

Predictors of Innovation

A considerable number of studies examined possible predictors of individual innovation (for reviews see Ford, 1996; King, 1990). Research addressed both individual and situational characteristics. With respect to individual characteristics the most prominent predictors of innovation are intrinsic motivation, domain-relevant skills, and creativity-relevant skills (Amabile, 1988). A consistent finding with respect to situational factors is that control at work, availability of resources, and supportive leadership are positively related to innovation (Amabile *et al.*, 1996; Scott and Bruce, 1994; West, 1987*b*). The effects of stressors in the work situation on innovation were relatively seldomly examined. We will refer to these studies later in this chapter.

Predictors of Personal Initiative: Job Characteristics, Individual Characteristics and their Relationship to Initiative

Frese (1996) developed a comprehensive prediction model of initiative. This theoretically driven model distinguishes between environmental supports, skills, individual characteristics, and orientations as predictors of initiative. Some parts of the model have been empirically tested. Results indicate that resources such as job control and complexity are relevant environmental supports (Frese *et al.*, 1996; Frese and Hilligloh, 1994). Control at work—opportunities to make relevant decisions about one's work and one's working conditions—is assumed to support initiative as it has an impact on employee's motivation to redefine their tasks in a broader way (thus, including extra-role goals), and on their sense of responsibility for their job. Furthermore, control at work makes it easier to leave the routine tracks of one's work. Job complexity advances the development of a high level of skills and knowledge which in turn helps to conceive of alternative ways of doing one's job (Frese *et al.*, 1996).

With respect to individual characteristics job qualification (Frese and Hilligloh, 1994), low psychological conservatism (Fay and Frese, 1997) and achievement motivation (Frese *et al.*, 1997) have been found to be predictors of initiative. Finally, motivational variables such as control aspirations (Frese *et al.*, 1994), change orientations (Frese and Plüddemann, 1993, Frese and Hilligloh, 1994), and self-efficacy (Speier and Frese, 1997, Frese and Hilligloh, 1994) support the unfolding of initiative.

Thus, initiative requires a minimum of control at work, otherwise independent action is impossible. A certain degree of qualification is necessary, otherwise there is a lack of ideas on alternatives to the usual procedures. Control aspirations are important as low control aspirations imply a rejection of responsibility: no out-of-the-ordinary action is taken when responsibility is perceived as threatening. Furthermore, initiative will only be taken when an individual is ready to cope with the potential changes in the environment that his actions are likely to evoke, and when he believes that he can affect the environment.

Stressors at Work: Action Theory as a Framework

We will use action theory as a framework to describe stressors (Hacker, 1986; Frese and Zapf, 1994). Within action theory actions are central and the way they are regulated in work processes. An action can be defined as a behavior that is oriented towards a goal. On a conceptual level, several phases within the action process are distinguished. An action starts with a goal, which is followed by orienting oneself and acquiring information, developing plans and deciding on one, executing the plan and monitoring its execution, and finally relating feedback to the goal in order to test whether the goal has been achieved.

Furthermore, action theory assumes that actions are regulated at various hierarchical levels (Frese and Zapf, 1994; Hacker, 1986), such as the sensorimotor level, level of flexible action pattern, intellectual and heuristical level. The levels of regulation differ in the degree to which conscious or non-conscious automated processes are involved.

Stressors are defined in relation to the regulation of actions: anything which *disturbs the regulation* of the action process is a stressor (Frese and Zapf, 1994; Semmer, 1984). A taxonomy of regulation problems distinguishes between three different factors resulting in disturbed regulation: (1) regulation obstacles; (2) regulation uncertainty; (3) overtaxing regulations (Frese and Zapf, 1994; Leitner *et al.*, 1987; Semmer, 1984).

Regulation Obstacles Regulation obstacle (Leitner *et al.*, 1987) is any event or condition 'that makes it harder or even impossible to pursue a goal or to regulate an action' (Frese and Zapf, 1994: 311). Without this obstacle, the action is 'intact'. Generally, regulation obstacles are stressors because they require additional efforts for task completion. Obstacles necessitate repetition of the action, force the actor to make detours, or they use up regulation capacity, subtracting it from the main task.

One can distinguish between interruptions and regulation difficulties. An interruption can be caused by disruptions of functions such as a computer breakdown, by people for example through phone calls, or by blockages. These interruptions are regulation obstacles because one has to restart the task again, or parts of the task already executed may be lost. Regulation difficulties appear when accessibility of relevant information is more difficult than necessary, or when movements need additional effort, for example due to inadequate tools.

Organizational problems can be regarded as regulation obstacles: material that fails to come in time or in the required quality causes interruptions of the action process. Social stressors such as hostile, arbitrary behavior of a supervisor or other social tensions are regulation obstacles as well: They divert attention from the main task to thoughts and worries about the relationships; therefore social stressors consume regulation capacity (Dunckel, 1991).

Regulation Uncertainty The working individual experiences regulation uncertainty when goals are badly specified, or when it is unknown which plans lead to the goal, what feedback is relevant, or when there is no or inadequate feedback. Instances of regulation uncertainty are qualitative overload (Frankenhaeuser and Gardell, 1976), role conflict, and role ambiguity (Kahn, 1973). Receiving contradicting assignments (such as: do your job extremely fast, but do not fall below the quality standards) causes a situation in which it is not clear which operations are able to accomplish both requirements; likewise, unclear task assignments make adequate goal development difficult.

Overtaking Regulations Regulations are taxed (and may be overtaxed) when actions have to be regulated with high speed or intensity. Typical strains on regulation are time pressure or quantitative overload, such as information overload. To ensure task accomplishment, more processing resources have to be allocated to regulation, which means that energy or concentration have to be increased.

Research on stressors and actions has predominantly used a framework that investigates the *negative effect of stressors on action*. Schönpflug and his co-workers however, turn the table around and consider the *stress producing effect of actions* (Schönpflug, 1985, 1986). Actions consume energy and require effort to set goals, plan, and process feedback, therefore, actions have to be regarded as potential stressors themselves (Frese and Zapf, 1994).

The Relationship between Stressors, Innovation, and Personal Initiative

The relationship between stressors, innovation and initiative will be described from three different perspectives: in a first approach we look at the detrimental effects of stressors by discussing how stressors impair the regulation of actions, hence, also the regulation of innovative and initiative actions. Second, we look at the reverse effect by considering in what respect innovation and initiative themselves can cause stressors, for example by evoking additional time pressure or organizational problems. Both relationships—stressors' negative effect on innovation and initiative and the reverse effect of actions on stressors—are depicted in Figure 8.1. Third, a model is developed that considers stressors to lead to the option for being innovative or taking initiative; this is shown in Figure 8.2. As a final point in this section, this submodel will be discussed in the framework of coping theory.

Stressors Reducing Innovation and Personal Initiative

Stressors can be detrimental to actions (arrow (a) in Figure 8.1). Generally, acts of innovation and initiative aim at improving work processes and procedures or preparing for future problems or demands. Thus, before innovation or initiative is started, opportunities for such actions have to be identified. Spotting these opportunities, for example by anticipating future circumstances, happens presumably in the course of long-term planning and of scanning processes. In the presence of a certain degree of stressors, all of the limited regulation capacity is needed to accomplish the task requirements and to deal with the stressors. This diminishes scanning and long-term planning (Frese and Zapf, 1994).

Fig. 8.1 Stressors as a hindrance to innovation and personal initiative, and the reverse effect of innovation and personal initiative on stressors

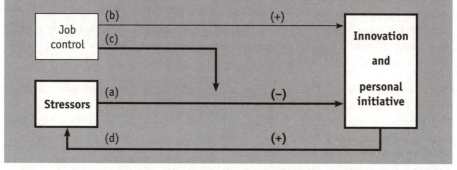

Farr and Ford (1990) pointed out that stressful work situations can impede role innovation. They argued that an organization must provide some 'slack' that allows an individual to think about the future. In situations of extreme workload in which one is only *re*-acting on immediate requests no time and possibilities are left for innovative, long-term thinking.

West and Altink (1996) described 'psychological safety' as an important prerequisite of individual innovation. They argue that in work situations in which employees feel unsafe, insecure, and threatened, innovation will be less likely to occur. Stressors might contribute to such unfavorable feelings; therefore, they can be seen as indirect barriers to innovation.

Thus, one mechanism suggests that stressors reduce the likelihood of identifying *opportunities* for innovation and initiative, thereby impeding these actions.

Furthermore, if we assume that stressors make action regulation generally more difficult, this should also apply to innovative and initiative actions. Innovation and initiative imply non-routine kind of actions. Next to goal development, it is necessary to engage in planning, which needs resources as no ready made action plans are available. These actions require a high amount of regulation capacity, which are especially vulnerable to regulation impairments.

Imagine a receptionist of a medical doctor's practice who has frequent difficulties with her computer. Busying herself with the time-consuming necessity of retrieving data and carrying on with her everyday work leaves her no room for initiative, for example for implementing changes in scheduling patients, which she might have already planned with her colleagues. Amabile *et al.* (1996) similarly suggest workload pressures and organizational impediments, such as conservatism and formal, rigid management structures, as obstacles to creativity and innovation. They argue that the production of novel ideas requires time for the exploration of alternative possibilities. If workload produces time constraints, creativity suffers.

Thus, a further way in which stressors are assumed to negatively affect innovation and initiative is by impeding the development and execution of plans.

Turning now to the environmental supports for innovation and initiative, we have pointed out that control at work is an important support for both activities. In addition, there may be interactions with stressors: high control at work allows a change of environmental conditions in order to reduce or remove the stressors (Frese, 1989). Thus, the negative effects of stressors on innovation and initiative are less severe under high job control conditions. Consequently, job control has a direct, positive effect on innovation and initiative (arrow (b) in Figure 8.1) and a *moderating* effect for the relationship between stressors and both actions (arrow (c) in Figure 8.1).

The Reverse Effect: Innovation and Personal Initiative Causing Stressors?

Schönpflug and colleagues argued that actions are factors that may themselves produce stressors and other problems: actions are effortful as they consume resources for preparation and execution, and actions can unintendedly aggravate problems or give rise to new ones (Schönpflug, 1985, 1986; Schulz and Schönpflug, 1982; also Frese and Zapf, 1994). In this section we follow this line of argumentation and apply it to innovative and initiative actions.

Stressors caused by actions can appear simultaneously with the action, or afterwards, with different duration (arrow (d) in Figure 8.1). First, we consider stressors that emerge concomitant with the action. We pointed out that all actions require cognitive resources, effort, and time; hence this applies also to innovation and initiative (Frese and Zapf, 1994). As a consequence of performing innovation or initiative as additional actions to the regular tasks, less time is left for accomplishing those. This can lead to time pressure, which is one case of overtaxing the regulation. If it is not possible to compensate for the time dedicated to such an additional action, an individual is forced to make a decision between the pursuit of the extra goal and the regular task. Then, the individual experiences role-conflict, which is an instance of regulation uncertainty. A further factor contributing to regulation uncertainty is novelty of the action: the individual knows what he or she wants to achieve with innovation or initiative, but not *how* to achieve it. This might cause organizational problems or other disruptions.

Furthermore, the social environment's evaluation of innovation and initiative is uncertain. Even when the outcomes are favorable, the implemented changes can cause undesired side effects, affecting colleagues or oneself; even simple changes of working routines can be a cause of annoyance. Worrying about the opinions of others or others' negative responses tax the regulation capacity. Additionally, initiative implies the pursuit of an extra-role goal. This frequently involves the acting individual going beyond its bound of authority which can give rise to conflicts with the supervisor.

Negative long-term effects of innovation and initiative are also possible, for example, initiative can cause role overload in the long term. If some initiative turned out to be successful and appreciated, and if the circumstances that induced this activity reoccur, it is quite possible that the person shows the same initiative again. Imagine your colleague starts to check your mail while you are on vacation. She prevents the breaking of deadlines, she informs the affected people about delayed answers. Since you valued this highly, it becomes likely that she will integrate what was initially an extra-role task into her role definition. Accepting several additional tasks can cause role overload. Beneficiaries of initiative develop expectations about future actions of the active colleague, which lead to a situation in which the active person cannot simply drop the additional tasks.

To summarize, innovation and initiative can both cause a wide array of stressors, independent of the success of the intended goal, emerging at different points in time in relation of the action and with a different duration. Thus, innovation and initiative can produce considerable costs for the acting individual.

Stressors as Options for Innovation and Personal Initiative

Stress research has demonstrated the detrimental effects of stressors on health, performance, and satisfaction (Kahn and Byosiere, 1991; Zapf et al., 1996). Without denying the negative effects of stressors, we now take the point of view that stressors can also have a positive effect because stressors are signals indicating that a process or environment is not optimal. Objectively, this signal points to the fact that something can be improved, that there is an option to intervene in order to change any facet of the situation related to the stressor. With the development of this model we enlarge the model of Farr and Ford (1990) on role innovation. Figure 8.2 describes how stressors might lead to innovation or initiative.

The appearance of a stressor is the starting point (arrow (a) in Figure 8.2). Farr and Ford (1990: 64, Figure 1) referred to this as 'perceived need to change'; here, we call it 'option for innovation and initiative'. Subsequent to recognizing the stressor as an option for intervention, a conscious goal can be developed to change the environment in order to eliminate or reduce the stressor.

Actions against the stressor can be taken by the person experiencing the stressor or by someone else who only observes the stressful encounter. There can be a considerable time lag between the perception of the option and the time of action: actions are not necessarily taken *in* the actually stressful situation; this is more likely to happen when the stressor is not operative, when there is room for thought and action. Thus, people can become active after the mere *anticipation* of a recurrent stressor.

Whether the stressor is actually *used* as an opportunity for intervention depends on several individual and situational characteristics. As already pointed out, qualifica-

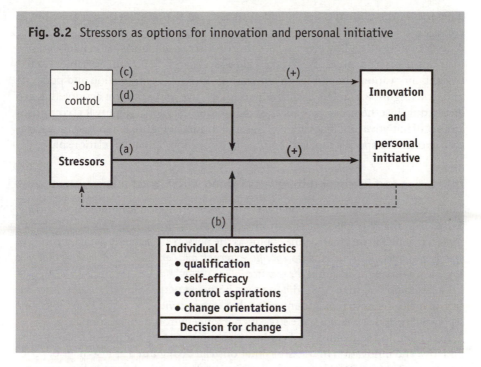

Fig. 8.2 Stressors as options for innovation and personal initiative

tion and motivational variables such as self-efficacy, change orientations and control aspirations are important individual prerequisites for innovation and initiative. This applies also to this specific incident of innovation or initiative. For example, an individual will only consider an innovative or initiative action against a stressor *under the condition that* she or he believes in her or his ability to manage the situation, thus, if she or he has sufficient self-efficacy. We suggest that these individual characteristics function as moderators in the relationship between the *option* for activity and *making use* of this option (arrow (b) in Figure 8.2).

Furthermore, the explicit wish to change the situation is a crucial precondition for action. The 'perceived payoff from change', as Farr and Ford (1990) named it, can be regarded as the major determinant of the decision. Even if the person shows all the important individual characteristics, he or she can make a deliberate decision against becoming active. One reason may be the anticipation of subsequent stressors as described above. The payoff is too small when the anticipated stressors outweigh the benefits.

A further variable influencing whether a stressor is used as an option for innovation and initiative is job control. The smaller the degree of job control, the more difficult it is for the individual to leave the working routine in order to intervene against a stressor. Thus, job control has both a direct positive effect on innovation and initiative (arrow (c) in Figure 8.2) and a moderator effect (arrow (d) in Figure 8.2).

In the previous section we described how innovation and initiative can give rise to stressors. The effect of innovation and initiative *on* stressors is here assumed to be different: as the activities are intended to remove the stressors, stressors should *decrease* in the long run, given that the innovative or initiative activities are successful. A deteriorating effect however, is—as a short-term consequence—also likely.

At this point it seems useful to take a closer look at the outcome variable—initiative and innovation: the model on stressors as options for innovation and personal initiative (Figure 8.2) refers exclusively to innovative and initiative actions that are directed against the stressor; in contrast to this, the first model (Figure 8.1) comprises any act of initiative and innovation. Thus, the model in Figure 8.2 should be considered as one very specific case in the stressor–innovation/initiative relationship.

Innovation and Personal Initiative as Coping with Stressful Encounters

The process described in the model on stressors as an option for innovation and initiative is in many respects similar to the process of coping. Lazarus and Folkman (1984: 141, italics in original) define coping as the person's *'constantly changing cognitive and behavioral efforts to manage specific external and/or internal demands that are appraised as taxing or exceeding the resources of the person'*.

Lazarus and Folkman (1984) differentiate between two coping strategies: *emotion-focused coping* seeks to regulate emotions that emerge with a stressor. *Problem-focused coping* is directed at changing the stressful person–environment relation.

According to the definition of coping, and supported by some empirical results, initiative and innovation in stressful situations can be regarded as instances of problem-focused coping. Problem-focused coping is often used when people experience work-related stress (Folkman *et al.*, 1986).

Folkman and colleagues (Folkman and Lazarus, 1980; Folkman *et al.*, 1986) suggested that problem-focused coping is used more strongly when an encounter is appraised as changeable; emotion-focused coping is more strongly employed when the troublesome situation is perceived as unchangeable. However, both forms of coping appear simultaneously in both changeable and unchangeable situations. This is similar to our notion that innovation or initiative taking can appear as a result of work stressors if the individual believes he or she has adequate means to manage them. Thus, innovation and initiative can be regarded as specific cases of problem-focused coping, a perspective also taken by Bunce and West (1996: 210, 211): 'Coping encompasses a broad range of responses which involve . . . dealing with the problem giving rise to the strain.'

However, there are also differences between innovation, initiative, and coping: first, innovative and initiative actions also occur when there is no stressor. Innovation and initiative can take place with the goal of making things better, or to improve any imperfection, irrespective of the existence of stressors.

Second, not every problem-focused coping strategy implies innovation or initiative. Imagine a production worker, who increasingly suffers from time pressure due to frequent machine breakdowns. When the machine stops functioning again, he uses problem-focused coping if he concentrates on things such as: 'Where am I going to find the toolsetter as quickly as possible? Is any colleague around who might be of help?' and searches then for help. But this is definitely not innovation (as it is not novel to the unit) nor initiative (as it is in-role behavior). If that very person, however, calls the toolsetter and asks to be *taught* how to repair the machine, then he takes initiative *and* uses problem-focused coping.

This example points to another crucial difference between initiative and coping. The person striving to be able to repair the machine himself to be independent from the toolssetter's service has a long-term focus: he prevents a loss of time in the future. Whereas long-term focus—in this case preventing the reoccurrence of the stressor— is one of the features of initiative, this is not necessarily true for coping: coping can be restricted to dealing with a currently manifest stressor.

Initiative and innovative approaches are usually taken when the stressor is not 'active'. Anticipation of a stressor and taking preventive means are forms of initiative and innovation. The theory of coping, however, relates the anticipation of stressors predominantly to negative emotions that need to be dealt with; preventive actions have only recently become an issue of interest (Aspinwall and Taylor, 1997)

Empirical data from a longitudinal study in East Germany (Frese *et al.*, 1997) support the overlap between innovation, initiative, and coping. The discussion above implies a positive relationship of both activities with problem-focused coping and a negative one with emotion-focused coping. Frese *et al.* (1997) report for an East and a West German sample correlations between a global measure of initiative and problem-focused coping of $r = .19$ ($p<.05$) and $r = .20$ ($p<.01$), respectively; the respective correlations with passive, emotion-focused coping are $r = -.17$ and $r = -.25$ (both $p<.01$). In the same samples, the specific measure of initiative at work has relationships of $r = .19$ and $r = .22$ with problem-focused coping, and $r = -.14$ and $r = -.18$ with emotion-focused coping (all $p<.01$); similar relationships were obtained for measures of interest in work innovation and executed innovations (with problem-focused coping: $r = .15$ to $r = .29$ (both $p<.01$); with emotion-focused coping: $r = -.09$, *ns*, to $r = -.18$ $p<.01$).[1]

Empirical Studies on Stressors, Innovation, and Initiative

Until now empirical research paid relatively little attention to possible relationships between stressors, innovation, and initiative. In this paragraph we want to review those few studies.

Innovation as Part of an Assigned Task

Amabile (1988) interviewed a total of 161 R&D scientists and marketing employees. Within a critical incident approach, respondents were asked to report cases of high and low creativity. By using content analysis, individual and environmental factors promoting and inhibiting creativity were identified. Twelve percent of the respondents mentioned the environmental factor 'pressure' as a promoter of creativity. In this context, pressure refers to 'a sense of urgency that is internally generated from

[1] Unpublished data: data on innovation stems from two different waves, assessed only in the East German sample.

181

competition with outside organizations, or from a general desire to accomplish something important' (Amabile, 1988: 147). At the same time, 33 percent of the respondents described time pressure (i.e. insufficient time for creative thinking; unrealistic time frames for the amount of work to be accomplished; high frequency of 'fire-fighting', Amabile, 1988: 148) as an inhibitor of creativity. Thus, this study suggests that pressure can have both positive and negative effects. Amabile concluded that pressure is a factor that has to be balanced: 'if there is no sense of time urgency, people may feel that their project is unimportant. If time pressure is too great, it may force people to take the simplest, most unimaginative route' (Amabile, 1988: 149).

Other studies examined the relationship between stressors and innovation with a correlational approach. Most of these studies concentrated on time pressure and workload pressure as the most prominent stressors.

Andrews and Farris (1972) examined the effect of time pressure on innovation in a sample of 78 scientists and engineers. Analysis revealed a positive correlation of $r = .25$ between experienced time pressure and innovation five years later. One might conclude that time pressure enhances innovation. However, average experienced time pressure was relatively low with 92 percent of the sample reporting no more than a moderate level of pressure. Furthermore, the scientists and engineers indicated how much experienced pressure deviated from subjectively optimal pressure. Analysis showed that innovation was highest for those persons in which experienced pressure matched the desired optimal level. When both too much or too little pressure were experienced, innovation was substantially lower. Stahl and Steeger (1977) studied the relationship between stressors and innovation in 154 US Air Force R&D scientists and engineers. No substantial relationships between various perceived pressure measures and peer ratings of innovation were found. All correlations were non-significant and did not exceed $r = \pm.15$.

Scott and Bruce (1994), examining innovative behavior in 172 technicians, engineers, and scientists reported a similar result. They found a correlation of $r = -.02$ between resource supply—including absence of time pressure—and innovation.

A study by Amabile et al. (1996) addressing team innovation provided some findings on the relationship between stressors and innovation. Managers were asked to nominate projects with the highest and lowest creativity they had been involved in during the previous three years. Subsequently managers evaluated—among other work environment variables—workload pressure in these projects. Within 141 pairs of high and low creativity projects work pressure was rated significantly higher in the low creativity projects. However, this finding could not be replicated in a smaller subsample in which only those 23 projects were included which met a more narrow innovation criterion. Furthermore, the effect size was small in both analyses.

Taken together, these results are rather inconsistent and suggest that there is neither a clear-cut negative nor a clear-cut positive relationship between time pressure and innovation. The weak correlations might be due to both negative and positive effects of time pressure on innovation (Amabile, 1988) or the curvilinear nature of the relationship (Andrews and Farris, 1972). These weak correlations do not speak against our model in which stressors were conceptualized both as hindrances and options for innovation and initiative. Rather, these studies indicate that it is worthwhile searching for possible moderators, such as control at work, that might affect the relationship between time pressure and innovation.

Role Innovation

In a study with 344 managers, Tsui and Barry (1986) examined the relationship between role stressors and managerial role behavior. Managerial role behavior was evaluated by managers' superiors, subordinates, and peers. Across all three rating groups, there was a negative relationship between role ambiguity and managerial entrepreneurship. Entrepreneurship included behaviors such as planning and implementing changes, initiating controlled changes, and solving problems by instituting needed changes (Tsui, 1984). Thus, entrepreneurship is conceptually relatively close to innovation and initiative. Role conflict was not related to managerial entrepreneurship.

In a longitudinal study, Munton and West (1995) studied the role innovation of job relocators. Role innovation (three months after moving) was predicted by self-esteem (three months before) and additionally related to concurrent mental health. Role innovation (six months after moving) was associated with concurrent self-esteem and concurrent mental health. Relocators with higher self-esteem and better mental health showed more role innovation than did relocators with lower self-esteem and low mental health scores.

The authors interpret their findings within a coping framework and suggest that 'role innovation might be an effective coping mechanism' (Munton and West, 1995: 372). However—since stressors were not explicitly measured in this study—two alternative explanations are plausible as well. First, a low strain level, i.e. high self-esteem and good mental health, might be a prerequisite for role innovation. Second, stressors might function as a third variable both resulting in high strain and impeding role innovation.

Ashforth and Saks (1996) examined the effects of socialization tactics on role innovation, role stressors (i.e. role conflict and role ambiguity), and stress symptoms. They reported a positive relationship between initial role conflict and role innovation six months later of $r = .22$. The correlation between initial role innovation on subsequent role conflict was $r = .16$. All correlations between role ambiguity and perceived stress symptoms on the one hand and role innovation on the other hand were small and non-significant. However, Ashforth and Saks (1996) interpret their findings in an organizational socialization framework with institutionalized (versus individualized) socialization tactics both resulting in low role conflict and low role innovation.

Bunce and West (1996) compared the effects of a traditional stress management program, focusing on cognitive–behavioral and arousal reduction techniques, to an innovation promotion program, encompassing the identification of work-related stressors and development of innovative responses to the stressors such as introducing new procedures. Three months after the program participants of the innovation promotion program showed less work-related strain than the stress management program participants. One year after intervention there was no more difference in strain between the two groups, but a significant increase in the level of innovation in the innovation promotion program group.

This study suggests that innovative responses towards stressors are possible and teachable with an innovation promotion program intervention. The effects on strain are less promising: one way of interpreting the lack of an effect on job strain is that changing work procedures, introducing new methods, improving skills etc., can represent a stressor itself, as we proposed as the 'reverse effect' of innovation and initiative (arrow (d) in Figure 8.1). This would reduce the potentially relieving effect of innovation. The authors themselves pointed out that an organizational performance measure would be an interesting additional dependent variable, as innovation might not produce an observable effect on strain, but on performance.

By summarizing the studies on stressors and role innovation, including managerial entrepreneurship, no clear-cut picture emerges. Role stressors were found to be both positively and negatively related with role innovation. There is a clear need for further research in which moderators including specific sample and task characteristics should be examined. Furthermore, it is necessary to include stressors other than role stressors into the empirical analyses.

Personal Initiative and Self-Reported Innovation

In a longitudinal study Fay and Sonnentag (1998) examined the relationship between stressors, job control, innovation and personal initiative. According to the stressors as options for innovation and personal initiative model (Figure 8.2), they hypothesized that stressors lead to an increase in innovation and initiative, with job control as a moderator. Unlike the model in Figure 8.2, individual characteristics were not included. Furthermore, they tested the effects of innovation and initiative on stressors, by relating both activities to changes in stressors (reverse effect).

Subjects were blue and white collar employees from the former East Germany ($n=128$–163). Stressors were operationalized as time pressure and concentration demands, job ambiguity, and organizational problems. Innovation was a questionnaire measure, asking for interest in innovation and executed innovation (Patchen, 1965), initiative was an interview measure assessing initiative at work (Frese *et al.*, 1996).

The 'stressor as option' hypothesis was examined using a hierarchical regression analysis approach: it was tested whether stressors at time n have a significant effect on *changes* of innovation and initiative from time n to time $n+1$. Furthermore, the effects of job control and its moderating effect on stressors were tested. Based on four waves of the longitudinal study, the analyses were executed for three time periods with initiative as the dependent variable, and for one time period with innovation as the dependent variable (this measure was only available for two waves). Two consecutive waves with time lags of one to two years were used.

Stressors were positively related to increases in initiative and innovation. The stressors explained 4–5 percent ($p<.05$) of the variance in changes in initiative, beyond what was explained by covariates (age, gender, socioeconomic status, job qualification), job control, and initial innovation. Stressors also had a positive effect on innovation: they explained an additional 2 percent ($p = .07$) of variance in changes in innovation beyond the covariates, job control, and the previous innovation. Both job control and the interaction terms (job control $\times$ stressors) had no significant effect, when controlling for the covariates.

The reverse effect was tested with the same hierarchical regression analyses approach, with stressors as the dependent variable and innovation and initiative as predictors. However, there was no effect of either activity on stressors.

This study lends support to the model of stressors being an option for innovative and initiative actions, while there was no evidence for the negative effects of these actions.

Implications for Future Research

We described the relationship between stressors, innovation, and initiative both in terms of a 'stressors as a hindrance' and a 'stressors as options' model. Furthermore, we always discussed the reverse effects of innovation and initiative on stressors. The combination of both models implies that there should be *both* positive and negative effects of stressors on innovation and initiative, and *both* positive and negative effects of those activities on stressors.

The studies reported on the relationship between stressors, innovation, and initiative gave altogether mixed results. Relating the studies to the two models presented, most studies used a rationale that is closest to the 'stressors as a hindrance' model. Given the complexity of the proposed relationships, most studies fall short of taking account of the reverse effects of innovation and initiative on stressors, or of a possible *positive* effect of stressors. Research that aims at disentangling these effects needs to use design methods different from those used in the studies presented above. For this, a more specific assessment of the dependent variables, innovation and initiative, is important.

First, studies placed within the stressors as a hindrance framework, looking for the proposed negative relationship between stressors, innovation, and initiative, need to confine the assessment of these activities to those that are *not* a response against a stressor; activities *directed against a stressor* should be excluded. We assume that innovation and initiative generally reduce under stressors, whereas concomitantly specific innovation or initiative actions against stressors increase. Therefore, these two types of innovation and initiative—directed against a stressor or not directed against one—have to be separated. Otherwise, the detrimental effects of stressors are undetectable due to the complex interplay of stressors and activities. Second, studying stressors from the perspective that they are 'options' for innovation and initiative likewise requires a specific dependent variable: only those innovative and initiative activities should be used as a dependent variable that are *directed against the specific stressor*.

According to both models, the reverse effects of innovation and initiative on stressors need to be included in empirical studies. In order to capture the consequences of these activities, short-term and long-term effects have to be examined. Specifically in the context of innovative and initiative actions carried out *against* a stressor, various variables are potentially affected: the initial stressor (which is expected to reduce), other stressors (possibly emerging or increasing), strain reactions and performance.

These suggestions pose high demands on researchers: they require a repeated measurement design; research participants indicating whether and what actions have been taken against a given stressor; whether and what effects these had on the environment; relating this highly subjective information to objective measures. Furthermore, several individual and job characteristics have to be taken into account as moderators.

Our approach is open to some enlargement. So far, we have only looked at *direct* effects of stressors on actions and vice-versa. Additionally, one might assume that stressors cause low mental health that in turn reduces the likelihood to show innovation or to take initiative. Thus, the descriptions of the rather complex interplay of stressors and activities left out the potential *mediating* variables: an individual's emotional reactions to stressors and activities, experience of strain, and effects on mental health. Future studies should take that into consideration.

With this chapter we want to encourage research with the rather uncommon perspective on 'stressors as options for innovation and personal initiative'. The study by Fay and Sonnentag (1998) indicates this to be a promising approach. Further support for this notion, however, should not tempt practitioners to feel free to ignore stressors as job holders themselves can deal with them. Instead, job design might actually need to focus more on the crucial moderators that support this active approach towards stressors.

References

Allen, N. J. and Meyer, J. P. (1990) 'Organizational socialization tactics: A longitudinal analysis of links to nowcomers' commitment and role orientation', *Academy of Management Journal*, 33, 847–858.

Amabile, T. M. (1988) A model of creativity and innovation in organizations. In B. M. Staw and L. L. Cummings (eds.), *Research in Organizational Behavior* (Vol. 10, pp. 123–167). Greenwich: JAI Press.

Amabile, T. M., Conti, R., Coon, H., Lazenby, J., and Herron, M. (1996) 'Assessing the work environment for creativity', *Academy of Management Journal*, 39, 1154–1184.

Ancona, D. G. and Caldwell, D. F. (1992) 'Demography and design: predictors of new product team performance', *Organization Science*, 3, 321–341.

Anderson, N. and King, N. (1993) Innovation in organizations. In C. L. Cooper and I. T. Robertson (eds.), *International Review of Industrial and Organizational Psychology* (Vol. 8, pp. 1–34). Chichester: Wiley.

Andrews, F. M. and Farris, G. F. (1972) 'Time pressure and performance of scientists and engineers: A five-year panel study', *Organizational Behavior and Human Performance*, 8, 185–200.

Ashforth, B. E. and Saks, A. M. (1996) 'Socialization tactics: Longitudinal effect on newcomer adjustment', *Academy of Management Journal*, 39, 149–178.

Aspinwall, L. G. and Taylor, S. E. (1997) 'A stitch in time: Self-regulation and proactive coping', *Psychological Bulletin*, 121, 417–436.

Bunce, D. and West, M. A. (1996) 'Stress management and innovation interventions at work', *Human Relations*, 49, 209–232.

Dunckel, H. (1991) Mehrfachbelastung und psychosoziale Gesundheit. In S. Greif, E. Bamberg, and N. Semmer (eds.), *Psychischer Stress am Arbeitsplatz* (pp. 154–167). Göttingen: Hogrefe.

Farr, J. L. and Ford, C. M. (1990) Individual innovation. In M. A. West and J. L. Farr (eds.), *Innovation and Creativity at Work: Psychological and Organizational Strategies* (pp. 63–80). Chichester: Wiley.

Fay, D. and Frese, M. (1997) *Conservatives at Work: Less Prepared for Future Work Demands?* (manuscript submitted for publication)

Fay, D., Böckel, A., Kamps, A., Wotschke, G., and Frese, M. (1998) *Personal Initiative and Organizational Leadership Behavior* (submitted).

Fay, D. and Sonnentag, S. (1998) *Stressors, Personal Initiative and Innovation* (submitted).

Folkman, S. and Lazarus, S. L. (1980) 'An analysis of coping in a middle-aged community sample', *Journal of Health and Social Behavior*, 21, 219–239.

Folkman, S., Lazarus, S. L., Dunkel-Schetter, C., DeLongis, A., and Gruen, R. J., (1986) 'Dynamics of a stressful encounter: Cognitive appraisal, coping, and encounter outcomes', *Journal of Personality and Social Psychology*, 50, 992–1003.

Ford, C. M. (1996) 'A theory of individual creative action in multiple social domains', *Academy of Management Journal*, 21, 1112–1142.

Frankenhaeuser, M. and Gardell, B. (1976) 'Underload and overload in working life: Outline of a multidisciplinary approach', *Journal of Human Stress*, 2, 35–46.

Frese, M. (1989) Theoretical models of control and health. in S. L. Sauter, J. H. Jr. and C. L. Cooper (eds.), *Job Control and Worker Health* (pp. 107–128). Chichester: Wiley.

Frese, M. (1996) Preparing work and organizational psychology for the 21st century: Self-reliance at work. Inaugural Speech at University of Amsterdam.

Frese, M. and Hilligloh, S. (1994) Eigeninitiative am Arbeitsplatz im Osten und Westen Deutschlands: Ergebnisse einer empirischen Untersuchung. In G. Trommsdorf (ed.), *Psychologische Aspekte des sozial-politischen Wandels in Ostdeutschland*, Berlin: Walter De Gruyter Verlag.

Frese, M., Kring, W., Soose, A., and Zempel, J. (1996), 'Personal initiative at work: Differences between East and West Germany', *Academy of Management Journal*, 39, 27–36.

Frese, M. and Plüddemann, K. (1993) 'Umstellungsbereitschaft im Osten und Westen Deutschlands: Inflexibilität als Gefahrenzeichen?' *Zeitschrift für Sozialpsychologie*, 24, 198–210.

Frese, M. and Zapf, D. (1994) Action as the core of work psychology: A German approach. In H. C. Triandis, M. D. Dunnette, and L. M. Hough (eds.), *Handbook of Industrial and Organizational Psychology* (Vol.4, 2nd edn, pp. 271–340). Palo Alto, CA: Consulting Psychologists Press.

Frese, M., Erbe-Heinbokel, M., Grefe, J., Rybowiak, V., and Weike, A. (1994) ' "Mir ist es lieber, wenn ich genau gesagt bekomme, was ich tun muß".—Probleme der Akzeptanz von Verantwortung und Handlungsspielraum in Ost und West'. *Zeitschrift für Arbeits- und Organisationspsychologie*, 38, 22–38.

Frese, M., Fay, D., Hilburger, T., Leng, K., and Tag, A. (1997) 'The concept of personal initiative: Operationalization, reliability and validity in two German samples', *Journal of Occupational and Organizational Psychology*, 70, 139–161.

George, J. M. and Brief, A. P. (1992) 'Feeling good—doing good: A conceptual analysis of the mood at work—organizational spontaneity relationship', *Psychological Bulletin*, 112, 310–329.

Hacker, W. (1986) *Arbeitspsychologie*. Bern, Switzerland: Huber.

Kahn, R. L. (1973) 'Conflict, ambiguity and overload: Three elements in job stress', *Occupational Mental Health*, 3, 2–9.

Kahn, R. L. and Byosiere, P. (1991) Stress in Organizations. In M. D. Dunnette and L. M. Hough (eds.), *Handbook of Industrial and Organizational Psychology* (Vol. 3, 2nd edn., pp. 571–650). Palo Alto, CA: Consulting Psychologists Press.

Kanter, R. M. (1984) *The Change Masters*. London: Routledge.

King, N. (1990) Innovation at work: The research literature. In M. A. West and J. L. Farr (eds.), *Innovation and Creativity at Work* (pp. 15–59). Chichester: Wiley.

Lazarus, R. S. and Folkman, S. (1984) *Stress, Appraisal, and Coping*. New York: Springer.

Leitner, K., Volpert, W., Greiner, B., Weber, W. G., and Hennes, K. (1987) *Analyse psychischer Belastung in der Arbeit. Das RHIA-Verfahren*. Köln: Verlag TÜV Rheinland.

Munton, A. G. and West, M. A. (1995) 'Innovations and personal change: Patterns of adjustment to relocation', *Journal of Organizational Behavior*, 16, 363–375.

Nicholson, N. (1984) 'A theory of work role transitions', *Administrative Science Quarterly*, 29, 172–191.

Organ, D. W. (1997) 'Organizational citizenship behavior: It's construct clean-up time', *Human Performance*, 10, 85–97.

Patchen, M. (1965) *Some Questionnaire Measures of Employee Motivation and Morale*. Michigan: Institute for Social Research.

Podsakoff, P. M. and MacKenzie, S. B. (1997) 'Impact of organizational citizenship behavior on organizational performance: A review and suggestions for future research', *Human Performance*, 10, 133–151.

Schönpflug, W. (1985) Goal directed behavior as a source of stress: Psychological origins and consequences of inefficiency. In M. Frese and J. Sabini (eds.), *Goal Directed Behavior: The Concept of Action in Psychology* (pp. 172–188). Hilldale, NJ: Erlbaum.

Schönpflug, W. (1986) Behavior economics as an approach to stress theory. In M. H. Appley and R. Trumbull (eds.), *Dynamics of Stress* (pp. 81–98). New York: Plenum Press.

Schulz, P. and Schönpflug, W. (1982) Regulatory activity during states of stress. In W. Krohne and L. Laux (eds.), *Achievement, Stress, and Anxiety* (pp. 51–73). Washington, DC: Hemisphere.

Scott, S. G., and Bruce, R. A. (1994) 'Determinants of innovative behavior: A path model of individual innovation in the workplace', *Academy of Management Journal*, 37, 580–607.

Semmer, N. (1984) *Streßbezogene Tätigkeitsanalyse*. Weinheim, Germany: Beltz.

Speier, C. and Frese, M. (1997) 'Generalized self-efficacy as a mediator and moderator between control and complexity at work and personal initiative: A longitudinal field study in East Germany', *Human Performance*, 10, 171–192.

Stahl, M. J. and Steeger, J. A. (1977) 'Innovation and productivity in R&D: Associated individual and organizational variables', *R&D Management*, 7, 71–76.

Staw, B. M. (1984) 'Organizational behavior: A review and reformulation of the field's outcome variables', *Annual Review of Psychology*, 35, 627–666.

Tsui, A. S. (1984) 'A role set analysis of managerial reputation', *Organizational Behavior and Human Performance*, 34, 64–96.

Tsui, A. S. and Barry, B. (1986) 'Interpersonal affect and rating errors', *Academy of Management Journal*, 29, 586–599.

West, M. A. (1987a) 'A measure of role innovation at work', *British Journal of Social Psychology*, 26, 83–85.

West, M. A. (1987b) 'Role innovation in the work of work', *British Journal of Social Psychology*, 26, 305–315.

West, M. A. and Altink, W. M. M. (1996) 'Innovation at work: individual, group, organizational, and socio-historical perspective', *European Journal of Work and Organizational Psychology*, 5, 3–11.

West, M. A. and Farr, J. L. (1990) Innovation at work. In M. A. West and J. L. Farr (eds.), *Innovation and Creativity at Work: Psychological and Organizational Strategies* (pp. 3– 13). Chichester: Wiley.

Zapf, D., Dormann, C., and Frese, M. (1996) 'Longitudinal studies in organizational stress research: A review of the literature with reference to methodological issues', *Journal of Occupational Health Psychology*, 2, 145–169.

9

Adverse Health Effects of
Effort–Reward Imbalance at Work:
Theory, Empirical Support, and Implications
for Prevention

Johannes Siegrist

Introduction

Although it is now widely recognized that 'stress' is the result of an interaction between environmental constraints or threats and individual coping resources the notion of 'organizational stress' seems to imply a causal role of specific environments such as organizations in the stress process. This notion may be too simplistic, bringing us back to the tradition of 'black box' approaches towards studying human behaviour. In fact, there is now clear evidence of individual differences in coping with organizational stressors as well as in a person's susceptibility for the health consequences of stressful experience (Cooper and Payne, 1991; Parkes, 1991; Weiner, 1992). On the other hand, stress-related health effects are more pronounced in individuals who participate in specific organizations, e.g. in particular work environments (see below). Therefore, a theoretical approach is needed which adequately addresses this person–environment interaction in the stress process.

The next section describes one such theoretical approach, the model of effort–reward imbalance at work. Furthermore, the potential significance of this approach is outlined in view of far-reaching current labour market developments. The section on theory is followed by a summary of currently available evidence on adverse health effects produced by effort–reward imbalance at work. In this research, health effects range from rather soft measures such as impaired subjective health, symptom experience, or sickness absence, to clinical conditions such as the prevalence of cardiovascular risk factors, the manifestation of cardiovascular disease, and premature mortality. In this context, the question of general, non-specific versus specific theoretical explanations of health outcomes is briefly discussed.

In the final section, consequences of current knowledge for the design and implementation of intervention measures are addressed, and a recently conducted pilot study on a worksite health promotion programme based on the theoretical model is described.

The range of conclusions to be drawn from this chapter may be limited due to the fact that its focus is on one type of organization only, i.e. organizations where paid work takes place. In general, organizations are best understood as goal-directed institutionalized patterns of activities that are characterized by some degree of division of work, of differentiation of roles and by explicit or implicit mechanisms of control. The impact an organization can exert on its members heavily depends on the importance of its goals, on the demands put on the individual, and on the sanctions and rewards available. In all three respects, organizations in which paid work takes place are particularly relevant, irrespective of whether the production sector or the service sector is analyzed.

This relevance emerges from the fact that work and employment define core societal goals and serve important personal functions. There are at least four reasons that account for the centrality of work and occupation in advanced societies.

First, having a job is a principal prerequisite for continuous income opportunities. Level of income determines a wide range of life chances. Secondly, training for a job and achievement of occupational status are the most important goals of primary and secondary socialization. It is through education, job training, and status acquisition that personal growth and development are realized, that a core social identity outside the family is acquired, and that intentional, goal directed activity in human life is shaped. Thirdly, occupation defines the most important criterion of social stratification in advanced societies. Amount of esteem and social approval in interpersonal life largely depend on type of job, professional training, and level of occupational achievement. Furthermore, type and quality of occupation, and especially the degree of self-direction at work, strongly influence personal attitudes and behavioral patterns in areas that are not directly related to work, such as leisure, family life, education, and political activity (Kohn and Schooler, 1983). Finally, occupational settings produce the most pervasive continuous demands during one's lifetime, and they absorb the largest amount of active time in adult life. Exposure to adverse job conditions carries the risk of ill-health by virtue of the amount of time spent and the quality of demands faced at the work-place. At the same time, occupational settings provide unique options to experience reward, esteem, success, and satisfaction. It is for these reasons that stress research in organizations where paid work takes place is of particular relevance both in theoretical and practical terms.

Theory

In most instances, theories emerge as a result of systematic observation, analytical thinking, and intuition. Theories are designed to identify those critical components within complex realities that determine relevant outcomes. Therefore, theories are instrumental in explaining or predicting observations. On this basis, they guide rational planning and systematic intervention. A theory is capable of producing new information as far as its predictions deviate from expectations that are based on already existing knowledge. Within the social and behavioral sciences the degree of generalization and formalization a theory can reach is limited. Therefore, so called 'middle-range theories' prevail in this area of research. In these theories, the range of conclusions is restricted, both with respect to time (e.g. stage of economic development of a society) and place (e.g. sociocultural context of a society). The following theoretical approach represents one such middle-range theory. Despite its limitations it generates a set of explanations or predictions and, thus, produces new information. Once its predictions are supported by empirical evidence (see next section) a theory is considered a useful guide for the development of new intervention techniques (see final section).

The basic notion of the model of the effort–reward imbalance bears some resemblance with the widely known expectancy value theory of motivation and with the theory of rational choice. Nevertheless, as some of its central predictions deviate from these theories, as will be explained in the following paragraphs, it is adequate to develop an original theoretical framework.

The core assumption of this model maintains that the work role in adult life defines a crucial link between self-regulatory functions such as self-esteem and self-efficacy and the social opportunity structure. In particular, the availability of an occupational status is associated with recurrent options of contributing and performing, of being rewarded or esteemed, and of belonging to some significant group (e.g. work colleagues). Yet these potentially beneficial effects of the work role on emotional and motivational self-regulation are contingent on a basic prerequisite of exchange in social life, that is, reciprocity. Effort at work is spent as part of a socially organized exchange process to which society at large contributes in terms of rewards. Societal rewards are distributed by three transmitter systems to the working population: money, esteem, and status control (see Figure 9.1). The model of effort–reward imbalance claims that lack of reciprocity between costs and gains (i.e. high-cost/low-gain conditions), define a state of emotional distress with special propensity to autonomic arousal and associated strain reactions (for a summary see also Siegrist, 1996).

Before explaining why sustained emotional distress is likely to occur under such conditions, the term status control needs to be introduced in more detail. The notion of status control evolved from our interest in those aspects of occupational life that threaten a person's self-regulatory functions, his or her sense of mastery, efficacy, and esteem by evoking strong recurrent negative emotions of fear, anger, or irritation (Siegrist, Siegrist and Weber, 1986). According to sociological theories of self and identity (Mead, 1934; Schuetz, 1962–64) such threats are likely to occur if the continuity of crucial social roles is interrupted or lost. Under these circumstances, control over basic interpersonal rewards is restricted, and as a consequence, self-esteem and emotional well-being are impaired.

For a large part of the adult population, occupational positions provide one such crucial social role. Threats to the continuity of occupational roles are assumed to produce sustained emotional distress. Most clearly, this is the case with job termination or job instability. However, related conditions of low reward and low security in occupational life may also be identified, such as forced occupational change, downward mobility, lack of promotion prospects, or jobs held with inconsistent educational background (status inconsistency). In all these conditions of low occupational status control in combination with high effort, basic reciprocity of costs and gains is lacking. Therefore, having a demanding, but unstable job, achieving at high level without being offered any promotion prospects, are examples of particularly stressful working contexts. In terms of the current developments of the labour market in a global economy, the emphasis on status control reflects the growing importance of fragmented job careers, of job instability, redundancy, and forced occupational mobility.

In Figure 9.1, three dimensions of occupational gratifications are distinguished: money, esteem or approval, and status control. Although I discussed the dimension of status control in some detail, it is nevertheless obvious that inadequate payment and lack of esteem and approval in association with high effort are similarly distressing experiences. In all these instances, high-cost/low-gain conditions are likely to elicit recurrent feelings of threat, anger, and depression or demoralization, which in turn evoke sustained autonomic arousal.

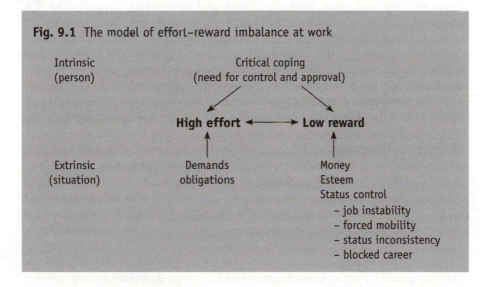

Fig. 9.1 The model of effort–reward imbalance at work

Intrinsic (person)

Critical coping (need for control and approval)

High effort ←→ **Low reward**

Extrinsic (situation)

Demands obligations

Money
Esteem
Status control
    – job instability
    – forced mobility
    – status inconsistency
    – blocked career

In line with the concept depicted in Figure 9.1, two different sources of high effort at work are defined, an extrinsic source, the demands on the job, and an intrinsic source, the motivations of the individual workers in a demanding situation. In this latter regard, the concept 'need for control' as a distinct individual pattern of coping with work demands was developed (Matschinger *et al.*, 1986).

This concept evolved from a critical analysis of the rather global pattern of Type A behavior. Need for control specifies those cognitive, emotional, and motivational components within the global concept of Type A behavior that are suspected of triggering enhanced arousal in demanding situations: individuals who score high on measures of need for control often tend to misjudge (i.e. overestimate or underestimate) demanding stimuli in their personal perception. It seems that both types of misjudgment are instrumental in eliciting excessive efforts and in providing opportunities to experience approval, success, and dominance. Although self-rewarding and successful over a period of years in adult life, and especially so in occupational life, high levels of need for control in the long run may precipitate states of exhaustion ('immersion'). Even so, it is likely that persons with high need for control spend high costs in terms of energy mobilization and job involvement even under conditions of relatively low gain. This may be explained partly by the characteristics of their perceptual and attributable style, partly by the self-gratifying experience of 'being in control' of a challenging situation. Therefore, an adequate assessment of the 'high cost' part of the equation requires information about either source of effort, extrinsic and intrinsic.

Before the measurement of this model is briefly discussed two further explications are needed. The first one concerns the question of why people should engage in such unfavorable trade-offs in their working life. In fact, a well-known psychological theory predicts that effort–reward imbalance is not maintained over a longer period of time and, thus, may not be of pathophysiologic importance. The expectancy value theory of motivation assumes that rational choice operates in individuals to achieve and maintain a balance between energy consumption and reward experience (Schönpflug and Batmann, 1989). High-cost/low-gain conditions are likely to be avoided or dismissed to maximize one's profit. At least, reduced expectancy operates to minimize one's efforts. This theory may be valid in many instances. Yet it does not take into account the social constraints under which individuals must take their decisions, especially the constraints associated with low occupational status control.

For instance, blue-collar workers with reduced opportunities of changing jobs will not minimize their effort at work even if their gain is low. The reason for this behavior is obvious: the possible costs produced by disengagement (e.g. the risk of being laid off or of facing downward mobility) by far outweigh the costs of accepting inadequate benefits. Thus, under defined conditions of low occupational status control, effort–reward imbalance is maintained contrary to the prediction derived from the expectancy value theory of motivation.

A second explication concerns the pathways of affective processing in high-cost/low-gain conditions. According to a widely discussed psychological theory, the cognitive theory of emotion developed by Lazarus (1991), cognitive appraisal or evaluation of an experienced stressor precedes any form of emotional response. In this view, negative emotions are the result of a multistage appraisal process, which includes the taxing of stressor properties and of a person's coping repertoire under exposure. Negative affect is considered a common reaction to conditions that exceed a person's coping abilities and thus threaten her or his self. Again, this theory would predict cognitive and behavioral adjustment to a high-cost/low-gain condition as a consequence of cognitive appraisal processes.

A recent debate on the cognitive theory of emotion revealed some limitations of this approach. There is growing evidence of rapid and direct pathways of affective information processing that bypass neocortical-limbic structures and, thus, are not subjected to conscious awareness (LeDoux, 1987).

Therefore, it is likely that affective processing is quite different from conscious computational processing. Or, as Gaillard and Wientjes (1993) argued,

In contrast to computational processing we have no control over the way in which emotional aspects of the information are processed. These processes are encapsulated and are largely unconscious. Only the results of this processing reach our consciousness. We may even feel anxious although we do not know why. . . . It is hardly possible to disregard the signals that are sent by our emotions. Strong negative emotions, in particular, have 'control precedence' relative to other signals reaching our consciousness (Gaillard and Wientjes, 1993: 268 f).

In this perspective, the negative effect associated with the experience of effort–reward imbalance at work may not necessarily be subjected to conscious appraisal, especially as it is a chronically recurrent everyday experience.

In our approach towards measuring effort–reward imbalance we take this argument into account. In a series of Likert-scaled items we assess the frequency and intensity of stressful experience elicited by specific conditions of high effort or low reward. We do not expect conscious appraisal to occur in every possible instance of a mismatch between effort and reward. Rather, we maintain that recurrent violations of internalized standards of matching elicit negative emotional reactions without related explicit reasoning and judgment. Therefore, a ratio between a sum score of items measuring effort (nominator) and a sum score of items measuring reward (denominator) is computed in the process of data analysis.

In Figure 9.2, a theoretical distribution of values of this ratio is demonstrated. Values <1.0 (section A) reflect a condition where subjectively assessed rewards are higher than efforts. Values = 1.0 reflect a balance between effort and reward (B). Values >1.0 (section C) reflect a critical condition of high effort and low reward.

In several studies using this measurement approach the prevalence of persons exhibiting score values >1.0 (section C) varies from 10 percent to 45 percent. Thus, the measurement approach identifies a substantial part of the workforce as being subjected to this type of 'organizational stress'.

Empirical Evidence

The following summary of empirical evidence is mainly based on three social epidemiological studies of employed middle aged populations. Two of these investigations use a prospective design, and one is a cross-sectional study. The first two studies were conducted under the authors' direction in German male blue-collar and white-collar workers while the third investigation, the well-known Whitehall II study in London, was directed by Michael Marmot (Marmot et al., 1991).

The first investigation is a 6.5 year prospective study of a cohort of 416 male blue-collar workers (ages 25–55, M=40.8±9.7). All men were free from overt coronary heart disease at entry. Medical and psychosocial data were collected at entry and three times during follow-up. Baseline psychosocial measures were used to explain the prevalence and change over time in major coronary risk factors and to predict new clinical events (Siegrist et al., 1990; Siegrist, 1996).

Fig. 9.2 Theoretical distribution of measures of effort–reward imbalance at work: A: values < 1.0 reflect a condition where subjectively assessed rewards are higher than efforts. B: values = 1.0 reflect a balance between effort and reward. C: values > 1.0 reflect the critical condition of high effort and low reward

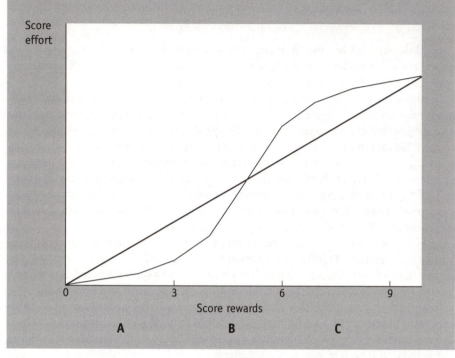

The second study to be reported was a cross-sectional analysis of associations between indicators of effort–reward imbalance at work and major coronary risk factors, such as hypertension, elevated fibrinogen and elevated atherogenic lipids in a sample of male middle managers ($n = 179$, ages 40–55, $M = 48.5\pm4.5$). This sample was remarkably homogeneous in terms of age and occupational status, and it was representative of the total group of middle managers of this age group in the enterprise. In both studies, epidemiological and clinical information was combined with psychophysiological information derived from a standardized psychomental stress test (Klein, 1995; Siegrist et al., 1997).

In the Whitehall II study 10,308 male and female civil servants, aged between 35 and 55 years, were examined prospectively. As there was no original measurement of effort–reward imbalance at phase 1 of this study, proxy measures had to be constructed for the crucial components of the model (Bosma et al., 1998). Newly reported coronary heart disease in a 5.3 years follow-up defines the criterion variable in this study.

Presentation of the main findings is organized into four paragraphs. In the first paragraph, evidence on the predictive power of an effort–reward imbalance with respect to the incidence of coronary heart disease in summarized. The second paragraph gives an overview of the explanations of the prevalence of selected cardiovascular risk factors provided by the model. In the third paragraph, associations between effort–reward imbalance and cardiovascular and hormonal reactivity to a standardized mental stress test are demonstrated. Finally, findings mainly derived from additional, most recent studies indicate the heuristic value of the model with regard to measures of subjective health, symptom experience, and sickness absence.

Coronary Heart Disease (CHD)

In the German blue-collar study based on more than 2,000 person-years 42 incident cases of CHD (acute myocardial infarction, sudden cardiac death, new CHD manifestation as evidenced by ECG) were documented. Table 9.1 presents the results of a multivariate logistic regression analysis. As can be seen, the co-manifestation of high effort and low reward at work is associated with a relative risk of 6.15 of new CHD in this cohort after adjusting for main confounders (Siegrist *et al.*, 1990, Siegrist and Peter, 1994).

Table 9.1 Logistic regression analysis: factors associated with CHD in a prospective study on blue-collar men (*n*=329)

Variable	Regression coefficient†		Multivariate odds ratio	95% CI
Age (≥ 46 years)	0.66	(0.36)	1.94	0.96–3.91
Blood pressure (≥ 140/90 mmHg)	0.78*	(0.38)	2.18	1.03–4.61
BMI (≥ 27 kg/m²)	−0.76*	(0.36)	0.47	0.23–0.96
High effort *or* low reward+	0.86*	(0.37)	2.38	1.15–4.91
High effort *and* low reward+	1.82**	(0.57)	6.15	2.01–18.82
Constant	2.87*	(0.39)	LR–chi²=228.16	d.f.=323

* $p<0.05$ **$p<0.01$
† All variables in model; each variable controlled for each other variable. SE of coefficient is given in parentheses.
+ Low reward: 'job insecurity' and/or 'status inconsistency'; high effort: 'immersion' (upper tertile of critical intrinsic effort as measured by 'need for control') and/or 'high work pressure'.

Source: Siegrist and Peter, 1994.

In the Whitehall II study, information on incident CHD was based on newly reported angina pectoris as measured by the Rose questionnaire and/or on doctor-diagnosed ischemia. Logistic regression analysis revealed odds ratios, adjusted for age, of 2.98 (1.48–5.99) for men and of 3.59 (1.10–11.7) for women defined by high cost/low gain at work. As endpoints, some 300 newly reported CHD cases in this sample entered this analysis (Bosma *et al.*, 1998). After adjusting for age, sex, employment grade, job control, negative affectivity and coronary risk factors, the odds ratio of any new CHD outcome was 2.15 (1.15–4.01) for those suffering from high effort and low reward (Bosma *et al.*, 1998).

A recently published paper on workplace conditions and mortality in Finland showed that the effect of stressful job conditions (high demands, low resources) on mortality and acute myocardial infarction depends on the level of economic reward (Lynch *et al.*, 1997). As the authors of this paper state, findings are consistent with the effort–reward imbalance model.

In summary, two independent prospective studies so far provide evidence on an independent effect of organizational stress, as measured by this model, on incident CHD. In view of the still rather high prevalence of ischemic heart disease in middle-aged populations these findings call for a new emphasis on work-related primary prevention (see below).

Cardiovascular Risk Factors

Associations between effort–reward imbalance and relevant cardiovascular risk factors such as hypertension and atherogenic lipids (especially high level of low-density-lipoprotein (LDL)—cholesterol) were found in the two German studies, the middle managers study and the blue-collar worker investigation.

For instance, the odds ratio of a co-manifestation of these two cardiovascular risk factors was 3.29 (1.11–9.77) in those suffering from effort–reward imbalance in the blue-collar study (Peter, 1991) and of similar magnitude in middle managers (Siegrist and Peter, 1996). Moreover, middle managers exposed to forced job change had a 2.94 (1.06–8.15) increased risk of being hypertensive (Siegrist and Peter, 1996). Those who suffered from a lack of reciprocal support and at the same time exhibited high need for approval (a measure of high intrinsic effort) showed significantly elevated levels of plasma fibrinogen (Siegrist *et al.*, 1997b).

Whereas findings reported so far are based on dichotomous information of health indicators additional results were obtained using continuous data on cardiovascular risk factors. One example concerns measures of LDL cholesterol in the middle managers study. In this sample, mean LDL cholesterol, adjusted for the effect of age, was significantly elevated in a psychosocial high risk group defined by high effort, lack of reciprocal support and lack of promotion prospects (174.8 mg dl^{-1} as compared to the grand mean of 141.7 mg dl^{-1}; $F = 3.9$; $p = 0.02$) (Siegrist *et al.*, 1997b).

These findings complement the above mentioned direct effects of chronic work stress on CHD by suggesting indirect pathways leading from chronic work stress to CHD via elevated cardiovascular risk factors.

Cardiovascular and Hormonal Reactivity

At present, direct evidence on biological processes linking sustained stressful experience (e.g. as defined by effort–reward imbalance) with indicators of cardiovascular pathology in humans is still poor. In this latter regard, the concept of heightened cardiovascular and hormonal reactivity to standardized mental stress was proposed and explored with special attention in experimental (Manuck *et al.*, 1995; Matthews *et al.*, 1989) and, more recently, in epidemiological studies (Everson *et al.*, 1997). This concept claims that heightened cardiovascular and hormonal responsiveness to experimentally induced mental stress in the long run results in the development of neurogenic hypertension and of atherosclerotic vascular lesions. Perhaps a more dynamic approach towards studying associations between chronic socio-emotional distress and reactivity to standardized mental stress is needed. For instance, it may well be that cardiovascular and hormonal reactions to acute challenge become compromised as a consequence of long-term taxing. It is well known from pharmacological studies that long-term administration of drugs results in attenuated reactions or even non-responsiveness due to diminished sensitivity or down-regulation of respective receptors in target organs. Similarly, long-term exposure to stressful conditions may be associated with reduced rather than heightened cardiovascular and hormonal responsiveness.

Following this argument we proposed the hypothesis that a high level of chronic distress due to effort–reward imbalance at work in middle-aged employed populations is associated with reduced rather than heightened maximal cardiovascular and hormonal responsiveness to a standardized challenge (Siegrist and Klein, 1990).

This hypothesis was tested in a sub-sample of 68 middle managers exposed to a modified version of the Stroop Colour-Word Interference Test. The main findings of the study are summarized in Figure 9.3. Results are based on two-factorial analysis of variance for each cardiovascular and hormonal parameter where defined confounding effects were taken into account. Adjusted means in delta (increase from baseline to peak) are given for the three work stress groups, i.e. tertiles of a summary measure of effort–reward imbalance. As can be seen, all associations are in the expected direction. However, associations are statistically significant only with respect to heart rate, adrenalin and cortisol.

In summary, reduced maximal task-elicited reactivity in heart rate, plasma adrenalin, and cortisol is found in a group of male middle managers defined by a high level of chronic work stress (high effort and low reward at work; Siegrist et al., 1997a). However, the relevance of attenuated autonomic and neurochemical stress responses for the development of cardiovascular dysfunction and disease remains to be explored. Reduced responsiveness may be interpreted as a sign of a compromised, overtaxed cardiovascular system. Alternatively, attenuated reactivity may also be considered instrumental in protecting a cardiovascular system from excessive strain. Further research will be needed to explore this issue.

Self-reported Health and Sickness Absence

In most recent investigations evidence was found of an explanatory role of effort–reward imbalance at work in reduced self-reported health as measured by the level of symptom experience. Currently unpublished findings show systematic associations of effort–reward imbalance with clusters of symptom experience in male and female bus drivers (R. Peter, personal communication). In addition, a recent study on hospital nurses revealed associations between effort–reward imbalance at work and two sub-scales of measures of burnout (emotional exhaustion and depersonalization (Maslach and Schaufeli, 1991; Ch. Killmer, personal communication)).

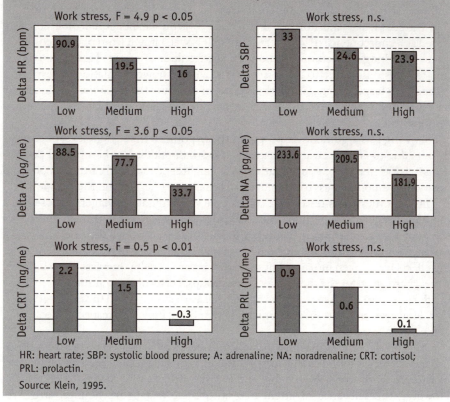

Fig. 9.3 Mean adjust delta values (difference peak–baseline) of cardiovascular and hormonal responses to standardized mental challenge according to level of chronic work stress (effort–reward imbalance), based on ANOVA

HR: heart rate; SBP: systolic blood pressure; A: adrenaline; NA: noradrenaline; CRT: cortisol; PRL: prolactin.

Source: Klein, 1995.

In the middle managers study information on sickness absence was available, and elevated risks of short-term absence, of number of absence episodes, and, to a lesser extent, of long-term absence were found under conditions of low occupational reward such as forced job change or status incongruence (i.e. discrepancy between efforts and achievements), but not under conditions of high effort (Peter and Siegrist, 1997).

This latter observation is of special interest because it may indicate differential predictive power of the model: the specific intensity of a negative effect resulting from high effort in combination with low reward may directly result in autonomic arousal and stress-related physiological responses, whereas a negative effect associated with low reward only may influence mood, motivation, and behavioral decision making (e.g. the decision to stay away from work). Certainly, the issue of differential prediction derived from a theoretical model calls for further research and analysis.

Given the considerable economic costs spent on a high level of sickness absence and impaired well-being these preliminary findings deserve further attention.

Implications for Prevention

As mentioned, theoretical concepts of organizational stress are useful in guiding and focusing intervention activities, e.g. in organization and personnel development. In this chapter, a new theoretical model of work-related stress was introduced, and empirical evidence on adverse subjective and objective health effects was summarized, with special reference to cardiovascular risk and disease.

In terms of public health impact it is interesting to know that in the studies conducted so far a proportion of subjects ranging from about 10 percent to about 45 percent were characterized by high effort–low reward conditions at work. Recent evidence suggests that the upper tertile of those scoring high on the effort–reward ratio (see Figure 9.2, section C) are at a clearly elevated risk of ill-health and disease. Taken as an estimate we may conclude that a proportion of initially healthy, middle-aged employed subjects ranging from at least 3 percent to about 15 percent are exposed to an elevated risk of future cardiovascular morbidity and/or impaired general health simply due to the fact that they suffer from a high level of effort–reward imbalance at work. For instance, the majority of reported odds ratios of CHD range from about 2.0 to about 4.0. This observation indicates that scoring high on effort–reward imbalance is associated with a two- to fourfold elevated risk of experiencing CHD or relevant precursors (such as a co-manifestation of hypertension and atherogenic lipids), compared to those who are not exposed to effort–reward imbalance.

These subjects can be identified with the help of the measurement device mentioned above, and special preventive efforts are indicated in these subgroups. Yet, worksite health promotion programmes designed for larger groups may also profit from this approach.

The theoretical model depicted in Figure 9.1 defines two levels of intervention: an interpersonal level where techniques of stress management and social skills in small group work take place (dimensions of intrinsic effort and of esteem reward; see Figure 9.1), and a structural level where measures of improved management within an organization, of changes in workload and in career opportunities are developed (dimensions of extrinsic effort, of financial rewards and of occupational status control; see Figure 9.1). Obviously, opportunities for structural measures are limited under the current economic constraints. In addition, all intervention measures derived from this model need to be tailored to meet the specific needs of respective target groups. Nevertheless, in view of reported adverse health effects consequences of this theoretical work for the practice of occupational health and safety are indicated, and they are already becoming visible in some instances. For instance, in the following paragraph, a recently conducted worksite intervention programme in professional drivers is briefly described. Results among others indicate that critical coping behavior (high need for control) can be successfully modified in a rather short time period in a group of highly stressed inner-city bus drivers.

Three groups of about eight participants were formed who met at regular intervals once a week for ninety minutes. The stress management program was not part of regular working hours, but was usually offered at the end of a working day. Twelve group sessions were provided, and each group was guided by an expert with extensive group experience. In its first part the program combined well-known elements (such as progressive muscular relaxation, self-observation and perception of arousal, coping with anger and self-assertiveness) with less established elements (such as a reduction of overcommitted work-related attitudes and behaviors; 'high need for control'). In its second part, the program addressed adverse job characteristics in terms of workload and occupational rewards and stimulated the development of suggestions for structural changes. Subsequently, these suggestions were discussed with superiors and, after the end of the group-based stress management program, they were dealt with by the official occupational health and safety committee of the bus drivers' company.

The program was offered to a small group of inner-city bus drivers aged 40–60 with at least 5 years of continuous job experience as a bus driver. A control group of similar size was defined within the same target population, and for ethical reasons the control group was offered the stress management programme after the study end, i.e. after twelve weeks.

During the study period a significant reduction in the mean score of the critical pattern of coping with job demands (high 'need for control') was reached in the intervention group, but no change was observed in the control group. Moreover, the substantially decreased mean score of need for control in the intervention group remained stable for at least three consecutive months, as a respective follow-up indicated (Aust *et al.*, 1997).

In summary, this pilot study demonstrates the beneficial effects on critical coping behavior following participation in a twelve weeks stress management program in a group of male inner-city bus drivers. The program combines individual and structural measures of stress reduction, and its rationale is based on a theoretical model. However, it is not possible to attribute the observed effect to specific elements within the intervention. While the major emphasis in this programme was put on the interpersonal level, the structural level nevertheless was addressed as well in the latter part of the program and, fortunately, in the period following the intervention where the company strenghtened its efforts of creating healthy working conditions.

Despite important new technological and organizational developments in the production sector and in the service sector of advanced economies organizational structures will persist that are characterized by high work demands in combination with relatively poor options of adequate salary, of esteem or approval, and of occupational status control (career development, job security). Although the prevalence of such unfavourable job conditions is higher among lower socioeconomic groups (Lynch *et al.*, 1997), they are not restricted to low-status populations. Rather, effort–reward imbalance at work defines a particularly stressful type of relative social deprivation whose effects on health are equally harmful in all those exposed.

It is possible that the intensity of work-related organizational distress and, thus, its adverse health effects, will diminish in the near future due to the fact that successful self-regulation in adulthood is increasingly experienced in societal areas other than work. Yet, as long as beneficial effects of such large-scale changes in sociocultural values and social psychological motivations are not demonstrated the policy implications of research on organizational stress in the work setting remain unchallenged. Moreover, it may well be that the particular type of relative social deprivation discussed in this chapter is not confined to the occupational context. If significant reward structures in adult social life extend beyond work adverse health effects in the long run may also follow this pattern. In fact, it will be a challenging task to explore to what extent the model of effort–reward imbalance may be helpful in understanding and preventing organizational stress in other settings.

References

Aust, B., Peter, R., and Siegrist, J. (1997) 'Stress management in bus drivers: a pilot study based on the model of effort–reward imbalance', *International Journal of Stress Management*, 4, 297–305.

Bosma, H., Peter, R., Siegrist, J., and Marmot, M. (1998) 'Two alternative job stress models and the risk of coronary heart disease', *American Journal of Public Health*, 88, 68–74.

Cooper, C. L. and Payne, R (eds). (1991) *Personality and Stress: Individual Differences in the Stress Process*. Chichester: Wiley.

Everson, S. A., Lynch, J. W., Chesney, M. A., Kaplan, G. A., Golberg, D. E., Shade, S. B., Cohen, R. D., Salonen, R., and Salonen, J. T. (1997) 'Interaction of work place demands and cardiovascular reactivity in progression of carotid atherosclerosis: population based study', *British Medical Journal*, 314, 553–558.

Gaillard, A. W. K. and Wientjes, C. J. E. (1993) A framework for the evaluation of work stress by physiological reactivity. In F. La Ferla and L. Levi (eds.), *A Healthier Work Environment* (pp. 266–282). Copenhagen: World Health Organization.

Klein, D. (1995) Der Einfluß chronischer Arbeitsbelastungen auf kardiovaskuläre und hormonelle Stressreaktivität unter standardisierter mentaler Belastung. Inaugural Dissertation, Faculty of Medicine, University of Marburg.

Kohn, M. and Schooler, C. (1983) *Work and Personality: An Inquiry into the Impact of Social Stratification*. Norwood, NJ: Ablex.

Lazarus, R. (1991) *Emotion and Adaptation*. New York: Oxford University Press.

LeDoux, J. E. (1987) Emotion. In F. Plum (ed.), *Handbook of Physiology: Nervous System V. Higher Function* (pp. 419–459). Washington DC: American Physiology Society.

Lynch, J., Krause, N., Kaplan, G. A., Tuomilehto, J., and Salonen, J. T. (1997) 'Workplace conditions, socioeconomic status, and the risk of mortality and acute myocardial infarction: The Kuopio ischemic heart disease risk factor study', *American Journal of Public Health*, 87, 617–622.

Manuck, S. B., Marsland, A. L., Kaplan, J. R., and Williams, J. K. (1995) 'The pathogenicity of behavior and its neuroendocrine mediation: An example from coronary artery disease', *Psychosomatic Medicine*, 57, 275–283.

Marmot, M. G., Davey Smith, G., Stansfeld, S., Patel, C., North, F., Head, J., White, I., Brunner, E., and Feeney, A. (1991) 'Health inequalities among British civil servants: The Whitehall II study', *Lancet*, 337, 1387–1393.

Maslach, C. and Schaufeli, W. B. (1991) Historical and conceptual development of burnout. In: W. B. Schaufeli, C. Maslach, and T. Marek (eds.), *Professional Burnout: Recent Developments in Theory and Research* (pp. 1–16) Washington DC: Taylor & Francis.

Matschinger, H., Siegrist, J., Siegrist, K., and Dittmann, K. H. (1986) Type A as a coping career: Towards a conceptual and methodological redefinition. In T. H. Schmidt, T. M. Dembroski, and G. Blümchen (eds.), *Biological and Psychological Factors in Cardiovascular Disease* (pp. 104–126). Berlin: Springer.

Matthews, K. A., Weiss, S. M., Detre, T., Dembroski, T. M., Falkner, B., Manuck, S. B., and Williams, R. B. (eds.) (1989) *Handbook of Stress, Reactivity, and Cardiovascular Disease*. New York: John Wiley and Sons.

Mead, G. H. (1934) *Mind, Self and Society*. Chicago: University of Chicago Press.

Parkes, K. R. (1991) Individual differences and work stress: Personality characteristics as moderators. In F. La Ferla and L. Levi (eds.), *A Healthier Work Environment* (pp. 122–142). Copenhagen: World Health Organization.

Peter, R. (1991) Berufliche Belastungen, Belastungsbewältigung und koronares Risiko bei Industriearbeitern (Occupational stress, coping and coronary risk in blue-collars) Münster: LIT Publishing Company.

Peter, R. and Siegrist, J. (1997) 'Chronic work stress, sickness absence, and hypertension in middle managers: General or specific sociological explanations?' *Social Science Medicine*, 45, 1111–1120.

Schönpflug, W. and Batmann, W. (1989) The costs and benefits of coping. In S. Fisher and J. Reason (eds.), *Handbook of Stress, Cognition and Health* (pp. 699–714). Chichester, Wiley.

Schuetz, A. (1962–64) *Collected Papers* (Vols. 1–3). The Hague: Nijhoff.

Siegrist, J. (1996) 'Adverse health effects of high-effort/low-reward conditions', *Journal of Occupational Health Psychology*, 1, 27–41.

Siegrist, J. and Klein, D. (1990) 'Occupational stress and cardiovascular reactivity in blue collar workers', *Work & Stress*, 4, 295–304.

Siegrist, J. and Peter, R. (1994) 'Job stressors and coping characteristics in work related disease: issues of validity', *Work & Stress*, 8, 130–140.

Siegrist, J. and Peter, R. (1996) 'Threat to occupational status control and cardiovascular risk', *Israeli Journal of Medical Science*, 32, 179–184.

Siegrist, J., Siegrist, K., and Weber, I. (1986) 'Sociological concepts in the etiology of chronic disease: the case of ischemic heart disease', *Social Science and Medicine*, 22, 247–253.

Siegrist, J., Peter, R., Junge, A., Cremer, P., and Seidel, D. (1990) 'Low status control, high effort at work and heart disease: prospective evidence from blue-collar men', *Social Science and Medicine*, 31, 1129–1136.

Siegrist, J., Klein, D., and Voigt, K. H. (1997a) 'Linking sociological with physiological data: the model of effort–reward imbalance at work', *Acta Physiologica Scandinavia*, 161, suppl. 640, 112–116.

Siegrist, J., Peter, R., Cremer, P., and Seidel, D. (1997b) 'Chronic work stress is associated with atherogenic lipids and elevated fibrinogen in middle-aged men', *Journal of Internal Medicine*, 242, 149–156.

Weiner, H. (1992) *Perturbing the Organism: The Biology of Stressful Experience*. Chicago: University of Chicago Press.

10

···

Job Characteristics in a Theoretical and Practical Health Context

Töres Theorell

Introduction

The aim is to decide which theoretical models should be used in the exploration of the work environment. On one extreme there is *the individual employee* who consults a psychologist or an occupational physician for symptoms of ill-health. In this case, the consulting practitioner needs a theoretical model which guides the consultation. It has to include all individual level factors that could be of relevance both to the explanation of the symptoms and to therapeutic interventions. On the other extreme there is *the management group* which is worried about the high prevalence of ill-health in the company. In this case, organizational factors that could have a collective importance to the health of the employees are relevant. Three important determining dimensions in the choice of theoretical model are individual/organizational, overview/ detailed and theoretical/practical. In this general context, the model that I am going to present is a two-stage model going from the organizational to the individual context. Its degree of complexity is relatively low. It does not pretend to cover all variation. Accordingly it should be characterized as an overview model. It has been used mainly in theory building but it could also be used as a framework for practical implication, although it has to be supplemented with practically oriented 'local' pieces of information.

Organizational Context

The first part of the model is presented in Figure 10.1a. This is an overview presentation of the organizational part of the model. It has two components. Within the inner circle there is the *demand–control–support model* originally proposed by Karasek (1979), subsequently supplemented by Johnson (1986) and translated into physiological health parameters by Theorell and Karasek (1996). The demand–control–support model deals primarily with the work content. Within the outer circle there is the *effort–reward model* proposed by Siegrist (1996). The effort–reward model represents the framework around the job situation. The two components supplement each other theoretically. The Karasek model deals mainly with factors that could be changed by means of organizational redesign. The Siegrist model deals with the balance between effort (which overlaps partly with the demand dimension in the Karasek model, see below) and reward factors, namely money, esteem, and social control.

Figure 10.1a shows an amalgamation of the work content factors included in the demand–control–support model with the effort–reward model.

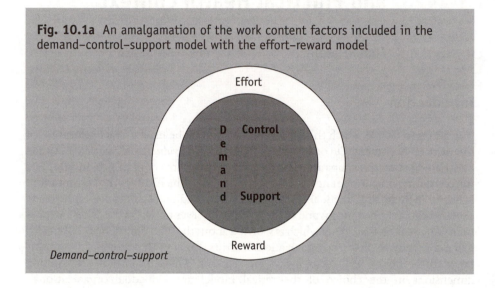

Fig. 10.1a An amalgamation of the work content factors included in the demand–control–support model with the effort–reward model

Theory

Karasek (1979) created a two-dimensional model amalgamating stress research traditions with alienation theory. The central concepts were building on previous analyses of division of labour, which emphasized the importance for the worker of influence over decisions and use of individual skill. These two factors were labeled authority over decisions and intellectual discretion, respectively. In factor analyses of mixed workers the two factors are mostly grouped together and Karasek reasoned that they were parts of a basic phenomenon which he labeled decision latitude. According to Karasek's theory, decision latitude interacts with psychological demands in generating long-term effects on health. Excessively high psychological demands are adverse to health only when decision latitude is low. When the decision latitude is high (and the worker can influence decisions regarding how and when to perform work tasks and also develop and use his own skills) excessive psychological demands may not be so harmful. This theory from an early stage incorporated social support at work (Karasek and Theorell, 1990), the importance of which had been discussed by other authors (see House, 1981). The role of the social support in the demand–control–support model was theoretically developed by Johnson (Johnson and Hall, 1988). Social support from superiors and workmates could serve as a buffer against the combination of high demands and low decision latitude. The worst combination—high demands, low decision latitude and low support—would have the most adverse health consequences (Johnson *et al.*, 1989).

Figure 10.1b shows the original demand–control model. As Karasek (1979) pointed out there are various combinations depending on psychological demands and decision latitude. In the ideal *relaxed* situation, there are no excessive demands and the decision latitude is good. In the opposite part of the diagram, the *active* situation, the demands are high but the decision latitude good. According to the theory this results in psychological growth and widening of the coping repertoire. In Karasek's early epidemiological studies the active job situation was associated with active leisure activities, and there is a theory which states that an active and challenging job stimulates active leisure. Part of this theory has been used in health psychology. An active job situation may stimulate an active health behavior. The combination of low demands and small decision latitude, i.e. a *passive* situation, on the other hand, is associated with loss of skill and atrophy of coping skills.

Fig. 10.1b Psychological demand/decision latitude model

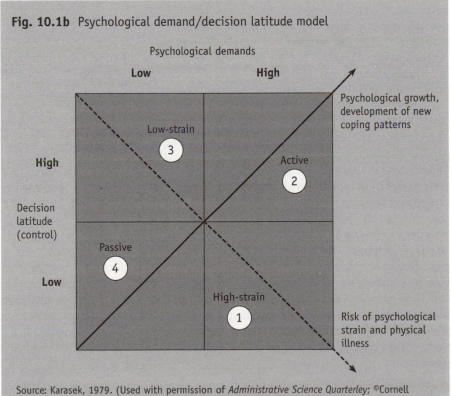

Source: Karasek, 1979. (Used with permission of *Administrative Science Quarterley*; ©Cornell University)

It should be emphasized that decision latitude has two components. In epidemiological studies of working men and women in the Western world the two factors cluster together. The first one, *authority over decisions*, is related to the potential that the employee has in deciding about his or her own work. In work organization terms this corresponds to flat or hierarchical structures. The other component, *intellectual discretion*, is related to the individual's control over the use of his or her own skills and the development of these. In work organizations with a good intellectual discretion, the employees are given good potential to use and develop their own skills. This enables them to take control in unexpected situations. Although the two components are mostly studied together in empirical research they could also be divided. They may have differential importance in relation to different health outcomes.

Measurement Issues

Although the demand–control–support theory has substantial face value in discussions with employees and companies there are problems associated with the measurement of it. The theory deals with the organizational framework. The basic dimensions could all be subject to organizational change: demands could be decreased, the two components of decision latitude could be improved (authority over decisions by improving the hierarchical structure of the company and intellectual discretion by job rotation and increased emphasis on development of competence) and social support could also be improved by means of structural changes (for instance in decisions regarding the goals of the company, principles for increased salary etc.). In the measurement of the basic constructs one is mostly limited to self-reports, although other alternatives are possible, such as expert ratings, aggregated measures based upon means from representative groups and independent observations. Self-reported measures could be biased. In particular measures of psychological demands have turned out to be methodologically problematic. Differences between individual descriptions of decision latitude are explained to a great extent by occupation. This means that this dimension is relatively robust when the general working population is studied. In the study of homogenous groups, the true variation in working conditions may be too small and in this case the standardized questionnaires are not appropriate and should be replaced by more focused 'local' or 'group specific' questionnaires. Differences between self-reported levels of psychological demands, on the other hand, seem to be more influenced by individual factors. Recent research indicates that it may be meaningful, particularly in service and care (occupations with frequent client or patient contacts) to differentiate between quantitative and qualitative demands (Söderfeldt, 1997). Social support at work seems to have a more 'individual' pattern—like psychological demands. For a more detailed discussion see Karasek and Theorell (1990) and Theorell and Karasek (1996).

Physiology

Physiological reactions were also incorporated into the theory (Karasek and Theorell, 1990). The basic idea was that the combination of high demands and low decision latitude would increase energy mobilization and at the same time inhibit protective—anabolic—processes. Poor social support could add to this adverse physiological reaction pattern. Part of these assumptions has been confirmed. At least for men (Theorell and Karasek, 1996, Pickering *et al.*, 1995), there is a clear relationship between job strain and blood pressure during working hours. This relationship also extends to blood pressure during sleep in some of the studies. The relationship is less clear for women. Conventional blood pressure measurement (after rest in the doctor's office) shows no or inconsistent relationships with job strain. Urinary catecholamine output has been related to low decision latitude and low support at work. Both blood pressure during activity and urinary catecholamine output could be regarded as indices of elevated arousal. The relationship between anabolism and job strain has been studied less extensively, although there is some evidence from a longitudinal study that increasing job strain is associated with decreasing plasma testosterone in men (Theorell *et al.*, 1990). The active and passive situations have been less extensively studied in relation to physiological reactions.

The importance to disease development of these psychophysiological reaction patterns in various combinations of psychological demands, decision latitude, and social support has been discussed in relation to coronary heart disease (Karasek and Theorell, 1990, Theorell and Karasek, 1996), gastrointestinal functional disorder (Westerberg and Theorell, 1997) and musculoskeletal disorder (Theorell, 1996).

Cardiovascular Disease Findings

Approximately 80 percent of the different published epidemiological studies have indicated that there is a clear relationship between low decision latitude and elevated coronary heart disease risk and that excessive psychological demands and low support may add to this risk (Theorell and Karasek, 1996). In a study of the working population in Sweden, workers made self-descriptions of work on one occasion and were subsequently followed with regard to cardiovascular mortality for eight years. The results indicated that men who belonged to the most favored 20 percent with regard to 'isostrain' (accordingly no excessive demands, high decision latitude and high support) lived on average eight years longer than the 20 percent of men in the least favored group (Johnson *et al.*, 1989). There was a tendency in the same direction for women although the findings were less pronounced. The findings were stronger when they were confined to men in blue-collar occupations than to white-collar men.

Of particular importance to job intervention research is that *decreased decision latitude* may be associated with increased risk within a five year period of development of myocardial infarction in middle-aged men (Theorell *et al.*, 1998). In a large area based case-referent study, decision latitude was measured by means of an indirect non-self-report method during each one of the ten years preceding a first myocardial infarction (MI). The same measurements were made in a population based matched referent non-MI sample during the same period. On the basis of this information the relative risk of developing a myocardial infarction could be calculated among working men and women who belonged to the 25 percent with the most pronounced decrease in decision latitude during the ten-year period. After adjustment for serum lipids, history of hypertension, smoking habits, social class and chest pain preceding the myocardial infarction, the relative risk of developing a myocardial infarction was clearly elevated among men. Deterioration of decision latitude was not associated with increased risk among working women although the combination of high demands and low decision latitude was as strong a risk factor among women as among men. The gender difference is probably explained by the lack of dynamics in the development of decision latitude among working women in Western society. Indeed, the most pronounced excess risk was found in 45–54 year old men who could still expect increasing decision latitude (mostly up to the age of 55). A 'premature' decrease may be perceived as particularly threatening in this group. The relative risk of developing a myocardial infarction in this age group of men was 1.8 (95 percent confidence interval 1.1–3.0). These findings may indicate a potential for disease prevention in this group of men by means of job redesign aiming at the prevention of decreased decision latitude—or helping these men to retain esteem and social control (in Siegrist's terms, see below).

Diseases other than Cardiovascular

With regard to functional *gastrointestinal disorders* (Westerberg and Theorell, 1997), there is also empirical evidence of a relationship between job strain and lack of social support on one hand and risk of illness on the other hand. In the case of *musculoskeletal disorders* (Theorell, 1996), some studies indicate relationships between illness symptoms and excessive psychological demands while others show relationships between illness symptoms and low decision latitude or low social support. Findings depend to a great extent on the samples studied, with different findings in office workers versus manual workers, in older versus younger, in men versus women, etc.

Relative Importance of Demand–Control–Support in a Public Health Context

Several authors have calculated the *etiological fraction* associated with job strain, the combination of high demands and low decision latitude. Etiological fraction refers to the proportion of cases that would have been avoided if the adverse conditions for the 'exposed' group (for instance, those 25 percent with the worst job strain using a combined measure) could be improved to the level of the remaining workers of the same age and gender group. A typical finding based upon self-reported work conditions in the latest Swedish epidemiological case-referent study of first myocardial infarctions (Theorell *et al.*, 1997) is the following (after adjustment for age, smoking habits, history of hypertension, chest pain preceding myocardial infarction, serum lipids, and social class):

Men aged 45–64 in full-time work:	7 percent
Men aged 45–54 in full-time work:	11 percent
Women aged 45–64 in full-time work:	13 percent

In a corresponding way the etiological fraction for loss of decision latitude (according to the definitions described above based upon indirect measurements) is:

Men aged 45–64 in full-time work:	7 percent
Men aged 45–54 in full-time work:	14 percent
Women aged 45–64 in full-time work:	No established relationship

These numbers indicate that the etiological fraction for the psychosocial job factors that we have discussed may be greater for men below age 55 than for older working men, and also that job strain may be even more important relatively speaking for women than for men. Since myocardial infarction has a lower incidence for women than for men in the working ages, the importance in absolute risk is less for women than for men. The etiological fraction associated with loss of decision latitude and job strain in men aged 45–54 is substantial and is comparable to the etiological fraction for elevated serum cholesterol, for instance.

Use of the Demand–Control–Support Model in Job Redesign

There is increasing evidence that the demand–control–support concept could be used successfully in job redesign. One of the first published controled evaluations was the one made by Jackson (1983). This author studied the effects of increased participation in decision making in a hospital outpatient facility using randomly assigned experimental and control working groups with a pretest and a six-month follow-up period. The job change intervention involved training all employees in participatory group problem solving techniques and a doubling or tripling of the number of scheduled staff meetings to two per month. Both of these components of the intervention may result in increased decision latitude and increased social support. The evaluation after the follow-up period showed that there was a significant drop in two job stressors related to decision making: role conflict and role ambiguity. There was also significantly reduced emotional strain, job dissatisfaction, absenteeism and intention to leave the job.

Strictly controlled evaluations of the health effects of job redesign are difficult or impossible to arrange in this field. Accordingly, most of the studies that have been published are unorthodox in the sense that there may be both individual and organizational components in the redesign, that the subjects in the groups to be compared may not be strictly comparable, because both experimental and control conditions may have been subject to redesign although to different degrees and finally because insuffiently long follow-up periods have been used. This makes it impossible to draw any final conclusions regarding the results. There are indications, however, that redesign aiming at increased decision latitude and/or social support may result in improved cardiovascular risk pattern with regard to lipids (Orth-Gomér *et al.*, 1994), decrease in sleep disturbance and gastrointestinal complaints (Wahlstedt and Edling, 1997) and decreased prevalence of pain in the upper part of the spine (Wahlstedt *et al.*, 1998). In several studies the aim of a job redesign focusing on decision latitude and social support has been improved production, for instance of care, but a beneficial consequence has also been decreased sick leave and improved health among employees. Examples of this have been studies of the care of the elderly (Arnetz, 1983) and of diabetes care (Lazes *et al.*, 1977).

Effort–Reward Imbalance

Theory and Measurement

According to Siegrist (see Siegrist, 1996) a crucial combination with regard to health consequences of job conditions is the degree to which the workers are rewarded for their efforts. When a high degree of effort is not corresponding to a high degree of reward emotional tensions arise and illness risk increases. Effort is the individual's response to the demands made upon him or her. These responses could be divided into *extrinsic* effort which refers to the individual's effort to cope with external demands and *intrinsic* effort which corresponds to the individual's own drive to fulfill his or her expectations. According to Siegrist and co-workers, the development of intrinsic effort follows a long-term track in the individual. Young employees without extensive work experience and with a high degree of 'vigour' get more and more commitments. Due to the increasing numbers of commitments there will be an increasing number of conflicts. If the individual is unable to decrease the number of commitments, 'immersion' will be the result in the old employee—with feelings of frustration and irritation some of which are components in 'hostility' and 'type A behavior'. A high level of psychological demands as part of the culture in a company may make the intrinsic efforts become internalized.

Although there is considerable overlap between extrinsic effort according to the effort–reward theory and psychological demands in the demand–control–support theory they are differently focused. While the demand–control–support is entirely organizationally oriented, the effort–reward model includes individual components. Reward is a composite measure of monetary rewards, esteem, and social control. Composite measures of effort–reward imbalance are based upon calculations of the ratio or the difference between scores for effort and reward, respectively.

Empirical Findings

The effort–reward model was formalized later than the demand–control–support model. Hence the literature is less extensive. Siegrist (1996) has summarized the empirical findings with regard to coronary heart disease. A prospective study of blue-collar workers has shown a significant association between effort–reward mismatch and myocardial infarction risk, and several studies have shown a relation between effort–reward imbalance on one hand and atherogenic lipid patterns and hypertension on the other hand.

Interestingly a recent unpublished study of British civil servants (men and women) has shown that both decision latitude and effort–reward imbalance contribute independently of one another to the risk of cardiovascular disease development (Bosma *et al.*, 1998). Thus the two models supplement each other.

Intervention Strategy Based upon Effort–Reward

Interventions based upon the effort–reward model have started. However, no published evaluation is available. The general principle is that rewards should be increased for a high degree of effort. This has been applied in many contexts. The most instrumental application is of course increased monetary reward. However, a more psychosocial application builds upon possibilities to increase esteem associated with the job as well as increased status control. All of these interventions are dealing with the framework around the job situation, not with the work content itself. The three reward dimensions are intercorrelated since increased monetary reward may increase both esteem and status control. The monetary possibility should be used with moderation since employers who are uninterested in a good working environment may 'buy themselves out'.

Interaction between Demand–Control–Support and Effort–Reward

In Figure 10.1a, the inner circle is affected by the outer one and vice-versa. If the demands are not balanced by reasonable decision latitude and support at work, there is a risk of a 'strain explosion'. The outer circle then becomes too narrow since the effort due to the strain is not balanced by sufficient reward. The outer circle cracks and 'volcanic eruption' results.

In the modern working world it is often difficult for a company to decrease demands (and extrinsic rewards resulting from them) although the personnel management and the occupational health care team should monitor quantitative demands carefully. It is becoming increasingly difficult to monitor quantity especially in large technically advanced companies in which many employees work part of their time at home at the computer. The tendency is that working hours are increasing in the whole industrialized world for this group of employees. It will be an important research goal for the near future to establish what amount of working hours may be harmful to health in different kinds of occupations.

With regard to health promoting factors, what is more important, reward or control and support? No uniform answer could be expected to this question. A good exploration of the work environment should include both components as well as others described in this book.

Individual Context

Figure 10.2 shows the individual context. The theoretical model introduced by Kagan and Levi (1971), and later modified by Theorell (1992), may be used for the analysis of the interaction between different classes of factors that are of relevance to the

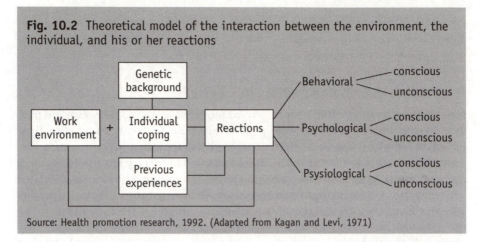

Fig. 10.2 Theoretical model of the interaction between the environment, the individual, and his or her reactions

Source: Health promotion research, 1992. (Adapted from Kagan and Levi, 1971)

relationship between working conditions and health. The individual coping patterns are determined partly by genetic factors and partly by experiences throughout life. Since genetic factors determine approximately one third of the variance in relevant components in coping patterns (see Lichtenstein, 1993), the environment is of considerable importance. The coping patterns are constantly changing somewhat due to our experiences. The figure shows that our psychological and physiological reactions to the external situation are stored as experiences which constitute part of our coping patterns. 'Good' experiences increase the likelihood that we react in a constructive way when we are faced with the same adversity next time and vice-versa. There are consistent relationships between decision latitude and coping pattern among employees—for instance, in a work site with small decision latitude the workers are unlikely to speak directly about unfair treatment to workmates and superiors (Theorell *et al.*, 1997). Accordingly, there is a dynamic interplay between individual coping pattern and psychosocial work environment.

Our experiences at work are embedded in our social context, and conditions outside work, such as social support from family and friends, are also important in determining the health effects of work conditions. Social support refers to the general support situation in life. Obviously there could be conflicts between at-work and outside-work support. When the work demands are increasing, conflicts with the family could arise. On the other hand, subjects with a large social network have access to a better social support both at work and outside work than others. Individual exploration of these factors is necessary in individual consulting.

Implications for Organizations

The model that I have described is not complete, either in individual counseling or in organizational contexts. It covers the basic underlying constructs: social support in life, previous experiences, demand–control and effort–reward.

In organizational counseling there is a whole set of other variables that should be covered, such as availability of external resources, career prospects (partially covered by the effort–reward balance factor as 'social control'), physical working conditions and organizational climate (see Cooper and Marshall, 1976). Furthermore, in the organizational context it is never sufficient to explore general global variables. There is also a need for 'local' and more focused information specific to the examined organization. The researcher or practitioner who does the exploration has to devote considerable energy to the exploration process itself. This process goes through several phases:

1. *Preparations* with exploratory interviews of key persons. A general theory or model such as the one presented in this chapter underlies these interviews. This early exploration phase also makes it possible to select relevant 'local' variables that are focused on the work site. In this phase it is necessary to anchor the exploration in all the relevant structures, employer, union, safety committee and employees. One also has to give considerable thought to choice of method. Self-administered questionnaires are only one method that could be considered. Face-to-face interviews or observations could be alternatives, particularly when the employees are likely to be unable to analyse the psychosocial situation or when there is increased risk for recall bias—for instance, lack of adequate complaining when there is widespread fear of being laid off. The role of the person/group that performs the exploration is also important. Whenever the employees perceive that there is a close tie between the employer and the group performing the exploration there will be increased risk of recall bias.

2. *Pilot studies* aiming at a more definite choice of methodology.

3. *Information seeking*—the actual distribution and collection of questionnaires, observations, interviews, medical examinations, etc.

4. *Feedback* which should be both individual and group oriented. The beneficial effects of individual feedback may be enforced if there is also attention to the organizational context. This means that the individual feedback should be accompanied by group feedback. The group feedback is based partly on characteristics of the work site that differentiate it from other similar work sites. Do you have more or less authority over decisions for employees here than in other similar work sites, for instance? Such differences, both positive and negative, could be an important stimulus to the next phase.

5. *Establishment of discussion groups*. In this phase it is necessary to structure work in a clear way. Discussion groups should be elected by the employees themselves, they should have clear deadlines for their work, they should produce written proposals for solutions, etc. This phase could take a long time—a successful implementation of an organizational change takes a high degree of patience and plenty of time, months and years rather than days and weeks.

The group in charge has to be prepared for conflicts during this phase. Conflicts regarding the solutions are an inevitable and necessary component of all organizational changes. If the organization is not prepared for this, there will be serious problems. The group in charge that becomes surprised when conflicts arise is not professional and should never have started the process! One has to be aware of this from the very first exploratory phases.

6. Formulation of new 'local' theory. The new ideas that arise during the work should ideally be spread. Other groups may be stimulated and mistakes may be avoided!

With regard to individual counseling there are also many other variables that have to be considered (Berridge *et al.*, 1997).

There is considerable difference in the way in which the demand–control–support model and the effort–reward model are translated into intervention programs. In the first case we are dealing with the organization of work. In redesigning work, decision latitude and support processes are stimulated whereas excessive demands are avoided. In the second case the focus is on rewards for effort. This may have important consequences for the attitudes towards the quality of the work environment among employers and employees. Some employers restrict their reasoning to monetary rewards and may consider the possibility of 'buying themselves out' of an unhealthy work environment. Although we have no empirical basis for making such a statement, traditions may favor this attitude more frequently among North American than among European employers—instead of improving the work environment the employer raises the salary. This may be unfortunate in the longer perspective since unhealthy work environments create damage to both productivity and health (see Karasek and Theorell, 1990). On the other hand, it is also true that a low salary may hurt self-esteem and social status among employees. These latter two components of reward could also be improved by non-monetary means. One example could be to improve the social status of a whole branch by explaining to a broader audience what the significance of this branch is to society as a whole. For instance, drivers of refuse vehicles may achieve higher status in the eyes of the people when it becomes clear that their work is important to the whole society. The same may be true of bus drivers, nurses, etc. The status of a whole group may be improved by advertisements or articles in newspapers. This is common when strikes are ongoing but could, of course, be arranged during other periods as well.

One problem with individual monetary rewards is that it may be difficult to formulate principles that will be accepted by all employees—what occupational behavior should be rewarded? This is particularly true in public service or health care in which emphasis on friendly behaviour to customers/patients may be in conflict with emphasis on quantity.

It is important for the organization to find the balance between different kinds of collective actions—esteem or organization orientated. There are several reasons why psychosocial organization work redesign has not been popular in work sites:

1. Both employers and employees may be afraid of conflicts that will arise during the process. A redesign process may be psychologically difficult to both and hence an alliance arises—neither wants the psychosocial factors to be properly handled on a collective level.

2. Psychosocial work redesign is time-consuming and there is no guarantee that it will result in improvement. Accordingly, the company may favor other processes.

3. Successful re-organization is often regarded as a 'company secret'. Hence, descriptions of such activities have been rare in the scientific literature. Most of the examples that have been described are from the public sector in which competition has been of smaller importance than in the private one. On the other hand, unsuc-

cessful re-organizations may be perceived as humiliating, and accordingly the organization does not want the description to be published for that reason. The result is that scientific description and analysis of work redesign is sparse. Hence, there is little scientific basis to rely on.

Despite all the difficulties there is growing evidence pointing to the potential benefit of improving work organization. The balance, however, is crucial. If rewards—monetary and social—are too low, a good work environment may not be enough because the employees feel offended and their social status is being jeopardized.

The other part of the model, the individual component, also has to be taken into account by the organization. If the basis of the change process is in the occupational health care organization this is self-evident. Occupational health care organizations, particularly in the Nordic countries, have considerable experience of a combined approach. As part of the psychosocial exploration each employee is subject to an interrogation (mostly by means of a self-administered questionnaire). He or she receives individual feedback both with regard to health (somatic and psychological) and psychosocial conditions. The individual information from all the participants is then summarized and a collective feedback process is also started. The two feedback processes enforce one another.

Conclusion

The two stage model that I have presented has its emphasis on the dynamic interplay between the individual and the work environment, between at-work and outside-work conditions and between genes and environment. It does not cover all the details in work organization that are necessary in practical work but it does lay the ground for basic analysis.

References

Arnetz, B. B. (1983) Psychophysiological effects of social understimulation in old age. Academic thesis, Karolinska Institute, Stockholm.

Berridge, J., Cooper, C. L., and Highley, C. (1997) *Employee Assistance Programmes and Workplace Counselling*. Chichester: John Wiley and Sons.

Bosma, H., Peter, R., Siegrist, J., and Marmot, M. (1998) 'Two alternative job stress models and the risk of coronary heart disease', *American Journal of Public Health*, 88, 68–74.

Cooper, C. L. and Marshall, J. (1976) 'Occupational sources of stress: A review of the literature relating to coronary heart disease and mental ill-health', *Journal of Occupational Psychology*, 49, 11–28.

House, J. (1981) *Work, Stress and Social Support*. Reading, MA: Addison-Wesley.

Jackson, S. (1983) 'Participation in decision making as a strategy for reducing job related strain', *Journal of Applied Psychology*, 68, 3–19.

Johnson, J. V. (1986) The impact of the workplace social support, job demands, and work control under cardiovascular disease in Sweden, Ph.D. dissertation, Johns Hopkins University. Distributed by Department of Psychology, University of Stockholm, Report No. 1-86.

Johnson, J. V. and Hall, E. M. (1988) 'Job strain, work place social support and cardiovascular disease: A cross-sectional study of a random sample of the Swedish working population', *American Journal of Public Health*, 78, 1336–1342.

Johnson, J., Hall, E., and Theorell, T. (1989) 'The combined effects of job strain and social isolation on the prevalence and mortality incidence of cardiovascular disease in a random sample of the Swedish male working population', *Scandinavian Journal of Work and Environmental Health*, 15, 271–279.

Kagan, A. R. and Levi, L. (1971) Adaptation of the psychosocial environment to man's abilities and needs. In L. Levi (ed.), *Society, Stress and Disease. The Psychosocial Environment and Psychosomatic Diseases* (pp. 388–404). London: Oxford University Press.

Karasek, R. A. (1979) 'Job demands, job decision latitude and mental strain: Implications for jobs redesign', *Administrative Science Quarterly*, 24, 285–307.

Karasek, R. A. and Theorell, T. (1990) *Healthy Work*. New York: Basic Books.

Lazes, P., Wasilewski, Y., and Redd, J. D. (1977) 'Improving outpatient care through participation; The Newark experiment in staff and patient involvement', *International Journal of Health Education*, 20, 61–68.

Lichtenstein, P. (1993) Genetic and environmental mediation of the association between psychosocial factors and health. Doctoral thesis. Karolinska Institute, Stockholm, Sweden.

Marmot, M., Bosma, H., Hemingway, H., Brunner, E., and Stansfield, S. (1997) 'Contribution of job control and other risk factors to social variations in coronary heart disease', *The Lancet*, 350, 235–239.

Orth-Gomér, K, Eriksson, I., Moser, V., Theorell, T., and Fredlund, P. (1994) 'Lipid lowering through stress management', *International Journal of Behavioural Medicine*, 1, 204–214.

Pickering, T. G., Schwartz, J. E., and James, G. D. (1995) 'Ambulatory blood pressure monitoring for evaluating the relationship between lifestyle, hypertension and cardiovascular risk', *Clinical and Experimental Pharmacology and Physiology*, 22, 226–231.

Siegrist, J. (1996) 'Adverse health effects of high effort/low reward conditions', *Journal of Occupational Health and Psychology*, 1, 27–41.

Söderfeldt, M. (1997) Burnout. Academic thesis, University of Lund. Meddelanden frén Socialhögskolan. Lund, Sweden.

Theorell, T. (1992) Health promotion in the workplace. In B. Badura and I. Kickbusch (eds.). *Health Promotion Research. Towards a New Social Epidemiology* (pp. 251–266). WHO Regional Publications European Series No. 37.

Theorell, T. (1996) Possible mechanisms behind the relationship between the demand–control–support model and disorders of the locomotor system. In S. D. Moon and S. L. Sauter (eds.), *Beyond Biomechanics: Psychosocial Aspects of Musculoskeletal Disorders in Office Work* (pp. 65–73). Taylor & Francis.

Theorell, T. and Karasek, R. A. (1996) 'Current issues relating to psychosocial job strain and cardiovascular disease research', *Journal of Occupational Health and Psychology*, 1, 9–26.

Theorell, T., Karasek, R. A., and Eneroth, P. (1990) 'Job strain variations in relation to plasma testosterone fluctuations in working men—a longitudinal study', *Journal of Internal Medicine*, 227, 31–36.

Theorell, T., Alfredsson. L., Westerholm,P., and Falck, B. (1997) Coping with unfair treatment at work—how does the coping pattern relate to risk of developing hypertension in middle-aged men and women? Manuscript, National Institute for Psychosocial Factors and Health, Stockholm.

Theorell, T., Tsutsumi, A., Hallquist, J., Reuterwall, C., Hogstedt, C., Fredlund, P., Emlund, N., Johnson, J., and the Stockholm Heart Epidemiology Program (SHEEP) (1998) 'Decision latitude, job strain, and myocardial infarction: a study of working men in Stockholm', *American Journal of Public Health*, 88, 382–388.

Wahlstedt, K. G. I. and Edling, C. (1998) 'Organizational changes at a postal sorting terminal—their effects upon work satisfaction, psychosomatic complaints and sick leave', *Work & Stress*, 11, 279–291.

Wahlstedt, K., Nygård, C. H., Kemmlert, K., Torgén, M., and Gerner Björkstén, M. (1996) 'The effect of work redesign on work environment and health in mail delivering. *Arbete och Hälsa*. In press.

Westerberg, L. and Theorell, T. (1997) 'Working conditions and family situation in relation to functional gastrointestinal disorders', *Scandinavian Journal of Primary Health Care*, 15, 76–81.

11

···

The Ethological Theory of Stress:
About Work Stress and Wisdom

Marc Schabracq

The Ethological Theory of Stress

People do not adapt to any situation: they specialize, select their environment from the pool of situations available to them, rearrange them—if possible—to their own taste and preferences, and adapt to them. So, human functioning is characterized by a specific ecology: an individual develops a relatively stable niche to live in. For example, most people live in only one house, together with only a few fixed family members; they have their daily, weekly, and yearly routines, interact with a very limited number of other people in customary ways, have their favorite ways of relaxing, and work in standardized ways and settings. The repetition inherent in such a life enables the actor to develop skills to handle a situation at a more or less 'automatic' level. In this way, attention can be focused on what is deemed important at that moment, such as the optimal performance of situated roles, the solution of specific task-related problems or further development of skills. Reality then becomes a sequence of familiar stretches of functioning, following a complex structure of temporal cycles. This results in a predictable life, which constitutes an appropriate home base for exploration and change. Attuned to our niches, we only need to follow well-specified and, sometimes abundantly signposted paths in familiar situations in order to become what we are and what we, in our own eyes, are supposed to be.

Such a niche triggers reminiscences of what, in ethology, is called a 'territory', a certain space that is taken care of by an animal. Within such a space, an animal can develop standardized behavioral sequences and knowledge to look after its vital needs. In these sequences, its skills are developed and attuned to the environmental characteristics. As such, an appropriate territory has crucial survival value. If necessary and possible, animals tend to defend their territories. This is accompanied by the activation of an emotional process (Rowell, 1972). Serious infractions and (partial) loss of territory lead to serious stress and ultimately, sometimes, to death. Of course, there are differences between animal territories and human niches. Most importantly, these are qualitative differences brought about by the use of signification and language, which allow us to redefine and reframe our niches. Though this provides us with more flexibility, infractions on and losses of (parts of) a niche evoke similar stress reactions in humans and other mammals (Eibl-Eibesfeldt, 1970).

Living in their own niche provides people with a semi-permanent system of relevant assumptions, meanings, images, goals, rules, templates for (interpersonal) procedures, skills, resources and equipment. This system gives them in each situation a small number of neatly arranged options, each with their own set of priorities (Schutz, 1970). Moreover, the system is organized in such a way that its borders can be guarded by some habitual, almost automatic scanning of a number of set-points (Frijda, 1986). As soon as some disturbance, threat or infringement is detected, its nature as well as the need for and availability of coping patterns are assessed (Lazarus, 1966). The system enables people to make plans, act in a meaningful and morally responsible way, and control their functioning in these situations and their outcomes in a socially acceptable way. We call this system 'integrity of individual functioning', or for short: 'integrity'. The concept of integrity has a respectable history in this field. It was used in similar ways by, for instance, Rümke (1939), Lecky (1945), Cofer and Appley (1964), Fromm (1955) and Ouwerkerk et al. (1994), while Erikson (1968) reserved it for the last life phase: integrity as the crown on the development of identity.

If needed and possible, people tend to defend their integrity in a way similar to territorial defence. Infringements on someone's integrity in a work situation, even by well-meant interventions to improve things, typically provoke stress and resistance. Of course, there are substantial individual differences in this respect. Some people need a completely structured environment, others need more space and challenges. In both cases, however, the intended outcome is an environment adapted to their specific configuration of abilities, values and needs, which is conducive to well-being and health.

Integrity encompasses an active process of signification. By means of mostly non-verbal relation proposals (Vrugt and Schabracq, 1991), people habitually apply social representations (Moscovici, 1984) to their own and other actors' activities in such a way that their meanings are shared. When such relation proposals and the social representations attached to them are accepted by the other actors, this results in a form of control: on the issue at hand they think and act as suggested by the first actor. This makes signification a great candidate for manipulation. For instance, meanings can be reframed, played up or down, or otherwise changed (Goffman, 1974). One can redefine causes, goals, strategies, rationales, actions and difficulties. In this way, redefinition and reframing can help a person to build up, adjust and defend his or her integrity: people can apply meanings that best serve their purposes. All this may enable one to reinforce, defend, rectify or even celebrate one's own actions, as well as to influence others' actions. As such, signification can be seen as a form of symbolic coping, that can have very real effects. On the other hand, a meaning, with its implications, that is enforced upon a person, against his or her will, can be experienced as an stress-generating infringement on one's integrity. Of course, the most important condition for successful redefining and reframing is that the definition must be accepted by one's relevant others. This does not have to be a matter of all or nothing:

the attitudes of relevant others can be explored and an acceptable new version can be negotiated. In order to be accepted, the new definition should have some internal logic, should not go against the implicit situational rules, and should not be too inconsistent with the other frames usually applied in that context. This is the world of (personal) politics. Ideally, the process of signification evolves into an integrated, consistent system of meanings, which serves one's goals in life, is open for further evolution and, at the same time, is attuned to the prevailing meanings and needs of the relevant others.

As situations are moral in nature, 'integrity' has a moral connotation also. The integrity involved in work can serve as an example here. Working in itself counts as a morally sound involvement. Moreover, it provides an opportunity to perform activities in the right way. As such, work forms a theatre to be good, both in a technical and a moral sense, by displaying a great number of valued personal qualities.

Subjectively, maintaining and developing integrity are experienced as living in the only reality possible at that moment. Performing a work task implies that this task becomes a full-blown reality: by its performance, it gets its full meaning; only then is it experienced by all involved as completely true and real. In addition, the organization within which this task was performed also becomes more real than it was before. To a smaller degree, the same applies to the society of which the organization is a part.

Submitting to the situational rules more or less automatically, actors tune in to the corresponding state of consciousness (Erickson et al., 1976). Following the right situational cues, one 'slides' from one situation into the next: attention is systematically not directed to places where, from a task perspective, there is nothing to attend to. Reality becomes in this way a journey through a landscape of realistic-looking backdrops, where a competent and attentive magician seems to go out of his way to make sure that our attention is diverted into an intended direction, each time it is about to be focused on something that is incompatible with task performance. Of course, this is living an illusion—a self-chosen and, partly, self-constructed illusion—but, then again, this appears to be the case with all experienced realities (James, 1890/1950; Burns, 1973).

In general, integrity leads to a sense of control, safety, self-efficacy and self-esteem and allows for a morally appropriate way of functioning in a manageable reality, as well as the development of an attractive identity. While integrity is conducive to well-being and health in general, as well as to good performance, inadequate forms of integrity are stressful. We distinguish three forms of inadequacy which each cause stress:

- underdevelopment of integrity;
- infringements on or losses of integrity;
- stress reactions caused by other stressors.

All three can be the result of some environmental change that one has not successfully incorporated into one's integrity. In the remainder of this section, I pay some more attention to the first two categories of stress sources.

Underdevelopment of integrity occurs when the task may have too little to offer to the task performer in the sense of challenges and goal attainment, and/or the task places too high demands on the task performer. So, tasks can be described in terms of a great number of bipolar dimensions. For each dimension, situated ranges can be specified within which the task can be optimally executed. This can be seen as a reflection of a very old and widely spread concept: the narrow path of virtue or the golden road of the middle, a central concept in Aristotle's 'Nicomachean ethics' as well as in classical Chinese and Christian thought. All these dimensions can affect the self-evidence and 'logic' of tasks: what the employee can, must, wants, and is allowed to do becomes problematic. Based on the bipolar nature of the dimensions, two kinds of loss of control can be distinguished, which can occur in diverse combinations.

First, loss of control can be caused by, for example, insufficient resources and equipment, poor ergonomical job characteristics, too high a work pace, too complex and too difficult tasks, too much task variety and too much autonomy. All these characteristics can, alone or in various combinations, lead to a state of task overload, which in its turn negatively affects what one is able and willing to do in order to attain the targets that one must attain. The task no longer corresponds to a personal theme; it becomes too complicated or too heavy to handle. Consequentially, the task disintegrates. Attention is diverted in a non-instrumental way: chaos and anomie take over and serious stress reactions may occur.

Secondly, the other pole of these dimensions can negatively influence what employees may do or, more specifically, are allowed to do. Examples are an imposed, too slow work pace, too easy and simple tasks, too little autonomy, too little task variety and too short work cycles. This restriction of the freedom of acting may lead to problems of underload, of a qualitative (no challenges, boring tasks) or quantitative nature (too little activity). The themes that one can realize by task performance are too insignificant: the task cannot provide sufficient meaning to the employee's presence at the work site and the employee realizes that the work is keeping him or her away from more meaningful and rewarding ways of functioning. Though this negatively affects the ability and willingness to perform the task in question, one must still perform it. In order to do so, one has to switch over to a more voluntary kind of attention: the employee has to force him- or herself to attend to the task. Such a forced form of attention soon becomes very tiring and can be sustained only for a limited period of time. The task does not mobilize sufficient processing capacity and attention is diverted to other activities that interfere with task performance (Shallice, 1978). The employees may experience concentration problems and feelings of irritation and boredom. If this leads to disruption of control over task performance, a stress process may be activated. Problems may be aggravated when the employee has high self-esteem, high work standards or high perceived self-efficacy.

Combinations of stressors from both categories, such as the combination of quantitative task overload and qualitative underload (the so-called high strain condition of Karasek and Theorell, 1990), may lead to an especially harmful condition.

The second form of inadequacy is a consequence of an infringement on or a loss of integrity, not counteracted by adequate coping activities.

As the environment of a task usually is highly familiar, it is possible to screen a task environment almost automatically for changes which demand attention, Lazarus' (1966) 'primary appraisal'. This also helps with Lazarus' 'secondary appraisal', i.e. the selection of a feasible coping pattern to deal with the stressor. In order to prevent interference, a task environment has to have certain characteristics at a neither too high nor too low degree (here too, the golden road of the middle applies!). At an experiential level, this is felt as a sense of trust and control, which allows the person in question to believe (James, 1890/1950) in the situated reality of the enactment of the work task. Of course, this sense of trust and control is co-determined by the nature of the task and personal preferences: what is too much or too little for some persons may be right for others.

When a task environment is disturbed, disrupted or changed, this leads to interference with the cognitive process necessary for ongoing task performance (Taylor, 1986). If not coped with, this may activate an emotional process which further interferes with adequate cognitive functioning and leads to loss of control over task performance. As one feels still obliged to perform at a normal level, such a loss can be an important source of stress. The following five characteristics of functional task environments can be distinguished (which can be considered as necessary conditions for the functionality of any kind of human reality):

- orderliness;
- compatibility of employees' values and convictions with organizational values and convictions;
- safety;
- participation in a social network;
- spill-over from and to other life domains.

The way people deal with all these stressors is dependent on a host of personal qualities, which are not a purely personal matter. All these qualities are related to the ways in which one deals with the specifics of (work) situations and their disturbances. In this way, they are to a high degree determined by the situational rule structures with which the individual identifies her- or himself. Only by being incarnated in situated action, these qualities are fully expressed. Consequentially, we do not see these personal qualities as characteristics of a person independent from his or her context.

To illustrate the ethological theory of stress described above, we pay attention to a number of work stressors, that are more or less typical for employees over forty. These are all partly forms of losses of integrity: losses of ability, motivation, role and rule structure are important sources of stress.

In Europe, North America, and Japan, the number of employees over 40 is increasing rapidly. This group forms an growing reserve of human capital, which, if deployed properly, may be of great strategic importance to almost any organization. In general, however, insufficient attention is paid to the possibilities of this group, at the expense of the organization at large as well as the individual employees involved. Moreover, the value of this potential will diminish further when nothing is done about it. This is mostly a matter of specific stressors of the second half of working life, holding serious threats to the employability, well-being and health of these employees. However, this is not an inevitable natural phenomenon but a consequence of the pursued policy and self-fulfilling prophecies evoked in this way. So the development of employees over 40 can be an important opportunity to organizations.

Notwithstanding the threats to the health and employability of employees over 40 (described in the second section of this chapter), the following studies show that the potential of these employees is a real one and provides a solid base for a different policy for the problems mentioned. So, nothing indicates a clear general decay of work performance of employees between 35 and 65 years (Waldman and Avolio, 1986; Sterns and Alexander, 1988; Cascio and McEnvoy, 1989; Warr, 1993). The health of older employees, as expressed in sick-leave numbers, does not give rise to big problems either. Though some abilities decline with ageing, others show further development (Thomae, 1993). In general, the decline of abilities (speed, bodily strength, stamina, sensory keenness, alternating attention) does not have serious limiting consequences for job performance. When employees get enough room to arrange their own work, they usually show sufficient reserves and other qualities to compensate for this decay (Baltes and Baltes, 1993). In particular, abilities based on knowledge and experience tend to improve with age (Schroots and Birren, 1993), while some elderly employees develop ways of coping with these specific stressors, which can be summarized under the denominator of wisdom and can be of great value to organizations (Schabracq and Winnubst, 1996).

In the second section, attention is paid to the aforementioned sources of stress and threats to employability characteristic of the second half of working life. In the subsequent section, the concept of wisdom is introduced as a conglomerate of coping techniques to deal with the different kinds of loss inherent in the stressors of the second section. A number of elements of wisdom are described. In the final section, it is indicated how personnel policies can be turned around in this respect.

Sources of Stress in the Second Half of Working Life

Stress has many undesirable manifestations affecting our functioning, development, and health. Though these effects can occur at all ages, they tend to be more serious in the second half of life, as people over 40, on average, are not in such good shape because of a lack of physical exercise. Their physiological reactivity tends to decrease, their physiological cycles tend to flatten and they need more time for recovery. In this respect, it is comforting to realize that most people over 40, compared to younger ones, have developed relatively effective coping procedures. Though 'normal' work stressors may affect the people who go through the second half of their working life as well, we here pay special attention to the specific sources of stress in the second half of the working life. Each of these can be described as a partial loss of integrity.

Loss of Youth

In middle age, people undergo bodily changes that indicate that youth is over. There are changes in skin, hair and general physique, as well as a decline in muscular strength, stamina and sensory functioning, changes that are often associated with a deeply felt loss of physical attractiveness (Janssen and Gerrichhauzen, 1995). As some of these changes are partly resulting from a lack of movement and physical exercise, as well as unhealthy eating and drinking habits, these can be taken care of accordingly. In addition, women are confronted with menopause and the loss of their reproductive potential, which can be experienced as the loss of a part of one's integrity.

Loss of youth also affects career perspective. Middle-aged employees are no longer juniors and are supposed to have acquired an established position, if not the summit of their career. However, as organizations have become flatter, the number of management jobs has decreased, while the number of middle-aged employees competing for these jobs has increased considerably in most Western countries and Japan (e.g. Offerman and Gowing, 1990). As a result, many middle-aged employees see their expectations thwarted: their efforts and adaptations, and the resulting inconveniences and unpleasantness, appear to have been in vain. Moreover, they do not get the respect or acknowledgment for past achievements they feel they have earned.

Generally speaking, the outlook on life changes for employees growing older. Having only a finite time to go, the importance of their work becomes more relative to them. The dreams and goals that used to make work into a seemingly logical route toward a better future, become less compelling. They do not expect substantial increases in income and prestige. Moreover, older employees tend to be more or less satisfied with their present life style. As their children have usually left the parental home, their level of expenditure has significantly decreased. In addition, older employees tend to grow weary of radical organizational changes and the adaptations these demand.

Loss of Parts of One's Identity

Taking on a (new) job sometimes may mean allowing oneself to be forced into a kind of behavioral and emotional mould. The inconveniences inherent in this are usually accepted in order to achieve future career goals that, at the moment, appear to be so valuable that these seem to make up for the inconveniences. The inconveniences are mostly dealt with by some form of denial (Breznitz, 1983), often combined with some identification with the oppressor to prevent feelings of alienation (Freud, 1971). This implies that there is no longer use for certain ways of functioning which may have been essential themes of the person's integrity. By abolishing those ways of functioning, one can actualize these basic themes only in less fruitful ways. If one stays in that job, one is at risk of either becoming a misfit, who pursues goals not adapted to the environment and who is exposed to the consequences of failure, or a person who is being left with an impoverished identity, no longer connected to certain basic needs. For example, in many organizations, persons who connect themselves strongly with themes such as perfection, originality, or diversion are at risk here. The same holds for persons who are at the wrong place in a certain organization: somebody who wants to dominate but cannot be boss, helpers who find nobody of relevance to help and experts who are not listened to.

Going through a series of such transitions, one may be left with a highly conventionalized and emotionally bleak form of functioning, which can be described as a state of stress, resulting from underdeveloped integrity (Schabracq and Cooper, in press). The individual may feel 'empty', 'hollow' and alienated. The person does what he or she has to do, but without much zeal, feeling bored and finding it hard to concentrate. Rewards become less meaningful. This state, called 'anhedonia', is probably hormonally determined (by high levels of corticosteroids) and suppresses appetite-driven learning processes (Willner, 1993).

At the same time, behavior may become more ritualistic, a form of displacement behavior which serves as a coping mechanism moderating the overall arousal level (Vrugt and Schabracq, 1991). Make-work and tidying may serve as examples here. Still, problems may arise when the individual has to adapt to fundamental changes. So, managing change may ask for ways of functioning that are no longer part of the repertory. The new situation then is experienced as unmanageable and threatening, resulting in a loss of integrity and control. Though it appears as if the abolished ways of functioning and their underlying needs have vanished altogether, they can usually be re-activated by some focused reflection or counseling (Bolen, 1989).

'Concentration of Experience': Loss of 'Transferability'

Employees identify with their jobs: the jobs become a part of themselves which they tend to hold on to for as long as possible. As a result, their abilities may develop only within the narrow limits of their jobs, a process called 'concentration of experience' (Thijssen, 1996) that can have important drawbacks. Career opportunities of persons subjected to concentration of experience tend to diminish. They cannot rise higher than their jobs or, in the best of cases, the top of their department. Also, they can be transferred less easily to other departments. This becomes especially consequential when their jobs disappear. Many elderly employees end up being stuck in their job, suffering from several ceiling effects ('golden cage syndrome', Peter's principle, being 'kicked upstairs', glass ceiling). As their jobs lose much of their meaning and no longer provide a useful structure for their integrity, they suffer from qualitative task underload, which may undermine their well-being and health.

Except for the costs of inefficient functioning, sick leave and replacement, such a development burdens the organization with an impairment of overall flexibility. In addition, younger employees see the advancement of their careers blocked and may decide to leave the organization.

Lack of Additional Training: Loss of Competence

While the world of work is changing faster than ever before, most employees over 40 get little or no additional training (Kerkhoff, 1993; Dresens, 1993; Boerlijst et al., 1993). As a result, their skills become obsolete at a fast rate. This is foremost a matter of organizational culture and its stereotyping and self-fulfilling prophecies. Training older employees is often, and mostly erroneously, considered as a bad investment, while a considerable number of employees over 40 shows persistent resistance to additional training. Several factors play a role here.

Some older employees associate additional training with an enforced and unwanted change in job design. Additionally, some of them fear that they are lagging behind so far that it will be impossible to catch up. Problems may also stem from the courses offered and the way they are given, as most training courses are not adapted to the specific needs of older employees. Last, some provide trainees with insufficient opportunities to practice their newly acquired skills and knowledge.

Lack of additional training may initially result in some form of qualitative overload, as the work becomes too difficult. However, in most cases someone else is appointed for the new parts of the task, leaving the older employee with an impoverished function, stripped of much of its meaning and structure. The older employee's integrity is affected and he or she may face qualitative, if not also quantitative, underload, which can activate a pernicious stress process, while the organization is burdened with an unproductive, overpaid and, probably, poorly motivated older employee. Proper additional training for older employees is the obvious solution (Schabracq and Winnubst, 1996).

Cohort Effects: Loss of Communality

People from forty to fifty belong to the baby-boom generation cohort (Becker, 1995). This generation has established its integrity within a youth culture, intentionally setting itself apart from mainstream culture. As such, they are often influenced by the ideas and ideals prevalent in that youth culture, such as the emphasis on communication, (sexual) freedom, self-actualization, democratic relationships, malleability of social structures, small scale 'alternative' enterprises and the essential goodness of man. At the same time, many of them have learned to be suspicious of economic and business life. As such, the baby boom generation is often seen as somewhat childish, irresponsible and soft by members of the older generation, while the younger generation looks upon them as overly idealistic, inefficient, and self-righteous. Many baby-boomers are now confronted with what they see as a reactionary culture, characterized by re-conventionalization, self-interest, dubious morality and a lack of meaning and purpose. Problems are bound to arise in the following areas:

- As youth itself is to them an important constituent of their identity, they find it hard to make the transition to 'proper' midlife roles.

- The emphasis on freedom, democratic relationships and nice ways to solve conflicts may lead to value conflicts about authority and leadership.

- The emphasis on self-actualization and meaningful activities may interfere with performing routine tasks which do not offer much opportunity for further development. As such, they may be more prone to qualitative task underload.

- Apart from being time and energy consuming, a strongly felt responsibility to live up to high standards in social relations may evoke negative feelings when one performs less well in this area, and lead to burnout symptoms.

- The second feminist wave took place within the baby-boom generation. The incomplete transition towards economic independence of women and household and child rearing tasks for men has created considerable turbulence and tension. For many women and some men of this generation this has led to double task load, interference with career opportunities and stress.

Employees from fifty to sixty-five belong to the so-called 'silent generation' (Becker, 1995). This generation is still powerful, as its members occupy many key positions in the upper levels of society. When older employees in the upper levels experience problems, they are often in a position to solve these problems themselves or find someone who can help them. This does not hold for the employees with a low level of formal schooling. A low level of formal schooling can activate a vicious circle of uninteresting jobs, little personal development (Kohn and Schooler, 1983; Bourdieu, 1986; Schaie and Schooler, 1989; Lee, 1991) and stereotyping (Vrugt and Schabracq, 1991). These are grave problems which, for the greater part, cannot be solved in a simple way.

The silent generation grew up in the era of the great depression, the Second World War and the first ten post-war years, which exposed them to more hardship than the younger generations. Having been taught to cope more by perseverance, denial and identification with the aggressor, they do not complain much and show fewer emotions than their younger colleagues. Also, as they seem less seriously affected by traumatic events, and carry on longer when they do not feel well, they become less visible to their superiors: their being there becomes more or less self-evident. When they experience serious difficulties, this may go on unnoticed for a long time. This may be a cause of their low average frequency and long mean duration of sick leave. These employees have, on average, learned to accept authority. Also, they were taught that age in itself deserves respect. And though most of them realize that much has changed in this respect, they still expect more respect from their younger colleagues, superiors, and subordinates than they usually get.

While the silent generation was born into a definite social class, church, and political party, all of which influenced their integrity, later generations had to make more choices about these issues. However, choosing one's own destiny and identity has become a necessity in our rapidly changing world of today. On average, older employees have less experience with these choices. Besides, they often have vaguely unpleasant feelings about it: though not a forbidden course of action, it is not felt to be completely right either. As a consequence these elderly people experience little control in this respect.

Though men and women are still far from being evenly represented in the higher levels of organizations, nowadays it is not uncommon to come across a female superior. Employees over fifty, male and female, often find it more difficult to work under a female superior.

Apart from the fact that the value orientation and attitudes of the baby-boom and silent generations can interfere with their well-being, health, and potential of adaptation, these may set these generations apart from the younger generations, as well as from each other, which can lead to conflicts and stereotyped perceptions. So they have to adjust their value orientations and attitudes in order to function well, which may imply a loss of structure.

Ageing of Networks: Loss of Relationships

Employees develop social networks of familiar and trusted people, with whom it is pleasant to be and who make everyday life manageable. One finds oneself protectors, and favorite subordinates and colleagues. Though pleasant in itself, this can be used also for giving and receiving information, warnings, advice, support, and factual help. As such, it is important for one's power position in the organization. It may be of help in case of promotion and impending dismissal. Moreover, a good network helps to prevent the activation of stress processes, makes stress less harmful and facilitates the recovery from stress-related complaints (Winnubst and Schabracq, 1996).

However, social networks age too: older employees are confronted with the loss of the ones who are of importance for them. This is also an emotional matter, involving feelings like grief, anxiety, depression, and bereavement. Because many elderly people do not make new friends as easily as they used to do, such losses leave them with an impoverished network. This leads, again, to a loss of integrity and role structure and of some of the yields of the network, such as control and pleasant emotional experiences. Moreover, many elderly people tend to have contact mostly with people of the same age as themselves. As such, these networks are the main medium for the age cohort effects. Apart from the obvious, negative consequences for the individuals involved, this process also affects the communication within the organization at large in a negative way.

Loss of Feedback

Some older employees get little or no feedback about their performance and so are exposed to a greater role ambiguity and isolation. Apart from these being stressors in their own right, they can be seen as other instances of loss of integrity and role structure. There are several reasons for this phenomenon. Because many elderly people hold the same job for many years, show on average a lower sick-leave frequency and tend to do their work without much complaining or other appeals for managerial attention—the silent generation especially has learned to be silent very well—the presence of these employees at the work site seems self-evident. Also, many managers and supervisors tend to experience some uneasiness in dealing with their older employees. Though managers and supervisors sometimes do not think very highly of some of them, they find that these older employees have acquired a certain status, based upon their seniority and contributions in the past. It may make it more difficult to manage these employees, as this may give rise to feelings of uneasiness. Consequently, some managers may simply avoid doing this.

Harmful Tasks: Loss of Work and Health

Many tasks are hard or downright harmful for elderly employees. As ageing goes together with a diminishing of mental processing speed, alternating attention, and physical strength, tasks that depend heavily on these abilities may cause problems for elderly workers. Obviously, elderly employees are seldom found in jobs like stock-jobber, air traffic controller, racing driver, or bouncer. Still, many elderly workers have to perform according to the same norms and standards as their considerably younger colleagues. In this respect, it is, especially for elderly employees, important to get enough autonomy to arrange one's own tasks. Other problems may stem from tasks involving a lot of repetitive physical activity leading to wear and tear of the musculoskeletal system, as well as from shiftwork which tends to become harder to sustain when one becomes older (Limborgh, 1995). In many cases these processes may lead to the impossibility to continue working in the same way. Again, this may lead to stress and loss of integrity and role structure.

Problems may also ensue from being exposed to work conditions characterized by few challenges, no possibilities for further development and little decision latitude for a very long period of time. Such conditions tend to lead to passivity in other life domains as well and pose serious threats to the well-being of health of the employees involved (Karasek and Theorell, 1990). This is not so much a matter of loss of role structure, but more of general underdevelopment of role structure and atrophy of integrity. In essence, this is another version of the problems described when identity is lost, above.

The Increase in Change: Loss of Continuity

The last decades are characterized by a rapid acceleration of change. Organizations have to adapt to these changes by changing themselves. As a rule, older employees find more difficulty with such changes.

Changes in an organizational culture imply changes in the prominence of certain values and objectives. Objectives such as skill perfection and professional freedom may become less prominent, though these may have been the reason for older employees joining the organization. These changes may leave them behind with work which, in their eyes, has been stripped of most of its challenges and meaning. Besides this loss, and the qualitative underload and stress resulting from it, they are confronted with demands to learn new skills which may not appeal to them. Though it is the easy way to see such a development as a personal motivation problem, and to act upon it accordingly, it is important to remember that its causes lie in the organizational change.

While most cultures are structured in such a way as to provide their members with a stable environment, the emphasis on change is a peculiarity of our culture. As a consequence, several generations already see the former generation as somewhat lagging behind and old-fashioned. Though this may be a typical case of stereotypical exaggeration for many older employees, it may still affect their jobs and integrity, as it influences the attitude of relevant others. In this way, the stereotype can become a self-fulfilling prophecy (see the discussion of stereotyping below).

The content of much organizational change may also cause problems for older employees. Organizations nowadays have had to become flatter, more flexible, less product-oriented, more client-oriented, etc. People working in such organizations have to become more decisive, more creative, and more entrepreneurial. Also, they are supposed to accept change as the normal state of things. In order to accomplish this, they are asked to behave as if they were completely free persons, who are working for themselves, and not for an organization owned by others. To older employees this remains more of a paradox. Moreover, many of them have effectively unlearned to act in such a way. So, many older employees come to work in an organization which is—to put it mildly—not very trustworthy to them. This can be another impairment of their integrity and the role structure available to them.

Stereotyping: Loss of Face and Self-esteem

One of the most consistent research findings is that older people differ greatly on almost every point (Belsky, 1990; Baltes and Baltes, 1993), because people live divergent lives, are congenitally different, and make different choices. So, people enter the last stage of their working life from different points of departure and they differ also in the developmental tasks that they have accomplished. This implies that everybody is not equally well prepared, willing, and able to engage in the challenges posed by the last stages of working life. Still, there exists a vigorous stereotype of older employees as an uniform group, characterized by low flexibility, strength, speed, and productivity, as well as by conservatism, bitterness, dependency, and passivity (Foner and Schwab, 1981; Belsky, 1990; Krijnen, 1996).

Older age is also associated with functional deficits, which may only be bettered by medical interventions (Baars, 1988). Since classical antiquity, people in the western world do not look forward to being old (Bennett and Eckman, 1973). For instance, the god of old age—Kronos in Greek, Saturn in Latin—was seen as cold, dry and unfriendly, and was traditionally associated with melancholy, prisons, and long-time loneliness (Biedermann, 1989). These stereotypes can be damaging to older employees in two ways.

First, in the case of blaming the victim, this kind of stereotyping leads attention away from solutions such as alterations of the work place, job redesign, training programs and better career policies. Because blaming the victim makes it possible to preserve a favorable image of the organization, these solutions may be obscured altogether. So, 'age cleansing' (that is removing the older employee from the organization) may look like the only feasible 'solution'.

Secondly, this kind of stereotyping tends to act like a self-fulfilling prophecy: older employees may learn to see themselves as problematic persons and may learn to find some compensation in it (less responsibility, lower standards, less demands, more claims for support on other parties). This process may aggravate the problem, because it may disturb the self-esteem of older employees. In the longer run, it may lead to impoverishment of their integrity and their jobs, as well as to task underload and stress.

Loss of Quality of Thinking under Stress

Stress reactions can act as stressors in their own right, which may also be more incapacitating for people over forty. An important point in this respect is that stress interferes with quality of thinking. This may be a matter of all kinds of intruding blanks, thoughts, feelings and events, which make it hard, if not impossible, to maintain a productive line of thinking. It may also be a matter of too rigid and constrained ways of thinking, focused on standard procedures, characterized by stereotypical conceptualization, black-and-white thinking and the absence of open questions, scrutinizing and reality testing, resulting in impoverished creativity. Often this second form is a kind of adaptation to an overly restricted work situation. Older employees who are for a long time exposed to such a situation are at a greater risk here. Also, employees over forty are more dependent on the use of their oversight, insight, relativization and their clear thinking to keep their work productive and innovative. In short, people over forty need more wisdom. This wisdom can also help to prevent or cure stress. However, we may run into a paradox here, as wisdom is not likely to evolve where stress prevails for some time.

Predicaments of Employees over Forty

Summarizing, it may be said that most employees over forty have to cope with one or several stress sources which can be defined as forms of lack or loss of role structure and integrity (Schuyt and Van de Klinkenberg, 1988): ageing goes together with having to resign from certain ways of functioning (Rümke, 1947). As such, graceful resignation and creating new, meaningful forms of integrity can be seen as crucial developmental tasks of employees over forty. This implies that these employees tend to be confronted with some relatively unstructured and ill-defined problems. According to Featherman et al. (1993), this is part of a general trend: throughout the life course, developmental tasks tend to become less well-structured.

Having to create new, meaningful role structures does not provide one with a well-defined goal state or a fixed path toward that goal state. Though one can learn from examples provided by colleagues, in essence, one still has to design one's own new role, and one has to do so in one's own way. Though this is an important developmental task, that has to be successfully accomplished in order to live a satisfactory life, people do not get much training and practice in such design tasks (Bono, 1990). In this respect, it is hardly surprising that some people fail in this respect and have to live in an impoverished and overly constricted reality.

As already indicated in the section discussing the loss of quality of thinking under stress, interpersonal differences in the successful accomplishment of this kind of developmental tasks are related to differences in wisdom, that is the degree to which one can, wants, and allows oneself to use certain cognitive abilities and skills.

Wisdom

The choice for the concept of wisdom is determined by its nice, positive ring and its connection to ageing: wisdom is one of the very few positive concepts associated with ageing. However, wisdom is hard to define in a simple way. Wisdom is more about perception than about logic; it is about potentiality, exploration, and creativity, an antidote to prejudice and fossilized thinking. Wisdom recognizes the possibility of different 'logical bubbles', i.e. localized domains of reality with their own frames of reference of axioms, rules, meanings, morality, and emotionality (Bono, 1996). Though all these aspects do play a role, such a description obviously does not make the concept less complex. In this chapter, the most important issues are the following three outcomes of wisdom.

First, wisdom leads to a 'greater picture' and 'sense of coherence' (Antonovsky, 1991). It concerns itself with the mutual determination of our functioning and our surroundings, our integrity. As such, it is about the lay-out of systems and subsystems, about their details and alternatives within the greater system (see the discussion on integration below). This greater picture allows an actor to act in a more deliberate and effective way.

Secondly, wisdom results in a pleasant-feeling state of equanimity and a certain ease of functioning and goal-accomplishment. This state is incompatible with strain and stress, and, as such, may be an excellent point of departure for preventing and counteracting stress. However, when stress takes over wisdom tends to wither away.

A third point is that, because wisdom is focused on design and designing (Bono, 1996), it can result in prevention, repair and replacement of losses of structure. As such, wisdom can be conceived as a conglomerate of coping techniques to counteract the effects of the stressors in the former section, as they all result in a loss of integrity.

Most of the elements and aspects of wisdom are inextricably connected to each other and often show considerable overlap. In this section, the following elements and aspects are described:

- maturity;
- detachment;
- inward turn;
- identifying and developing personal themes;
- improved integration of diverse information;
- more focused working;
- motivating;
- life plan.

Maturity

A precondition for wisdom consists of the accomplishment of maturity resulting from the successful attainment of the principal developmental tasks of middle age (Rümke, 1947).

First, one has to solve unfinished problems of the personal past. This can be a matter of unresolved conflicts, ways of coping that have become obsolete, traumatic incidents one has not come to grips with, and goals one had or has to relinquish. Unfinished problems like these tend to tie up processing resources at the expense of the available processing capacity. That is why their solution may contribute to an

increase of the processing capacity available for designing and leading a more meaningful life. This may ask for the help of a counselor or psychotherapist.

A second task concerns facing and accepting one's own mortality. True acceptance
of one's own death leads to the option of what Heidegger (1962) has called 'being to
death' ('sein zum Tode'). This means living authentically and experiencing every
moment as if it were your last one. Near death experiences are an example here, as
they enable one to experience and use the time left in a more aware and pleasurable
way. Moreover, from such a perspective petty anxieties and preoccupations become
less limiting.

Other developmental tasks are about accepting the loss of one's youth, the decay
of physical and mental capacities, and the inevitability of guilt, loss, and suffering.

Success in these developmental tasks enables one to loosen up and let go of things
in order to lead a life that is better geared to one's own basic needs and talents, more
focused on the here and now, and allowing for more relativization. In general, successful accomplishment of these developmental tasks helps to get a view of the
greater picture and a taste of the feelings of easy functioning associated with wisdom. These tasks can be addressed in the context of a self-management program.
Whether these are actually accomplished depends, of course, on the employee in
question.

Detachment

Wisdom is characterized by a basic attitude and disposition of detachment.
Detachment implies a sense of peace and serenity, stemming from a flexible but
solid integration in the here and now. The person involved is not blindly engaged in
pursuing future goals, knowing that goals can be altered or given up when they
turn out to be unattainable or when more attractive options turn up. A detached
person is neither involved in fruitless attempts to undo the past, as he or she under-
stands that the past and the present stemming from it are not subject to change, and
can only serve as learning material for future actions. So, detachment means accepting the responsibility for the status quo as the point of departure for shaping the
future.

This state allows one to toss around thoughts, relativize, ask oneself questions,
look for and explore inconsistencies and contradictions, and change at will one's own
point of view. So, one can search, design, and execute alternatives; and one can accept
all of them, alternate between them, combine them, pick only one, etc. (Bono, 1996).
In short, one can open up new opportunities, chances, and challenges (Cavanaugh
and McGuire, 1994), in order to create appropriate niches for the design of new or better adapted structures.

Detachment is not *per se* something exotic that is out of reach for normal mortals.
Detachment can be taught and practiced, for instance within the context of a self-
management program. Practicing some method of 'thinking of nothing in particular' (meditation, relaxation exercises, hypnosis, alpha training, yoga, running) helps
one to enter a state of mental calm which allows for the thinking processes mentioned above.

Inward Turn

Another important element of wisdom is the so-called inward turn, a concept that found its place in a number of prominent theories of adult development (Sinnott, 1994). The inward turn consists of a form of gradual cognitive restructuring, which is supposed to take place during and after midlife (Jepson and Labouvie-Vief, 1992; Baltes and Baltes, 1993). The inward turn implies that the person involved lives more in his or her thoughts and fantasies, and somewhat less in the outer world at hand. Two factors are important here.

One factor is that older persons can apply more elaborate scripts and schemas. This allows them to handle many tasks and situated roles almost automatically, which leaves them with sufficient processing capacity to turn their attention inwards. Another factor with the same effect may be the loss of role structure mentioned before, which means that the person involved finds himself in situations that provide insufficient cues to bind his attention.

The inward turn implies that the people involved spend more time musing, thinking of nothing in particular. From a different perspective, this can be described as a way of functioning which is related to meditation or contemplation. Such a way of mental functioning also can be used in a more focused and goal-directed way, for instance to refresh and centre oneself.

Other applications, described by Stokvis (1946) as a form of self-suggestion, are techniques of programming oneself to reinforce a more goal-directed and effortless way of working, without interference from disturbing thoughts or feelings. Variants of such an approach are also applied in sports psychology under the denominator mental preparation. As such a way of working provides optimal outcomes at low costs in effort, they are especially appropriate for older employees who have to be sparing in energy expenditure.

The combination of detachment and inward turn can also lead to more attention for one's own integrity, to self-reflection and self-monitoring. Pursued in a systematic way, it may contribute to a better quality of choices, decisions, and goal-setting. A useful method in this respect is the focusing technique (Gendlin, 1981). Instigating a dialogue between different parts of a person as practiced in Gestalt therapy can be of help here too.

Identifying and Developing Personal Themes

As far as socialization leads to the underdevelopment of basic personal themes, it may result in an impoverished life for the person involved (see the discussion on loss of identity above). Being a misfit or leading to a bleak life of conformism and little creativity are possible outcomes here. Learning about one's basic themes, finding better outlets for them and re-activating them, often with the help of a professional, can re-energize the integrity of the person in question.

The underdevelopment of themes can also be a consequence of overdevelopment of other themes, resulting in an activity which is too narrowly focused. As the underdevelopment of these other themes may lead to some critical limitations in one's behavior repertory, developing them can help to enrich one's repertory of actions and to reinforce one's freedom of action. Learning about one's basic themes and motives is important here.

Assessment of themes and motives is an important issue in self-management programs. Essentially, this is an instance of the inward turn. This can be done in different ways. Practicing some detachment, reflecting, applying focusing techniques, writing a conscientious autobiography, counseling, and discussing results of paper-and-pencil personality tests can all be of help here. Identifying one's personal themes provides one with more insight into personal assumptions and underlying values, as well as a better understanding of one's group roles, personal pitfalls based upon an exaggeration of a certain theme, and typical theme-bound stressors (Palmer, 1988; Ofman, 1992). Once the most important themes are identified, they may serve as a safe home base, from which one can explore other ways of functioning. Formulating a concise wording of one's main reason, motive or goal for living can be useful here. Once formulated, it may be used as a yardstick or touchstone for evaluating one's actions. Moreover, identifying the main personal theme may also lead to a clarification of one's value orientation. As this orientation determines one's room to move and the main guidelines, such a clarification can be crucial in shaping one's future.

Learning about such themes may also lead to a more precise perception of the habitual conduct of other people. Their attitudes and behaviour become more predictable and one can come to a better understanding in what moves them and what may be their most effective rewards and punishments.

An example of an actualization of an underdeveloped part in some male persons is an increase in attention for the relational sides of life, such as giving attention and care (which, according to Baltes and Baltes, 1993, may be due to a decreased production of male hormones). Such a development is conducive to better relationships, a better social network and more social support, and can prevent or soften the occurrence of stress. It may take place spontaneously, but often can be furthered by extra instruction and attention.

Improved Integration of Diverse Information

The 'inward turn' enables some persons to integrate different domains of knowledge and competence in a better way. This can be a matter of making better connections between abstract suppositions on the one hand and concrete issues, needed for dealing with the situated state of affairs, on the other (Jepson and Labouvie-Vief, 1992). This can only be accomplished if one is completely immersed in one's thoughts and there are no intruding thoughts, feelings, or blanks. A useful technique here is lowering one's own activation to a level of alpha EEG waves, and to take it from there to explore certain lines of thought without interference (Silva and Goldman, 1988). Such a state of mind is also more appropriate for dealing with fussy sets (Bono, 1996).

Another aspect relevant here is that people when they grow older become more involved in finding and defining problems, and less in solving well-specified problems (Featherman et al., 1993). According to Featherman et al., creatively designing a problem is of crucial importance in solving the ill-structured and ill-defined problems inherent in elderly employees' developmental tasks. It is also the first step in design-ing new structures.

Because the effects of these forms of integration depend on the quality and quantity of one's knowledge, wisdom has more meaning when an actor disposes of a broad gen-eral knowledge, enabling him or her to relate knowledge from different disciplines (Kramer and Bacelar, 1994). An improved integration of information can have several positive effects on the quality of mental functioning and integrity (Bono, 1996).

First, the view may become broader (helicopter view). A broader picture implies a shift from focusing on separate events and simple cause–effect attributions to a more systems-oriented way of thinking (Senge, 1992). This allows an actor to get a grip on underlying mechanisms, which may provide one with the leverage to steer some of its outcomes.

Secondly, the view may become deeper. On the one hand, it becomes richer in detail. As the person involved is more aware of different values and assumptions, he or she can distinguish, enter and leave different individual or group-bound realities (De Bono's logical bubbles mentioned before), experiencing their points of view and logic, without losing the overall picture. On the other hand, the time horizon widens (Jaques, 1986). Exploring different options, one can think in greater time entities. This is particularly useful for designing strategies and fundamental changes that encompass many years, which is highly important for every organization.

Thirdly, the view may become richer, in the sense that more potential alternatives are taken into account. This faculty is one of the outcomes of greater detachment described above.

The improved integration of information has its costs in processing capacity and time. For instance, Kemper *et al.* (1993: 138) point out that the lower working memory thresholds for all kinds of cognitive material may very well be the cause of the well-documented slowing down of the working memory (Salthouse, 1992).

Motivating

As was mentioned before, the development of wisdom implies that the person involved gets a different attitude to and a better understanding of others. Also it was indicated that goal-setting may improve as a result of more self-reflection, while the processes underlying seemingly separate events are said to be better understood as well. Together this attitude and these abilities enable one to motivate others for com-mon causes. Motivating takes place by providing an inspiring future vision and by stimulating the other to develop initiatives to realize this attractive vision (Senge, 1992). The latter is foremost a matter of asking questions, creating challenges and opportunities, and giving responsibility (Aubrey and Cohen, 1995). Though ability to motivate others may be useful to anybody, this applies even more when one gets older and somewhat less energetic and strong.

Life Plan

During the latter career stages, it becomes clearer which goals can and cannot be reached. The persons involved may reorient themselves and say goodbye to what proved to be unattainable. This asks for a new life plan, based on who one really is and wants to be, and on the options and limitations of external reality. The elements of wisdom described so far can be integrated into such a plan. The persons involved have to draw up the balance of their life (Featherman et al., 1993) in order to determine what they still want to pursue. This is about what they can and want to do, within what they are allowed and allow themselves to do. Formulating and executing a life plan can be seen as redesigning one's integrity: redesigning priorities, main issues, and the value orientation for one's further development. The concise wording of one's main life theme, mentioned in the discussion above on personal themes can be a helpful tool here.

A good life plan is not confined to one's job, career, and professional development. Relationships with other people and other societal institutions play a crucial role too. What can you contribute, what can you mean to others? The reward consists of the relationships you choose and their outcomes, such as for instance social support.

Another feature of a good life plan is that it is not harmful to one's well-being and health. So, it must be well-balanced over the different life domains. One should learn to get enough pleasure and rest and to deal with one's own and others' stress processes. And one should seek some physical exercise (swimming, running) and practise some form of thinking of nothing in particular (swimming and running will do too). Essentially, a plan such as this one is a general coping program. It allows for a life of further development, without unnecessary stress. As such, it can be an outcome of a self-management program, which also pays attention to the elements of wisdom described in this section.

Last, a life plan must be used with sufficient detachment: sometimes there are impossibilities and sometimes a more promising vista will appear. Both cases may call for an adaptation of the plan.

Organizational Policy

What can an organization do to improve integrity and to counteract and prevent the stressors described above in the section devoted to the sources of stress? Also, what can it do to promote the development of wisdom, as described in the previous section? This section describes an exemplary approach. As such, it is based on a report written for a trading firm with a rapidly aging work force, which is typical of many other corporations these days.

Development of Objectives

First the management team itself formulates an unambiguous global vision on the future of their aging personnel. This vision is elaborated in well-defined objectives and a strategy. A special workshop with an external expert can be useful. Several points have to be taken into account.

The main objective is to ensure that all employees develop their integrity, their abilities and skills so that they are able to adapt in their own way to the changes the organization is going through. This means that everybody has to pursue a career that capitalizes on their own talents and (age-bound) competencies, in a way that is compatible with the greater organizational picture. Such a career should provide challenging tasks, with enough room for further development, but without undue stress and health risks.

An important element—because it is the main basis of the problematic—is facing how stereotyping older employees and its silent effects on the organizational policy have contributed substantially to the present problems. One of the indications of possible stereotyping is a, probably justified, concern that special policies focusing on older employees will lead to stigmatizing. Though becoming aware of stereotyping is a matter of the whole company, the management team has a clear modeling function. Later, this becomes foremost a task for middle management, who have to implement the policy. Still later, all personnel, younger and older, get involved in this.

Another element of the objective is the individualized character of the policy to be followed. A policy to take care of the ageing of employees can only be successful if it is geared to the great individual differences. The simplest way to realize this is to give employees enough information, time, and attention to enable them to make their own decisions, set their own goals in a way compatible with the organizational goals and rules. Also, these employees are the best experts when it comes to their own integrity and working conditions, while they are also the ones who are most motivated to take good decisions. So, everyone has to take care of their own development and employability. Obviously, such an approach can only be successful if the organization gives enough freedom and opportunities to learn and practice.

Interventions

When the management team has agreed on objectives and strategy, they should communicate these immediately and clearly to the organization at large (by special meetings, circular letters, special attention to the issue in team discussions of progress and periodical dyadic meetings with one's superior, etc.). The most important policy modification can consist of executing the organization's own human resource management with more consistency for all age groups. This also prevents interventions from being seen as stigmatizing. Also it may be of help when the management team elaborates and communicates a clear organizational vision and mission as a context for individual development.

It is recommended that a special task force be instituted, which includes key representatives of all parties involved (management team, internal P&O professionals, middle management, shop floor) and an external facilitator. The task force is responsible for the design and implementation of the policy and reports periodically to the management team.

Though such a policy essentially addresses all age groups in the same way, it may imply considerable changes for employees over forty. For instance, as the latter group will be the target of real career policy now, they will be involved (again) in:

- periodical meetings with the immediate superior about performance, well-being, changes, training needs and career;

- job and task changes:
  - job redesign (for example in autonomous teams),
  - job rotation,
  - secondment in another organization,
  - temporary projects;
- changes in terms of employment:
  - individualized working hours,
  - study leave and sabbatical leave,
  - cafeteria plans for pay, fringe benefits, and pensions;
- additional work-related and general training and education.

It is of crucial importance that employees have a big say in designing their own job and career. Employees over forty may need some extra information, time and attention from P&O and their direct superiors. Some special training or coaching can be of help here too.

Special Training Programs

Special training programs focus on self-management for employees of different age groups. This can be an entry program for new and mostly young employees. Training in self-management and enculturation in the organization is then integrated in one program. Another program is tailored to employees who have done the same job now for a considerable time and who are confronted by a high workload and insufficient time for reflection and further development. This program focuses first on prevention of the stressors discussed in the second section of this chapter and the development of some of the abilities mentioned in the third section. Last, there is a program focusing on employees over forty, with comparable objectives, though also directed to counteracting the stressors discussed in the second section.

All self-management programs follow one general format. First the trainees survey what they can and want to do: they explore their talents and special themes, and the opportunities and limitations that ensue. Some of the elements of wisdom are introduced and practiced in special exercises. There is also an introduction of some version of the factors described in the second section above and their impact on one's life. A management representative gives an overview of the management team vision of the future and the opportunities it provides to the trainees. Then, trainees try to get a better overall picture of the organization, its purpose, culture, and external environment. The program results in a plan, in which they design, in dialogue with the organization, their contribution to the organization for the next seven years. Also group members indicate how they can and will help and support each other in this respect. An additional option is the instigation of projects focusing on implementation of some part of the policy, for which the trainees themselves have to find sponsors in the organization. Techniques used include:

- relaxation, imagination, and focusing exercises, among others focused on centered working and self-monitoring;

- questionnaires about personal themes (assumptions, contributions to teams, pitfalls, stressors);
- writing assignments focusing on the analysis of one's integrity and the organization, and keeping a diary;
- discussions, brainstorm sessions, and a feedback exercise;
- individual consultations with a psychologist.

Apart from self-management training, it is recommended that some training be given to the people who have to implement this policy, the direct superiors of the employees involved. Two subject areas are crucial here: learning to deal with stereotyping and learning to play a role as coach, and managing from a perspective of subsidiarity (Handy, 1995) instead of one of positional power.

References

Antonovsky, A. (1991) The structural sources of salutogenic strengths. In C. L. Cooper and R. Payne (eds.) *Personality and Stress: Individual Differences in the Stress Process* (pp. 67–104). Chichester: Wiley and Sons.

Aubrey, R. and Cohen, P. M. (1995) *Working Wisdom*. San Francisco: Jossey-Bass Publishers.

Baars, J. (1988) De sociale constitutie van de ouderdom. (The social constitution of old age). In C. P. M. Knipscheer, J. Baars and M. Severijns (eds.) *Uitzicht op ouder worden: een verkenning van nieuwe rollen (A View of Growing Old: an Exploration of New Roles)* (pp. 21–36). Assen: Van Gorcum.

Baltes, P. B. and Baltes, M. G. (1993) Psychological perspectives on successful aging. In P. B. Baltes and M. G. Baltes (eds.) *Successful Aging. Perspectives from the Social Sciences* (pp. 1–34). Cambridge: Cambridge University Press.

Becker, H. A. (1995) De demografie van ontgroening en vergrijzing (The demographics of Aging). In J. A. M. Winnubst, M. J. Schabracq, J. Gerrichhauzen and A. Kampermann (eds.) *Arbeid, levensloop en gezondheid (Labour, Life Cycle and Health)* (pp. 27–41). Heerlen: OU / Utrecht: Lemma.

Belsky, J. K. (1990) *The Psychology of Aging.* (2nd edn.) Pacific Grove, CA: Brooks / Cole Publishing Company.

Bennett, R. and Eckman, J. (1973) Attitudes towards aging. In C. Eisendorfer and M. P. Lawton (eds.) *The Psychology of Adult Development and Aging.* Washington: APA.

Biedermann, H. (1989) *Knaurs Lexicon der Symbole (Knaur's Lexicon of Symbols).* Knaur, Munich.

Boerlijst, J. G., Heijden, B. I. J. M. van, and Assen, A. van (1993) *Veertig-plussers in de onderneming (People over 40 in the Corporation).* Assen: Van Gorcum.

Bolen, J. S. (1989) *Gods in Every Man.* New York: Harper and Row.

Bono, E. de (1990) *I am Right, you are Wrong.* London: Viking.

Bono, E. de (1996) *Textbook of Wisdom.* Harmondsworth: Penguin Books.

Bourdieu, P. (1986) The forms of capital. In J. G. Richardson (ed.) *Handbook of Theory and Research for the Sociology of Education.* New York: Greenwood Press.

Breznitz, S. (ed.) (1983) *The Denial of Stress.* New York: International Universities Press.

Burns, E. (1973) *Theatricality.* New York: Harper & Row.

Cascio, W. F. and McEnvoy, G. M. (1989) 'Cumulative evidence of the relationship between employee age and job performance', *Journal of Applied Psychology,* 74, 11–17.

Cavanaugh, J. C. and McGuire, L. C. (1994) Chaos theory as a framework for understanding adult lifespan learning. In J. D. Sinnott (ed.) *Interdisciplinary Handbook of Adult Lifespan Learning* (pp. 3–21). Westport CN: Greenwood Press.

Cofer, C. N. and Appley, M. H. (1964) *Motivation: Theory and Research*. New York: J. Wiley & Sons.

Dresens, C. S. H. H. (1993) *Geschikt voor alle leeftijden (Fit for all Ages)*. Lelystad: Koninklijke Vermande.

Eibl-Eibesfeldt, I. von (1970) *Ethology, The Biology of Behavior*. New York: Holt, Rinehart & Winston.

Erickson, M. H., Rossi, E. J., and Rossi, S. I. (1976) *Hypnotic Realities*. London: J. Wiley & Sons.

Erikson, E. (1968) *Youth, Identity and Crisis*. New York: Norton.

Featherman, D. L., Smith, J., and Patterson, J. G. (1993) Successful aging in a post-retired society. In P. B. Baltes and M. G. Baltes (eds.) *Successful Aging. Perspectives from the Social Sciences*. Cambridge: Cambridge University Press.

Foner, A. and Schwab, K. (1981) *Aging and Retirement*. Belmont, CA: Wadsworth.

Freud, A. (1971) *Das Ich und die Abwehrmechanismen (The Ego and the Defense Mechanisms)*. München: Kindler.

Frijda, N. H. (1986) *The Emotions*. Cambridge: Cambridge University Press.

Fromm, E. (1955) *The Sane Society*. New York: Rinehart.

Gendlin, E. T. (1981) *Focusing*. New York: Bantam Books.

Goffman, E. (1974) *Frame Analysis*. New York: Harper & Row.

Handy, C. (1995) *The Age of Paradox*. Boston: Harvard Business Press.

Heidegger, M. (1962) *Being and Time*. (Translated by J. Macquarrie and E. Robinson) New York: Harper & Row.

James, W. (1890/1950) *The Principles of Psychology*. New York: Dover.

Janssen, P. and Gerrichhauzen, J. (1995) De middenloopbaan- en middenleven-fase (The mid-career and midlife stage). In J. A. M.Winnubst, M. J. Schabracq, J. Gerrichhauzen and A. Kampermann (eds.), *Arbeid, levensloop en gezondheid (Labour, Life Cycle and Health)*. Heerlen: Open Universiteit.

Jaques, E. (1986) 'The development of intellectual capability: a discussion of stratified systems theory', *The Journal of Applied Behavioral Science*, 22, 361–383.

Jepson, K. J. and Labouvie-Vief, G. (1992) Symbolic processing of youth and elders. In R. L. West and J. D. Sinnott (eds.) *Everyday Memory and Aging* (pp. 124–137). New York: Springer Verlag.

Karasek, R. A. and Theorell, T. (1990) *Healthy Work. Stress, Productivity and the Reconstruction of Working Life*. New York: Basic Books.

Kemper, S., Kynette, D. and Norman, S. (1993) Age differences in spoken language. In R. L. West and J. D. Sinnott (eds.) *Everyday Memory and Aging* (pp. 138–152). New York: Springer Verlag.

Kerkhoff, W. H. C. (1993) *De oudere werknemer: Strategisch 40+-beleid (The Elderly Worker: Strategic 40+ Policies)*. Deventer: Kluwer Bedrijfswetenschappen.

Kohn, M. L. and Schooler, C. (1983) *Work and Personality: A Study. An Inquiry into the Impact of Social Stratification*. Norwood, NJ: Ablex.

Kramer, D. A. and Bacelar, W. T. (1994) The educated adult in today's world: wisdom and the mature learner. In J. D. Sinnott (ed.) *Interdisciplinary Handbook of Adult Lifespan Learning* (pp. 31–50). Westport, CN: Greenwood Press.

Krijnen, M. A. (1996) Beeldvorming over ouderen (Representations of the Elderly). In M. A. Krijnen and M. J. Schabracq (eds.). *Werkend ouder worden (Ageing at Work)* (pp. 17–29). Utrecht: Lemma.

Lazarus, R. S. (1966) *Psychological Stress and the Coping Process*. New York: McGraw-Hill.

Lecky, P. (1945) *Self-consistency: A Theory of Personality*. New York: Island Press.

Lee, J. S. (1991) *Abstraction and Aging. A Social Psychological Analysis*. New York: Springer Verlag.

Limborgh, C. van (1995) Ploegendienst en Variabele Dienstroosters (Shift work and variable ros-ters) In M. J. Schabracq, J. A. M. Winnubst, A. C. Perreijn, and J. Gerrichhauzen (eds.) *Mentale Belasting (Mental Load)* (pp. 301–320). Utrecht: Lemma.

Moscovici, S. (1984) The phenomenon of social representation. In R. M. Farr and S. Moscovici (eds.) *Social Representations* (pp. 3–69). Cambridge: Cambridge University Press.

Offerman, L. and Gowing, M. (1990) 'Organizations of the future', *American Psychologist*, 45, 95–108.

Ofman, D. (1992) *Bezieling en Kwaliteit in Organizations (Inspiration and Quality in Organizations)*. Cothen, NL: Servire.

Ouwerkerk, R. van, Meijman, T., and Mulder, B. (1994) *Arbeidspsychologie en taakanalyse (Work Psychology and Task Analysis)*. Utrecht: Lemma.

Palmer, H. (1988) *The Enneagram*. New York: Harper Collins Publishers.

Rowell, T. (1972) *Social Behaviour of Monkeys*. Harmondsworth: Penguin Books.

Rümke, H. C. (1947) *Levenstijdperken van de man (Life Stages of the Male)*. Amsterdam: De Arbeiderspers.

Salthouse, T. A. (1992) *Mechanisms of Age-Cognition Relations in Adulthood*. Hillsdale, NJ: Lawrence Erlbaum Associates.

Schabracq, M. J. and Cooper, C. L. (1998) Toward a phenomenological framework for work and organization stress. *Human Relations*, 51, 625–648.

Schabracq, M. J. and Winnubst, J. A. M. (1996) Senior employees. In M. J. Schabracq, J. A. M. Winnubst and C. L. Cooper (eds.) *Handbook of Work and Health Psychology* (pp. 275–294). Chichester: J. Wiley & Sons.

Schabracq, M. J., Cooper, C. L., and Winnubst, J. A. M. (1996) Work and health psychology: towards a theoretical framework. In M. J. Schabracq, J. A. M. Winnubst, and C. L. Cooper (eds.) *Handbook of Work and Health Psychology* (pp. 3–29). Chichester: J. Wiley & Sons.

Schaie, K. W. and Schooler, C. (eds.) (1989) *Social Structure and Aging*. Hillsdale, NJ: Lawrence Erlbaum & Associates.

Schroots, J. J. F. and Birren, J. E. (1993) Theoretical issues and basic questions in the planning of lon-gitudinal studies of health and aging. In J. J. F. Schroots (ed.) *Aging, Health and Competence* (pp. 4–34). Amsterdam: Elsevier.

Schutz, A. (1970) *On Phenomenology and Social Relations*. Chicago: University of Chicago Press.

Schuyt, T. and Klinkenberg, T. van de (1988) Helpen en de zuigkracht van de macht (Helping and the pull of power). In C. P. M. Knipscheer, J. Baars, and M. Severijns (eds.) *Uitzicht op ouder wor-den: een verkenning van nieuwe rollen (A View on Growing Old: An Exploration of New Roles)* (pp.53–64). Assen: Van Gorcum.

Senge, P. M. (1992) *The Fifth Dimension*. London: Century Business.

Shallice, T. (1978) The dominant action system: An information-processing approach to conscious-ness. In K. S. Pope and J. L. Singer (eds.), *The Stream of Consciousness*. New York: Plenum Press.

Silva, J. and Goldman, B. (1988) *The Silva Mind Control Method of Mental Dynamics*. New York: Pocket Books.

Sinnott, J. D. (1994) The relationship of postformal thought, adult learning, and life span development. In J. D. Sinnott (ed.), *Interdisciplinary Handbook of Adult Lifespan Learning* (pp. 105–119). Westport, CN: Greenwood Press.

Sterns, H. and Alexander, R. (1988) Performance appraisal of the older worker. In H. Dennis (ed.) *Fourteen Steps to Managing an Aging Workforce* (pp. 85–93). Lexington, MA: Lexington Books.

Stokvis, B. B. (1946) *Psychologie der suggestie en autosuggestie (Psychology of Suggestion and Autosuggestion)*. Lochem: De Tijdstroom.

Taylor, S. E. (1986) *Health Psychology*. New York: Random House.

Thijssen, J. G. L. (1996) *Leren, leeftijd en loopbaanperspectief* (Learning, age and career perspective) dissertation. Tilburg: KUB.

Thomae, H. (1993) Foreword. In J. J. F. Schroots (ed.) *Aging, Health and Competence*. (pp. xi–xiii). Amsterdam: Elsevier.

Vrugt, A. J. and Schabracq, M. J. (1991) *Vanzelfsprekend gedrag. Opstellen over nonverbale communicatie (Behaviour that goes without saying. Essays on Nonverbal Communication)*. Amsterdam/Meppel: Boom.

Waldman, D. and Avolio, B. (1986) 'A meta-analysis of age differences in job performance', *Journal of Applied Psychology*, 71, 33–38.

Warr, P. (1993) *Age and Job Performance*. European Symposium on Work and Aging, Amsterdam: UvA, p. 17.

Willner, P. (1993) Animal models of stress: An overview. In S. C. Stanford and P. Salmon (eds.) *Stress. From Synapse to Syndrome* (pp. 145–165). London: Academic Press.

Winnubst, J. A. M. and Schabracq, M. J. (1996) Social support, stress and organizations. In M. J. Schabracq, J. A. M. Winnubst, and C. L. Cooper (eds.) *Handbook of Work and Health Psychology* (pp. 87–102). Chichester: J. Wiley & Sons.

12

The Theory of Preventive Stress
Management in Organizations

Jonathan D. Quick, James Campbell Quick, and
Debra L. Nelson

Introduction

The theory of preventive stress management in organizations begins with the translation and integration of concepts from public health and preventive medicine. These
concepts are then overlaid on to an organizational stress process framework, from
which the theory is derived. This chapter is organized into four major sections
addressing specific aspects of the theory of preventive stress management in organizations. The first section describes the theory, beginning with the preventive medicine model. Concepts from this model are superimposed on to the stress process in
organizations framework, thus effecting the preventive stress management model.
This section also includes two sets of testable hypotheses, which form the core of the
theory, and research related to each set of hypotheses. In the second section, diagnostic, prevention, and stress management implications of the theory are discussed,
including surveillance indicators added to the original model. The third section presents idiographic research from two organizations: ICI-Zeneca Pharmaceuticals and
the United States Air Force. The fourth section discusses the implications of the
theory for future research. The conclusion discusses Sisyphus, dynamic self-reliance,
and the relationship of theory, beliefs, and observations.

A Theory of Prevention

To introduce the theory of preventive stress management in organizations, we begin
with a description of the preventive medicine model, followed by an explanation of
the stress process in organizations. The preventive stress management model is
based on the translation of the preventive medicine model and its overlay onto the
stress process in an organization framework. While organizational stress is not pre-

cisely defined for the purposes of this chapter, preventive stress management is defined as follows (Quick and Quick, 1984: 13).

Preventive stress management is an organizational philosophy and set of principles which employs specific methods for promoting individual and organizational health while preventing individual and organizational distress.

As a basic philosophy, preventive stress management consists of basic ideas, beliefs and principles to achieve good health and high performance in organizations. The basic ideas and beliefs are embodied in five guiding principles.

1. Individual and organizational health are interdependent.
2. Leaders have a responsibility for individual and organizational health.
3. Individual and organizational distress are not inevitable.
4. Each individual and organization reacts uniquely to stress.
5. Organizations are ever-changing, dynamic entities.

This chapter extends this philosophy and these principles into a theory by deducing two sets of empirically testable hypotheses, one set of hypotheses from the stress process in organizations framework and the second set of hypotheses from the preventive stress management model.

The Preventive Medicine Model

Preventive medicine is a relatively young branch of medicine aimed at prevention of health problems and disorders, illnesses, diseases, and epidemics (Last and Wallace, 1992). Early in the twentieth century, Harvard President Charles W. Eliot was instrumental in encouraging Harvard Medical School to be a leader in preventive medicine. A popular result of this effort was a series of lectures during the first decade of this century on sanitation, contagion, and other public health topics (Benison *et al.*, 1987: 117). The health risks in the early 1900s were primarily acute, such as influenza, as opposed to chronic, such as cardiovascular disease. With the success of the war on acute diseases, the public health and preventive medicine battle-field shifted to the chronic diseases and health promotion (Cohen, 1985; Foss and Rothenberg, 1987).

In contrast to the acute and infectious diseases, chronic diseases do not arise suddenly. Rather, chronic diseases develop gradually through a progression of stages, a 'natural life history'. The natural life history of most diseases is one of evolution through stages of susceptibility, early illness, and finally advanced or disabling disease. Progress through these three stages may be illustrated with coronary artery disease. At the stage of susceptibility, the individual is healthy, but is exposed to certain health risks or precursors to illness, such as a sedentary life (i.e. lack of physical activity and exercise) or cigarette smoking. If these health risks lead to the development of arteriosclerotic plaques in the coronary arteries, the individual is at the stage of early or preclinical disease in which few, if any, symptoms are present. As the disease advances, it becomes symptomatic or clinical disease. Angina pectoris and heart attacks are advanced manifestations of coronary artery disease. This natural life history of a chronic disease is not inevitable and there is growing evidence for natural protective mechanisms and defenses enabling individuals to maintain their health even when exposed to health risks. These natural defenses and homeostatic processes were first discussed by Cannon (1932).

Public health encompasses a broad array of health protection activities inspired by the practice of viewing illnesses within a social context, as President Eliot did (Benison *et al.*, 1987; Ewart, 1991). The predominant diagnostic model in public health involves the interaction between a host (the individual), an agent (health-damaging organism or substance), and the environment. One fundamental concept of preventive medicine is the opportunity for preventive and treatment intervention at each stage in the life history of a disease. Preventive interventions aim to slow, stop, or reverse the progression of disease. *Primary prevention* is designed to protect health at the stage of susceptibility by eliminating or reducing the impact of health risks; it is prevention before the onset of disease or disorder (Winett, 1995). *Secondary prevention* is designed for early detection of disease and prompt, early intervention to correct departures from health (Last, 1988). *Tertiary prevention* is therapeutic and designed to treat symptoms or advanced disease, to alleviate discomfort, and to restore function (Last, 1988).

The Stress Process in Organizations

Walter B. Cannon was the first to identify the stress response, labeling it the 'emergency reaction'. His view of its roots in 'the fighting emotions' set the stage for its identification as the fight-or-flight response (Cannon, 1929). Subsequently, Hans Selye's environmental stress investigations found the release of adrenal-gland hormones to be a chief result of stress, normally leading to appropriate adaptation to stressful situations (Selye, 1976a). However, the adaptation mechanism may malfunction and cause one or more diseases of maladaptation, such as cardiovascular disease or arthritis. Selye's (1973, 1976b) General Adaptation Syndrome (GAS) included three stages: alarm, resistance, and exhaustion. While the alarm stage of the GAS is what Cannon labeled the emergency reaction, it is in the resistance stage of the GAS where an individual struggles, fights, and is exposed to health risk and distress. Finally, the exhaustion stage is where collapse occurs.

Kahn *et al.* (1964) drew attention to the psychology of stress by focusing attention on the psychosocial demands of role conflict and role ambiguity as environmental stressors for people in organizations. They showed how conflict and confusion can lead to individual distress and strain, with their associated organizational costs. Lazarus drew attention to another aspect of the psychology of stress by introducing cognitive appraisal and coping (Lazarus *et al.*, 1985). This line of research identified the role of individual differences in the perceptions of demands and stressors, leading one person to see an opportunity or challenge where another sees a threat.

Stress Process Hypotheses   Taken together, the medical foundations and psychological elaborations of the stress concept lay the groundwork for describing the stress process in organizations. The core elements of the stress process are: (1) organizational demands and stressors, which lead to (2) the stress response, resulting in (3) eustressful or distressful consequences (Quick, Quick, Nelson and Hurrell, 1997: 4–5; Selye, 1976a: 15). *Organizational demands and stressors* are the physical or psychological triggers for *the stress response*. The stress response is the generalized, patterned, unconscious mobilization of the body's natural energy resources and results from the combined action of the sympathetic nervous and endocrine systems. The stress response enables individuals to manage organizational demands and stressors. *Eustressful* consequences of stressful experiences or events are healthy, positive, and constructive while *distressful* consequences are unhealthy, negative, and destructive. The relationships among these constructs are expressed in two hypotheses.

Hypothesis 1:   Intense, frequent, prolonged organizational demands increase the stress response in people at work.

Hypothesis 2:   Intense, frequent, prolonged elicitation of the stress response increases the risk and incidence rates of distressful health consequences.

Modifiers of the stress response help account for variance in consequences across individuals, influencing whether the consequences are eustressful or distressful. These dispositional factors and individual difference modifiers influence vulnerability and help account for significant portions of the explained variance in consequences. Of the numerous modifiers of the stress response, Type A/B Behaviour Pattern (TABP/TBBP) (Jenkins, 1997), hardiness (Ouellette, 1997), positive/negative affect (Burke *et al.*, 1993) and self-reliance (J. C. Quick *et al.*, 1996) may be among the most influential moderators. Wofford and Daly (1997) suggest that cognitive–affective stress propensity (CASP), which is a latent reactivity variable, may underlie these more manifest modifiers. For example, individuals high in CASP might possess more Type A Behavior Pattern, less hardiness, more negative affect, and less self-reliance, thus predisposing them to greater risk of distress. Or, individuals low in CASP might possess more Type B Behavior Pattern, more hardiness, more positive affect, and more self-reliance, thus immunizing them against the risk of distress. Because the stress response is a general response involving psychological as well as somatic (bodily) responses, there are parallel physiological susceptibility (Schwartz *et al.*, 1996) and natural protective, immunizing mechanisms and defenses (Ursin, 1997).

Hypothesis 3:   Individuals high in vulnerability modifiers are at greater risk of distress than individuals low in vulnerability modifiers.

Corollary: Individuals high in protective mechanisms and defenses are immunized against the risk of distress more than individuals low in these factors.

Research Related to Hypotheses 1, 2, and 3   Table 12.1 includes nine studies related to hypotheses 1, 2, and 3. In addition, the first several decades of basic physiological and

Table 12.1 Nine studies related to hypotheses 1, 2, and 3

	Context/setting	Data collection method	Findings	Source
Hypothesis 1: Organization demands	60 white-collar workers in managerial and non-managerial positions at the Volvo plant in Gothenburg	Self-reports of work load, including interviews and surveys; physical exams measuring neuroendocrine and cardiovascular functioning over 2–12 hour periods	Physiological arousal indicated by norepinephrine was high under periods of work and home stress. Specifically, females and males had high levels at work; men's dropped off at home while women's continued to rise at home. Blood pressure and epinephrine levels showed the same trend	Frankenhaeuser, 1991
	Two samples of males: 1) blue collar cohorts from a 6½ year prospective study 2) middle managers	Physical measurements of medical and psychosocial data; epidemiological and clinical information	Work pressure was associated with AMI and SCD with an odds ratio of 3.45. Work pressure was associated with AMI*, SCD**, or CHD*** with odds ratio of 2.54	Siegrist, 1996
	Random sample of working male populations in Sweden and America. Swedish data were longitudinal.	Recent national surveys in the USA and Sweden measuring job decision latitude, job demands, mental strain indicators (similar to the Mental Status Index)	In both countries, workers with jobs low in decision latitude and high in job demands report factors associated with job strain: exhaustion, trouble awakening mornings, depression, nervousness, anxiety, insomnia plus alternatives to the model: pill consumption and sick days. Longitudinal data indicate that positive job changes moderate these negative effects over time	Karasek, 1979

250

	Sample	Measures	Findings	Citation
Hypothesis 2: Individual stress	Husband/wife pairs with husbands employed as senior administrators at correctional institutions	Existing and created measures of husband's occupational demands, well-being, perceived type A behavior of husbands, stressful life events, negative affective states, impact of husband's job on home and family, life satisfaction, psychosomatic symptoms, marital satisfaction, social support, coping behaviors, and health and life style behaviors	Greater occupational demands on husbands were associated with lower levels of satisfaction and well-being of wives, including decreased marital satisfaction and increased psychosomatic symptoms, smoking, and alcohol use	Burke, Weir and DuWors, 1980
	Data collected from a sample of teachers, principals, department heads within a single school board over a 1-year time interval	Existing and created measures of work setting, social support, sources of stress, negative attitude change, and work outcomes, as well as the Maslach Burnout Inventory	Work setting and stress were correlated with negative attitude change (burnout). Certain stresses associated with one's occupational role were significant contributors to emotional exhaustion in both women and men when measured one year later	Burke and Greenglass, 1995
	Men from civilian, non-institutionalized population in the USA, aged 18–79	Job Characteristic Estimation System; Health Examination Survey; Health and Nutrition Examination Survey	Occupations with low decision latitude and high psychological workload are associated with past myocardial infarction for male workers	Karasek et al., 1988
Hypothesis 3: Individual differences	Middle- and upper-level managers of a large utility company	Adaptation of Schedule of Life Events; Seriousness of Illness Survey; portions of: Alienation Test and California Life Goals Evaluation Schedule	Stressful life events are associated with increases in symptomology, hardiness decreases likelihood of symptom onset, especially in high stress events	Kobasa, Maddi, and Kahn, 1982

Table 12.1 *cont.*

Context/setting	Data collection method	Findings	Source
Mentally and physically healthy and successful graduates of Harvard College (3 classes)	Open-ended questionnaires; serial physical exams; evaluation by psychiatrist; Thematic Apperception Test	Pessimistic explanatory style (stable, global, and internal explanations for bad events) predicts physical illness two to three decades later	Peterson, Seligman and Vaillant, 1988
Three groups of Air Force trainees: a regular group of men, a regular group of women and a group of problem trainees (clinically diagnosed with medical or behavioral problems)	Portions of: Self-Reliance Inventory, General Health Questionnaire, Symptoms Checklist 90-R; scales for burnout and self-esteem	Descriminator self-reliance is a predictor of success during the course of basic military training. Strong relationships among self-reliance, self-esteem, and burnout	Quick *et al.*, 1996

* Acute myocardial infarction.   ** Sudden cardiac death.   *** Subclinical coronary heart disease.

medical stress research established many of the sympathetic nervous system and endocrine system pathways to arousal of the stress response as a result of a wide variety of demands and stressors (Cannon, 1915/1929, 1932, 1935; Selye, 1976b, 1976c), providing the general underpinning support for hypothesis 1. Frankenhaeuser's (1991) discussion of several studies provides the most direct evidence confirming the effects of workload and work-related demands on neuroendocrine arousal and the stress response. Hypothesis 2 encompasses a wide range of manifest forms of distress. The three hypothesis 2 studies in Table 1 display some of this range, from the adverse effect of work demands on family life (Burke *et al.*, 1980) to the debilitating effects of burnout (Burke and Greenglass, 1995) and the potentially lethal effects of myocardial infarctions (Karasek *et al.*, 1988). The three hypothesis 3 studies in Table 1 show the beneficial effects of protective factors such as hardiness (Kobasa, Maddi and Kahn, 1982) and self-reliance (J. C. Quick *et al.*, 1996) and the adverse effects of vulnerability factors such as pessimism (Peterson *et al.*, 1988).

The Translation of Prevention into an Organizational Stress Context

The preventive stress management model results from the translation of the preventive medicine model and its overlay onto the stress process in an organizational framework, as shown in Figure 12.1. The impact of organizational demands proceeds through three stages, providing an opportunity for preventive intervention. While early or preclinical disease begins in the second stage of the *preventive medicine model*, disorder, distress, and strain do not begin until the third stage of the *preventive stress management model*. This is an important distinction between the two models. While stage two stress responses are basically healthy, they do possess some health risk.

The Prevention Hypotheses The preventive interventions in both models are intended to be parallel. *Primary prevention* aims to reduce, modify, or otherwise manage organizational demands and stressors to enhance health and reduce distress. *Secondary prevention* aims to modify individual stress responses to necessary and inevitable organizational demands. *Tertiary prevention* attempts to minimize the amount of residual individual and organizational distress not averted by primary or secondary prevention, or a combination of the two. Understanding organizational stress is important in order to reduce the distress and strain too often associated with stress in organizations. Primary, secondary, and/or tertiary preventive stress management programs are strategies for preventing job strain and channeling job stress into healthy, productive outcomes (Quick and Quick, 1997). The preventive stress management model in Figure 12.1 leads to the following hypotheses:

Hypothesis 4:   Primary prevention interventions to reduce, modify, or manage the intensity, frequency, and/or duration of organizational demands reduce the stress response in people at work.

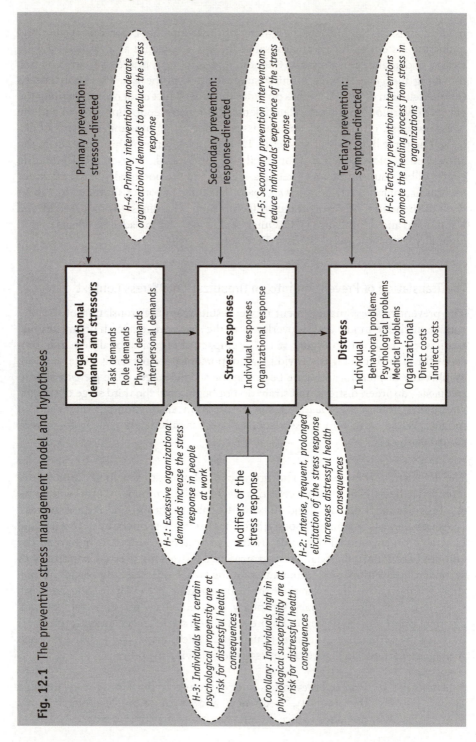

Fig. 12.1 The preventive stress management model and hypotheses

Hypothesis 5:   Secondary prevention interventions to moderate individuals' stress responses reduce the intensity, frequency, and/or duration of the individuals' experience of the stress response.

Hypothesis 6:   Tertiary prevention interventions to minimize distress and provide therapy shorten and improve the healing process from stressful or traumatic events in organizations.

Research Related to Hypotheses 4, 5, and 6   Table 12.2 presents six studies related to hypotheses 4, 5, and 6. Additional idiographic research in support of comprehensive organizational prevention interventions is presented in the third section of this chapter and in Karasek and Theorell (1990). The two studies related to hypothesis 4 show the beneficial effects of increasing control through job redesign (Karasek, 1990) and designing a team-oriented work environment (Terra, 1995). Additional research tends to focus on the efficacy of specific primary prevention strategies for individuals, such as learned optimism (Seligman, 1990), transformational coping (Maddi, 1995), changing TABP (Roskies, 1987), and social support (House *et al.*, 1988; J. D. Quick *et al.*, 1996). As suggested in Table 12.2, there is more empirical research on secondary prevention strategies for individuals, which bears on hypothesis 5. While learned optimism may be a primary prevention strategy for individuals, spiritual faith and hope are secondary prevention strategies because they alter how the individual responds (Sethi and Seligman, 1993). Relaxation and exercise are well established secondary strategies for individual preventive stress management, as indicated in Table 12.2 (Pauley *et al.*, 1982; Toivanen *et al.*, 1993). There is the least evidence for support of hypothesis 6 and only one study is included in Table 12.2. While there is an argument for the use of expressive writing and confiding in others as secondary prevention strategies (Pennebaker, 1990), these clearly become tertiary prevention or treatment strategies when related to a work trauma such as job loss (Spera, Buhrfeind and Pennebaker, 1994). Hypothesis 6 deals with clinical psychology and medicine as much as organizational behavior and management. Thus, one may need to turn to the clinical literature on the treatment of executives (Moss, 1981), post-traumatic crisis intervention (Braverman, 1992), or grief workshops for co-worker suicides (Adkins, 1995).

Implications of the Theory for Diagnosis, Prevention, and Surveillance

This section discusses the implications of the theory of preventive stress management for diagnosis and prevention. First, the section presents a process for organizational stress diagnosis. Second, the section discusses prevention and stress management. Finally, we extend the preventive stress management model by incorporating public health surveillance indicators.

Organizational Stress Diagnosis

Diagnosis is an essential prerequisite to preventive or treatment interventions within the preventive stress management model. Figure 12.2 sets forth a process for

Table 12.2 Six studies related to hypotheses 4, 5, and 6

	Context/intervention	Data collection method	Findings	Source
Hypothesis 4: Primary prevention	White collar workers who were members of Sweden's Federation of White Collar Unions	Six indicators of physical illness and three indicators of psychological distress were developed; measures of change influence and decision latitude changes	Increased control and participation on the job could reduce illness, especially coronary heart disease, among males	Karasek, 1990
	Workers in a metal can industry plant in the Netherlands/Job redesign, implementation of self-managing work teams	Local management reports; archival data	Sickness absenteeism decreased by 50% over 5 years; flexibility improved; productivity increased significantly; workers better qualified, informed, and motivated	Terra, 1995
Hypothesis 5: Secondary prevention	US residents adhering to 9 major religions, divided into 3 groups: fundamentalists, moderates, and liberals	Attributional Style Questionnaire; Beck Depression Inventory, religious survey	Optimism, religious hope, religious influence in daily life, and religious involvement are greater for fundamentalists than for moderates, and greater for moderates than for liberals	Sethi and Seligman, 1993

Women hospital cleaners and women bank employees	Longitudinal measures, over a 6-month period, of cardiac autonomic nervous function; stress questionnaire or interview at time 3	Both groups experienced psychophysical distress during stressful periods in their workplace, which influenced subjects' health. Engaging in repeated relaxation preserved the health of the subjects	Toivanen et al., 1993
Xerox employees interested in joining a new Health Fitness Center	Longitudinal (14 weeks) measures include a portion of the State-Trait Anxiety Inventory; a measure of self-concept; physiological tests such as skinfold measurements, submaximal physical work capacity test, blood samples	Significant improvements in triglycerides and total cholesterol, resting heart rate, systolic blood pressure, predicted VO_2 MAX, self-concept, and trait anxiety	Pauley et al., 1982
Hypothesis 6: Tertiary prevention			
Former professional male employees who worked for a large computer and electronics firm	Health questionnaire; Transition-Search Behavior Questionnaire, a daily questionnaire	Subjects who wrote about the trauma of losing their jobs were more likely to find reemployment soon after the study than the control subjects	Spera et al., 1994

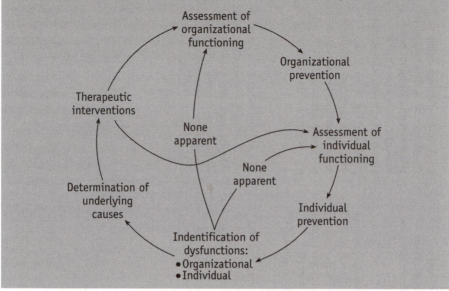

Fig. 12.2 The process of organizational stress diagnosis. From Preventive Stress Management in Organizations (p. 114) by J. C. Quick, J. D. Quick, D. L. Nelson, and J. J. Hurrell, Jr. Copyright 1997 by the American Psychological Association, Washington, DC. Reprinted with permission.

organizational stress diagnosis. The diagnostic process shown in the figure rests on two assumptions. First, organizational stress diagnosis is an interdisciplinary process requiring representation and contributions from medicine, organizational science, and psychology. Second, organizational diagnosis is an interpretative process that does not achieve closure. Rather, a diagnostic statement becomes a working hypothesis as a basis for data development and analysis, subject to modification in light of new data and information.

Organization stress diagnosis draws on a variety of diagnostic methods, including interviews, questionnaires, and observational techniques. Many modifiers of the stress response can also be systematically assessed. These include social support, personality factors (e.g. hardiness, locus of control, optimism–pessimism), individual physiological susceptibility, gender, and a number of other factors (see chapter 3, Quick *et al.*, 1997 for a review).

Strategies for Preventive Stress Management

Organizational stress diagnosis should lead to preventive interventions aimed at improving individual and organizational functioning. The theory of preventive stress management in organizations is built on a prevention framework which offers a scheme for organizing and applying a wide range of individual and organizational

Fig. 12.3 Preventive strategies and surveillance indicators for organizational stress

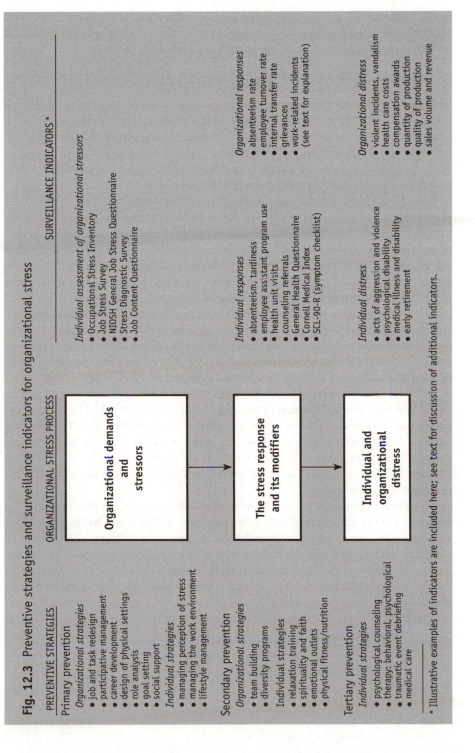

PREVENTIVE STRATEGIES

Primary prevention

Organizational strategies
- job and task redesign
- participative management
- career development
- design of physical settings
- role analysis
- goal setting
- social support

Individual strategies
- managing perception of stress
- managing the work environment
- lifestyle management

Secondary prevention

Organizational strategies
- team building
- diversity programs

Individual strategies
- relaxation training
- spirituality and faith
- emotional outlets
- physical fitness/nutrition

Tertiary prevention

Individual strategies
- psychological counseling
- therapy: behavioral, psychological
- traumatic event debriefing
- medical care

ORGANIZATIONAL STRESS PROCESS

Organizational demands and stressors

The stress response and its modifiers

Individual and organizational distress

SURVEILLANCE INDICATORS *

Individual assessment of organizational stressors
- Occupational Stress Inventory
- Job Stress Survey
- NIOSH General Job Stress Questionnaire
- Stress Diagnostic Survey
- Job Content Questionnaire

Individual responses
- absenteeism, tardiness
- employee assistant program use
- health unit visits
- counseling referrals
- General Health Questionnaire
- Cornell Medical Index
- SCL-90-R (symptom checklist)

Individual distress
- acts of aggression and violence
- psychological disability
- medical illness and disability
- early retirement

Organizational responses
- absenteeism rate
- employee turnover rate
- internal transfer rate
- grievances
- work-related incidents (see text for explanation)

Organizational distress
- violent incidents, vandalism
- health care costs
- compensation awards
- quantity of production
- quality of production
- sales volume and revenue

* Illustrative examples of indicators are included here; see text for discussion of additional indicators.

stress management strategies at three discrete places in the organizational stress process, as indicated in Figure 12.1. Figure 12.3 sets forth a set of specific preventive strategies, organized by primary, secondary, and tertiary prevention.

Surveillance Indicators for Monitoring Organizational Stress

The theory of preventive stress management also lends itself to a systematic approach to surveillance and monitoring, which are important functions in occupational health and preventive medicine (Ordin, 1992). Surveillance indicators provide information about organizational stressors, stress responses, and signs of individual and organizational distress. Examples of each of these categories of surveillance indicators are given in the right hand column of Figure 12.3.

Surveillance indicators are the foundation of an evidence-based approach to the preventive management of workplace stress. Indicators can be used to assess the causes, patterns, trends, and means for preventing adverse individual and organizational consequences of stress. They can be used to assess the impact of preventive interventions; to compare stressors, stress responses, or symptoms of distress among different divisions or locations within an individual organization; or to make comparisons across companies or across industries.

Diagnostic methods should be valid, reliable and feasible. They should produce results that are intuitively clear and meaningful to senior management. A recent review of organizational stress diagnosis (Quick *et al.*, 1997: chapters 6 and 7) considers basic concepts and provides a detailed survey of numerous stress-related diagnostic instruments, including each of the survey instruments listed in Figure 12.3.

In Figure 12.3 the instruments listed under 'Individual Assessment of Organizational Stressors' as well as several of the items listed under 'Individual Responses' are survey questionnaires. When used for surveillance purposes these questionnaires are administered periodically—every two years, for example—to the same sample group. Organizational health centers have been developed in the US Air Force (Adkins and Schwartz, 1996), one of whose roles is to monitor organizational health through regular surveys.

Absenteeism, counseling referrals, employee turnover rate, production statistics, and several of the other surveillance indicators listed in Figure 12.3 can be gathered on an ongoing basis and tracked as monthly rates. There are a variety of work-related incidents whose rates may be used as surveillance indicators, depending on the nature of the company. These incidents include strikes, work stoppages, accidents, unscheduled machine downtime, overuse of materials and supplies, and inventory shrinkages.

Idiographic Research Related to the Theory

This section presents two idiographic organizational research cases relevant to the theory. The first is the case of ICI-Zeneca Pharmaceuticals, a British-based pharmaceutical unit of Imperial Chemical Industries (ICI) with global operating locations. The second is the case of the US Air Force, a military organization with global operations and bases. Idiographic research offers a more holistic, detailed, and comprehensive consideration of the stresses and strains within an organization (Levinson *et al.*, 1972; Quick, 1997). The ICI-Zeneca case examines an organization experiencing stress in the midst of growth and expansion while the US Air Force case focuses on an organization going through force reductions and downsizing. There are also exemplary idiographic research studies of very distressed organizations which have experienced tragedy, such as Union Carbide in Bhopal (Shrivastava, 1987).

Occupational Health in ICI-Zeneca Pharmaceuticals

ICI-Zeneca Pharmaceuticals is one example of an effective preventive stress management program (Teasdale and McKeown, 1994). ICI-Zeneca Pharmaceuticals' experience with stress at work began in the mid-1980s when stress-related illness reports to the Occupational Health Department exhibited a disturbing upward trend. The company was in a growth period which led to manufacturing operations in seventeen countries, sales in 130 countries, and major operations in the UK, the USA, Continental Western Europe, and Japan by 1992. ICI-Zeneca's research identified twelve likely reasons for increased stress, including organizational change, the rapid growth, increasing complexity, an international thrust, profit and production pressure, new work overload, and high quality work expectations.

The Chief Executive Officer's Letter   ICI-Zeneca's CEO sent all department heads a letter discussing the stress associated with increasing business demands. The intent of the letter was to sensitize all managers to the risk of serious problems for employees subject to stress overloads; to clarify the positive value of good stress to employee job satisfaction, motivation and good performance; and to emphasize continuous surveillance of workload, priorities, and reasonable timescales. The CEO pointed out that if work takes up more than a reasonable proportion of an individual's total life, for an extended period, the company is unlikely to benefit in the long term.

ICI-Zeneca's Stress Management Strategy   The company developed a six level stress management strategy, using prevention and treatment interventions. Because of the disturbing upward trend in stress-related illnesses and disorders, the first level of intervention was treatment of the stress-induced casualties. The second level engaged public health surveillance activities to detect other casualties, better defining the extent of the problem within the company. The third level of the strategy legitimized stress as a concern by senior management. Levels four and five of the strategy increased awareness of stress and stress-related disorders throughout the company, teaching behavioral, emotional, and cognitive skills for effective stress management. Level six in the strategy aimed to improve the organizational culture.

Measurable Benefits for ICI-Zeneca   ICI-Zeneca tracked a number of measurable, as well as less tangible, benefits of the stress management strategy. Two of the evaluation measures were the General Health Questionnaire (GHQ) and medical, psychological, or referral visits. The GHQ was administered to employees over a period of three to four months before and after they attended a workshop. Scores on the GHQ improved 15–20 percent between the first and second administration of the test. In addition, the number of referrals to psychiatrists or psychologists and self-referrals to the ICI Medical Centres or their own family doctors' clinics were tracked over a 10-year period. This measure showed an increase over the years before the stress management strategy and workshops, and a decrease during the years which followed.

Organizational Health in the United States Air Force

Joyce Adkins, a member of the US Air Force Biomedical Science Corps (Adkins, 1995, 1996; Adkins and Schwartz, 1996), has focused attention on organizational health as a leadership challenge. She has used transactional psychology, public health concepts, and a preventive stress management intervention framework to assess and enhance the health of various operational and support units in the US Air Force. An organizational health center (OHC) is a key concept she pioneered. The mission of an OHC is to maximize human potential and productivity through optimal physical, behavioral, and organizational health. The aim of an OHC is systemic organizational intervention, through a menu of specific primary, secondary, and tertiary prevention interventions, to improve working conditions; to monitor psychological disorders and risk factors at work; to provide information, education and training; and to enrich the psychological health services for all employees.

Sacramento Air Logistics Center Adkins (1995) first implemented an OHC at the Sacramento Air Logistics Center. The OHC had a dual focus on mission performance and personnel well-being (Hickox, 1994). Her preliminary research data showed tangible results in the first year of operation (Adkins, 1995). First, a total cost reduction in workers' compensation of 3.91 percent, compared to a near doubling of baseline data between 1985 and 1993. This is a savings equal to $289,099. Second, medical visits/health care utilization for job-related illness and injury decreased by 12 percent, with a savings for lost productivity alone of $150,918. Third, there was a decrease in premature mortality rate and associated productive years' lost savings of $5.4 million (120 productive years times $45,000 per year average annual accelerated labor cost), resulting from a decrease of ten behaviorally-related deaths.

Air Force Safety Center Adkins extended elements of the OHC concept throughout the US Air Force after a move to the Air Force Safety Center, especially with regard to organizational assessment, diagnosis, and surveillance. For example, she collected occupational stress data measuring occupational demands and stressors, personal strain and distress, and stress management and coping strategies in five US Air Force organizations: two air depot maintenance centers, two pilot training wings, and one air combat unit (Quick *et al.*, 1997: 280–281). Her data showed more conflict and ambiguity demands as well as greater vocational, psychological, and interpersonal strain in the maintenance organizations compared to the other three organizations. Her data also showed more responsibility demands in the air combat unit compared to the other four organizations, without greater strain responses in that unit, thus suggesting a possible moderating effect of hardiness.

Stressed Systems Study Further examination of organizational health in the US Air Force was undertaken through a two-year Stressed Systems Study (Grier, 1997). The Air Staff's operations tempo (OPTEMO) and personnel tempo (PERSTEMPO) research was aimed at analyzing the demands and stress placed on US Air Force personnel and equipment as a result of the dramatic downsizing of the military services in the USA combined with an increase in assigned tasks over the same time period. The stresses and strains within the US Air Force are significantly different during the period of force reductions in the 1990s than they were during the post-Vietnam, Regean-era build up period (Quick *et al.*, 1983).

Priorities for Future Research

Globalization of trade in goods and services is heightening competition in nearly every sector of the national economies of Europe, North America, and other developed countries. This in turn is leading to even greater emphasis on productivity, to restructuring, to downsizing/rightsizing of organizations, and to the insecurity associated with more flexible labor market practices (Cascio, 1995; Gowing *et al.*, 1998). The nature of work and character of the workplace are also evolving with the shift from manufacturing to service jobs, with greater diversity in the workforce, and with increased emphasis on teamwork (Nelson *et al.*, in press).

These changes mean increases in organizational demands and individual stressors. At the same time, pressure to contain costs is forcing companies to scrutinize expenditures for organizational stress diagnosis, employee assistance programs and other programs aimed at primary, secondary, or tertiary prevention of individual and organization stress. Sound research to support the theory of preventive stress management in organizations is, therefore, a matter of concern to senior executives as well as to academic researchers. Both the focus and the quality of research are important.

Focus of Research

Where should future research focus in preventive stress management? Among the six hypotheses and one corollary presented earlier in this chapter, the level of supporting evidence varied considerably. The need for additional research also varies among the hypotheses. Hypotheses 1 and 2 are concerned with the causal linkages among organizational stressors, stress responses, and distress within individuals and organizations. Additional research can deepen our understanding of the dynamics of organizational stress and it can always be useful for convincing skeptical executives that organizational stress should concern them. Yet, these causal linkages are relatively well-established and research on these hypotheses is perhaps a lower priority.

Hypothesis 3 and its Corollary are concerned with individual psychological and physiological susceptibility to the risk of organizational demands and stressors leading to adverse consequences. Here the evidence is less well-developed. Preventive measures generally have their greatest impact when targeted toward high-risk individuals and situations. For example, are individuals with Type A behavior more prone to respond to work demands and pressures with anger and hostility? Additional research linking individual susceptibility to adverse individual and organizational consequences could be of great value.

The most challenging but potentially most beneficial focus for future research is on hypotheses 4, 5, and 6. These hypotheses concern the impact of alternative strategies for primary, secondary, and tertiary prevention. As outlined in the left column of Figure 12.3, these strategies are numerous and diverse. Which are most effective in reducing the organizational and individual consequences of stress? Under what circumstances is each strategy the most effective? Equally important, how can organizations best structure themselves to undertake preventive management measures and what is the cost to the organization of undertaking particular strategies? A review of the evidence shows that while considerable progress has been made in the evaluation of individual-level interventions, there has been little progress in evaluating organizational-level interventions (Nelson *et al.*, in press).

Quality of Research

The quality of future research is important for studies undertaken on any of the predictions. But the research methods are especially important for hypotheses 4, 5, and 6 each of which concerns intervention research. Descriptive case studies with no before–after measures and no comparison group are the weakest designs; studies with randomized comparison groups and repeated before–after measures are the strongest, but most difficult to execute, designs (Mohr, 1992). Time-series analysis (Cook and Campbell, 1979), with frequent repeat measures beginning well before and continuing well after the intervention, is a powerful quasi-experimental alternative which is under-utilized in the management and stress management literature. One of the strengths of the ICI-Zeneca was the 10-year time-series analysis which related stress management training to a measurable decrease in psychological referrals.

In addition to the basic study design, the choice of measurement instruments is critical. Earlier reference was made to the wide range of instruments and indicators for measuring organizational stressors, organizational stress, individual stress, and modifiers of the response to stress. In addition to the basic criteria of validity, reliability and feasibility, measures must be appropriate to the type of intervention being studied and the same measures must be used consistently throughout the study. Studies that evaluate individual-level interventions, for example, have progressed in considering a wider range of outcome measures. Biochemical changes such as catecholamines, angiotensin, renin, and aldosterone have been evaluated, and some studies have included evaluations of health care costs (Murphy, 1996).

Conclusion

Organizational stress concerns the issues of human struggle and suffering at work. Preventive stress management offers an organizational philosophy and methods for managing this problem to improve health and performance at work. Some organizational stress is both inevitable and desirable. The intent of preventive stress management is to maximize eustress and performance, to minimize distress, but not to eliminate stress. While this is an ongoing process, people at work need not be left with the problem of Sisyphus, king of Corinth in Greek mythology. Sisyphus was left in a state of perpetual, hopeless, joyless struggle after he tricked Death and was condemned to push a rock endlessly up a hill, only to have the rock always roll back down before the task was finished. Alternatively, people at work may develop dynamic self-reliance (Frese, 1997), moving towards growth and higher mastery in their portfolio of stress management skills. At the limit of that portfolio, *The Book of Job* offers yet one more option: act with faith and just belief. Weick (1987) suggests that belief, not scepticism, precedes observation. Further, 'if theories are significant beliefs that affect what we see, then theories should be adopted more to maximise what we see than to summarise what we have already seen' (Weick, 1987: 122). The theory of preventive stress management offers a framework within which to expand our view of the stress process and, more importantly, our possible action options for intervention to enhance health in organizations.

The authors would like to thank Anna Florey for extensive editorial comments, Joyce Adkins and David Mack for suggestions on early drafts of this chapter, and Thomas A. Wright for a thorough reading and thoughtful suggestions on a near final draft. We thank Anna Florey for her help and preparation of the tables and figures. We thank David Mack for his review and preparation of the references.

References

Adkins, J. A. (1995) Occupational stress: A leadership challenge. Paper presented at the Air Force Material Command Horizons Conference, Albuquerque, NM, February.

Adkins, J. A. (1996) Continuum of occupational violence prevention. Paper presented at the Eleventh Annual Conference of the Society for Organizational and Industrial Psychology, San Diego, CA, April.

Adkins, J. A. and Schwartz, D. (1996) Organizational health: An organizational systems perspective. Paper presented at the Third Biennial International Conference on Advances in Management, Boston, MA, June.

Benison, S. Barger, A. C., and Wolfe, E. L. (1987) *Walter B. Cannon: The Life and Times of a Young Scientist.* Cambridge, MA: Belknap Press.

Braverman, M. (1992) Posttrauma crisis intervention in the workplace. In J. C. Quick, L. R. Murphy, and J. J. Hurrell, *Stress and Well-being at Work* (pp. 299–316). Washington, DC: American Psychological Association.

Burke, M. J., Brief, A. P., and George, J. M. (1993) 'The role of negative affectivity in understanding relations between self-reports of stressors and strains: A comment on the applied psychology literature', *Journal of Applied Psychology*, 78, 402–412.

Burke, R. J. and Greenglass, E. R. (1995) 'A longitudinal examination of the Cherniss model of psychological burnout', *Social Science and Medicine*, 40, (10), 1357–1363.

Burke, R. J., Weir, T., and DuWors, R. E., Jr. (1980) 'Work demands on administrators and spouse well-being', *Human Relations*, 33, 253–278.

Cannon, W. B. (1929) *Bodily Changes in Pain, Hunger, Fear and Rage*. New York: D. Appleton-Century. (Original work published 1915.)

Cannon, W. B. (1932) *The Wisdom of the Body*. New York: W. W. Norton.

Cannon, W. B. (1935) 'Stresses and strains of homeostasis', *The American Journal of the Medical Sciences*, 189 (1), 1–14.

Cascio, W. F. (1995) 'Whither industrial and organizational psychology in a changing world of work?' *American Psychologist*, 50, 929–939.

Cohen, W. S. (1985) 'Health promotion in the workplace: A prescription for good health', *American Psychologist*, 40 (2), 213–216.

Cohen, S. and Edwards, J. R. (1989) Personality characteristics as moderators of the relationship between stress and disorder. In W. J. Neufeld (ed.), *Advances in the Investigation of Psychological Stress* (pp. 235–283). New York: Wiley.

Cook, T. D. and D. T. Campbell. (1979) *Quasi-experimentation Design and Analysis Issues for Field Settings*. Boston: Houghton Mifflin Company.

Ewart, C. K. (1991) 'Social action theory for a public health psychology', *American Psychologist*, 46, (9), 931–946.

Foss, L. and Rothenberg, K. (1987) *The Second Medical Revolution: From Biomedical to Infomedical*. Boston, MA: New Science Library.

Frankenhaeuser, M. (1991) 'The psychophysiology of workload, stress, and health: Comparison between the sexes', *Annals of Behavioral Medicine*, 13, (4), 197–204.

Frese, M. (1997) Dynamic self-reliance: An important concept for work in the twenty-first century. In C. L. Cooper and S. E. Jackson (eds.) *Creating Tomorrow's Organizations: A Handbook for Future Research in Organizational Behavior* (pp. 399–416). Chichester, England: Wiley.

Gowing, M., Kraft, J, and Quick, J. C. (1998) *The New Organizational Reality: Downsizing, Restructuring, and Revitalization*. Washington, DC: American Psychological Association.

Grier, P. (1997) 'Stressed Systems', *Air Force Magazine*, 80 (7), 52–55.

Hickox, K. (1994) 'Content and competitive', *Airman*, January, 31–33.

House, J. S., Landis, K. R., and Umberson, D. (1988) 'Social relationships and health', *Science*, 241, 540–545.

Jenkins, C. D. (1997) Type A/B behaviour pattern. In J. M. Stellman (ed.) *ILO Encyclopaedia of Occupational Health and Safety*, 34, 41–42. Geneva, Switzerland: International Labour Office and Chicago: Rand McNally.

Kahn, R. L., Wolfe, R. P., Quinn, R. P., Snoek, J. D., and Rosenthal, R. A. (1964) *Organizational Stress: Studies in Role Conflict and Ambiguity*. New York: Wiley.

Karasek, R. A. (1979) 'Job demands, job decision latitude, and mental strain: Implication for job design', *Administrative Science Quarterly*, 24, 285–308.

Karasek, R. A. (1990) 'Lower health risk with increased job control among white collar workers', *Journal of Organizational Behaviour*, 11, 171–185.

Karasek, R. A. and Theorell, T. (1990) *Healthy Work*. New York: Basic Books.

Karasek, R. A., Theorell, T., Schwartz, J. E., Schnall, P. L., Pieper, C. F., and Michela, J. L. (1988) 'Job characteristics in relation to the prevalence of myocardial infarction in the US health examination survey (HES) and the health and nutrition examination survey (HANES)', *American Journal of Public Health*, 78, 910–918.

Kobasa, S. C., Maddi, S. R., and Kahn, S. (l982) 'Hardiness and health: A prospective study', *Journal of Personality and Social Psychology*, 42, 168–177.

Last, J. M. (1988) *A Dictionary of Epidemiology* (2nd edn.) New York: International Epidemiological Association.

Last, J. M. and Wallace, R. B. (eds.) (1992) *Public Health and Preventive Medicine* (13th edn.). Norwalk, CN: Appleton & Lange.

Lazarus, R. S., DeLongis, A., Folkman, S., and Gruen, R. (1985) 'Stress and adaptational outcomes: The problem of confounded measures', *American Psychologist*, 40, 770–779.

Levinson, H., Molinari, J., and Spohn, A. G. (1972) *Organizational Diagnosis*. Cambridge, MA: Harvard University Press.

Maddi, S. R. (1995) Workplace hardiness for these turbulent times. Paper presented at the Academy of Management, Vancouver, BC, Canada, August.

Mohr, L. B. (1992) *Impact Analysis for Programme Evaluation*. Newbury Park: Sage Publications.

Moss, L. (1981) *Management Stress*. Reading, MA: Addison-Wesley.

Murphy, L. R. (1996) 'Stress management in work settings: A critical review of the health effects', *American Journal of Health Promotion*, 11, 112–135.

Nelson, D. L., Quick, J. C., and Simmons, B. L. (in press) Preventive management of work stress: Current themes and future challenge. In A. Baum, T. Revenson, and J. Singer (eds.) *Handbook of Health Psychology*, Mahwah, NJ.: Lawrence Erlbaum Associates.

Ordin, D. L. (1992) Surveillance, monitoring, and screening in occupational health. In J. Last and R. B. Wallace (eds.), *Maxcy–Rosenau–Last public health and preventive medicine* (13th edn., pp. 551–558). Norwalk, CT: Appleton & Lange.

Ouellette, S. (1997) Hardiness. In J. M. Stellman (ed.) *ILO Encyclopaedia of Occupational Health and Safety*, 34, 42–43. Geneva, Switzerland: International Labour Office and Chicago: Rand McNally.

Pauley, J. T., Palmer, J. A., Wright, C. C., and Pfeiffer, H. (1982) 'The effect of a 14-week employee fitness program on selected physiological and psychological parameters', *Journal of Occupational Medicine*, 24, 457–463.

Pennebaker, J. W. (1990) *Opening Up: The Healing Power of Confiding in Others*. New York: Avon Books.

Peterson, C., Seligman, M. E. P., and Vaillant, G. E. (1988) 'Pessimistic explanatory style is a risk factor for physical illness: A thirty-five-year longitudinal study', *Journal of Personality and Social Psychology*, 55, 23–27.

Quick, J. C. (1997) Idiographic research in organizational behavior. In C. L. Cooper and S. E. Jackson (eds.) *Creating Tomorrow's Organizations: A Handbook for Future Research in Organizational Behavior* (pp. 475–492). Chichester, England: Wiley.

Quick, J. C. and Quick, J. D. (1984) *Organizational Stress and Preventive Management*. New York: McGraw-Hill.

Quick, J. C. and Quick, J. D. (1997) Stress management programs. In L. H. Peters, S. A. Youngblood, and C. R. Greer (eds.), *The Blackwell Dictionary of Human Resource Management*. Oxford, England: Blackwell.

Quick, J. C., Shannon, C. and Quick, J. D. (1983) 'Managing stress in the Air Force: An ounce of prevention!' *Air University Review*, 34, 76–83.

Quick, J. C., Joplin, J. R., Nelson, D. L., Mangelsdorff, A. D., and Fiedler, E. (1996) 'Self-reliance and military service training outcomes', *Journal of Military Psychology*, 8, 279–293.

Quick, J. C., Quick, J. D., Nelson, D. L., and Hurrell, J. J. Jr. (1997) *Preventive Stress Management in Organizations*. Washington, DC: American Psychological Association. (Original work published in 1984 by J. C. Quick and J. D. Quick.)

Quick, J. D., Nelson, D. L., Matuszek, A. C., Whittington, J. L., and Quick, J. C. (1996) Social support, secure attachments, and health. In C. Cooper (ed.), *Handbook of Stress, Medicine, and Health* (pp. 269–287). Boca Raton, FL: CRC Press.

Roskies, E. (1987) *Stress Management for the Healthy Type A: Theory and Practice.* New York: Guilford Press.

Shrivastava, P. (1987) *Bhopal: Anatomy of a Crisis.* Cambridge, MA: Ballinger.

Schwartz, J. E. Pickering, T. G., and Landsbergis, P. A. (1996) 'Work-related stress and blood pressure: Current theoretical models and considerations from a behavioral medicine perspective', *Journal of Occupational Health Psychology,* 1, 287–310.

Seligman, M. E. P. (1990) *Learned Optimism.* New York: Alfred A. Knopf.

Selye, H. (1973) 'Evolution of the stress concept', *American Scientist,* 61 (6), 692–699.

Selye, H. (1976a) *Stress in Health and Disease.* Boston: Butterworths.

Selye, H. (1976b) *The Stress of Life* (2nd edn.) New York: McGraw-Hill. (Original work published 1956.)

Selye, H. (1976c) 'Forty years of stress research: Principal remaining problems and misconceptions', *Canadian Medical Association Journal,* 115, 53–56.

Sethi, S. and Seligman, M. E. P. (1993) 'Optimism and fundamentalism', *Psychological Science,* 4, 256–269.

Siegel, B. S. (1990) *Love, Medicine and Miracles: Lessons Learned about Self-healing from a Surgeon's Experience with Exceptional Patients.* New York: Harper Perennial.

Siegrist, J. (1996) 'Adverse health effects of high-effort/low-reward conditions', *Journal of Occupational Health Psychology,* 1, 27–41.

Spera, S. P., Buhrfeind, E. D., and Pennebaker, J. W. (1994) 'Expressive writing and coping with job loss', *Academy of Management Journal,* 37 (3), 722–733.

Teasdale, E. L. and McKeown, S. (1994) Managing stress at work: The ICI-Zeneca Pharmaceuticals experience 1986–1993. In C. L. Cooper and S. Williams (eds.), *Creating Healthy Work Organizations* (pp. 133–165). Chichester: Wiley.

Terra, N. (1995) The prevention of job stress by redesigning jobs and implementing self-regulated teams. In L. R. Murphy, J. J. Hurrell, S. L. Sauter, and G. P. Keita, (eds.) *Job Stress Interventions* (pp. 265–293). Washington, DC: American Psychological Association.

Toivanen, H., Lansimies, E., Jokela, V., and Hanninen, O. (1993) 'Impact of regular relaxation training on the cardiac autonomic nervous system of hospital cleaners and bank employees', *Scandinavian Journal of Work, Environment and Health,* 19, 319–325.

Ursin, H. (1997) Immunological reactions. In J. M. Stellman (ed.) *ILO Encyclopaedia of Occupational Health and Safety,* 34, 57–58. Geneva, Switzerland: International Labour Office and Chicago: Rand McNally.

Weick, K. (1987) 'Organizational culture as a source of high reliability', *California Management Review,* 29 (2), 112–127.

Whetton, D. A. and Cameron, K. S. (1995) *Developing Management Skills: Managing Stress* (3rd edn.). New York: Harper Collins.

Winett, R. A. (1995) 'A framework for health promotion and disease prevention and programs', *American Psychologist,* 50 (5), 341–350.

Wofford, J. C. and Daly, P. (1997) 'A cognitive process approach to understanding individual differences in stress response propensity', *Journal of Occupational Health Psychology,* 2, 134–147.

Index